Business Communication

3E

BETTY S. JOHNSON
Stephen F. Austin State University

MARSHA L. BAYLESS
Stephen F. Austin State University

DAME

THOMSON LEARNING

Australia · Canada · Mexico · Singapore · Spain · United Kingdom · United States

Business Communicating—Third Edition, by Betty S. Johnson and Marsha L. Bayless
Desktop Publishing: Sheryl New
Artist: Pam Porter
Cover Design by South-Western College Publishing
Printer: Globus Printing

Printed in the United States of America
2 3 4 5 6   05 04 03 02 01

For more information contact Thomson Learning Custom Publishing, 5191 Natorp Blvd., Mason, Ohio 45040, 1-800-355-9983 or find us on the Internet at
http://www.custom.thomsonlearning.com

For permission to use material from this text or product, contact us by:
• **telephone: 1-800-730-2214**
• **fax: 1-800-730-2215**
• **web: http://www.thomsonrights.com**
ISBN 0-324-10946-6
Library of Congress Catalog Card No. 01-131654

This book is printed on acid-free paper.

OVERVIEW

Welcome to the third edition of *Business Communication*. At the conclusion of your course, you will have a comprehensive understanding of the elements of business communication. Success in business communication equals success in business. This textbook will help you improve your communication skills in preparation for further business courses as well as for the workplace.

Business Communication integrates factors that impact business communication such as technology, ethics, legal issues, and multicultural and international elements in the first three chapters of the text. These components are then interwoven throughout the remaining 14 chapters of the textbook.

Each chapter starts with **Critical Thinking Applications** that will provide you with the opportunity to think about some specific business communication challenges. The applications can be used for discussion or for class assignments such as electronic mail, for posting on a class discussion group, speaking assignments, or writing assignments. At the beginning of each chapter you will also find **Chapter Objectives** that will give you a list of the key components that will be discussed in the chapter.

The textbook is divided into six areas of business communication. **Factors Impacting Communication in Business** discusses communication theory, communication channels, and societal issues of communication.

Oral communication is discussed in **Components to Enhance Oral Communication.** The chapters focus on speaking skills, listening skills, and team communication.

Elements of Business Research includes the information needed to research and prepare business reports. Facets including the research problem, collecting research data, analyzing data, presenting data visually through graphics, and writing effective reports are presented. The APA (American Psychological Association) citation style is presented in chapter 8. Alternative citation styles of MLA (Modern Language Association) and Chicago Style are included in Appendix B.

Letters and memos are discussed in **Framework for Successful Business Writing.** The theory of writing business documents is explored as well as specific guidelines for positive, negative, and persuasive messages.

Employment communication is presented in **Strategies for Employment Communication**. Several styles of resumes including chronological, functional, combination, and electronic are presented. Ideas for application letters to accompany the resume are included. Tips and techniques for employment interviews are also included.

The reference section of the textbook called **Guides to Effective Composition** includes four appendices. Appendix A includes a review of grammar and punctuation principles to enhance your writing. A summary of formats for reports, memos, and letters is included in Appendix B. A list of commonly misspelled words is included in Appendix C. Similar but frequently confusing words are described in Appendix D.

A study guide that includes review questions and additional business communication activities is available. The instructor's manual contains an extensive test bank and suggested problem solutions. Over 200 visuals are available in Powerpoint format.

ACKNOWLEDGMENTS

We would like to express our appreciation to our students at Stephen F. Austin State University and to those faculty and students at other universities who used the first and second editions of our textbook and provided valuable feedback for this improved third edition.

Especially, we would like to thank our colleagues Ms. Judi Biss and Dr. Susan Jennings for their support of our textbook and ideas for improving both the textbook and the study guide. We would also like to acknowledge Dr. E. Ruth Carroll at Georgia Southern University who also made suggestions after her students used the textbook.

We would like to dedicate this edition of the textbook to the memory of our colleague Dr. Christine Monica Irvine who was a strong supporter of the first two editions of this textbook. We miss you and your encouragement, Chris.

We welcome your ideas for improving this textbook. Please send your remarks to our e-mail addresses bjohnson@sfasu.edu or mbayless@sfasu.edu.

Betty S. Johnson
Marsha L. Bayless

BRIEF TABLE OF CONTENTS

Factors Impacting Communication in Business

Components to Enhance Oral Communication

Elements of Business Research

Framework for Successful Business Writing

Strategies for Employment Communication

Guides to Effective Composition

TABLE OF CONTENTS

Chapter 3 Examining Societal Issues of Communication 35

Components to Enhance Oral Communication

Chapter 4 Strengthening Speaking Skills 55

Elements of Business Research

Guides to Effective Composition

EXPLORING THE COMMUNICATION PROCESS

Critical Thinking Applications

- What factors prevent you from being an effective communicator?

- Who is responsible for the success of a communication exchange? The speaker or the listener?

- Why would a company emphasize both written and oral communication in its orientation process for new employees?

CHAPTER OBJECTIVES

After studying this chapter, you should be able to:

1. Define communication and describe the basic process of communication.
2. Contrast verbal and nonverbal forms of communication.
3. Identify three primary barriers to effective communication.
4. Describe the prerequisites for effective communication.
5. Characterize the information flow within organizations.

THE IMPORTANCE OF COMMUNICATION

Congratulations! You already have good communication skills or you would not be ready for a college text focused on business communication. The purpose of this text is to improve your communication skills to better prepare you for a successful transition to other business courses and to the workplace.

A recent study of alumni of a college of business asked the question, "How valuable is the business communication course?" The same question was asked about all of the other business courses required of all business majors. The alumni marked business communication as THE MOST VALUABLE course placing it above all other required business courses. In this study there was no difference in the ranking based on major–all majors agreed.

You have learned to communicate in a variety of ways using both verbal (words) and nonverbal (symbols or gestures) means. You have learned to share information, emotions, and attitudes—at some times more successfully than at others. These experiences serve as the foundation for your business communication studies.

Although you have been communicating since you were an infant, the study of communication generally and business communication specifically is important to your success in the business world.

Most communication authorities believe that typically Americans spend about 70 percent of their active hours communicating verbally—listening, speaking, and/or writing. Many studies indicate between 40 and 60 percent of the work time is spent in communication activities.

Business communications require tact when dealing with mistakes or misunderstandings. The majority of communication activities from checking e-mail (electronic mail) to talking on the phone to writing memos to attending committee meetings to speaking with colleagues require daily use of effective business communication skills.

Through the years many philosophers have reflected on the nature and value of communication in our society. Many of their ideas can be related to current beliefs about the role of communication in the workplace.

Thoughts on Communication

The two words "information" and "communication" are often used interchangeably, but they signify quite different things. Information is giving out; communication is getting through.—**Sydney J. Harris**

Transport of the mails, transport of the human voice, transport of flickering pictures—in this century as in others our highest accomplishments still have the single aim of bringing men together.—**Antoine de Saint-Exupéry**

Two prisoners whose cells adjoin communicate with each other by knocking on the wall. The wall is the thing which separates them but is also their means of communication....—**Simone Weil**

The Basic Process of Communication

To communicate effectively, we need at least a partial understanding of the communication process. First, we must understand the meaning of the word *communication.* The dictionary lists several definitions for the word *communication.* The root word *communicate,* however, comes from the Latin word *communis,* meaning common. Thus, for successful communication we are trying to meet on common ground, at least momentarily, with the receivers of our message. We are trying to establish a common basis for sharing information, attitudes, ideas, and understanding.

Some specialists treat communication in two categories—**intrapersonal** (within oneself) and **interpersonal** (between or among individuals). Do we actually *communicate* within ourselves? Or do we *study* or *analyze* our thoughts, our knowledge, and our attitudes and feelings? Self-analysis is, of course, important. We need to analyze ourselves in order to improve various traits, to try to determine how others perceive us, and to bolster our self-esteem.

Although self-analysis is important, communication is interaction. If there is no reception of the message or if the message has no effect, successful communication has not occurred. Communication is the sharing of thoughts, information, and emotions. With this definition in mind, we can diagram the communication process as shown in Figure 1-1.

Message senders determine first the thought, the information, or the feeling they want to transmit; often two of these are combined. Then they choose the media and channels to use. They hope that the symbols, media and channels they choose have the same meanings for the receivers as they have for the senders. If that situation exists, accurate communication has likely occurred.

The receiver must interpret or decode the words or symbols to give meaning to them. If the sender and the receiver share a common understanding of the meanings of the words and symbols, the message should be successful. The words and the symbols chosen, however, do not always have the same meanings for the message senders and for the receivers. A shouted command of "you can't leave that POV here" may be difficult for the receiver to interpret. Does the receiver know that POV stands for privately owned vehicle?

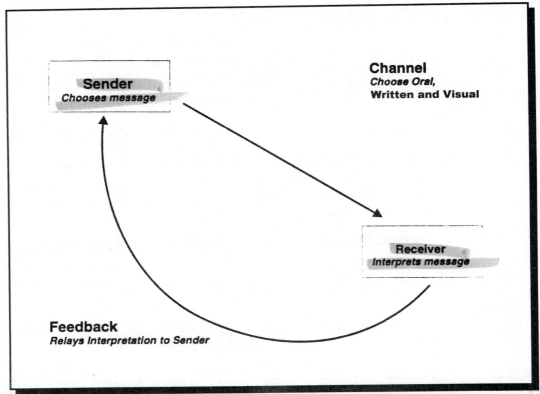

Figure 1-1. The Communication Process

The feedback the sender receives from the receiver is one method of determining whether the receiver understood the message as intended. Successful communication requires some degree of feedback. Feedback may be positive or negative. If positive feedback is received—the receivers nod their heads in agreement with the sender—the sender assumes the receivers understood the message as intended. If negative feedback—such as a frown or a puzzled look—occurs, the sender usually tries again with different words or symbols to express the message. Consequently, the communication process is complex, frequently requiring many cycles to complete a simple message. Because of this complexity, we do not expect to attain perfection; but we strive to achieve effectiveness. Studying the information in this book and applying it in all our situations will help us to communicate effectively.

When preparing to transmit a message, we should give careful consideration to the purpose of the message and to the receivers. If we want to give positive news, we use one approach. If we want to send negative news, we use a different approach. The content, the tone, and the wording of our messages differ for various receivers. If, for example, we write or talk to someone who knows very little about a topic, we need to include more facts and illustrations than are needed if the receiver is well informed on that particular topic. More is said about considering the purpose and the receivers in later chapters of this book.

Forms of Communication

To transmit our information, thoughts, and feelings effectively, we may use a verbal form (written or spoken words), nonverbal form (signals or sounds with no words), or a combination of these two.

Verbal

Verbal messages can be sent by speaking or by writing. Most oral communication is carried out in face-to-face situations either on a one-to-one basis or within a larger group. Among the numerous instances in which oral communication predominates are training sessions and committee meetings. Telephone conversations also are used extensively, of course, in transacting business.

Letters, memorandums, and reports are perhaps the most frequently used forms of written business communication. Manuals, brochures, catalogs, advertisements, and newsletters are also used widely. These written messages, as well as oral presentations, are given thorough coverage in this book.

Nonverbal Communication

A nonverbal form of communication serves well for transmitting certain messages and is often used spontaneously. Nonverbal communication is the exchange of meaning that occurs in the absence of the spoken word. For example, at a busy location, you might summon a taxi by waving your arm.

We transmit nonverbal messages constantly—consciously or subconsciously. Some frequently used forms of nonverbal communication are sight, touch, sound, kinesics, and time. A few illustrations of each of these categories are given here.

Sight. Visual forms of nonverbal communication channels are illustrated in these examples: A person attending an auction usually raises a hand or uses facial expressions to indicate to the auctioneer a desire to bid. College students sometimes start looking at their watches or stowing their belongings in backpacks to remind the professor that it is almost time for the class period to end.

Traffic signal lights are examples of visual nonverbal communication. Motorists know the meanings of the red, yellow, and green colors in the light. They can also identify a graffiti-splattered stop sign by its shape.

People making oral presentations may have their confidence reinforced by listeners who smile or nod in a way that indicates approval of the manner in which the oral presentation is being made. Such gestures are especially reassuring to speakers who believe the persons making the gestures are competent to judge the quality of the oral presentation. Using words to express approval would not be appropriate in an instance such as this, yet this nonverbal form can be used quite effectively.

Touch. A handshake—a gesture given little thought by many people—is an example of touch as an effective form of nonverbal communication. A firm handshake by persons who are being introduced to each other suggests warmth or amicable personality. On the other hand, a handshake given because of obligation, such as to congratulate an opponent who won the contest, is likely to express a feeling that is somewhat less exuberant. In some cultures handshakes are not common, but other gestures of touching play a similar role. In some countries, for example, a hug or a kiss on each cheek may play a role equivalent to that of a firm handshake in the United States.

Because people interpret touching in different ways, care should be exercised when touching others in the workplace. A hug or a pat on the back may be offensive to some and may even be considered harassment.

Sound. Ringing a doorbell, speaking in a pleasant tone of voice to indicate approval or speaking in a sarcastic tone of voice to signify disapproval, and listening for a dial tone before dialing a telephone number are among the many uses of sound as a form of nonverbal communication.

Emergency vehicles such as police cars, fire trucks, and ambulances are equipped with special sound devices that alert us they are approaching. These sounds tell motorists they need to clear traffic lanes so the vehicles can pass safely.

Stores, factories, hospitals, schools, and other organizations have chimes or bells that have specific meaning for their employees. For example, a long steady bell tone signals the end of the class in many schools whereas two short bells repeated three times signal fire alarms. Similar codes may be used to page medical team members to various sites within the hospital. The sounds alert quickly those who need to know of an emergency and are not offensive to others within their range. Sound is used as an effective form of nonverbal communication more often than many of us realize.

Kinesics. Kinesics are body movements to which people attach meaning. Two common types of body movements that are used to communicate nonverbally are ***illustrators*** and ***regulators***. Illustrators usually accompany the spoken word. For example, when giving directions to the library, you may raise your arm and point while saying, "Go down the stairs and through the double glass doors; turn right and walk about a block. The library is on the left." Pointing to the markerboard or other visual aid while talking, the teacher uses both verbal and nonverbal (kinesic) communication.

Regulators are subconscious movements that are somewhat difficult for us to control; therefore, when the messages sent by these regulators conflict with the verbal messages, the nonverbal messages are usually thought to be more accurate. Swinging one's leg while seated or tapping a foot indicates nervousness or annoyance. Similarly, moist palms suggest one's nervous state. Failure to maintain good eye contact with your receivers or holding both hands tightly clasped in your lap makes them think you have something to hide or that you are being less than honest with them. Crossed arms and a solid stance tend to represent a closed mind—a situation where the receivers refuse to listen to your position. Your sitting erect and leaning slightly forward in your chair notifies the speaker you are paying close attention to the conversation; similarly, reclining in the chair with feet extended indicates you are less interested. What are you telling your instructor about your interest in this class by the way you sit in your chair?

Time. The use of time is a form of nonverbal communication. If you repeatedly look at your watch while talking with someone, you are nonverbally relating that you do not have much time to share in this conversation. If you are habitually late, you are indicating that you think you and your time are more important than the person or persons you keep waiting.

The ways you spend your time express your priorities. You cannot say honestly you did not have time to study for your exam. More accurately, you can say you thought other activities were more important, and you chose not to spend your time studying.

The forms of nonverbal communication mentioned here, as well as many others, can be combined with words to produce effective oral and written communication in business and in social situations.

Combined Forms of Communication

A nonverbal message can be transmitted with no verbal message accompanying it. A verbal message, on the other hand, is accompanied by a nonverbal message. Voice tone, pronunciation, facial expressions, gestures, and other nonverbal forms accompany oral messages. Handwriting style, punctuation, and appearance of the page are among the numerous nonverbal symbols that accompany written messages. The nonverbal message that accompanies the verbal message receives more attention. An often-heard comment, for example, is, "*What* was said did not affect us nearly as much as the *way* it was said." Based on the voice tone, the same words may be sincere, sarcastic, or noncommital. Consider the sentence "You look nice today." What meaning could it carry?

Among the many forms of nonverbal communication that can be combined with written words to transmit a message effectively are punctuation marks; different fonts and effects such as bold, italics, and underlines; color; spacing on a page; stationery quality; and/or handwriting style. An exclamation mark at the end of a sentence may indicate the mood of the writer, or it may draw attention to the importance or the severity of a situation. Underlining or boldfacing a word or a group of words calls attention to that part of a message. Varying the line lengths accomplishes the same purpose.

Sometimes nonverbal communication supports the verbal communication: Stephanie Graves smiled as she congratulated her assistant. Sometimes the two forms contradict each other: Tim Clarkson said with a disgruntled voice that he is excited about the proposed reorganization of the company. When verbal and nonverbal messages conflict, the receiver is more likely to believe the nonverbal message because nonverbal messages are more difficult to control and are, therefore, perceived to be more accurate.

Barriers to Communication

Communication is not only essential, but it is also enjoyable. Yet many barriers to the process add to its complexity. Some of the communication barriers are physical, some are language related, and others are psychological.

Physical Barriers

People who are uncomfortable because of fatigue, hunger, illness, limited space, temperature of the environment, or other reasons can neither send nor receive messages as well as they could if they were comfortable. Also, the appearance of the communication medium has an effect on the recipient. When a message is poorly printed or uses poor spacing or is presented in handwriting that is hard to read, the receiver has difficulty concentrating on the content. Likewise, inappropriate attire of a speaker or poor delivery of the message makes it hard for the listener to concentrate on the content.

Numerous other physical distractions such as whispering, coughing, and shuffling of papers, as well as traffic and other outside noises, are barriers to effective communication. Poor lighting and poor acoustics are frequently encountered. An extensive list of other physical communication barriers could be made.

Language Barriers

Misspelling, incorrect pronunciation, and poor choice of words are common barriers to effective communication. Of these three, poor choice of words is perhaps the most serious. Readers and listeners do not know the meanings of all the words they see or hear; and because many words have more than one meaning, the meaning the message sender intended to convey may not be the meaning the reader or listener receives. Using idioms (expressions unique to a particular region) may confuse your receiver. Idioms, such as *cut the lights,* may mean one thing to a person in one particular region, yet something else to persons in another place. Trite words or the overuse of a contemporary appropriate word or phrase such as *basically, like*, *okay*, *whatever*, and *you know* can be so distracting that it becomes a major communication barrier.

Words—whether spoken or written—should be chosen carefully to fit the particular situation at hand and the communicators involved. Because of backgrounds and experiences, people tend to perceive different meanings of words. The owner of a luxury car and the owner of a compact car, for example, may listen as a salesperson describes a sedan. One listener might perceive the sedan as a little car; the other, a big car.

Psychological Barriers

A negative feeling concerning a message that is transmitted can affect adversely the message sender or the receiver. The sender is likely to exhibit a negative feeling either consciously or subconsciously and thereby present the message ineffectively. Similarly, a receiver who has a negative feeling may receive the message ineffectively or not accept it at all even though the words and the accompanying nonverbal channels are clearly understood.

Let's assume winter is Michael's favorite season because he enjoys skiing and he requests vacation time in February. Could he easily accept the advantages his supervisor may point out for rescheduling his vacation for summer? He probably would have trouble concentrating on those advantages as much as he should.

Positive feelings also affect communicators and can sometimes influence a message sender to present information so that the negative features are not apparent to the receiver. Similarly, a receiver who has positive feelings about a situation may possibly hear the words used to explain negative features yet still not actually comprehend them.

Even though there are many barriers to communication, the communication process can be effective. Continuing to study in order to sharpen communication skills will pay rich dividends.

Prerequisites for Effective Communication

As we have discussed, a primary requirement for communicating effectively is at least a partial understanding of, as well as an appreciation for, the communication process. Other prerequisites for effective communication follow:

1. Consider the receiver.
2. Understand the problem or situation.
3. Select and phrase words carefully.
4. Consider cultural, ethical, and legal issues.

Consider the Receiver

When speaking or writing, try to put yourself in the receiver's place by looking at the situation from that person's point of view. How would you view the situation if you were the receiver? Would you expect an adjustment, a refund, or some other course of action?

By attempting to see the situation as your receiver would, you will be better prepared to select appropriate words and media for the communication.

Understand the Problem or Situation

A thorough knowledge of the situation leading to communication helps you to understand the statements others make orally or in writing, and it helps you to decide what to say or write. In business you usually understand the conditions that exist, and you have access to information about the receivers of your message. Completing the exercises and the problems in this book, though, will require you to use your imagination to a greater extent than is necessary in real situations.

Select and Phrase Words Carefully

You need to be familiar with the terms used in connection with the business transactions you handle so that you can transmit your ideas in an appropriate way and so that you can interpret precisely the ideas you receive by listening or by reading. Strive always to increase your knowledge of words, especially those pertaining to your field of work. Since people think in words, the larger the vocabulary you have, the better you can formulate and express ideas. Likewise, a good vocabulary helps you to understand the messages you receive.

To communicate accurately, use good grammar. Errors in sentence structure, in spelling, in punctuation, and in pronunciation can make a message convey ideas or information different from what is intended. Additionally, your credibility is damaged. If your messages contain careless errors, the receiver will believe all of your work will be careless and unreliable. For example, would you want to have your insurance coverage with a company that did not spell your name correctly on the policies? Will you even have insurance coverage should you need it?

You can enhance the quality of your business messages by studying the following chapters and the reference section of this book. You can, of course, get further help by referring to any one of many grammar books or reference books.

Consider Cultural, Ethical, and Legal Issues

The cultural experiences of both the sender and the receiver influence the meaning assigned to communication messages. The sender should be considerate of the culture in which the receiver conducts business and should respect those expectations. Ethical and legal considerations must also be weighed in communication activities. Just as you need to have the right attitude about the receiver and to have the correct information to communicate, you also need to consider both the ethical and the legal implications of your communication. Because your communication represents your organization, the organization may be legally responsible for the messages you send. Chapter 3 discusses these implications in greater detail.

Communication Flow In Organizations

Within the business organization, communication flows in different directions. That flow may be *external* (to individuals who are not within the company) or *internal* (to people who are within the company). To be successful, persons must communicate effectively with both groups.

External Communication

Because a primary objective of an organization is to provide products or services, communication with individuals and groups outside the organization is required. A manufacturer has to acquire raw materials, hire personnel, and possibly obtain transportation services before products can be finished. Consulting services also may be required from time to time for efficient operation. Writing letters to customers and prospective customers, talking on the telephone, conversing in face-to-face situations, preparing television and radio advertisements, and other communication activities are necessary for selling finished products.

Speeches to civic clubs, professional meetings, schools, and similar groups are some of the many external communication activities of organizations. These activities help to create, to maintain, and to promote good public relations—a vital characteristic of successful organizations.

Internal Communication

Employees in organizations communicate constantly among themselves. Constant communication is required for giving and receiving instructions, for announcing plans, for reporting activities and progress, for procuring supplies and services, for distributing products and services, for hiring and training personnel, and for numerous other activities.

A very important reason for constant internal communication is to maintain good morale. When employee morale is good, more production is accomplished; and fewer problems arise. All employees should be well informed on matters that pertain to them, and they should always feel confident that the information they need will be available when they need it. Effective communication among the organizational personnel is perhaps the greatest contributor to good morale. This communication may follow either formal or informal paths.

Formal Paths. Formal communication paths carry messages that are sent intentionally along the lines of authority and responsibility depicted in the company's organization chart. An organization chart shows relationships and positions of responsibility within an organization. Figure 1-2 shows a partial organization chart.

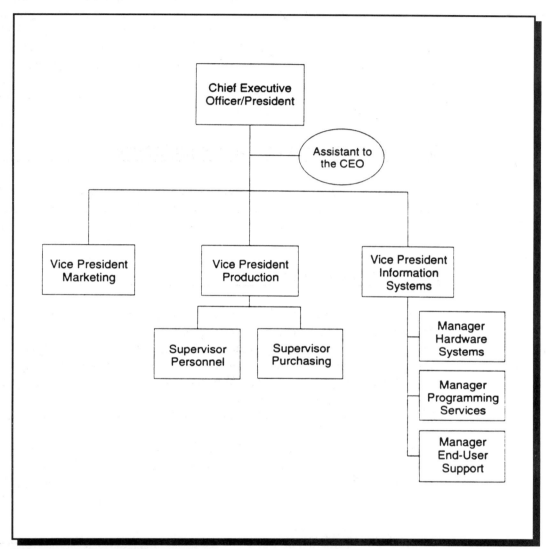

Figure 1-2. Organization Chart

Messages may be sent routinely or for special occasions, and they usually go in one of three directions: downward, upward, or horizontal.

Downward messages flow from persons who hold positions nearer the top of the organization chart to persons who hold positions on lower levels. For example, the president may send an information memorandum to a vice-president, a congratulatory or a condolence letter to a sales representative, an e-mail message to a staff assistant, or a set of instructions to several maintenance employees. Bulletin boards—electronic and physical—provided they are arranged well and are kept up to date—are good channels for sending messages to several people.

The downward messages may be oral. They may be sent by telephone or by teleconference, or they may be sent in personal conversations. These conversations may take place in a manager's office, at an employee's workstation, or at various other places. Public address systems, staff meetings, and committee meetings afford opportunities to disseminate information to groups. Managers often need to tell groups about new branches, strikes, layoffs, new products, and so on.

Seldom is a message transmitted downward without involving upward transmission of other messages. These responses are often called feedback.

Upward messages flow from persons who hold positions nearer the bottom of the organization chart to persons who hold positions on higher levels. An assistant manager, for example, may send a memorandum to the manager of that department. Sales associates may—through conversation or a telephone call or in writing—send messages to their sales manager. Any message, whether oral or written, that is sent from a person on a lower level of the organization chart to a person on a higher level is a part of upward communication.

Upward communication is promoted to stimulate and encourage creativity, innovations, and the expression of new ideas. Another reason for promoting upward communication is to understand the feelings of the employees. When the morale is high, the managers want to know about it. When employees have grievances or are merely curious about a situation, the managers want to know that so they can supply the needed information.

Many messages take a **horizontal** path between individuals at the same level within the organization. As an example, the manager of the Production Department may need to send messages to and receive messages from the manager of the Transportation Department. Also, an assembly-line worker may likely communicate with other assembly-line workers. Horizontal communication takes place often among employees at all levels of the organizational structure.

Informal Paths. Even though formal communication paths are essential in small organizations as well as in large ones, informal communication takes place in all groups and is extremely important. Informal communication is often called the "grapevine" because communication frequently occurs in clusters. Like messages of a formal nature, informal messages may flow in downward, upward, and horizontal directions; however, the informal paths are less structured and are more spontaneous than are the formal paths. Figure 1-3 shows an example of how informal communication may travel among employees at various levels within an organization.

Informal communication patterns are more likely to form on the basis of personalities, locations, and circumstances than on position within the organization. For example, if Erica, the Vice President for Internal Affairs carpools with Terrence, a systems analyst, and Frederick, the legal affairs representative, the three will likely communicate about company activities while enroute. They are not at the same levels within the organization and may not necessarily have formal communication needs. When Terrence gets to work, he may share some of the things he learned in the carpool conversations with his associates in the computer center. Then that same information may be shared over coffee when the five departmental secretaries, including the one from the computer center, get together. People who take their breaks at the same time will talk informally regardless of their organizational position.

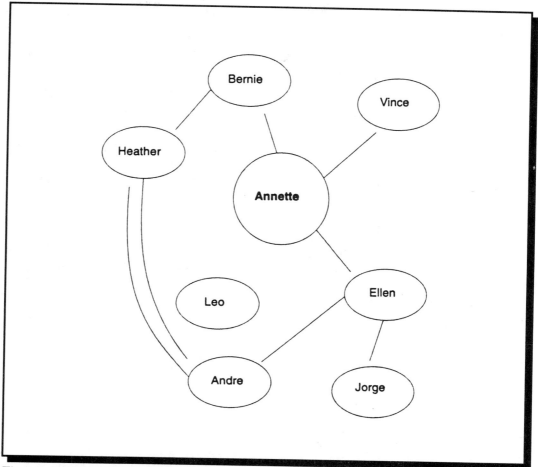

Figure 1-3. Typical Paths of Informal Communication

Informal messages can flow **downward** between any two levels or among a variety of levels on the organization chart. A top-ranking executive's speaking to an assembly-line worker in a corridor or elsewhere is an example of informal oral communication that can have a positive effect on both communicators.

A supervisor may go to the desk of a systems analyst, a sales representative, or another employee to congratulate the employee on a successful venture or to express appreciation for good work. The coffee break is also a good place to communicate informally. Dozens of other opportunities exist daily for effective informal downward flow of messages.

Informality does much to break down communication barriers between people on different levels of the organization structure. Several trends in business such as business casual dress provide a more informal work environment that can encourage informal communication.

Like **upward**-flowing formal messages, informal messages go from people on a lower level to others on upper levels of the organization chart. These messages can flow between any two levels: they can go to the next level up or to even higher levels. Perceptive managers create situations to encourage upward communication. They try to stimulate employees to be creative and innovative and to express their feelings about working conditions.

Company-sponsored activities such as social events, wellness programs, and athletic teams provide excellent opportunities for informal communication among personnel from all levels of the organizational structure. In a casual setting, some barriers to communication may be reduced.

Frequent informal communication among personnel enables them to get to know one another and to understand the desires, ambitions, elations, doubts, and other feelings of superiors, peers, and subordinates. For high morale, which leads to greater efficiency, various types of situations can be created to promote informal communication.

Even though managers develop situations to encourage frequent informal communication among personnel on various levels of the organization, people tend to join others at their own level for coffee breaks and other occasions that provide opportunities for informal communication. This practice helps the workers to understand the work, needs, aspirations, and so on of their peers. Also, they benefit from these informal exchanges of facts, ideas, feelings, and so on by learning ways to perform their duties more efficiently. These employees can, at the same time, vent frustrations and discuss rumors as well as facts that they learn through the "grapevine," which thrives within any major group.

Communication is a complex process and requires careful planning. A study of the organization and format of business messages described in this text will enable you to become an effective communicator.

DISCUSSION

1. What must the sender and the receiver have in common for successful communication?

2. How can silence coupled with the absence of gestures and facial expressions be a medium of communication?

3. What steps can people take to improve their ability to communicate?

4. Describe barriers that were not mentioned in this chapter that you believe negatively affect communication.

5. What are several situations that could be developed to promote informal communication among personnel within an organization?

6. Why is the "grapevine" a suitable name for the informal communication structure that exists in most organizations?

EXERCISES

1. Observe two people communicating. Analyze both the sender's and the receiver's verbal and nonverbal communication. Describe your findings to the class.

2. To test the importance of feedback in the communication process, try the following exercise: As a friend is talking to you, do not give feedback. Do not speak and do not use nonverbal communication; that is, do not nod your head, smile, frown, and so on. Observe your friend's response to your lack of response! Tell your friend about your experiment. Report your findings to the class.

3. Watch a videotape of a television program or movie. First watch the tape with the sound turned off. What can you understand from the nonverbal messages you see? Next, watch the tape with sound. Were you accurate in your nonverbal communication? Discuss your findings with the class.

4. Establish an e-mail account if you do not already have one. Send a message to your instructor or a fellow class member that discusses a communication situation you have encountered that would tie in with one of the concepts discussed in this chapter.

5. Several quotations were listed that discussed communication. Use a book of quotations or a computer program to find other quotations that you think would be of value in describing communication. Be ready to e-mail your quotation to your instructor or discuss your findings.

CHOOSING COMMUNICATION CHANNELS

■ Of the technologies available for communicating in business today, which one is the most essential? Justify your choice.

■ You have prepared a new contract with a higher salary for one of your employees at a branch location. What factors should be considered as you decide whether to fax the contract to the branch location?

■ Regarding job offers, it has been said that good news comes by telephone and bad news by letter. Do you agree? How does the selected channel affect your perception?

SELECTING THE COMMUNICATION CHANNEL

The purpose of a business communication message is to convey meaning in an accurate, effective manner. The business communicator must make several choices before actually sending the message to the audience.

First, you must choose the precise words and nonverbal mediums for the message; then you must select the most effective way of creating your message; and finally, you must determine the most appropriate channel for transmitting this message to your intended receiver. Technology plays a significant role in message creation and channel selection.

Using Technology in Business Communication

Changes in technology have affected businesses and business communication ever since Alexander Graham Bell said, "Mr. Watson, I need you." Technology has become increasingly important in recent years.

Some of the available technologies that assist business people in their communication activities are computer technology, Internet, electronic mail, voice mail, facsimile machines, teleconferencing, and portable communication devices such as cellular telephones, pagers, and personal digital assistants. These technologies support the creation, distribution, and reception of business communication.

To illustrate the impact of technology and the diversity of communication channels, examine the communication activities of Manager Matt, a typical business person as listed in Figure 2-1.

Defining the Communication Channel

In the example of Matt's typical workday, numerous communication channels and technologies were used. Consider this example as well. One day the manager noticed that several employees seemed to be treating customers in a very casual, offhand manner. The manager would like all customers to feel that their concerns are important and would like

A Communication Day in the Life of Manager Matt

6:30 a.m.	Before dressing for work, Matt checks the local weather forecast on the Internet. While he is at his computer, he also checks the status of his stock portfolio. Then he turns to his personal digital assistant to refresh his memory of his day's schedule.
7:25 a.m.	During his half hour commute to work, Matt uses a cellular phone to check his voice mail for any changes that have occurred in his appointments and meeting schedule.
7:55 a.m.	Matt meets a co-worker in the parking lot and talks about sports, the weather, and an upcoming meeting during the walk to the building.
8:05 a.m.	Turning to his office computer, Matt first checks his e-mail and finds he has 12 new messages–three from his boss. He quickly scans the subject lines and finds that the location has been changed for an afternoon meeting. Although he replies to four messages, deletes two messages after reading them, and moves three to other folders for future reference, he doesn't have time to read three of the messages. The unread messages stay in his inbox folder.
8:30 a.m.	Matt greets his first appointment of the day–the department's web master. In the course of the conversation, Matt selects several photos to be scanned for possible addition to the company web page. He must check his computer twice for information as well as make two phone calls to clarify the situation.
9:00 a.m.	Matt takes the elevator to his first meeting of the day. Fortunately, he remembered to print a copy of the agenda which was included as an attachment in one of his e-mail messages that morning.
10:15 a.m.	Returning from his morning break, Matt learns that several people are still unclear about the new vacation policy. Turning to his computer again, he creates a memo clarifying the situation, and faxes it to the branch offices.
10:30 a.m.	Matt opens and reads his mail. He has two letters from clients, a memo from the HR department regarding a change in employee benefits, and three advertising brochures.
11:00 a.m.	Matt accesses the Internet to do some research for his 4 p.m. meeting.
12:00 noon	Matt joins a group of colleagues at a nearby restaurant for lunch. His pager beeps as soon as he orders. By the time he excuses himself and responds to the page, he has two more pager messages. Lunch is short!

Figure 2-1. Communication Day in the Life of Manager Matt

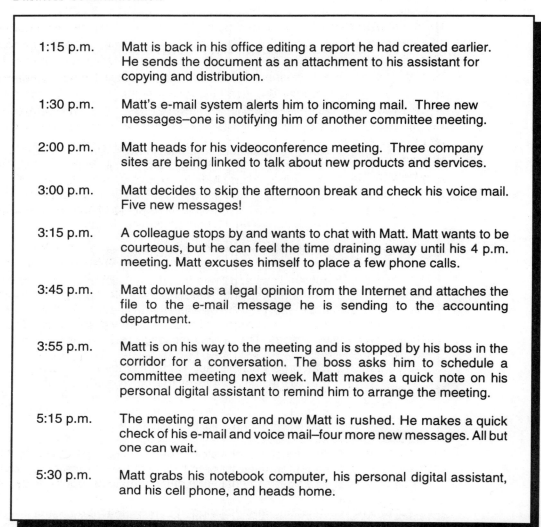

1:15 p.m.	Matt is back in his office editing a report he had created earlier. He sends the document as an attachment to his assistant for copying and distribution.
1:30 p.m.	Matt's e-mail system alerts him to incoming mail. Three new messages—one is notifying him of another committee meeting.
2:00 p.m.	Matt heads for his videoconference meeting. Three company sites are being linked to talk about new products and services.
3:00 p.m.	Matt decides to skip the afternoon break and check his voice mail. Five new messages!
3:15 p.m.	A colleague stops by and wants to chat with Matt. Matt wants to be courteous, but he can feel the time draining away until his 4 p.m. meeting. Matt excuses himself to place a few phone calls.
3:45 p.m.	Matt downloads a legal opinion from the Internet and attaches the file to the e-mail message he is sending to the accounting department.
3:55 p.m.	Matt is on his way to the meeting and is stopped by his boss in the corridor for a conversation. The boss asks him to schedule a committee meeting next week. Matt makes a quick note on his personal digital assistant to remind him to arrange the meeting.
5:15 p.m.	The meeting ran over and now Matt is rushed. He makes a quick check of his e-mail and voice mail—four more new messages. All but one can wait.
5:30 p.m.	Matt grabs his notebook computer, his personal digital assistant, and his cell phone, and heads home.

Figure 2-1. Continued

all employees to realize that customer satisfaction is vital to company profits. The manager has decided that it would be a good idea to discuss these concerns with the employees. After the manager has decided what to say, the next step is to determine how to create and send the message. How should the manager send the message?

A *communication channel* is the path along which a message is sent. Three broad types of communication channels are *oral, written, and visual*. Technology has expanded each of these types of channels and provided additional avenues for creating and sending messages effectively.

Oral Channels

Oral channels are face-to-face conversations, telephone calls, voice mail, and group discussion. An advantage of an oral channel is immediate feedback and interaction during the communication process. In the preceding example, if the manager would like to discuss treatment of customers with a specific employee or with a group of employees and would like feedback and/or suggestions from the group, an oral channel may be a good choice. Oral channels can be quite time consuming, however, for the manager. For example, a manager who wishes to talk face-to-face individually with ten employees must plan to spend quite a bit of time in the communication process.

A further concern exists when determining how and when all employees should receive the information. If a supervisor wishes to discuss vacation schedules individually with employees on a face-to-face basis, a few persons may realize that they were the last few the supervisor talked with rather than the first few. Those individuals may feel slighted because they were the last to know about the vacation communication. Such a communication scenario can be especially difficult if one of the first employees to find out about the vacation schedule immediately tells others whom the supervisor hasn't had a chance to talk with yet.

Face-to-Face Communication. In face-to-face communication, one person speaks directly to another. Communicating face-to-face allows immediate feedback. In addition, the message can be tailored for each individual. Some individuals, for example, may prefer to hear negative news right away, while others would be happier if the speaker provided reasons before giving the negative news.

Face-to-face communication also allows the sender and the receiver to study nonverbal messages and to better interpret the nonverbal signals that accompany the verbal message. Quite often, however, it is easy for the communicators to get off the subject and to spend too much time discussing irrelevant matters. In addition, a certain amount of time is usually spent socializing and answering questions such as "How is your family?" or "Are you having a good week?" Seldom can the face-to-face meeting start immediately with the topic at hand.

Telephone Communication. Communicating by telephone may be a more effective use of time than communicating face-to-face. When communicating by telephone, each person can provide feedback, even when the people are at different geographic locations.

A disadvantage of telephone communication is "telephone tag" which occurs when two persons keep leaving messages as they try to reach each other. As communicators can not see each other, telephone communication does not provide ample opportunity for the persons to interpret nonverbal cues which is another disadvantage. For that reason, if messages or instructions are quite complex, communicating over the telephone may not provide the best results.

Voice Mail. Voice mail is an alternative to telephone communication. One obvious advantage of voice mail is the automatic answering of telephones when the intended receiver is using the telephone or is unavailable to answer incoming calls. Before this technology, companies that received a large number of calls hired one or more receptionists to answer the phone and transfer calls to or take messages for the appropriate persons.

The caller can leave a message that can later be recalled by the person who was unable to take the phone call. Using voice mail can help to reduce "telephone tag." The best use of voice mail, though, is for simple announcements or easily understood requests.

When leaving a message by voice mail, the sender cannot interact with the intended receiver. With some voice mail systems, it may be difficult to determine when callers accessed their messages or whether they received them at all.

When an organization installs voice mail, each person who has a telephone is given a voice mail box. Messages can be left if no one answers the extension. A difference from a telephone answering machine is that the individual who receives the messages can forward them to one or several other individuals, can store them permanently, or on some systems, may print them if a hard copy is needed.

In some voice mail systems, a message left for internal telephone callers may be different from the one left for external callers. For example, in a system used at a metropolitan newspaper, each user may design two different messages. Callers within the company may receive a message like "This is Jeff. I am running around the place fixing computers! Leave a message and I will get back to you." The message may be more formal for callers phoning from outside the company such as "This is Jeff Linwood. I am unavailable at the moment, but will be happy to return your call."

Voice mail, combined with upgraded telephone technology, has greatly simplified the telephone answering process. For example, a credit-card customer with a concern about the balance of an account, may call the toll free number of the credit card company. The phone is answered by a recorded message that mentions the name of the company and gives instructions for using voice mail. After listening to the instructions, the customer may push "1" for an account balance. The customer can then key in the credit card number. Frequently, a code word is required for security purposes. A recorded voice then states the current balance, the date the account was last paid, the amount of the last payment, and the amount of remaining credit. The message may even be repeated if the caller wishes. The caller can receive all of this information and more without talking to a person.

Another voice mail system was designed for a service organization that received 10,000 phone calls a month. The organization listed a four-digit code on each brochure or piece of correspondence it distributed. Callers were then asked to call in and could direct their voice mail to the appropriate voice mailbox by keying the four-digit code after the initial phone message was received.

Some callers think that interacting with a computer answering device is intimidating and/or impersonal. In deciding on the appropriate use of voice mail, each organization must balance its efforts for fast, efficient service with the customers' needs.

Communication by voice mail requires the sender of the message to state clearly and concisely the main points of the message as well as to relate what action is expected from the message receiver.

Group Communication. The sender may choose to convey messages to a group at one time. The committee chairperson, for example, may want to communicate with all the members at a meeting. The meeting may be a conventional one with all members physically present or it may combine technology for a teleconference in a meeting room with participants in different locations or by computer conference. While communicating with a group may provide feedback, group dynamics may encourage some members of the group to speak out, while others remain silent.

One advantage of communicating with a group is that all members receive the message at the same time. The sender must be careful, however, when conveying negative news to a group. For example, assembling several people and telling them that their jobs are being eliminated may be ineffective communication.

Written Channels

The message sender can choose a written channel such as a letter, an electronic mail message, a memo, or a report. These channels are effective for conveying messages that contain many steps. The written channel can provide clarity that the other channels cannot have. Written messages are more formal and especially useful in documenting transactions with clients and customers. Some communicators use an oral channel for initial contact and decisions and then send a follow-up written document to confirm the information provided through one of the other channels.

Letter. Communicating by letter is an accepted business practice. Often a letter is used to follow up an earlier form of communication. The sender can spell out conditions or concerns to which the recipient can respond. Usually, a letter is used to communicate with those outside the company or when a formal method of communication within the company is expected.

Application letters, letters offering positions, and letters accepting positions are often written. These uses of formal written channels can be very important in the employment process as companies must often be able to justify any hiring or promotion decisions.

Letters are sometimes more costly than other communication mediums because of the labor involved. Contrary to popular opinion, sending a letter costs more than *just* first-class postage! When considerations such as the costs of the executives' time, cost of administrative support (if used), of supplies such as stationery and printer toner, and overhead costs are factored into the total cost of a letter, an average business letter could cost well over $12.

Sending a letter may require several days for the communication process to occur as delivery by the U.S. Postal Service or by private mailing services may take up to 10 days for delivery. Additionally, if the same letter is sent to many people, it is likely that it will not reach all the addressees at the same time.

Electronic-mail (e-mail). Perhaps one of the fastest growing areas of business communication is electronic mail (e-mail). In recent years, however, e-mail has made its way on to virtually all computer networks. E-mail may be sent internally to people on a local area network or externally around the world through a wide area network of telephone lines and modems.

E-mail can be compared to voice mail. The sender of the message sends it to the electronic mailbox of the receiver. Again, no immediate interaction or feedback takes place. As with voice mail, e-mail can be a quick method to communicate. A message can be sent to several addresses at one time.

Two of the big advantages of electronic communication are convenience and speed. Using this type of communication, the senders can transmit the messages whenever they wish. The receivers then respond at their convenience. Other advantages of e-mail are listed in Figure 2-2.

You could compare electronic communication to checking your postal mailbox. You may not check your mail at the same time every day. When you do check your mail, you may decide not to open all the letters at one time. Electronic communication carries a similar convenience factor. A difference between the two, however, is that electronic communication is much faster than postal mail. If someone has a question and needs a quick response, the message receiver can respond quickly with an electronic channel.

Each person using e-mail has an electronic address. The user accesses the system and sends messages to individuals or to groups, forwards mail, saves mail in appropriate file folders, and prints a hard copy of mail if necessary. Features of e-mail packages vary. Many packages allow senders to label their messages with a priority level such as high, medium, or low.

E-mail can be used well for more complex instructions or for scheduling meeting dates and times. In most e-mail systems, the recipient can print a copy of the message. Having a hard copy of a complex message contributes to accurate communication at a later time. E-mail can also be useful when you know the recipient is difficult to reach by telephone. The sender can quickly transmit the message and then wait for a response from the receiver—a technique that may be quicker than repeated attempts at phoning.

While e-mail has many distinct advantages, the disadvantages of electronic communication should also be considered. Company monitoring and computer hackers are two disadvantages. Many companies reserve the right to randomly monitor employees' electronic communication. Some companies limit e-mail use to business purposes only, while others permit personal messages on a limited basis. For this reason many people have more than one e-mail address using one for business communication and one for personal communication. Computer hackers may access one's personal e-mail mailbox; therefore, use caution when sending confidential information electronically. Other disadvantages are discussed in Figure 2-2.

Electronic Mail

Advantages

- Electronic messages may be sent more quickly than hard copy messages.
- Messages are more informal.
- A message may be sent to several people at one time.
- Messages may be sent at any time regardless of time zone differences of recipients.
- Messages may be sent conveniently to people who are difficult to reach by telephone.
- Messages may be saved and stored electronically in designated folders for easy reference.
- An address book (mailing list) can be developed for frequently used addresses.

Disadvantages

- Because messages may be composed and sent quickly, errors in spelling, grammar, and accuracy may occur.
- Electronic messages may be considered less important than letters and reports.
- Access to e-mail may be limited for some people who do not have ready access to a computer.
- Electronic transmission failure or erroneous e-mail addresses may result in undeliverable mail.
- E-mail mailboxes can become cluttered with junk messages that distract from relevant messages.
- E-mail messages may not be private because of company monitoring or unauthorized access to personal mailboxes.

Figure 2-2. Electronic Mail

In one case, an executive of a major corporation indicated that e-mail was the lifeblood of his organization. Offices were located across the country and e-mail tied them all together. Changes in schedules and plans were easily conveyed instantly via e-mail to all the offices. He noted that he always read electronic messages from his boss first!

When using e-mail follow these general guidelines:

- Consider the type of message you are sending; use e-mail for quick, informal messages. Detailed instructions should be included as an attachment that can be easily printed by the receiver.
- Reserve formal and/or confidential messages for a printed letter or memo.
- Clearly state the subject on the subject line so that the receiver will know the general subject content without opening the message.
- Send a separate e-mail message for each item you wish to discuss. If you include several issues in one message, it is easy for one point to be overlooked.
- Be sure to use correct spelling, grammar, and sentence structure. Check your message for accuracy. Informality is no substitute for inaccuracy.
- Personalize your message by including the receiver's name early in the message as a salutation or within the first sentence.
- Use upper- and lower-case letters as the message is easier to read. Typing a message in all capital letters is considered SHOUTING and should be avoided.
- Answer e-mail messages promptly if a response is appropriate. Don't feel obligated to respond to e-mail messages that don't require a response as this creates unnecessary or junk e-mail for the other person.
- Do answer e-mail messages when the sender may question whether you have read the message. For example, if this is your first message from an external person, a simple response expressing thanks for the message will tell the sender that the message was received.
- Limit message distribution to people who need to receive your message.
- Observe the organizational chain of command. Do not send e-mail messages to people to whom you would not send print copies.
- Use discretion in forwarding messages, as the original sender may not want the message shared with others. In fact, in some instances, you may wish to contact the original sender to ask for permission to forward the message.
- Remember your e-mail message can easily be forwarded to others or printed to become a written document; therefore, avoid saying things that you do not want publicized!
- Avoid "flaming"—saying things in anger that you wouldn't write in hard copy.
- Include your name in the body of your message; your e-mail address may not clearly identify you to the recipient. Although your e-mail may have a signature feature, other e-mail systems may not be able to read your signature feature.
- Determine whether a message was sent to a Listserv before using the reply function of your e-mail. A Listserv is a special distribution list that sends all messages and all responses to those messages to a group of people. Therefore, using the reply function will automatically send your message to all people on the Listserv.

Memo. Memos are normally used within a company and may be written in a more informal writing style than is used in letters. Memos frequently contain technical terms easily understood by those within the company.

Memos can be sent to individuals or can be posted in a common area such as on a bulletin board. They can be most effective for complex issues. For example, if a company is considering a new health plan, a memo about the plan could be studied carefully by the recipients and shared with family members.

Report. Reports vary in length from short, informal reports to long, formal ones. A report describes an examination of a particular issue and may include recommendations for action. When a report is completed, it is often distributed to one person or to several.

When evaluating complex or controversial issues, a written report is perhaps the most effective means of communicating. Recipients have an opportunity to study the information in detail. Issues of report writing will be discussed in Part Three of this text.

Visual Channels

The slogan "a picture is worth a thousand words" can have importance in communication. Technology such as facsimile machines, e-mail, and the Internet are effective visual channels in that they convey images, diagrams, photographs, and sketches that can assist in communication. Although not exclusively visual, these technologies rely heavily on visual images for communication purposes.

If the communicator believes that a visual image will enhance clarity, a channel that will accommodate visuals must be selected. In addition to the various technologies mentioned above, nonverbal communication, photographs, and graphic images are visual channels of communication.

Nonverbal communication. As discussed in Chapter 1, nonverbal communication enables people to communicate without words. Whether through body movements, the use of time or space, or physical appearance, we all communicate daily nonverbally. First impressions of people are usually made based on visual communication.

Photographs and graphic images. Photographs and graphs frequently communicate more precisely than words. In business communication, visual aids may be included in reports, as e-mail attachments, or on a web page. These images may replace or supplement the written word.

Facsimile Machine. Fax communication is one of the fastest-growing areas of communication technology. Communicating by fax can be quick and inexpensive. Fax machines can transmit diagrams or other visual material very effectively.

In one company, a sales manager was traveling to a site he had not visited. He knew how to get to the city, but wasn't sure of the specific location. A map that he requested be faxed to him helped him easily find the new site.

Some companies have satellite communication facilities that link remote sites. A fax machine in both locations helps them in exchanging last-minute information or for taking a closer look at ideas.

Many companies use fax between different locations in the same city and when communicating with other businesses in the same local calling area. Costs for fax transmission increase when long-distance phone charges are added. Many faxes can be sent in the evening or at night, however, to save on long distance charges.

Confidentiality is a concern with fax machines when many machines are located in a common area rather than in an employee's private office.

The Internet. The Internet is widely used by businesses and for personal use as well. Usage of the Internet is expected to continue to grow significantly in the next few years. Many local service providers, (telephone or cable television systems), provide access to customers to use the Internet to browse the World Wide Web, to retrieve databases, and to use electronic-mail.

An increasing number of business users now provide varied company information on their own home pages on the ***World Wide Web***. A site for a company would provide a showcase available to any user of the World Wide Web.

Using Web browser software, such as Internet Explorer or Netscape, you can search the Web for topics or for specific company sites. By using a search engine, such as Yahoo, Alta Vista, Magellan, or Lycos, and entering key words of specific topics or categories you can find corresponding web sites. These searches are extremely valuable in research and for locating specific topics of interest.

Choosing the Best Communication Channel

As a sender prepares to transmit the message, the choice of channel becomes important. When choosing the channel, the sender should weigh the rate of transmission speed, the value of simultaneous communication, the need for privacy, the interaction of communicators, the requirements for message accuracy, the importance of nonverbal cues, the legality of a message record, the technology access of both persons, the cost of the message, and the use of a visual approach. Consider the following list.

Questions to Answer When Selecting the Communication Channel

✔ What speed is needed for transmission?
✔ Is simultaneous communication to all persons important?
✔ Should the message be private?
✔ Will interaction at the time the message is delivered be important?
✔ Is the message complex or difficult to understand?
✔ Are nonverbal cues necessary when the message is delivered or received?
✔ Should a written record be kept of the message?
✔ Does the recipient have access to the communication channel?
✔ Is cost a factor?
✔ Would a graphic or visual message be better than another form?

Transmission Speed

How important is speed to communication? The fastest methods of communication may be telephone or face-to-face. These options will vary, however, depending on the situation. Telephone communication is not fast if the sender is unable to contact the intended receiver. Face-to-face communication is not fast if the proposed recipient is not available.

An e-mail message is faster than a business letter. A letter or a memo may actually be faster than e-mail, however, if the recipient checks a fixed mailbox more frequently than an electronic one.

Simultaneous Communication

Should all the proposed recipients learn about the message at the same time? Communicating individually by telephone or face-to-face may take a considerable amount of time.

If the goal is for all the recipients to get the message at the same time, the sender may wish to post a memo or send out individual memos. Sending the same message to a large group by e-mail or voice mail would be effective if those who are out-of-town on business check voice mail and/or e-mail wherever they are.

Privacy

Is the message one that should be conveyed in the privacy of an office? A team manager of a professional sport learned that he was fired when the message came across his fax machine. He would have preferred to receive this information both privately and in a more personal manner. Some messages should be related in private.

Could a company employee receive a letter that was not placed in an envelope, thus allowing others to read the letter before the employee saw it? Was a confidential message sent by e-mail that may be reviewed by the computer systems operator at a later time?

All of these issues of privacy relate to the communication channel. On sensitive or potentially sensitive issues, the message sender should choose the most secure channel.

Interaction

Interaction can occur as the message is being delivered, or it can be a response after the message has been delivered. The greatest chance for interaction exists in a telephone or face-to-face message. If the senders want immediate interaction, they should choose a channel that allows interaction. Voice mail and e-mail provide for limited interaction. Interaction has to be delayed when a letter, a memo, or a report is sent.

Message Accuracy

Accuracy in communication results in fewer communication mistakes. Some messages such as those announcing times and places for meetings are easy for the recipients to comprehend, and they are easy to record. A message to the maintenance crew describing exactly how a room is to be set up for a meeting, however, may be more complicated. If you meet face-to-face with the chief of the crew and go over the details, you may have better results than talking over the phone because you can show the chief what you have in mind. However, if the meeting is a few weeks away, you may find that it would be a better idea to send a memo summarizing your meeting so that the accuracy of the message can be maintained.

The more complex the message, the more opportunities for error. In order to ensure accuracy, the message sender should choose a channel that matches the complexity of the message. Complex messages should be in writing. A memo, a letter, an e-mail communication, or a fax would be best for this type of message. If the instructions are longer than a couple of paragraphs, a channel that produces a hard copy of the document for easy reference would probably be the best choice. The recipient can then have a hard copy of the document to refer to as needed.

Nonverbal Cues

Receiving nonverbal cues during the communication process may be important for the message sender. For example, a manager might be able to judge how negative news is being received by seeing the expression on the recipient's face. If such nonverbal cues are important, the sender should choose a channel that allows for such interaction. If, for example, a manager can relocate a promising supervisor to either of two locations, a face-to-face meeting may be needed so that the manager can pick up clues as to which location seems more interesting to the supervisor.

Message Record

In some instances, the communicator wishes to have an official record that a message was sent to a person. For example, during an employee evaluation, the supervisor may communicate orally with the employee about areas of concern. The supervisor may then wish to document that meeting with a memo or letter to provide a record of the communication.

If documentation of communication is important, the telephone and face-to-face communication would not be the best channels. A letter, memo, fax, or e-mail message can all serve as good documentation choices.

Technology Access

Some communication channels may not be available to every sender. For example, a fax can be sent only if the recipient has a fax machine and if the fax is on-line. An executive of one organization who preferred to fax orders in the evenings when phone charges were lower indicated that many companies turned off their fax machines when everyone left the office in the afternoon. In those cases, a fax could not be sent until the next day.

Many companies have e-mail for communicating within the organization. Voice mail is usually available to external and internal communicators. A message sender can send an e-mail message or a voice mail message to only those customers or fellow employees who have access to these technologies.

Cost

If the choice of the communication channel is not based on one or more of the factors already discussed, cost can be a significant factor. A business letter or memo will be more expensive to send than voice mail or e-mail. Face-to-face communication can be quite expensive if the executive's time is factored into determining the cost.

Fax communication can be expensive if long distance phone charges as well as supplies are included in the total cost. One organization, however, has found that faxing a document long distance averages only 27 cents per page. In that case, faxing a one page document would actually be cheaper than sending it by U.S. mail.

Legal and Ethical Considerations

When preparing a message and selecting a communication channel, the communicators must also consider legal and ethical factors.

Legal

A primary concern for business communicators is whether a legal violation occurs in a communication process. If communicators are involved in hiring a new employee, for example, the communication channel used could have legal implications since procedures for hiring should be the same for all candidates. In the initial process, communicators should not choose to telephone some candidates, send letters to some, and ignore others. Such actions could expose the communicators and their companies to possible legal action based on discrimination.

The communicators should be consistent and should choose the same channel for all candidates at each round of the hiring process. At the first level, the communicators may choose to write a letter to each candidate. As the top candidates are selected, the communicators may wish to phone each candidate or hold face-to-face interviews with the top few. Consistency in channel usage is very important.

Communicating consistently with employees is a major concern for business executives. If, for example, some employees are always warned about their behavior in private conferences while other employees are always warned in group communication or in front of others, legal consequences may ensue. Some employees may successfully contend that they were treated differently from the others.

Legal concerns also exist when communicating with customers. For example, if customers are interested in purchasing a cordless phone with an integrated answering machine, they may have several questions about the product. If a buying decision is based on information provided by a company representative, and it is later determined that the model was misrepresented, the company may have a legal problem to address that was caused by communication error.

Ethical

While it may be legal to fire someone by sending a fax message, that process does not seem ethical. Ethics are those standards that govern the way in which both individuals and businesses conduct themselves. Ethical standards should remain a concern for all employees when choosing appropriate channels of communication.

Privacy is an important ethical concern in communication. Some employees may not wish information such as medical conditions known to other employees. Ethically, a company may decide that medical conditions or other personal information is private. Choosing a less-secure channel, therefore, such as voice mail or fax may not be a good choice when discussing private issues.

Communicators should consider the ethics of situations when selecting a communication channel.

DISCUSSION

1. What technologies are important in business today?

2. Discuss the connection between the use of technology and the most appropriate communication channel.

3. Describe changes that have occurred in business that have resulted from changing technology.

4. When would e-mail be a good choice as a communication channel?

5. Give some examples of how communication by voice mail could be conducted.

6. Why is the message receiver's access to technology important? Provide an example.

7. How can technology eliminate the wasted time associated with telephone tag?

8. Which oral communication channel seems most effective in a situation requiring tact?

9. When should a written channel such as a letter be selected?

10. What channels would provide the speediest communication?

EXERCISES

1. Visit a local business to discover which of the technologies discussed in this chapter are used in the business's communication activities. You may wish to focus on one or two technologies such as fax, voice, or e-mail. Be prepared to report your findings to the class.

2. Using the *Communication Day in the Life of Manager Matt* as a guide, interview an executive and write his/her business communication scenario. Compare and contrast the

two communicators. Alternatively, analyze Matt's lifestyle based on his daily activities. How does technology impact his life?

3. Interview someone in business or on your campus who uses e-mail on a daily basis and ask what he or she likes and/or dislikes about using e-mail. Summarize your interview for the class.

4. Establish your own e-mail account, if you have not already done so. As a team project with three or four other class members, send e-mail messages to one another. Each of you should discuss what you think is a current "hot" issue on campus. Respond to each message you receive. Summarize your responses for your instructor.

5. If your college has voice mail, you and three or four other class members could leave messages for one another. Perhaps you may wish to discuss plans for an upcoming weekend or vacation. Respond to each voice mail message you receive. Summarize the results of this project for your instructor.

6. Scan a photograph or graphic image or download one from the Internet. Be prepared to discuss the process you used.

PROBLEMS

1. For each of the following situations, identify the most appropriate communication channel and technology to use.

   a. Ben just returned to the office after a visit to the emergency room with his 10-year old daughter who broke her arm. His supervisor Madeline has to notify him today that his expected promotion is not going to happen. What channel do you recommend for Madeline?

   b. Julio noticed a job opening posted on the company bulletin board. The notice said that interested persons should contact the company personnel office. What communication channels could he use in this instance? What would you recommend?

   c. One of the employees in your department is getting married. You have been appointed as head of a committee to plan an appropriate event for those in the department to honor the future newlywed. What would be an appropriate channel to communicate with the other members of your committee? What would be a good channel to notify the twenty other members of the department?

   d. Rachel picked the wrong communication channel for her message. She sent a scathing message about her boss to her co-worker Steve. Unfortunately, Rachel inadvertently sent the message by e-mail to all the members of the department *including* her boss. Are there any good options for Rachel now? Should she try any other communication channels? Report your decision to the rest of the class.

   e. Michael just called from the hospital to say that his wife had been killed in an automobile accident. Michael's wife was friends with many of the other employees. What would be the best way to notify the other employees?

f. The XYZ company phoned for some price information. Justin wanted to do this price quote just right. After he had researched the prices, carefully typed his cover letter, and mailed the quote first-class mail, he learned that a competitor won the order by quickly faxing some information in a rather informal style. Did Justin pick the wrong channel?

g. Everard just received word that budgets are being slashed and that the new computers that Lorna and Lincoln were expecting will not be purchased. What should Everard do?

h. In the carpool on the way to work Bryan learned that two of the other departments were getting increases in their budgets but he hadn't heard about any increase for his department. Should he notify his department head?

EXAMINING SOCIETAL ISSUES OF COMMUNICATION

- A fellow employee went "beyond the call of duty" to help you complete an important task. You would like to recognize the person's effort by giving him/her a small gift of appreciation. Is this an acceptable business practice? Why or why not?

- You are working on a project and decide that there are some great photos and clip art that you can download from the World Wide Web to insert in your report. You also find a few good cartoons in the paper. Are there any legal/ethical issues involved in using photos, clip art, and/or cartoons?

- What are your responsibilities as a guest at a business dinner?

CHAPTER OBJECTIVES

After studying this chapter, you should be able to:

1. Define international and muticultural communication.
2. List factors that relate to cultural understanding.
3. Define ethics and contrast ethical and legal issues.
4. Apply the Business Ethics Paradigm to decision making.
5. Value the importance of business etiquette.

UNDERSTANDING SOCIETAL FACTORS IN COMMUNICATION

Businesses and business people do not operate independently. As we engage in our daily work activities, we must interact with people within our organization, with clients and suppliers, and with society in general. Technology has not only improved the ease of communication; it has expanded our communication frontiers. Today we are communicating more easily with others throughout the world.

International and Multicultural Communication

Effective communication is as much a key to success in transacting business with the people of various nations as it is in transacting business at home. For that reason, this chapter was designed to help improve your communication skills among various cultures.

One myth held by many citizens of the United States is that it is not important to learn about other countries or cultures because it is information that will never be used. Today's business communicator, however, must be aware of the differences in international and multicultural communication in order to be successful.

International communication involves communication with those in other countries. Many companies in the United States conduct business with customers in other countries. In addition, many businesspeople travel or live in other countries which requires a greater understanding of other life styles.

Multicultural or intercultural communication occurs between people in the same country but who are from different cultural groups. Demographics in the United States have changed rapidly in the past few years. As the country changes, so does the multicultural diversity of the workplace. A thorough understanding of different cultures is a workplace requirement for the successful business person.

Developing Cultural Understanding

The biggest difficulty in communicating with others either internationally or inter-culturally is a lack of understanding of another culture's attitudes and beliefs. In learning about communication theory, you found that barriers could exist which caused communication difficulties. Such barriers are especially difficult when communicating with those of other cultures.

We all see the world through the lens of our own experiences. To understand the experiences of others you must take some additional steps and look at several areas for cultural understanding. The areas include awareness, language, customs, nonverbal communication, time, and space (shown in Figure 3-1).

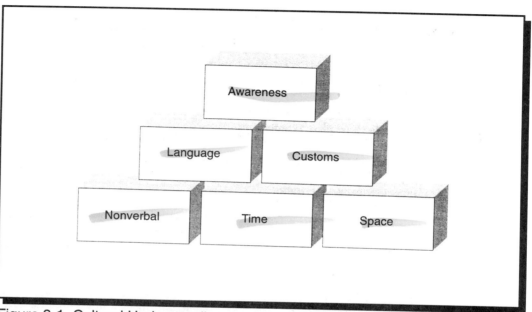

Figure 3-1. Cultural Understanding

✳ *Awareness.* The one component which will lead to success in understanding all of the others is the awareness that people are different. A recognition of these differences will lead you to alternate means of communication. If your communication message does not appear to arrive as you expected, you may wish to try a different approach. For example, if you tell someone you plan to be "out of pocket" until next week, they may not be sure of your meaning. A different choice of words may be required for better understanding.

One business consultant working in Germany asked the computer operator what was the most difficult problem she had with a popular word processing package. She said that the most difficult concept was working with inches. Her background was all with the metric system. Once aware of the problem, the consultant was able to show the operator how to change the onscreen measurement from inches to the metric centimeters.

Another important issue to awareness is to develop an attitude that being different does not mean being *wrong*. A "do it my way or hit the highway" philosophy will rarely lead to success in the international arena.

✳ *Language.* English is known as the universally accepted business language. As levels of English proficiency vary widely in our own country, language differences occur in communicating with individuals from other countries. Even among English speaking countries variances occur in slang and spelling.

Americans are at a disadvantage in the global market in language proficiency—most speak only English. For those with language proficiency, the most common other language is Spanish. Our language proficiency as a nation does not fare well when compared to Europeans who are often comfortable with three or four languages.

If you have an opportunity to enhance your language skills or to add such skills by learning another language, you will increase your ability to communicate in the global workplace.

Customs. Customs are different in various countries. U.S. business people frequently greet each other with a hand shake. In other countries nods, bows, or hugs may serve the same purpose. Customs also vary within cultural and gender groups. Most women in the U.S. are less comfortable with shaking hands than are men. Part of this difference may be attributed to custom. In a social setting women frequently greet each other without hand shakes while men routinely greet each other with hand shakes.

In some Middle Eastern countries eating with the left hand or touching someone with that hand is not acceptable as the left hand is considered unclean. Hopefully, the left-handed business executive heading for the Middle East will be aware of this custom.

In Japan presenting the business card is quite different than the U.S. custom which usually involves accepting the card and putting it into one's pocket—often without a glance at the card. The Japanese will have the information inscribed on both sides of the card—one side in Japanese and the other usually in English. The card is presented with both hands and a bow. The receiver is to take the card with both hands and read it carefully. In effect the business card is to be treated with respect; don't use it to write a handy phone number on the back!

Customs also include such things as the importance of the family, eating patterns, and degree of formality. The important thing to remember is that customs are different and one should be aware of those differences when communicating with those from cultures that are not your own.

Nonverbal. Gestures are used by people to communicate nonverbally or to supplement the spoken word. Frequently, gestures are used when language difficulties occur. However, gestures vary across cultures. A gesture to summon a server in a restaurant might be acceptable in one culture but considered rude in another.

One traveler who was hitchhiking in another country found that his thumbs up signal was getting no results except angry glares. He later discovered that the gesture he was using was an obscene one—no wonder he had no opportunities to catch a ride!

Another traveler who spoke no German was trying to indicate that she wanted one of the items in a German market. When she held up her forefinger, she always managed to get two items. To order one item, she should hold up her thumb rather than her forefinger. The best advice on gestures is to observe those in the culture around you and make no gestures unless you are sure what they mean.

Another nonverbal communication signal is eye contact. In some cultural groups within the U.S., direct eye contact is seen as disrespectful and rude. Other groups consider someone who will not meet their eyes as shifty and untrustworthy. Obviously, the communication will be improved if both groups understand the signals of the other.

Time. Time is considered differently in various cultures. In the United States, time is valued and meetings are expected to start on time and proceed directly to business.

Several college students were asked how long they would wait for a friend who was supposed to meet them at noon for lunch. The majority of students said they would wait no more than fifteen minutes for the friend to arrive. Several indicated that if they had to wait for longer than five or ten minutes, the first thing they expected to hear was a reason for the delay. In some cultures delays of half an hour or more are common. Patience with time delays is something those in the U.S. need to develop when communicating with some cultures.

In Latin and South American countries, time is usually a less important factor. Individuals from those cultures expect to spend time getting to know a person and a company and are not anxious to do business right away. This can be a frustrating experience for a business person who expects to fly down to a country for a one-day visit or who plans to conduct all of the business in a one-hour meeting.

✳ *Space.* The amount of space a person prefers around them is also a result of cultural background. Space can be divided into four realms 1) *intimate* space of 18 inches or less; 2) *personal* space of 18 inches to 4 feet; 3) *social* space of 4 feet to 8 feet; and 4) *public* space of greater than 8 feet. For most U.S. citizens, intimate space is reserved for close family members such as a spouse or children; personal space is for close friends; and social space is the most comfortable distance for other people.

If someone comes too close to you, you are tempted to step away from them so that more space can be maintained. In some environments such as movie theaters and on planes and buses, seating is fixed at a distance of less than 18 inches. In that case many Americans prefer to have an empty space between the seats.

In other cultures such as Asian and Middle Eastern, a closer sense of space is used. Therefore, an American may feel somewhat nervous when those from other cultures encroach on the space the American feels is needed. When a group of American students were asked, "What is the ideal number of people on an elevator?," several responded with no one but yourself. Another popular choice was three people so you wouldn't feel trapped in an elevator with one other person. Certainly, most elevators will hold a much larger group.

Acknowledging Cultural Diversity

Stereotypes. Stereotypes are images we build and apply to a group of people based on characteristics found in a few individuals. *Stereotypes* can be a barrier to communication because they block a better understanding of a group. Here are some stereotypes by state:

State Name	Characteristics
Texas	Wear cowboy hats and boots. Own oil wells. Only listen to country music.
California	Live on the beach. Know how to surf. Are blonde. Always trying strange things.
New York	Talk too fast with accents. Are rude. Drive cabs.
Florida	Full of drug dealers and retired people. Lots of tourists. Always sunny.

In looking at the stereotypical characteristics by state, the question is "Are all people from a state like that?" The answer, of course, is no. In addition, it is easy for negative stereotypes to end up on such lists. The same tendency toward pointing out the negative could appear on any list you could make of cultural stereotypes. Negative impressions do not assist in communication.

You should try to look beyond stereotypes to the individual person in order to make the judgments you need to communicate. This is not an easy process and is one that a communicator must always work on.

History of Cultural Groups. The United States is somewhat unique in its mix of cultural and ethnic groups in society. Japan, for example, is a homogeneous society composed of 99 percent Japanese. For some years the United States prided itself on being a "melting pot" for the cultures of the world which somehow implies that we were able to turn everyone into a stereotypical "American." A clearer picture might be that each cultural and ethnic group adds to the "portrait" of America which is like a never ending mural being painted on a wall. The mural grows and changes and reflects the society. America's diversity has also served as its strength. The ability to adjust to change and flexibility should be America's strong points in the globalization of business.

With so many diverse cultures, communication challenges exist everywhere. Those in the U.S. must make a sincere effort to understand those groups in our own culture which will make it easier to apply these efforts to those cultures in other countries.

Learn About Others. In order to better understand others, you should make the attempt to learn about other cultures and to experience them whenever possible. In turn, you may wish to share your culture with others who are not aware of its patterns.

You may learn about another culture by talking to members of that culture, by participating in cultural events, and by learning about books, plays, movies, and music. As you learn about one culture, you will then wish to learn about others. You can continue to learn about different groups as you experience business contacts.

Through your communication efforts to learn as much as you can about other countries and cultures, you can become successful when working in either an international environment or one that is culturally diverse.

Ethical and Legal Considerations

We have seen the importance of culture in communication. However, other considerations also influence communication decisions. Among the factors to consider are the ethical and legal implications of each message sent.   What is ethics? The root word of ethics is from the Greek word, *ethos*, meaning character or custom. Ethics can be defined as a set of moral principles or rules of conduct that govern the way people behave. The ability to differentiate between right and wrong or good and bad is another interpretation of ethics. While that definition is generally accepted by most, few can really agree as to what right and wrong really mean. Who determines what is right and what is wrong? By what standard do we measure our decisions?

Personal values serve as the basis for one's ethical framework. Those values are determined in part by your environment, by religious experiences, by philosophical beliefs, and by your viewpoints. Because we have all had different experiences, we may have different values. If we say that each person may define ethics and ethical behavior to match his or her personal set of values, no standard would exist. Society, however, identifies certain behaviors that are considered appropriate, while other behaviors are not considered appropriate.

Business ethics are business decisions based on society's perception of ethical behavior. Sometimes those decisions are not clear cut. For example, as a supervisor are you ethically obligated to tell your employees everything you know about the company's decision to downsize? Are you obligated to the company not to tell the employees about future decisions that may adversely affect their employment?

The dilemma of conflicting values and responsibilities is further complicated by the numerous laws affecting businesses. Although different, both ethical and legal considerations are required for effective communication.

Contrasting Ethical and Legal Issues

Closely associated with ethics is the question of legality. Before you can decide whether an issue is ethical, you must first decide if the issue is legal. Although an action is legal, it may not be ethical. Is it legal to misrepresent your product to a customer? Is it ethical? What are the ramifications of such a decision?

Although ethical and legal decisions are frequently grouped together, differences exist between the two. Ethical decisions are based on moral reasoning whereas legal decisions are based on mandates provided within the laws governing us. To better understand the significance of each, consider the following examples.

Ethical Errors	Legal Errors
Accepting more credit than is justified for your work on a group project	Taking the work of another and using it as though you created it yourself (plagiarism)
Reporting your progress on a project as being nearer completion than it is	Installing copies of software programs for which you have no license
Failing to keep a confidence	Failing to fulfill a contract

Ethical and legal decisions must serve as the basis for all communication. A basic framework for ethical decision making and a knowledge of the laws impacting your communication is fundamental to successful communication.

Within the framework one chooses to apply in resolving an ethical decision, individual values help determine the appropriate decision. One's values may be formed in part by environment, by culture, by philosophy and in part by theology. Regardless of its origin, every person has a set of values to use in making decisions.

Values Affecting Ethical Decision Making

Society in general, and most people individually, value honesty, integrity, and respect. Ethical decision makers will recognize and honor these values in their evaluation of each situation.

Honesty. Ethical people are honest people. They practice **honesty** in both word and deed. Communications are truthful, accurate, and fair. Honesty avoids deceptions, half-truths, and omission of key information.

Being honest does not give one the right to be rude. Tact is also appropriate in communication exchanges. If the truth contains negative information, it is appropriate to state the message in the passive voice. Consider the following statements. Both are honest. One, however, shields the receiver's pride.

Accusatory (Active voice)	**Tactful (Passive voice)**
You didn't complete the project on time.	The project was not completed as scheduled.

Tact is rubbing out another's mistake instead of rubbing it in.
–*Farmer's Almanac*

Integrity. **Integrity** is an especially important ethical value because it encompasses commitment, loyalty, justice, and promise-keeping. To be ethical, you must be committed to your beliefs and be willing to stand for them. A certain degree of loyalty is expected of friends, family, employees and employers. Promise-keeping refers to your ability to carefully consider whether you are willing and able to fulfill the promise in spite of unknown or future events that could make it difficult, detrimental, or impossible.

> Javan was elected to the position of vice-president for his professional organization. He accepted the position with the understanding that he would move to the office of president the following year.
>
> After serving for most of the year, Javan decided his interests and responsibilities had changed. He resigned because he no longer wanted to be an officer. His decision violated the ethical value of integrity--he was not loyal to those who had elected him to assume the responsibility for the organization.

You are responsible for your actions and your decisions; therefore, you should consider the potential consequences prior to taking the action and then be willing to take responsibility for your decisions. Responsibility also includes your community/civic responsibility. As a member of society, you are responsible to a certain degree for the overall public good. Your contribution to protecting or improving society is called social conscience.

Respect. The value of **respect** imposes a moral duty to treat all persons with consideration. An ethical person exercises personal, official, and managerial authority in a way that provides others with the information they need to make informed decisions. The rights and opinions of others are also regarded. This means we recognize and honor all persons' right to be independent, while maintaining their self-determination, privacy, and dignity.

The Ethical Decision Making Process

Making ethical decisions is not easy and does not come automatically. You must consciously work at making appropriate ethical decisions. You use a problem-solving approach to arrive at any decision; incorporate the ethical issues into that same decision making model. The basic steps of the Business Ethics Paradigm should assist you in reaching a decision that is both ethical and legal.

The Business Ethics Paradigm

I. What are the facts?
    A. Gather as much information as possible about the issue.
    B. Classify those facts relative to their importance on this decision.
II. Identify possible solutions.
III. Evaluate each solution by answering these questions:
    A. Is this action legal? If not, go to the next alternative.
    B. How will this decision affect the company?
        1. What costs will be associated with the decision?
        2. What benefits are associated with the decision?
    C. How will this decision affect others?
        1. What will be the effect on other employees?
        2. What will be the effect on customers?
        3. What will be the effect on society?
    D. How will this decision affect me?
        1. Will I feel good about this decision?
        2. Can I live with the consequences of this decision?
        3. Will my reputation be jeopardized?
        4. Will my reputation be enhanced?
    E. Would I want others to make similar decisions affecting me and my company?
IV. Select the most appropriate solution given your answers.
V. Communicate your decision.

While there are few solutions that are completely right or completely wrong, you must carefully weigh all alternatives and be ready to justify your decision should the need arise.

Ethical Issues in Communication

Although business ethics as a subject merits expanded study in the form of complete courses or degree programs, ethical business communication deserves our attention here. Careful thought should be given not only to the messages you prepare, but also to consequences of your communication. Verbal and nonverbal messages may communicate unethically. Consider the ethical expectation our receivers have of our written, oral, and visual messages.

Written Communication. Written communication carries a great ethical responsibility. Readers expect our communication to be honest, truthful, accurate, straightforward, and fair. Do not attempt to deceive or mislead the reader by covert or overt statements, by playing on one's emotions, or by visually misrepresenting data.

Covert statements deliberately mislead or deceive the reader by stating false information. To describe a medium-priced, medium-quality product as "the best on the market" is a covert statement. The product may be "one of the best on the market at that price;" but is not "the best on the market."

Overt statements deceive the reader by omitting key facts: perhaps you do not lie, but you do not tell the whole truth. To write a personnel recommendation for Shane stating he has above average work skills when you wouldn't consider rehiring him if given the opportunity is deceptive. Perhaps your statement is true in that Shane has above average work skills, but his people skills leave a lot to be desired.

Playing on the reader's **emotions** presents another ethical issue in letter writing. While it is appropriate to indicate the emotional benefit of your product/proposal in certain situations, be cautious about creating sympathy, fear or other strong emotions to prompt the reader to respond as you suggest. For example, do not imply that death is imminent if the reader does not buy and install your smoke detector.

When analyzing and presenting data, it may be tempting to massage the data to reflect the position that you wish to take. Consider the following survey data for example. Surveys were sent to 250 members of a professional association; 48 people responded. Of the 48 that responded, 25 favored a dues increase. Is it ethical to report that the majority of the members support a dues increase when actually only 10 percent of the members responded affirmatively?

Certain ethical issues relate directly to electronic communication and the technology that supports it. The use of company e-mail and voice mail for personal business raises ethical issues. Many companies have established guidelines for appropriate usage of electronic mail while others have not. Some companies, for example, permit personal use of e-mail after official work hours. Others require that e-mail only be used for business purposes.

While e-mail is personal, it is *not necessarily* private. As employers provide computers, network connections, and e-mail software, several courts have ruled that employers have the right to monitor employees' e-mail. Therefore, you must treat your electronic messages with the same concern for ethical statements as your other written messages. Do not let your e-mail come back to haunt you.

E-mail enables us to send and receive messages easily. We can also post messages that we have received on electronic bulletin boards or forward messages we have received to another person quite easily. Questions of ethical conduct arise when one forwards messages without the sender's knowledge. If Carrie sends Richard an e-mail message, he shouldn't forward it to Krystel and Kathy without Carrie's consent. Likewise, Richard shouldn't post a message he has received to an electronic bulletin board.

Oral Communication. Many of the issues described in written communication also pertain to oral communication. However, oral communication has certain ethical implications that are unique. For example, honoring one's word, although there is no written record of the commitment, is considered ethical.

Using nonverbal communication to contradict spoken communication may raise ethical issues. You may say "Susie is dependable" in different tones. You may use a positive tone, indicating that she is in fact dependable, or you may use a sarcastic tone implying she is not at all dependable. Your choice of words and tone could lead to an unethical exchange of information.

Visual Communication

Technology makes it easy to access information and to copy it in to documents. A great deal of information can be downloaded from the World Wide Web. Special care should be taken when accessing information which may by protected by copyright. For example, the photo you copy from the World Wide Web into a newsletter you are planning to distribute may be protected–requiring you to legally pay a fee to use the photo.

Other written techniques that may raise ethical issues are **organizational** and **visual presentations** of data. To emphasize a point, use a simple sentence or the independent clause of a complex sentence. Although accurately reported, a point subordinated in a dependent clause may be under emphasized. To intentionally subordinate important points to sway the reader is questionable from an ethical standpoint.

Visually presenting graphs and charts that are incorrectly proportioned may give the reader the impression that one area is more important (performed better, etc.) than the other areas.

Many other ethical communication issues exist. These will be discussed in other chapters throughout the text.

Legal Issues in Communication

When following the Business Ethics Paradigm, your decisions should be legal as well as ethical. Remember that one of the questions you must answer in making an ethical decision is to determine whether the alternative is legal. You will be faced with both legal and ethical communication issues affecting you and your company.

Legal Responsibilities of Employees. You represent the company when you communicate on its behalf. Therefore, the company is legally responsible for your comments. Your promises, commitments, accusations, or threats are just as binding for the company as are the commitments made by any of the company officers. Commitments from either may result in legal action for the company. When you communicate for your company, be aware of any legal requirements, company policies, and precedents that have been set. Collect the facts and document the circumstances for your communication. When communicating, differentiate between facts and opinions.

As a result of the many legal requirements, some companies have established guide letters to assist employees in preparing sensitive communication. These guides, although not necessarily form letters, have been carefully reviewed by legal counsel to certify that the communication is appropriate.

Also of concern to communicators is the possibility that their files of letters, memos, reports, and/or notes may become public record in legal disputes. Through subpoenas and by deposition, your records may become documentation for or against your company. It is important, therefore, that you maintain accurate and complete records of your communications.

Legislation with Communication Implications. While it is not feasible to discuss all the laws that are relevant to business communications, the most common topics are described here. Business communicators must be knowledgeable not only of these laws but

also of all laws governing their communications. Numerous other texts and resource books as well as legal counsel can provide a more thorough coverage of the topic.

Specific legislation governs many areas of business. Among those areas are employment, advertising, product guarantees, credit, collections, copyrights, privacy, and defamation. While this list is not intended to be inclusive, it has many communication implications.

Because Title VII of the Civil Rights Act protects against discrimination based on race, color, sex, religion, or national origin, **employment communication** should not request such information. Those interviewing job applicants should be particularly knowledgeable of the legal restraints and organize their remarks accordingly. Comments and questions, written or oral, should focus exclusively on bona fide occupational qualifications (BFOQ). Assume a delivery service requires drivers to lift packages weighing up to 70 pounds. It can specify that the applicant must be able to lift 70 pounds. It cannot, however, restrict the position to males (because they can normally lift more than females).

There are specific **truth in advertising** laws that specify what you can and cannot say in your advertising. Such laws certainly should govern the written communication between the customer and the company. Do not promise merchandise or services that you cannot deliver. In addition, you should not promise discounts or merchandise that you are not authorized to offer.

Warranties and guarantees must be written in clear, understandable language. The Consumer Product Warranty Act and Federal Trade Commission Improvement Act of 1975 prohibits ambiguous language and vague statements when providing product guarantees. Assume the promotional materials for an E-Z Clip lawn mower states, "The first lawn mower with a five-year warranty!" If the five-year warranty actually covers only the blade assembly and the remainder of the mower has only a one-year warranty, the E-Z Clip Corporation would be violating the Consumer Product Warranty Act.

Credit decisions are protected under the Fair Credit Billing Act of 1974. Exercise care when determining credit worthiness and evaluations. As with employment, discriminating because of race, religion, color, or national origin is prohibited. Additional factors that cannot be used include age, marital status, and family plans. Reasons given for denying credit must not relate to one of these factors.

When attempting to collect unpaid accounts, use the **Fair Debt Collection Practices Act of 1978** as a guide. This act specifies when and how you may contact a debtor. A series of collection letters are usually prepared ranging from gentle reminders to statements of legal action. These letters should be written and reviewed by legal representatives before being sent. Guide letters are particularly appropriate for both credit and collection series.

Creative and artistic works may be **copyrighted.** The copyright prevents others from using a created work without permission. Except with limited "fair use" privileges usually reserved for educational institutions, copyrighted work cannot be copied without permission. Copyrights apply to written materials (textbooks, novels, reference manuals), audio recordings, and computer software.

Privacy issues affect both the employer and the employee. Employers have the legal responsibility to maintain certain employee data—age, marital status, health history, etc.—in a confidential manner. Employees have the responsibility to keep company issues such as copyrights, patents, product development of future plans, confidential.

Privacy rights extend to communication in that written communications are said to belong to the sender and the receiver. Use of such communication without permission is unlawful.

To speak or to write unfounded derogatory remarks about another individual is **defamation**. Such oral remarks are called **slander**; written remarks are **libel**. Both slander and libel may result in monetary damages being awarded to the wronged party.

Recommendations and references about current or past employees pose one of the greatest potentials for slander/libel action. When writing a reference letter, be very careful to state facts that can be documented. When it is necessary to state an opinion, indicate that the comment is an opinion. Give opinions only when they can be substantiated.

Ethics and the Law in a Global Perspective

Citizens of the United States are bound by the laws of this country. Even in trade with other countries, U.S. citizens must follow the laws of their home country. The customs or culture of a particular country may endorse activities that are not considered ethical or legal business practices in the United States. Therefore, we cannot legally engage in these activities. For example, U.S. business people cannot exercise bribery even though it is considered a way of doing business in some countries.

Trade agreements with certain countries specify certain standards of acceptable behavior. Business people should be very careful to follow the standards of the agreement.

Ethical and legal issues are so complex and diverse that it is difficult to address all areas that apply to communication. The successful communicator will, however, carefully weigh each decision to determine whether it is legal and ethical before preparing written, oral, or electronic communication. Watch for further discussions of ethical and legal issues throughout the text.

Business Etiquette

Another societal issue affecting communication is basic business etiquette. Also called image or impression management, etiquette involves the very basic way we communicate our acceptance, appreciation, and respect for others. Certain etiquette rules are documented whereas others are unwritten, but nevertheless as important. Areas of business etiquette affecting communication include dress codes, introductions, business dining, interpersonal relationships with colleagues, and technology etiquette.

Dress Codes

Some companies may have written dress codes specifying appropriate dress for their employees. Other companies, however, may not have a published dress code. Nevertheless, a dress code exists. Successful employees quickly learn both the written and unwritten rules of business dress for their organization. While dark suits and ties may be the standard in some organizations, other companies may prefer the more relaxed business casual attire.

Regardless of the formality of the dress, employers expect employees to be neat, clean, and well groomed. Employees who violate express or implied codes will communicate a less than favorable image to their supervisors, to their colleagues, and to their customers.

Business casual dress usually refers to slacks, sports shirts, or casual dresses. It does not include jeans, shorts, sweatshirts, windsuits, or tattered or frayed clothing.

Suggestive clothing should be avoided. This includes clothing that is too tight, skirts that are extremely short, or tops that are low-cut.

A good rule to follow in determining appropriate attire for a particular organization is to observe what supervisors wear and pattern your wardrobe accordingly.

Introductions

A first impression is often the most lasting impression. Therefore, introductions and greetings are particularly important for successful interaction. Be careful to introduce others with whom you are meeting. If a colleague fails to introduce you, wait for an appropriate time and introduce yourself.

When introducing two individuals of differing ranks, remember to present the lower ranking person to the higher ranking person. When introducing persons of equal rank, age is an appropriate distinction. Introduce the younger person to the older one by including the older person's name first in the introduction. When introducing a customer or client to a person within your organization, use the client's name first in the introduction. If possible, include a statement about each person to help them become better acquainted.

In the United States, shaking hands is the acceptable business greeting regardless of gender. When introduced to a person, extend your hand; establish eye contact, and repeat the person's last name. Do not automatically assume that you should use the first name unless invited to do so. Repeating the name serves two purposes: the other person will appreciate your interest and you are more likely to remember the name if you speak it orally. If you have been given a statement about the other person, comment on something that you may have in common or of general interest. Do not appear to be interrogating the person as people do not necessarily want to share their life histories in business introductions.

Some Thoughts on Manners

You can get through life with bad manners, but it's easier with good manners.
–Lillian Gish

Life is not so short but that there is always time for courtesy.**–Ralph Waldo Emerson**

Manners are a sensitive awareness of the feelings of others. If you have that awareness, you have good manners, no matter what fork you use.**–Emily Post**

Business Dining

Basic table manners make positive impressions in business dining. When you are invited to participate in a business meal, remember these basic tips:

► Arrive on time.
► Wait for your host to indicate your seat.
► Don't put your elbows or personal items (purse, briefcase, cell phone, etc.) on the table.
► Wait until the host unfolds the napkin and places it in the lap before doing likewise.

- ► Don't order the most expensive items on the menu.
- ► Avoid food items that are difficult to eat such as spaghetti, ribs, or corn on the cob.
- ► Follow the lead of your host regarding alcoholic beverages.
- ► Chew with your mouth closed.
- ► Don't talk while chewing food.
- ► Select the appropriate utensil for your food. In most place settings, select the outside fork or spoon and move inward with each course of your meal.
- ► Place your fork and knife across your plate to indicate you are finished.
- ► After you have finished, put your napkin on the table; don't refold it.
- ► Engage in casual conversation during the meal. Avoid controversial topics.
- ► Be a good listener as well as a good conversationalist.
- ► Thank your host at the conclusion of the meal.
- ► Follow up with a written thank you note within two days.

Interpersonal Relationships with Colleagues

Frequently, you will be involved in social interactions with colleagues. These activities may include business dining, lunches, company picnics, or parties. Basic business etiquette applies in these settings as well.

When attending a company function, find out the appropriate dress. Does casual dress refer to shorts or to dress slacks? Is the function a formal one?

Engage in conversations that are not strictly business based. Few people want to spend their social hours talking about office problems. Be well informed on current events so that you can speak intelligently about them. Other appropriate topics may include recent bestsellers, sports, travel, or hobbies. You may develop good friends through the workplace.

Use caution, however, when engaging in romantic relationships with colleagues. Too frequently, relationships do not last. Then you would be faced with a difficult or embarrassing situation in the workplace. Be especially cautious about relationships with superiors or subordinates. Claims of preferential treatment or harassment may cause jealously among coworkers and may place you in a legal or ethical dilemma.

Technology Etiquette

Other basic forms of business etiquette apply to the use of technology. Be considerate of others as you use your telephone, cell phone, pager, voice mail, fax machine, or laptop computer.

Answer your **telephone** by the fourth ring. Identify yourself and your business. Listen carefully for caller's name and business affiliation. Do not yell into the mouthpiece. Keep a notepad and pen close by for making notes during the conversation. If you are given a name or telephone number, repeat it to the caller to be certain you have recorded it correctly. Speak in a conversational voice. End your calls with a cordial ending. Do not hang up abruptly.

Cellular telephones and **pagers** have created the need for specific courtesies not only to the party with whom you are speaking, but also to those people around you during your conversations. Turn off the ringer on your telephone during meetings and in public places such as restaurants, churches or theaters. Respect the rights of those about you. Speak softly;

do not yell into the mouthpiece. Except in extenuating circumstances, do not place or receive calls while you are engaged in a face-to-face conversation. Keep your conversations short. Use your phone with caution while driving or operating equipment.

Create a professional message for your **answering machine and/or voice mail**. Identify yourself. Indicate how the caller can reach you–through a voice message, by contacting you at a different number, or by leaving a message with another person. Be sure to tell the caller when you plan to return and when you will respond to their call.

Similarly, be thoughtful when using a **fax machine**. Include a cover page stating the name of the intended recipient. Don't fax long, unannounced, and perhaps, unwelcomed, documents. Because fax machines may be situated in public areas, do not fax confidential information unless the receiver has requested you to do so.

And finally, be considerate when using your **laptop computer** in a public space. Do not infringe on the space of others who are forced to sit near you (as in an airplane).

An awareness of the societal issues of communication specifically relating to international, intercultural, ethical and legal issues is a valuable asset to successful business communication. Understanding the value of business etiquette is key to developing successful business relationships.

DISCUSSION

1. What steps would you take to learn something about a cultural group?

2. What customs not listed in the text do you think influence communication?

3. What ethnic groups exist in your community?

4. Do stereotypes have any value?

5. Contrast the ethical and legal issues affecting communication.

6. Describe how cultural or environmental values affect ethical decision making.

7. Investigate legislation not discussed in this chapter that affects communication.

8. How can incorrect business etiquette impact your success?

EXERCISES

1. A team of three or more students could participate in this exercise. Select at least three countries and compose a list of stereotypes for citizens of that country. Now compose a list of stereotypes for Americans. Compare the lists. What is the value of the stereotypes, if any? Be prepared to present your results in an oral presentation to the rest of the class.

2. Select an ethnic group of your choice. Do some research to discover the following:
   a. What is the history of this group in the United States?
   b. Name three significant leaders. What were their contributions?
   c. Name at least one author or actor/actress who has served as a role model for the ethnic group.
   d. What are unique customs of the group?
   Report your findings in a manner directed by your instructor.

3. Complete assignment No. 2 except use a different country rather than an ethnic group.

4. Watch several television shows and/or movies. How is the cultural group of your choice portrayed. What are the positive and the negative factors? Do you think such media have an impact on the perception of cultural groups? Be prepared to report your findings to the class.

5. Interview two people from a cultural group. Ask them to describe their customs and culture. Be ready to report to the class.

6. Interview a business executive to determine the impact of business etiquette on executive success.

7. Send an e-mail message to your instructor describing a business etiquette dilemma that you or a friend has experienced.

PROBLEMS

1. Based on your personal experience, describe an international or intercultural experience that caused you difficulties in communication. Be prepared to role play the situation or describe it in an e-mail message.

2. Assume that your company is sending you to a country of your choice for two weeks. You will have to make all of the arrangements for the visit. How will you travel there, what will the budget be, what travel documents (passport, visa) will you need, and of what holidays and customs should you be aware. Create a profile or memo about your trip that you will share with your supervisor.

3. You have been asked to give a tour of your community to a group of visitors from another country. You decide what country. You will have an afternoon in your community to give them a feeling for the area. Develop an itinerary with a rationale for your choice of sites. Be prepared to discuss your ideas with the class or to prepare a memo for the instructor.

4. Access the Internet or World Wide Web and use a search feature to locate information about a culture or country of your choice. You should have at least ten sites. Be prepared to discuss your findings with the class or to send an electronic message to your instructor. You may wish to do this activity with a partner.

5. Describe a personal ethical or legal dilemma that you or someone you know has faced in the workplace. What were the facts and what action was taken? How did it fit with the concepts discussed in this chapter? Be prepared to discuss the situation in class or through e-mail.

6. For each of the following situations, determine the most ethical and legal solution. Support your decisions with your rationale. Be prepared to address the issue in a report to the class or to your instructor.

    a. Staci is rushed at work and can't get everything done on the new job. She uses a new spreadsheet package at work. Although she has a computer at home which will run the spreadsheet package, she does not own the program. Should Staci make a copy of the spreadsheet program to put on the home computer so work can be done at home?

    b. Leisha takes a number of prescription medications for a chronic health problem. So far she has not said anything to her fellow workers about her health problems. The company has just announced that random drug testing will soon begin. Those employees with positive drug tests may be terminated. What should Leisha do?

    c. Jackson is employed at a company which has received several government contracts for equipment. On his current project, Jackson notices several things which are not being done according to the guidelines for equipment. One of the most important is that safety inspections are not thorough which may result in unsafe equipment leaving the plant. Jackson needs his job. What should he do?

    d. Arnie really liked his job until his new supervisor arrived. Although Arnie did not expect to have any problems with having a woman in the position, she soon began making suggestive remarks to Arnie. He had the feeling that she was interested in him in a non-business way. She asked Arnie to work late alone with her a number of times which he did. Now she wants him to come to her home on Saturday night for dinner. He doesn't think the meeting is for business and doesn't want to go. What should he do about his supervisor?

    e. As a new supervisor, you have found a series of cartoons in a business magazine which appear to be very motivational. You intend to photocopy the three pages for all fifty of your employees. Is this a correct use of copyrighted material?

    f. You have been somewhat cautious about sending any controversial material by electronic mail. You have a co-worker, however, who is always talking about the opinions she is expressing about the company and her boss over e-mail. Is e-mail as private as U.S. postal service mail? Do you have any advice for your co-worker?

    g. You are employed in the insurance department of the company. In processing new insurance claims, you notice that one of the executives of the company has been diagnosed as HIV positive. You think this information is too important to keep secret. What should you do?

h. Sally Jane works for an employer who is always making sexual innuendos about Sally Jane in front of other people. Today when she wore a new dress to work, her boss said, "Hey, look at this hot little lady! When do you get off work? Ha, Ha!" He also has "kidded" her about sleeping with clients to get more company business. Sally Jane doesn't like the hostile atmosphere and it is causing her to be less productive. What should Sally Jane do?

i. Bill was hoping to get a promotion which would provide a higher salary. When the promotion did not come through, Bill was very disappointed. He has decided to take office supplies from work to home because he does work at home, and he didn't get the promotion so the company owes him something. You are Bill's co-worker. What should you do?

j. Bruce has worked for his company for four years. Although everything seemed to go very well at the beginning of that time, he is becoming more and more annoyed with events at the company. He has expressed his unhappiness to his father who tells him he is not "loyal" to his company. Bruce's dad worked for one company for 30 years prior to his retirement. What should Bruce do about his dissatisfaction with his job?

k. Adrian is a member of the X generation. He loves computers and works with them all of the time. He can't understand his boss who is part of the baby-boomer generation. His boss tries to avoid everything to do with computers. This disagreement causes difficulties in work arrangements. What can Adrian do?

l. Amy's job is structured so that at some times she has little work to do. Her employers want her to look busy even if she is not busy, so they have asked her not to read books or magazines on the job. Her employers have said that she can work with the computer. Amy found a neat game program from a friend of a friend and installed it on her computer at work. She has spent many enjoyable hours with the game. However, she now suspects she may have brought in a computer virus. What should she do?

m. Ellie just arrived at the reception for the new clients. She only knows two people in the room and they seem busy talking to people. She feels a little awkward and unsure about what to do. What etiquette suggestions do you have for her?

n. Cliff is now working on a multimedia system at work which lets him make computer presentations more interesting by inserting clips of popular songs, movies, and photographs. Cliff is making an action adventure type of computer promotion and plans to include several clips from a popular movie. What ethical and legal considerations should Cliff know about?

STRENGTHENING SPEAKING SKILLS

Critical Thinking Applications

- Investigate ethical and legal issues of business speaking. Develop guidelines for planned and unplanned speaking activities.

- Should business presentations be conducted in the sender's or the receiver's primary language? Justify your answer. What differences must be considered when communicating in a second language?

CHAPTER OBJECTIVES

After studying this chapter, you should be able to:

1. Describe differences among casual, responsive, and organized speaking.
2. Prepare, organize, and practice an oral presentation.
3. Improve your current speaking techniques.
4. Deliver an effective oral presentation.
5. Prepare a team presentation.

SPEAKING IN BUSINESS

The majority of those in business spend a significant portion of their working day communicating orally. They frequently communicate orally with their associates and with the general public. The effectiveness of this communication plays a major role in the successful operation of business enterprises. For that reason, anyone planning a career in business is wise to devote the time and the effort required to raise oral communication skills to the highest possible level.

The communicator can be involved in several approaches to speaking: casual, responsive, or organized.

Casual Speaking

The casual approach to speaking occurs when you are speaking but have not planned or practiced what you intend to say. Conversations are a frequent application of the casual approach to speaking. Although most business conversations focus on a task to be accomplished, a portion of the conversation is usually social in nature. Such social questions as "Did you see the game last night?" or "Did you read the editorial in the paper?" are often asked in casual speaking.

You might also ask about family or hobbies in this type of communication. The reason for these types of questions is that most people prefer this type of opening conversation which serves as an extended greeting before focusing on the task at hand. In some cultures, the social questions may be an important part of the success of the total conversation.

Responsive Speaking

Responsive communication occurs when you are responding to others who are speaking to you. Effective listening is an important component to responsive communication. If you are not listening to the person who is speaking to you, you will have a difficult time responding successfully. At one time or another, we have all been caught day-dreaming when someone asked us a question. As we snap back to reality, we have the sinking sensation that we have missed something!

Although most responsive communication is unplanned, it can be anticipated. If you are working on a negotiation team which is working on salary issues, you can assume that someone not on the committee might ask how things are going. This type of question can be anticipated. You may not wish to discuss the proceedings of the team until a specified time—therefore, you need to decide what your response to such questions might be. Your goal is to be tactful but not to reveal information. Some of the hardest questions may come from your friends who expect you to answer because of that friendship. Having an appropriate answer ready before the question arises can be very helpful to your speaking success.

Organized Speaking

Organized speaking takes place when you are asked to prepare an oral presentation. The presentation may be for a few individuals or for a large group; it may be formal or informal; it may be long or short. In all cases, you have just been assigned the task that most individuals face with dread. Studies indicate that the fear of speaking in front of a group rates high on the list of human fears. What can you do if you feel this type of fear when assigned an oral presentation? You can gain confidence as well as control your fear of speaking by preparing and practicing for your oral presentation.

Preparing the Oral Presentation

When you are asked to make an oral presentation, you need to plan your preparation by evaluating a number of issues. A speaker who uses thorough planning before the presentation is on the road to a successful presentation.

Audience Analysis

The first thing the speaker must do is to analyze who will be in the audience. Consider such factors as age, educational background, interests, income, area of the country, and most importantly—level of subject knowledge.

If the speaker is presenting information on investments, then the age, interests, and income of the audience are important. For example, employees in their early twenties may be less interested in retirement than those in their fifties. The speaker will want to relate the importance of retirement to those of all ages. If speakers address technology issues, they must know the level of their audience. For example, if they assume that the audience knows nothing about computers, their presentations may be too basic and cause the audience to lose interest. The same thing can happen if the presentation begins at a point that is too far advanced for the audience.

The speaker must also develop *credibility* with the audience. Credibility is the extent to which the audience believes that the speaker has the knowledge and ability to discuss the topic at hand. The speaker can demonstrate credibility through qualifications, appropriate examples and illustrations, and interaction with the audience.

Research

Most presentations will require some research on the part of the speaker. The research may involve visiting the library, accessing the Internet, examining company files, or interviewing other professionals. Part of the planning process is for the speaker to determine what information is readily available and what will require some research. Presenting correct, current information adds to the credibility of the speaker while giving incorrect or outdated data does the opposite. See the example that follows:

Be Accurate With Data

The speaker was discussing employee benefits for the next year. The new year's figures were based on increases in base figures from two years ago rather than from last year's figures. This error was obvious to the audience when they looked at the labels on the visuals that supported the presentation. The incorrect data would affect the entire presentation.

Be Accurate With Quotes

When attending an opening address at a national conference, the keynote speaker held the audience in his grasp. Then he said, "As Shakespeare said, 'The child is father of the man'." He immediately lost the attention of at least one member of the audience who thought, "Shakespeare didn't say that!" It took another fifteen minutes for the listener to figure out that the quote should have been attributed to William Wordsworth.

Perhaps you might think this is a minor item—but the speaker lost that audience member for at least fifteen minutes because of an error in research. Most speakers cannot afford distractions caused by their own choice of words.

Examples, Stories, Analogies

One way a speaker can make the oral presentation more interesting and more memorable is to use examples, stories, and/or analogies to illustrate key points. When discussing appropriate ways to work with customers, the speaker might use examples of how customers were *not* treated correctly and any consequences which may have resulted. Such stories may remain longer in the memory of the listener than any list of points. For that reason, the speaker must carefully select examples that will illustrate the points intended. Such items should be as carefully planned as any other portion of the text and should relate to the topic under discussion.

When planning the presentation, the speaker should avoid adding jokes to the presentation. Few business speakers have the ability to tell jokes successfully to an audience. In addition, jokes are often offensive to certain segments of the audience. Jokes can be like time bombs, especially, if the speaker has not analyzed the audience correctly. Uncomfortable laughter or silence may follow the offensive joke.

Word Choice

The speaker should select a vocabulary that will suit the sophistication of the audience. You can see an excellent example of this technique during the next televised political race. Observe the candidate speaking in front of different audiences and see if you can detect any subtle differences in speaking styles. Certainly, if your audience doesn't understand your words, you will have difficulty communicating with them.

Correct grammar is also a must for the speaker. Most listeners can quickly pick up on errors in grammar which may make them question your capability and credibility.

Organizing the Oral Presentation

A good beginning is extremely important in organizing the presentation. Not all speeches should begin the same way. However, the introduction should preview the presentation. In other words, *give an overview of the presentation in the introduction.*

Get the listeners' favorable attention early. You may wish to use an example or story. Other ways to attain the listeners' attention—after you have acknowledged the introductory remarks—are beginning with a startling fact, by reading or reciting an applicable quotation, by telling a short story, or by asking a question that will stimulate interest. The title of your presentation should also be revealed to the audience.

After getting the listeners' attention by your preferred manner, mention the subtopics of your speech. For some occasions, you may present a significant point that is to be supported in the body of your presentation. Presenting that point in such a way that the listeners know to expect elaboration later helps to keep them listening.

Body

In the body of the speech, present the three or four major points you chose. Use the style and techniques that best fit the topic, the audience, and you. You might wish to *compare and contrast* points, to discuss *several options* or courses of action, or to examine the topic in a *chronological manner*. If the subject is complex and your time is limited, you may wish to focus on only a few facets of the issue.

Visual Aids

For a speech in which you use graphics, you can use a computer, an overhead projector, a flip chart, a handout, or a combination of these media to present them. Keep the graphics clear, simple, and easy to read.

Make sure that all lines are clear and that all letters and figures are clear and large enough to be read easily by every person in the audience. One guideline is to include *no more than seven lines with seven words each on any single visual*.

Don't try to show too much information in any one graphic. Showing several graphics with a few lines on each one is much better than showing a few graphics with a great deal of information on each one.

Graphics which are projected should be in *landscape* style—with the words running across the longest side of the page. Using *landscape* style allows all viewers to see the graphics more clearly. Using a ***portrait*** style—where the words run across the short side of the page—can often cause words at the bottom of the page to be too low on the projection screen making it difficult for some audience members to see them.

Making your own graphics with care compliments the listeners by letting them know you care enough about them to spend sufficient time preparing for your presentation. Well-done graphics also give you a sense of confidence about your material. Items such as *bullet charts* which list key ideas or points also help to keep your presentation on track.

While graphics are desirable for many presentations, you should not use them so much that they detract from you—the star of the show. Display a graphic only while you want the listeners to look at it. Whether or not you use graphics in your speech, present your chosen three or four major points in a logical sequence. This sequence often builds to a climax, which is the time to stop.

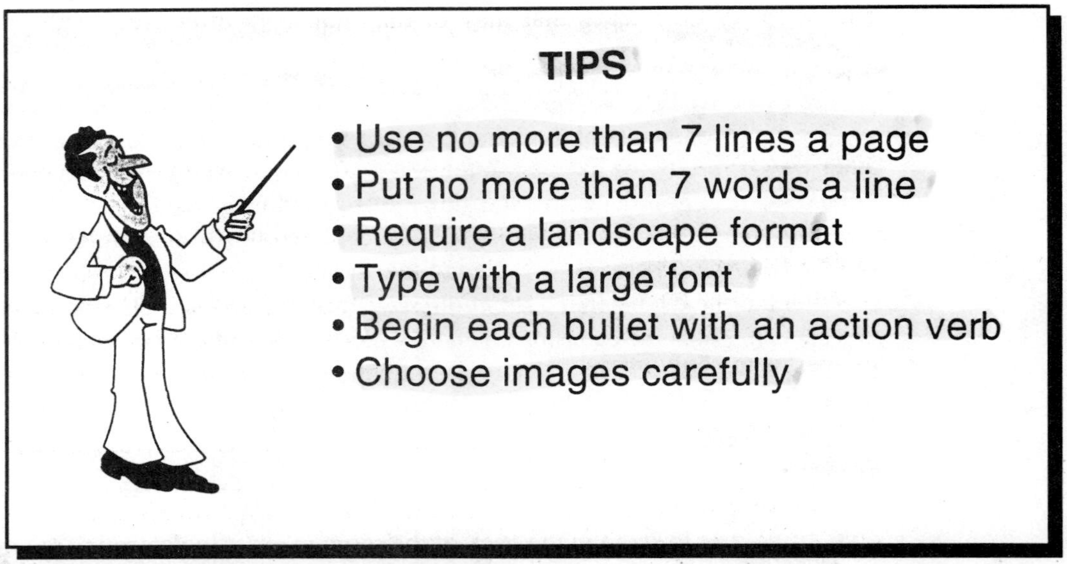

TIPS
- Use no more than 7 lines a page
- Put no more than 7 words a line
- Require a landscape format
- Type with a large font
- Begin each bullet with an action verb
- Choose images carefully

Figure 4-1. Make Visuals Easy to Read

Conclusion

The conclusion of a presentation is just as important as the beginning. Whether your presentation leads to a climax or you simply complete the presentation of well-supported major points, end the speech smoothly—not abruptly. Usually, you should ***summarize*** the significant points by mentioning them briefly so that the listeners can easily relate to them. As listeners often remember the last things they hear, a summary of the key ideas also helps the listeners to remember what you said.

Questions

Most business presenters must be prepared to answer questions from the audience. Questions may take the form of requests to clarify information that has been presented or requests for additional information that was not discussed. Sometimes an audience member will state another point of view or provide an example that supports or disagrees with a point the presenter has made. Just as presenters plan the presentation, they can also anticipate the types of questions that may be asked and have responses in mind.

After the planning steps have been completed, the speaker is ready to practice the presentation.

Practicing the Oral Presentation

Just as preparation is the first step in the design of your oral presentation and organization is the second step, practice is the third step. Practice will give you more confidence and ease your fears of speaking. In addition, practice will let you see if your presentation has any rough spots that may need additional work. You will also have the chance to try techniques that may or may not work effectively without practice. Your practice will be more effective with the input of a peer or friend. Be sure to cover the following areas in your practice procedures.

Environment

You should examine the location where you will give your presentation, if possible. An understanding of the size of the room, seating arrangement, and lighting will help you in practicing your presentation. Be sure that any special equipment you intend to use such as a computer projection system or a television and VCR is available and that you know how to operate the equipment.

Voice Projection

You should speak loudly enough and clearly enough for all audience members to hear you. Ask a peer to stand in the back of the room in order to determine how well your voice projects. Many facilities have microphones. If you intend to use a microphone, practice speaking into it. Again, ask a peer to determine how well the sound reaches the back of the room. If you intend to move from one location to another during your presentation, you should check to see if the microphone can also move with you or if a portable microphone is available.

The tone of your voice can also have an impact on the success of your presentation. Avoid speaking in a shrill voice or droning in a monotone. If you attempt to memorize your speech or read it, your voice will more likely assume a monotone. Instead, use note cards only for your key points throughout the presentation. Your voice should project enthusiasm and confidence during your presentation. Those qualities lend a positive note to the presentation. Certainly, if the speaker appears to be bored with the topic, how can the audience be interested?

Pronunciation

The way you speak can impact your listeners. Many words have more than one correct way of pronunciation. Perhaps most difficulties occur with place names which might be pronounced differently in different geographical areas. For example, one of the major rivers in Kansas is pronounced as the Ar-*kansas* River. When the same river reaches the Arkansas border, the pronunciation changes to Ar-kan-*saw* River. Selecting the non-preferred pronunciation in either state marks the speaker as using an incorrect pronunciation.

Timing

Practicing a presentation gives you an opportunity to see how long your presentation will be. Time limits are frequently a factor in presentations. If you have been asked to give a five-minute presentation at a meeting, your audience will expect you to stay within that time limit. If you go over that time, your presentation may be cut short before you have an opportunity to discuss all of your points. Keep in mind that an actual presentation may be shorter than the one you conducted in practice—nervous presenters often speak more quickly during the actual presentation than in practice.

Part of your practice of the presentation should focus on the pace with which you present the material. Silence can be an effective reinforcer of your points. You may wish to make a point, pause for a few seconds, and then proceed with further discussion of the points.

Questions

A good way to practice answering questions is to have a peer ask you questions. Be sure you give yourself a chance to think through a question before answering it. A helpful strategy is to repeat the question before you answer it. This technique has two advantages. First, you will have additional time to think of an appropriate answer. Second, all of the members of the audience will hear the question you are answering. Frequently, if someone in the front of the audience asks a question, those in the back may not hear the question so your answer makes less sense.

You will also want to decide how much of your presentation time should be available for answering questions. For example, if you have thirty minutes, you may decide to speak for twenty minutes and answer questions for the other ten. If you feel that few individuals will have questions about your presentation, you might wish to speak for twenty-five minutes and allow five minutes for questions. When the time for questions is nearly over, you may wish to end it gracefully by answering "one last question."

Visuals

You should check your visuals for clarity. Project them at the front of the room and then walk to the back of the room to see how they look. Are the visuals clear and easy to read? Will they help the audience in understanding your topic? Do you need to turn down the lights for better visibility? Where are the light switches, how do they work, and can someone operate them for you?

Critique

In order to improve your presentation, you will want to critique your practice session. You can do this through self-analysis as you proceed through the presentation—what seems to work well, what does not. You can also ask a peer or friend whose opinion you trust to evaluate your work and offer suggestions. A peer may notice something that you do not.

The best way to evaluate your performance is to videotape it. By examining the videotape, you can determine if you used any distracting mannerisms (such as touching your hair or looking down at the floor). You can also check your word choice to be sure correct grammar and precise words were used. In addition, you can see if your examples, stories, and analogies were accurate. A checklist such as the following one may be helpful.

Checklist for an Effective Oral Presentation

Item	Good	Acceptable	Needs Work
1. Maintain eye contact with audience—look at several individuals located throughout the audience.			
2. Use nonverbal communication—your appearance matches the speaking situation.			
3. Adjust your voice—volume, enthusiasm, confidence.			
4. Speak clearly and distinctly.			
5. Use correct grammar and word choice.			
6. Study the audience—be flexible enough to change presentation if problems develop.			
7. Check the timing to see if it is accurate.			
8. Evaluate introduction and conclusion for strength.			
9. Develop rapport with audience.			
10. Ask for feedback.			

When you get ready to deliver your actual presentation, take four or five deep breaths and then move to the front of your audience with a smile. Remember that the people in the audience want you to feel comfortable and to do well; they are on your side. After you go to the lectern, wait a few seconds to begin your presentation. Try to make the audience feel comfortable; this will help you to relax. Don't mention that you feel uncomfortable. In fact, don't say anything negative about yourself.

The Team Presentation

You may be called upon to give a team oral presentation. The basic components of planning and practicing will still be your best guidelines to a successful presentation. However, you will have some extra factors to consider in a team presentation.

Appearance

A professional appearance is one of the factors that can increase your credibility as a speaker. Your appearance must be appropriate for both your audience and your presentation. Special challenges occur in a team presentation. The team should be attired in a coordinating look. For example, you would not want one team member in a suit and tie, another in business casual dress, with yet another wearing shorts. While identical clothes or outfits are not required, the team should look like a team. For example, all members could wear professional business dress or casual business dress, if appropriate.

Interaction

The team members must decide how the individual team members will be introduced during the presentation and who will be speaking in what sequence. Perhaps, instead of one presenter speaking directly after another, an interactive style is used where two or more speakers present material by interacting with one another. Select a style that is appropriate to both the team members and the presentation.

Time

A team presentation requires additional time for practice when compared to an individual presentation. It is more critical that a team practice so that each team member uses the appropriate amount of time. For example, one four person team began their presentation that was to be 15 minutes in total length. The first speaker spoke for 11 minutes leaving 4 minutes for the remaining three team members. The disarray and lack of practice was evident to everyone in the audience.

Another issue related to time is the display of the visual aids. Which team member will show what aids? If a presentation graphics program is used, the team members will need to coordinate their efforts to present a professional team presentation. The issue of addressing questions should also be discussed. Which team members will respond to the questions, if asked? Clarification of this point before the presentation will make a smoother transition for the team when the question phase begins.

Situations for Speaking

The techniques you learned for oral presentations can be adapted to other speaking situations. You will have an opportunity to use oral communication in a number of business activities such as the following:

Face to Face Communication

You will use oral communication techniques when communicating in person with others. Here are some types of *face-to-face* communication.

Conversations. Business conversations serve a number of worthwhile purposes. Among the purposes are these: (1) they help to maintain a high level of morale, (2) they help to maintain good public relations, (3) they provide a brief break that promotes greater efficiency, and (4) they often lead to improved procedures.

Social situations as well as counseling sessions and other business communication arise often in most business offices. Good conversationalists are good listeners. They pay careful attention to what they hear, and they respond appropriately. They respond by looking into the eyes of the speaker part of the time—but usually not all the time—and by using facial expressions, gestures, and tone of voice and by making oral comments. They express their thoughts clearly and interestingly. As they move from topic to topic, they use good transition; and they share participation with others in the group. They reach a happy medium between the amount of time they spend talking and the amount of time they spend listening.

Interviews. Interviews are carefully planned oral conversations. Before conducting an interview, the interviewer determines the kinds of questions to ask and the question sequence. Some of the questions may be written so they will be stated the same way for more than one interview. Other questions are suggested by the interviewee's responses. And, of course, the questions and the responses lead to discussion that is expected, but is not planned specifically.

Interviewers ordinarily do most of the talking, but they want the interviewees (those being interviewed) to talk, too. The amount of talking expected of an interviewee depends on the purpose of the interview. If it is for employment, for example, the interviewer wants to learn as much as can be learned about the interviewee in the time available. The interviewee may have questions to ask and should ask them at the appropriate times. Some of the questions come naturally in the discussion of various topics that are raised, and others should come near the end of the session when the interviewer asks for questions.

Introductions. You will have the opportunity to perform many introductions in your business career. Some introductions are to introduce a client to others in your firm or to introduce employees to each other. You may also be asked to introduce a speaker to an audience.

A speaker's introduction has a significant effect on the audience. When you introduce a speaker, your job is to tell the audience enough about the speaker's qualifications and background to create interest in the speech. Let's say the topic is "Restaurant Management." If the speaker has written books or journal articles on this subject, emphasize them. If the speaker has managed restaurants successfully in other locations, mention these activities. You may mention the speaker's formal education for restaurant management, and you may also point out awards and other types of recognition received, as well as memberships in related organizations.

The introduction may contain some humor, but humor is not a requirement. By giving an appropriate introduction confidently, you help the speaker to feel confident. State your comments clearly and at an easy-to-hear pace. Pronounce the speaker's name clearly and correctly and then sit down.

Instructions. You will have the opportunity to give instructions during your business career. Sometimes directions that you thought were very clear will result in a less than perfect result. What happened? In order for your instructions to be effective, you should tell the employees what the instructions will cover and should make the employees feel comfortable enough to ask you questions.

Instructions are most effective at that time when the employees realize a need to receive them. Try to give instructions where the recipient can easily hear you. Keep the instructions in a logical, sequential order. If the process is complex, you may encourage the employee to write down the steps for later reference. When you are finished giving instructions, you may wish to see if the employee really understood you. One technique is to have the person restate the instructions in his or her own words.

How Simple Should Instructions Be?

When giving instructions, you may expect that the listeners already know things that they do not. A supervisor in a rush handed an employee a document and said "I need ten copies for my meeting—stapled." The employee quickly returned with the copied item. Upon closer examination, however, the supervisor realized that the employee had stapled ten copies of page one together, ten copies of page two together, etc. Certainly the supervisor could not distribute a complete copy to each participant in the meeting as they were stapled! The instructions were obviously not basic enough.

Electronic Communication

When communicating electronically, at times you will have an opportunity to use oral communication.

Telephone and Voice Mail. Some business workers feel like they spend most of their day on the telephone. Telephone conversations can be a quick way to communicate because neither party has to move to the location of the other. When speaking on the phone, you would like your voice to be clear and pleasant.

A business telephone call is different from a casual call to friends and relatives—you may wish to plan a business call. In fact, you may wish to jot down key points or questions you want to ask in the phone call. Such a list is especially important if you must leave a message for someone to call you back. Certainly, you don't want to forget your questions by the time your call is returned.

The same planning technique is important when using voice mail. If you are leaving a message requesting information, you need to leave all the pertinent facts so the recipient can answer your questions easily. You should also speak clearly and be sure to identify yourself in your message.

Conference Calls. Conference calls are very effective in some situations. Instead of having just two people engaged in the telephone conversation, participants may speak to and hear comments from all that are involved in the conference call. Time and money can be saved by making a conference call instead of having all the participants travel to one physical location. Participants in a conference call must be careful to identify themselves as they speak, especially when several individuals are communicating.

Interactive Television Communication. Many companies have invested in special communication rooms which feature video capabilities. One urban company found that a great deal of work time was lost when employees had to travel back and forth to two facilities located fifteen miles apart. After they built a television communication center, those who needed to talk to each other met in similar rooms at each site. Through video, they could see and communicate with each other by direct phone line link. At the end of the year, the company found that the amount of time lost to travel had been greatly reduced.

Many educational institutions are also using interactive television to provide instruction in many locations. For example, an instructor might be in a classroom in one city while students may be located in several other cities. All are linked electronically together for the class session.

Group Communication

You may be asked to assume a leadership role when communicating with groups both within the organization and outside the company.

Moderating Meetings. If you are in charge of conducting a meeting, you need to be sure that you are prepared. Most meetings follow an *agenda* which is a list with a sequence of topics in the order in which they will be addressed. As the moderator of a meeting, you will wish to prepare the agenda and distribute it before the meeting or at the meeting. At the beginning of the meeting you may wish to ask if any of the participants have agenda items that have not been mentioned. If you decide to change the order of topics, you should tell the audience what you are doing.

Be sure that the facilities for the meeting are also prepared. Does the meeting room have sufficient chairs in the arrangement you prefer? Will the temperature and lighting in the room be acceptable? You can think of other questions as you prepare the facility for the meeting.

As moderator of the meeting you should see that the meeting begins and ends on time. If it appears that the meeting will take longer than scheduled, you may wish to ask the group if they wish to continue for a specified length of time or if they prefer to reschedule the meeting for another time. You can understand the importance of ending on time if you equate a meeting with your class session. How do you feel when an instructor continues to hold class after the time the class is scheduled to end? Do you find yourself paying less attention? Perhaps you are anxious to get to your next class, to lunch, or to work. The same anxiety occurs in meetings which run longer than expected.

Demonstrations. Oral communication situations include demonstrations of various kinds. Salespersons frequently demonstrate the uses or the operation of the products, appliances, or machines they sell. Employees give demonstrations for understudies, new employees, and visitors to their offices. Before you begin a demonstration of any type, make sure that you are thoroughly familiar with the items you are to handle and that you have all the necessary supplies, electrical outlets, and so on required for an efficient demonstration.

Move through the various steps quickly enough to make it obvious that you are well qualified for your task, but move slowly enough to permit the observers to understand each step. Even though you must spend a good portion of the time looking at the items you are demonstrating, look directly into the eyes of the observers during each pause and while you answer questions they ask.

Because you cannot face the audience all the time during a demonstration, be especially careful to enunciate clearly and to talk loudly enough to be heard easily. You can enhance the effectiveness of a demonstration by telling the observers what to expect before you actually begin the demonstration. Then a quick review after you finish increases still further the effectiveness of the demonstration. Allowing an interested observer to go through each step under your guidance often pays rich dividends when you have finished a demonstration for the purpose of making a sale or of teaching an employee to perform a certain task.

Developing speaking effectiveness can be summarized into three activities: **preparing, organizing**, and **practicing**. Techniques reviewed in this chapter can help you in all of your business communication.

DISCUSSION

1. Why should a speaker look at the people in the audience when making an oral presentation?

2. What can speakers do to help themselves relax before an audience?

3. Based on presentations you have heard, what are some of the characteristics of a good speaker? What are some of the characteristics of a poor speaker?

4. What tips would you give someone who has to give instructions?

5. List some of the ways a team presentation may differ from an individual presentation.

EXERCISES

1. The following activity is a *speaking exercise* which should be conducted with a number of people.

Just a Minute to Think Quick and Speak Up

Divide the people into groups of five or six. Appoint one person in each group as the group leader–volunteers are nice.

The teacher will be the timer for all groups. A list of topics will be provided similar to the one below. The group leader or whoever he or she appoints will begin by speaking on the selected topic to the other group members for one minute. The speaker can remain seated. The purpose is to become comfortable by thinking quickly and speaking up in front of a small group. The one rule for this activity is that once the teacher tells all the speakers to begin, each speaker must speak for the full minute–don't stop half way through the time!

The second step is for the group members to select one of their members to think quick and speak up in front of the class on a selected topic.

You can use these topics or you can brainstorm in your group to select some topics of your own.

1. The movie critic: give a review of a movie you have seen recently.

2. Your idea of a good vacation spot.

3. Your favorite or least favorite advertisement.

4. A sports figure or sports team you like.

5. If you became a sudden millionaire, what would you do?

6. Give an update on the best show in television.

7. The best things about living in Texas (or state of your choice).

8. Your favorite holiday.

9. The best place to eat out.

10. Your favorite musical artist.

PROBLEMS

1. Revise the following visual to make it more effective.

> **5 Steps to Create a Better Work Environment**
>
> 1. Appropriate chairs and desks to reduce strain.
>
> 2. The lightning should be sufficient.
>
> 3. Barriers to Reduce Excessive Noise.
>
> 4. Periodic brakes during the day.
>
> 5. Smoking only in designated outdoor areas.

2. Prepare a short demonstration of a product you might sell to others. Be sure you include the important features and allow an opportunity for questions. Be ready to give your demonstration to the class.

3. Assume that you would like to invite your favorite college instructor to speak at a function of your organization. Write an appropriate introduction which would be suitable for the situation.

4. You are involved in the search for a new faculty member for the department where your major is located. Prepare a list of about ten interview questions which will be asked of all the applicants.

5. As the program chair for your organization, you have composed a list of topics that your members would want to hear about. Find class members who might like to prepare an oral presentation of five to eight minutes on these topics.

Job termination. You've been fired. Now what?

Computer virus. Your computer is doing strange things. Is it a virus?

Life insurance. You have no life insurance. Do you need it?

Job search. You would like a job in a certain city. What should you do first?

Social contact. You are interested in dating a co-worker. What are your options?

Travel. You are making your first business-related trip. What are some guidelines?

Smoking. A co-worker's is smoking in a nondesignated area. What should you do?

Harassment. You think your co-workers are treating you unfairly. What do you think you should do?

Technology. You are interested in a new technology. Describe it and its benefits.

International. You may do business with another country. Select an appropriate country and report on it.

---

6. You have been asked to address a group of thirty college freshmen. Your topic is "Tips on Adjusting to College Life." Design an appropriate oral presentation—you have been assigned twenty minutes on the program.

7. Phone at least three friends and ask them to critique your telephone voice for tone and clarity. Be ready to either write a memo or to report your findings to the class.

8. Use the World Wide Web to research information on a product or service of your choice. In addition, find information about at least two other competing products or services. Be ready to give a short presentation on your results. Hint: Use a search engine of your choice on this assignment.

9. Plan a team presentation. Begin by brainstorming about possible business topics. Develop a list of at least five topics. Prioritize them. Decide which topic you will choose. Do appropriate research on this topic. Organize and be prepared to give a presentation with appropriate visual support.

10. Find three Internet sites that discuss a hobby, interest, or specific area of business. Prepare three to five visuals using a presentation graphics software package such as Powerpoint. Be prepared to make a presentation or to discuss your visuals.

REFINING LISTENING SKILLS

■ Describe a real-life scenario where listening skills made an impact.

■ How has technology affected the need for listening skills?

CHAPTER OBJECTIVES

After studying this chapter, you should be able to:

1. Describe five types of listening.
2. Define barriers to effective listening.
3. Utilize techniques for improving listening.
4. List factors in good listening management.

THE IMPORTANCE OF LISTENING

The four fundamental activities of communication are writing, reading, speaking, and listening. In business programs of study, more instruction is devoted to improving writing skills than to any of the others, yet listening is perhaps the activity that is used the greatest part of the time in business. Studies have shown that managers spend more than 50 percent of their working day listening. Also, other business personnel spend a major portion of their time listening.

In business we listen to customers, to clients, to co-workers, to stockholders, to labor union representatives, to government officials, to suppliers, and to the general public. Among the business situations in which we listen are face-to-face conversations, telephone calls, speeches, sales talks, demonstrations, committee meetings, staff meetings, oral reports, briefings, conventions, training programs, and management development programs.

Executives have realized the importance of listening and are placing greater emphasis on the improvement of listening skills. Effective listening helps to promote good morale, to relieve tension, to show respect, and to motivate others.

Listening relates to speaking in the way that reading relates to writing: when we listen, we receive meaning from sounds that we hear; when we read, we receive meaning from symbols that we see. We can see words yet not actually read them. When we see words that we do not know the meanings of, we readily realize we are not receiving the message that was recorded. Similarly, from time to time we look at familiar words on a page of a book, a report, or other document and do not grasp the recorded message.

Haven't you sometimes returned to a reading task after being interrupted by a telephone call or another activity and read several sentences—even several paragraphs—before recalling having read that page before the interruption? Likewise, we often hear words spoken in a face-to-face conversation, on the telephone, or on the radio and suddenly realize we have not received the message that was made up by those words. By bearing these situations in mind, we are aware that seeing is not reading and that hearing is not listening. Reading and listening involve *thinking* in addition to seeing and hearing. We use our brains to give meaning to the words we see or hear and thus receive the message those words convey.

Types of Listening

All listening is not the same. In fact, at least five types of listening—casual, active, empathic, selective and critical—are used to achieve our purposes. Frequently, you may find yourself switching from one type of listening to another as a speaker catches your interest.

Casual Listening

Casual listening is listening primarily for enjoyment rather than for courtesy, empathy, or understanding. You might almost call this type of listening background listening. You are aware of it, but you are not always fully focused on what you are hearing. Enjoying music on tape or radio while performing a task is one example of casual listening. When you listen to a television program, you may use casual listening. Some people use casual listening when their talkative friends speak to them.

Active Listening

Active listening requires the listener to respond either verbally or nonverbally to the speaker. Active listening can take place when two people are conducting a conversation or when one person gives instructions and another responds to those instructions.

Empathic Listening

In empathic listening the listener tries to empathize or understand the feelings of the person talking. The listener wisely studies the nonverbal signals as well as the words that are spoken. An adjustment manager's listening to an irate customer's request for a refund is one example of empathic listening in business. Empathic listening is also used when listening to those who have suffered disappointments such as loss of job, loss of family member, or other trauma. If you can relate to the situations of those individuals, you will be using empathic listening.

Selective Listening

Selective listening takes place when the listener hears only selected parts of a conversation or other information. At the beginning of the semester most instructors discuss the course syllabi. One student may focus on the types of tests to be given, while another is trying to determine what the attendance requirements will be, and a third is interested in the number of papers or speaking assignments. If the three students discussed what they heard about the course, you might find three different perceptions. Often an intense focus on one idea or thought results in selective listening.

Critical Listening

When involved in critical listening, the listener not only receives information but also analyzes it and evaluates it. Critical listening is perhaps the most difficult type of listening to do because the listener is trying to listen and analyze at the same time. An example of critical listening may be when you are asked a question during a job interview—you have to both listen to the question and begin preparing what you hope will be an acceptable response.

We often combine two or more types of listening for one occasion. The occasion may be that of conversing, interviewing, attending a meeting, giving instructions, and so on. For whatever purpose we are listening, the ability to listen effectively is important. See the following list for typical cues which may signal a switch in listening types.

Type of Listening	Cue Which May Indicate Type of Listening
Casual	"...and after that she said...and then she said..."
Active	"Don't you agree on this issue?"
Empathic	"I have a right to be upset, don't I?"
Selective	"The following information will be on the exam."
Critical	"Your job responsibilities will include..."

The road to good listening ability is not smooth; numerous rough spots, or barriers, confront us. Some of them are presented in this chapter. Tips for improving listening ability follow a discussion of the barriers.

Barriers

As business communicators, we face various barriers to effective listening. Some are created by the speaker; some, by the listener; and some, by other persons, or by things. Here are some of the frequently encountered barriers:

1. Differences between speaking and hearing rates
2. Discomfort
3. Emotions
4. Controversial words
5. Limited attention span
6. Limited vocabulary
7. Multiple meanings for words
8. Desire to talk
9. Excessive note taking
10. Interruptions
11. Telephone problems
12. Hearing and seeing difficulties
13. Appearance of the speaker
14. Distracting gestures
15. Poor speech habits

These barriers to effective listening are discussed as they apply to some of the business communication situations.

Differences Between Speaking and Hearing Rates

Perhaps the most serious barrier to effective listening results from our ability to give meaning to a greater number of words in a given time than the number of words that are transmitted to us. Because the average speaking rate is about 125 words a minute and we can absorb more than 400 words a minute, a significant amount of time is available to allow our minds to wander.

For this reason, we often begin to daydream. Daydreaming can become a habit. To minimize the amount of time spent in daydreaming, we can force ourselves to continue listening if we relate what we hear to what we know and to what we have experienced. Thinking about experiences and expectations while hearing a speaker's words helps to enable us to listen effectively.

Discomfort

People usually have trouble listening well when they are not comfortable. Being tired, hungry, cold, hot, or ill can lead to ineffective listening. The environment in the room where one is listening can have an impact. For instance, uncomfortable seating makes listening difficult.

Why Is It Hard to Concentrate?

Delaney Jensen was in a rush to attend a 1 p.m. meeting. On this hot summer day, he ate a big lunch at a small restaurant three blocks away. At the meeting the room is crowded with colleagues, and it seems like the air conditioning is not working at its normal cool level. Delaney finds himself drifting off and having a hard time focusing on the business of the meeting. His physical discomfort is interfering with listening.

Emotions

To listen well, emotions have to be controlled. In any communication situation—a face-to-face conversation, a speech to a large group, a telephone conversation, an interview, and others—a listener who is biased or has a prejudiced feeling about the communication topic likely listens to only a few of the spoken words. Also anger, fear, and embarrassment set up strong barriers to effective listening.

Positive emotions—elation or an urge to laugh—also present barriers to listening. Negative or positive emotions can be present at the beginning of a listening period, or they may develop during a communication situation.

Controversial Words

People who are offended by a speaker's use of certain words tend to stop listening to the message. Words with negative political, ethnic, or gender overtones offend many listeners.

For example, using the pronouns *he*, *him*, and *his* generically offends some listeners. At the same time, others in the audience are not offended by the word choice.

While it is impossible to know all the words that are disliked by various people, skilled communicators do not use words that are known to be offensive to many people.

Limited Attention Span

Attention spans vary among communicators, and each person's attention span varies according to existing conditions. A person who is in a hurry to move to another location or is eager to discuss another topic has a shorter attention span than when these conditions do not exist.

Other factors that tend to limit a listener's attention span are fatigue, communication topic, attitude toward the other communicators, personality of the other communicators, and time of day. Listening ability may decrease sharply right before lunch or before the end of the work day. Obviously, listening ceases when the listener's attention-span limit is reached.

Limited Vocabulary

When the person talking uses a word with which we are not familiar, our listening efficiency is impaired. If the unfamiliar word is a key word in the idea or concept being presented, we may miss the entire concept. When the trend of thought is broken, listeners are prone to lose interest in the topic and to think about something else. Thus, daydreaming may begin.

Vocabulary Counts

I attended a conference where the speaker talked about using the ***sneakernet***. As this was a meeting on computer networking, I thought I should perhaps know the term—I didn't, and neither did the person next to me. The next day in a different session the term was explained. A ***sneakernet*** operates when you save a document on a disk, put on your sneakers and walk down the hall to another computer, and then load the disk on the machine!

Assume a co-worker comes stomping back to her desk with the statement "I will never get a new computer as long as that Luddite is in charge!" will you understand the meaning?

The larger the vocabulary we have, especially those words that relate to the discussion topic, the better we can listen. We can continue to get meaning from the spoken words rather than to concentrate on the words themselves.

Multiple Meanings for Words

Numerous everyday words in the English language have more than one meaning each. The listeners who know only one of the meanings think of that one meaning, of course; and those who know more than one of the meanings sometimes wonder which meaning the speaker intended to convey. In some contexts the listeners cannot readily determine which meaning is intended by the word.

Questions then arise in the minds of the listeners and thus diminish listening effectiveness. For example, at what time of day do you eat dinner? Some would argue that the meal is served at noon while others would say dinner is served in the evening. If a word has more than one clear meaning, another choice would be better.

Desire to Talk

In face-to-face conversations, in telephone conversations, and in large group meetings, as well as in other situations involving oral communication, listeners are often eager to talk. They want to give an illustration of the idea being discussed, they want to ask a question, or they want to speak for some other reason. Thinking about what they want to say prevents their listening carefully to what is being said by someone else. You have probably noticed, for example, that some people jump into a conversation by saying something which does not appear to relate to what the others have been talking about. In those cases, frequently the speaker has been too busy deciding what to say that he or she has not noticed that the conversation has moved on to a different topic.

Excessive Note Taking

One way listeners can overcome the barrier of wanting to talk is to write notes so that their thoughts will not escape them before they get an opportunity to talk. Taking too many notes, however, is a strong barrier to effective listening. The listeners who attempt to write everything—or most of everything—the speakers say keep themselves so busy writing that they cannot listen carefully to all the ideas the speakers express.

Notetakers should practice listening for key concepts rather than trying to capture all of the speaker's words. A technique to try is to write down only what you think are the main ideas from a presentation. Then ask a fellow attendee to see if you agreed on all of the main points.

Interruptions

Focus is very important to successful listening. When the listener is disturbed to the extent that the focus is lost or directed to another topic, successful listening stops. Interruptions of any kind are barriers to good listening as indicated in the following example.

Interruptions Cause Problems

Juan Guerrera was explaining a new accounting procedure which was rather complex to his superior Branch Northrup. After five minutes, the phone rang distracting Mr. Northrup as he dealt with the phone call. Juan started to explain again when an express package for which Mr. Northrup was waiting was delivered. After another attempt by Juan, Mr. Northrup was reminded that he would be late for a meeting if he didn't leave immediately. Juan did not feel that Mr. Northrup had a good grasp of the new procedure due to all of the interruptions which took place.

Telephone Problems

The previously mentioned barriers to effective listening that apply to face-to-face conversations, interviews, and other oral communication situations apply equally to telephone calls. Special barriers to listening on the telephone arise because of poor connections, defective equipment, and the speakers' telephone voice.

Telephone Voice

Tamara Porter noticed that everyone with whom she spoke on the phone asked her to "speak up" or to "repeat that." Finally, a friend to whom she spoke on the telephone told Tamara that her voice was so soft that it did not carry over the phone well. After Tamara practiced speaking more loudly on the telephone, she felt the situation was improved.

As telephone use continues to increase, overcoming these special barriers becomes more important.

More speakers are leaving messages with voice mail than ever before. When you listen to a voice mail message, you would like to know the name of the caller, when the call was made, what the message is, and what action you are to take. Some callers need practice in leaving successful voice mail messages.

Hearing and Seeing Challenges

Meanings cannot be given to words unless they are received—heard or seen. And if words are received inaccurately, incorrect meaning is given to them. People who have normal hearing and seeing ability experience diminished listening power when they cannot see or hear the speaker or see the items that are used to enhance the spoken words. Examples of such items are small type on graphics for presentations to large groups, blocking of a listener's view by an individual or item, and distracting gestures in any oral communication situation.

Shrill voices are difficult for listeners to absorb. Also, voices that are too soft or too loud make listening a challenge. A monotone creates boredom and can, therefore, detract from listening effectiveness.

The noise level in a particular area may be so high that hearing is difficult. The noise may come from people who are talking either inside or outside the room in which oral communication occurs. Coughing and the shuffling of papers inside the room, the hum of equipment, loud music, the noise of vehicles, and audible sounds from outside a building are frequent barriers to good listening.

Image of the Speaker

A first impression can be a powerful tool for a speaker. If your image matches the expectations of your listeners, one barrier to communication will be easily removed. Many companies hold retreats where casual dress is permitted or even have certain days of the week where employees are urged to dress casually.

However, a person who arrived in cut-off shorts and an old t-shirt to speak to a group of formally dressed executives might encounter image problems. When the person who was inappropriately dressed was communicating, others might have difficulty getting beyond the appearance barrier to listening.

Additional factors affecting the image of the speaker include grammar, word choice, knowledge of subject, and speaking style. The combination of these factors along with appearance set an image for the speaker. Therefore, any time the image of a speaker is not what the listeners expect it to be, listening effectiveness is decreased.

Distracting Gestures

Mannerisms and gestures are often barriers to effective listening. While focused arm movements can enhance a presentation, idle habits can distract the listener. When a speaker jingles change or keys while speaking, the listener may be distracted. Similarly, a speaker who paces back and forth may be distracting.

What Was That Again?

Dillon Winston attended an executive conference where the speaker was sharing information about future product developments. Dillon was interested in the topic but found himself spending a great deal of time watching the speaker either rock back and forth on the heels of his shoes or pace back and forth in the front of the room. These physical gestures distracted Dillon from the content of the speaker's talk.

Poor Speech Habits

A major barrier to effective listening is poor speech habits. While no one is expected to be able to pronounce all words correctly or to talk with no errors in grammar, good oral communication should not contain excessive mispronunciations and errors in grammar. When through a "slip of the lip" speakers make an error, it is usually best for them to ignore the error and to continue talking. The listeners pay little attention to isolated errors.

For a word that has more than one equally good correct pronunciation, speakers ordinarily use the pronunciation that seems natural to them because they hear it often. If speakers know, however, that their pronunciation of a specific word is not familiar to a listener or to a particular group of listeners, they are wise to use the pronunciation that the listeners expect to hear. Otherwise, attention is called to the delivery rather than to the content of the message. Similarly, accents are troublesome for listeners. An example is the pronunciation of New Orleans. Some speakers say "New **OR**leans," others say "New **OR**le**ANS**," while others say "New **Allins**."

Another distraction that affects listening adversely is the use of "filler" sounds, words, and phrases. Examples are *um, uh, okay, like, and, and a, I mean*, and *you know*. The "fillers" come during breaks between statements when the speaker should remain silent.

Studying barriers to effective listening may suggest ways to overcome them. Some ways in which listening effectiveness can be improved are presented next.

Tips for Improvement

Identifying barriers to effective listening, wanting to overcome them, and constantly applying the following tips will help us to improve our listening skills:

1. Resolve to improve.
2. Develop the right attitude.
3. Know what to expect.
4. Know the speaker's background.
5. Develop a good vocabulary.
6. Stop talking.
7. Choose a good place to sit.
8. Reduce distractions.
9. Help the speaker to relax.
10. Listen for ideas rather than for details.
11. Control emotions.
12. Observe nonverbal cues.
13. Don't jump to conclusions.
14. Take notes of key ideas.
15. Provide feedback.

These tips for improving listening skills are discussed as they apply to some of the oral communication situations that occur often in business.

Resolve to Improve

All of us have bad habits, and breaking them is unlikely unless we first realize we have them. Then we have to want to break them. If you are a poor listener, you can improve your listening skills if you want to do so. Once you have resolved to improve, you will have to work at it. Listening effectively is hard work.

To improve, concentrate. As you receive ideas, relate them to your own experiences. Remain on guard, though, to limit the relationships you make to those you can process in the amount of time available because of your ability to absorb words faster than you hear them. Don't let yourself daydream when you should be listening.

Develop the Right Attitude

Whether an employment contract is being discussed during a coffee break, a sales demonstration is underway for a group of prospective customers, or someone is talking for any other occasion, those in the audience are expected to listen. To listen effectively, they have to have the right attitude. Persons who have biased or prejudiced feelings toward or against any topic are handicapped. They may miss worthwhile ideas they could use advantageously only because their prejudiced ideas are too strongly ingrained to permit them to accept the worthwhile ideas being expressed. For effective listening, those who hear the presentation have to repress preconceived ideas while hearing spoken words.

Know What to Expect

In any oral communication situation, listening effectiveness is enhanced when the listeners know what to expect. Appropriate information about the topic before the event or an overview of the presentation's content will clarify matters for the audience.

What Is a Network?

Two executives attended a special conference put on by vendors of computer products related to the technical issues of computer networks. The executives knew that their knowledge was limited—in fact, on the long drive to the conference location they were studying information about networks. As they prepared to attend the first session, they thought that they would at least recognize the terminology which was to be used.

To their dismay, the session focused completely on different types of wire that could be used for networking—in great detail! The executives had expected a different session and felt intimidated by their lack of knowledge.

Know the Speaker's Background

Experts are not perfect. When you know, however, that the person to whom you are listening is an expert on the topic being discussed, you may listen carefully. If you know very little or nothing about the speaker's background, you may decide early in the communication that some statements are poorly supported, and thus you listen less effectively than you would if you knew the speaker is highly qualified.

Gaining information about the background of a speaker is often worthwhile.

Develop a Good Vocabulary

Gestures, tone of voice, and other nonverbal communication media convey meaning; but words are required for conveying some ideas. A listener who is not familiar with the words a speaker uses does not receive the message the speaker intends to transmit.

Words have numerous definitions. Often, listeners need to know the various definitions in order to receive a message correctly. Both speaking and listening competence is reduced if the listener has to ask for clarification because of not knowing the meaning of a word. Unfortunately, many listeners don't ask for definitions; they just guess at the meaning.

To strengthen your listening skills, build a large vocabulary. Learn especially the terms that apply to situations about which you often communicate.

Stop Talking

Almost no listening takes place by a person who is talking. To listen well, remain silent until the person talking reaches a good stopping point. Knowing when to talk and when to stay quiet is important.

There is a time to talk and a time to listen. Communicators who know when to do either are fortunate.

Empathy Can Be a Plus

Lisa Rouen was concerned about the possibility of her earning an upcoming promotion to a higher level position. Although she had submitted the necessary paperwork to apply for the promotion, she was still nervous. She decided to talk to her mentor Gina Lyle. Gina assumed an empathetic role. She listened to all of Lisa's preparations and concerns and supplied positive feedback. After Lisa had discussed the promotion with Gina, she felt relieved. In this situation, Gina's role was to be a listener rather than a speaker.

Choose a Good Place to Sit

Seeing a speaker's facial expressions and gestures contributes to good listening. Also, seeing graphics, items being demonstrated, and other objects a speaker uses to enhance the delivery of an oral message contributes to good listening. For this reason, choose a place to sit that will enable you to see as well as to hear. Sitting beside a speaker in a conference room may not be the best choice because you will not be able to easily see the presentation. Select a place you believe is as free of distractions as possible.

For some occasions the place where you sit helps the speaker to relax. For example, a subordinate may sense a communication barrier if the superior sits behind a desk with the subordinate sitting on the opposite side for an interview. To minimize tension and to promote listening, both participants may sit on a sofa or in chairs away from the superior's desk.

Reduce Distractions

You can take the initiative to reduce distractions to listening by avoiding typical distractions. By sitting near the front of a room, listeners in a large audience eliminate many of the distractions created by others in the group. Choosing a chair next to the door may cause you listening difficulties as people enter and leave the room after the speaker begins. Sitting far from doors and windows minimizes the effect of distractions outside the meeting room.

Speakers create many distractions whether they are speaking in a one-to-one situation or to a group of any size. Voice qualities, dress, posture, gestures, accents, and other characteristics of a speaker often distract listeners. When encountering distractions of any kind, try harder than usual to concentrate on the message content and wait until the message has been received to think about the distractions.

Help the Speaker to Relax

Ordinarily, speakers who feel comfortable create fewer distractions and present their ideas more effectively than do those who are ill at ease. Do what you can, therefore, to help them. Your pleasant facial expressions, relaxed posture, and friendly gestures to respond to spoken words contribute to relaxation for the speakers.

Employees often feel somewhat tense when discussing problems with a superior. Encouraging them to talk briefly about a topic with which they feel comfortable sometimes enables them to relax before discussing the problem. Thus they listen more effectively to the message being sent to them. At the beginning of an interview, a job interviewer will frequently ask an applicant about something they might have in common so that applicant can be a little more relaxed in the interview.

Listen for Ideas Rather Than for Details

Often, listeners who attempt to absorb many details miss good ideas. Likewise, those who pay much attention to delivery style—accent, word choice, mannerisms, and so on—do not receive some points of the message being transmitted. To listen well, therefore, listen for ideas rather than for details or delivery.

Control Emotions

We are not expected to agree with everything we hear. When we disagree, though, with what someone is saying, we should control our emotions in order to receive the entire message being transmitted. Becoming angry or impatient makes listening more difficult than it is when we control our emotions. Avoid losing control of emotions because you do not like the message content or because you object to the words or the nonverbal mediums used to convey the message.

If a company has announced that it will be downsizing its work force, the employees may have trouble controlling emotions such as fear they may lose their jobs or anger at the company executives. Keeping our emotions under control until after messages have been sent enables us to listen more effectively than we otherwise could.

Observe Nonverbal Cues

Observing the nonverbal cues of speakers in addition to hearing their words contributes to effective listening. Does the sales representative, for example, use gestures that seem to contradict the statements made about a product that is being promoted? Does the labor relations director use a tone of voice that helps to convince listeners that what is being said is true? Sometimes the nonverbal messages that accompany verbal messages are the more important.

For greater listening effectiveness, therefore, observe carefully the nonverbal communication of the people who are talking.

Don't Jump to Conclusions

Maintain an open mind throughout the listening period. Persons who jump to conclusions before the speakers say all they intend to say about a topic stop listening. Different, valid conclusions may be drawn by those who listen to the entire message before drawing a conclusion.

Take Notes

Taking notes improves listening in some oral communication situations, but don't take too many notes. Jot down words or sentence fragments that will serve as reminders when you refer to them later.

Suppose you want to respond to something that was said by a speaker. Rather than continuing to think about what you want to say and thus not listen to what is being said, write enough notes to use as a reminder of what you want to say and then listen until the appropriate time comes for you to respond. Taking excessive notes, however, requires too much time and thought to permit you to listen to all the message.

Provide Feedback

By responding at appropriate times, you tend to listen more effectively than if you remain passive throughout the oral communication session. You may provide feedback to the speaker in several ways. In conversations, interviews, and so on, you may add information to what has been said. You may ask questions about parts of the topic that have not been discussed, or you may ask for clarification of ideas that have been presented.

Using facial expressions, making gestures, laughing, and applauding are among the ways listeners can provide feedback. Active involvement usually stimulates others to communicate and keeps you listening effectively.

One of the listening tasks where feedback is most important is during the giving and receiving of instructions. As you listen to instructions, you may wish to ask questions to clarify information. Doing so effectively will save time when the task is completed correctly the first time.

Listening Management

Managing so that listening effectiveness can be improved is important for four reasons: (1) people, especially business personnel, spend a major portion of their time listening, (2) many people listen ineffectively, (3) little has been done to help people to improve listening skills, and (4) effective listening is essential—not only for following instructions, but also for learning, for maintaining good morale, and for maintaining good public relations.

As a competent member of the business work force, you will be wise to schedule oral communication situations—staff meetings, employment interviews, appraisal interviews, employee conferences, committee meetings, and the myriad other oral communication situations—at the right time and for the right place. A group meeting, for example, is usually less effective on Friday afternoon than on another day. A one-to-one conference with an employee may be less effective near the middle of the employee's most productive period of the workday than at another time.

Giving instructions at the time the listeners need them promotes good listening. The listeners, therefore, are able to apply immediately what they hear.

Making appointments to communicate with others contributes much to their listening effectiveness. If superiors are especially busy and have not scheduled a time to talk about a subordinate's concerns, they tend not to listen effectively and therefore do not give proper attention to the concerns as quickly as they otherwise would.

Group meetings should be scheduled for rooms that are removed from excessive noise or movement inside or outside the building. One-to-one meetings should be held in places where hearing is easy, and they should be held in places where the communicators feel somewhat relaxed. Steps should be taken to avoid interruptions in oral communication situations.

A very important point for managers to keep in mind is that they should schedule no meeting unless there is strong evidence that it will be worthwhile for those who attend. Attending a few meetings that are not beneficial tends to hamper listening effectiveness in later meetings.

The Listener and Speaker Relationship

Showing sincere consideration for others is always, of course, a good practice to follow. Courtesy, tact, and sincerity are commendable traits of successful business executives. Exhibiting these characteristics in oral communication is especially worthwhile. Listeners should show proper consideration to the speakers by making talking easy for them. Those who talk should show proper consideration to the listeners by making listening easy for them.

DISCUSSION

1. What is the difference between hearing and listening?

2. Why has little been done to teach people to improve their listening skills?

3. What are some barriers to effective listening that were not mentioned in this chapter?

4. What are some listening barriers you have encountered recently?

5. What are some ways (not mentioned in the chapter) for improving listening skills?

6. Which do you expect *you* will do more—speak or listen?

EXERCISES

1. The following activity is a *listening exercise* which should be conducted with a number of people. Try this activity to see how well *you* do in giving and receiving instructions. Determine the importance of feedback.

The Artist and the Director

Divide the group up into two person teams. Ask one member of each team to leave the room—*the Artist*. The remaining team member is *the Director*. The coordinator of the activity should draw a figure such as a cabinet, a car, or an animal on the board. Ask each ***Director*** to jot down a note of how to draw the item. Erase or cover the board.

When ***the Artists*** return to the room, place the chairs so that the members of the team will be back to back. ***The Director*** will now provide instructions to ***the Artist*** to draw the item mentioned. ***The Director*** cannot tell ***the Artist*** what the item is nor can any clues be given. For example, if the item is a pizza, ***the Director*** can not say—"It is something you can have delivered to eat." In this round of the activity ***the Artist*** can ask no questions and ***the Director*** cannot watch what ***the Artist*** is doing—no feedback. When ***the Artist*** is finished, ***the Director*** can see how well the directions worked.

In round two, the team members trade places and the new ***Artists*** leave the room. The coordinator draws another object—one which is more difficult. This time—although the chairs are still back to back and ***the Director*** cannot see ***the Artist's*** work—***the Artist*** can ask questions of ***the Director***. For example, "How long is the line?"

In the third round, either team member can be ***the Artist***. The most complex item is drawn. When ***the Artist*** returns to the room, the chairs are moved side by side and ***the Director*** can watch what ***the Artist*** is doing and provide feedback. In addition, ***the Artist*** can ask questions as in round two and ***the Director*** can give answers.

PROBLEMS

1. Select two partners. Work as a team and listen to an oral presentation—a TV newscast, a radio newscast, or other speech—and after a few hours have passed, compare your notes on what you remember from the presentation. Be ready to share your findings with the class.

2. People are frequently asked to give directions. Write a set of directions directing a person from your classroom to another building of your choice on the campus. You may wish to test your directions by speaking them to another class member and having that student follow them to arrive at the building.

3. Consider your listening habits in one of your classes. Analyze the place where you normally sit. Are there distractions? If so, what are they? Is your chair a good location for listening? Compare your listening effectiveness in the class with your effectiveness in another class. What factors were different? Write a brief memo to your teacher describing your analysis.

4. Use the criteria in this chapter to analyze the technique of a speaker you recently heard (do *not* choose your business communication instructor). Select at least five items and evaluate the speaker on those categories. Write a brief memo listing your findings.

5. Search the Internet for ideas and topics relating to improving listening skills. Compose a list of at least five sites where you can find helpful information. Be prepared to report by e-mail to the instructor or to give a report to the class.

6. Listen to a presentation by a public figure that you do not like. This could be a talkshow host, a politician, or someone else that you have negative emotions about. When listening, attempt to overcome your emotions by focusing on the content of the presentation. What were the key points? You may wish to ask another person to listen to the same presentation to see if you had similar results. Be prepared to discuss your findings.

7. Listen to a presentation and look for all of the nonverbal communication. Does any of the nonverbal communication disagree with the spoken words? Does any of the nonverbal communication support the spoken words? How would you evaluate the speaker's nonverbal communication. Prepare an e-mail discussing your results.

8. If you completed Exercise 1, compose an e-mail discussing what you thought was worthwhile about the activity. Send it to your instructor.

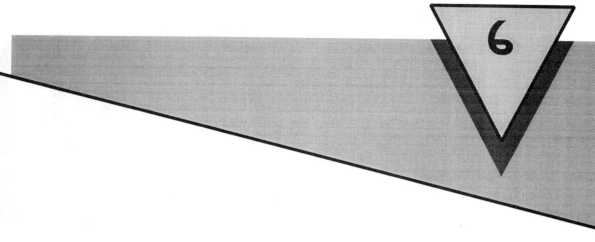

USING TEAM COMMUNICATION

Critical Thinking Applications

■ How does a diverse workforce impact communication in teams?

■ Investigate and discuss techniques of business etiquette that promote team building within an organization.

TEAMS IN BUSINESS

While success in team communication and team performance has always been important in business, an increased emphasis has been placed on cooperation in the workplace within the past ten years. Repeatedly, company representatives are stressing the importance of hiring those who understand how to work in a team environment.

Successful team communication provides an opportunity for several ideas to be shared and developed. The best ideas may then be further developed and implemented.

The purpose of this chapter is to discuss the importance of teams to business, the cooperative focus of teams, the dynamics of team interaction, and effective team procedures.

Importance of Teams

In many cases the story of business success in America has involved the tales of rugged individualists like Henry Ford who defied all the odds and the current thinking of the day to first mass produce the automobile. While the entrepreneurial spirit still lives in the United States, many companies have also seen the value of the team environment to business success.

Team responses provide a diversity of ideas, concept ownership, global perspectives, and personal growth among employees.

More Ideas

In an effective team environment, many ideas are generated through synergism. *Synergism* takes place when individuals working together can develop more ideas than can the same individuals working alone. One person's idea serves as a bridge or connection to another individual's idea. An example of synergism might be when a team discusses fund-raising activities. Each individual might have an idea or two. However, when all the ideas are discussed, other ideas which were not proposed by any specific person might form as a result of the team interaction.

Ownership of Ideas

When an individual presents an idea or plan, normally the idea is associated with that person. Sometimes an idea might succeed or fail based on the personality and position of the person who proposed it rather than the merits of the idea itself. In a team environment ideas should be developed so that all participants can share in the ideas and the ownership belongs to the team rather than to an individual. Team ideas, therefore, may receive more support because they are not attributed to a single person. As all of the team members retain ownership of the idea, they may be more willing to advocate the idea outside of the group.

Global Environment Strategy

Other countries, including Japan, have long used a team environment throughout business. Groups defined as quality circles have helped Japan move from a reputation as a producer of poor-quality goods after World War II to a reputation as a producer of high-quality goods today. In a quality circle, all levels of production staff are involved in discussing improvements in quality. Together the team works out problems to produce a better product.

As businesses in the United States continue to provide products to a global marketplace, adopting the successful team techniques implemented by others may be one way of remaining competitive in a global environment.

Personal Growth

One of the advantages of team participation is the opportunity for each member to grow and develop within the group. Successful completion of a team assignment may lead to more challenging responsibilities as other members of the team see the commitment and involvement of each team member. In addition, by working with others with different knowledge, you can learn new valuable skills. The isolationist who cannot perform effectively in a team environment may have difficulty progressing in the company.

Focus on Cooperation

Most jobs in today's leading businesses focus on cooperation throughout the organization. Cooperation has a number of benefits for the employee and the company. The most important are sharing results, providing social contact, and directing competition toward the competitor.

Shared Results

A cooperative work environment provides an opportunity to share both successes and defeats of business. Some business jobs are more stressful than others. One way to lessen stress may be to share it among the work team. In fact, the team is responsible for the success or defeat. A similar example may be found in sports when no one person is responsible for victory or defeat; in fact, the entire team is responsible for each victory.

Social Contact

Cooperation in the workplace provides an opportunity for social contact with others. In earlier generations, the social contact which human beings enjoy was provided by extended families or friends outside of the workplace. With families more geographically dispersed as well as with busy work schedules, employees turn to the workplace itself for social contact. One criteria, therefore, for selecting your next job might be—would I enjoy being around the people I work with outside of the work day? If the answer is no, you may have to develop your friendships outside of the workplace.

Directed Competition

Competition is a healthy part of business. Without competition products would never be changed or improved. One of the biggest reasons that technology has changed so rapidly over the past few years has been that major vendors have competed with each other to produce better and better products while many prices have actually dropped.

What a company must do is foster a cooperative attitude within the company so that the competitive spirit is actually directed toward the competition. For example, the primary goal for the automotive sales team should not be how many cars can each of the sales staff sell, but rather how many of the company's cars can be sold instead of the competitor's cars. When a cooperative spirit is used within the company, the company as a whole can become more competitive. If competition is not directed in the right direction, employees can waste time, energy, and resources competing among themselves.

Dynamics of Groups

By the time you leave college you will probably have had several opportunities to work in a group environment as part of a team. You may be able to select your fellow team members or you may be assigned to a team. In the workplace both procedures are used to develop groups. You will find your team performance more effective if you understand the dynamics of groups. The following factors influence team dynamics: life of the group, standards of behavior, composition, size, and roles.

Life of the Group

Most groups have either a short-term or a long-term life span. Short-term groups exist to complete the assigned task. Most class projects require groups which seldom meet for longer than the length of the course. Short-term groups usually have less focus on social activities and more on completing a specific task.

Long-term groups are those that continue for longer than a year. A company ball team, a standing committee, a board of directors, or a long-term task force are examples of long-term groups. Members of long-term groups will frequently expend more effort on social activities particularly during the formation of the group. This socialization enables team members to be more cohesive throughout the life of the group. In college, a number of students who join a team their first year may maintain active membership throughout their college career. Social interaction in such groups can be vital to their longevity and success.

Standards of Behavior

Most groups quickly establish expected standards for the behavior of the group. Expected standards may relate to meeting length, meeting place, dress code, and other behaviors. A team that establishes its meeting time as ten minutes before class in the hallway outside the classroom will have an expected standard of rushed meetings. While such meetings may occur, if they become the expected standard, the team will be less effective as tasks cannot be successfully completed in that time frame.

Standards of behavior will develop in any group. You may wish to work with other team members to develop the standards that you think will be appropriate for your group.

What Is Standard Behavior for a Group?

One group of students decided to meet casually every two weeks on Wednesday evening for dinner. They would discuss how each person was doing and provide any assistance or advice of interest to the other group members. The number of students in the group varied from six to nine. Not all students attended each meeting. Each meeting was held in a different restaurant in town.

The standards of behavior for this group were the meeting time and the fact that the meeting varied from place to place. Another standard was that attendance was not required but requested. Any student could bring up any issue. All team members understood and accepted these standards of behavior resulting in an effective support group.

Team Composition

Most groups or task forces in business are established with a purpose including certain activities to accomplish. The greater the *diversity* of the group, the more ideas that are generated. If a large law firm decides to study the issue of employee compensation, a team of five senior law partners may not be the best team to consider all the issues because it lacks diversity. A team composed of the firm's financial manager, three attorneys with different levels of seniority, and a representative of the support staff may provide a wider range of opinions.

If you have an opportunity to select your own team in a business course, you should also look for *expertise*. Which members of the proposed team can provide computer skills, which can provide research skills, and which are good communicators. You may wish to consider individuals of different gender, cultures, and ethnic groups to add perspective to your team.

If you select your team based strictly on your friends or on people you know, you may wish you had individuals with different expertise by the time the project is finished. In one business communication class, ten members of the same fraternity were enrolled in the class. The class members had an opportunity to express their partner choice. Nine of the fraternity members were divided into three groups of three. The tenth member was assigned to a team with non-fraternity members. At the conclusion of the project, several of the fraternity members felt that a different team composition would have been better while the reluctant tenth fraternity member was pleased with his outside team experience.

Another factor to consider in team formation is the ***position*** of the individual in the workplace. For example, if an executive is placed on the committee, employees at lower levels may feel obliged to agree with the executive because of that person's position in the company rather than because they support the executive's viewpoint in team discussions.

Some factors can be used to counter this ***position*** effect. For example, the executive should not sit behind a desk or at the front of the room or head of the table, rather a circular arrangement should be used. In addition, the composition of the team can help. For example, three employees at the same level in the company may be appointed to the team while only one executive is appointed to the group. Such an action may encourage the employees to speak their own thoughts.

Size of Team

The size of the team will vary with the complexity of the task. However, the ideal team size is *five to seven* members. An odd number of members is recommended so that if a team decides to vote on issues, tie votes will not occur. Usually five to seven members provide enough diversity in the team to serve as effective problem solvers. Groups larger than ten members often discourage the discussion and interaction which can take place in smaller teams. Scheduling meetings also becomes more difficult with larger groups.

A more popular size of groups for business courses is three to five members. Most projects can be handled by a team of four students. In the workplace, times can be arranged for team meetings during the course of the work day. Scheduling meetings for class groups can be difficult, however, so the larger the group, the more difficult it may be for the team to meet.

Roles in Teams

As a team meets and develops its own identity, different roles emerge. Although not all groups will include these members or these members will not be formally identified, they can be found frequently in team development. The roles can be summarized as *task director, social director, cooperative member, individualist member*, and *floater*.

Task Director. The Task Director's goal is to get the job done. In a team setting, the Task Director is one who continually focuses the team on what has to be done next to accomplish the goal. Some team members may see the Task Director as pushy or as a dictator. However, without a Task Director the team will probably have difficulty finishing the assigned job.

Social Director. As discussed earlier, a cooperative environment provides an environment where social contact is important. The social director may be interested in social activities for the group. The social director may be interested in the personal lives of the team members and may ask about hobbies or interests. Some team members may view the social director as one who is always wandering off the topic and "wasting" time with things not related to the assigned job. The social director is important, however, because human beings enjoy social exchange and will work less effectively if they do not have rapport with other team members.

<u>*Cooperative Member*</u>. The cooperative member may be a follower of either the task director or the social director. The cooperative member wants to do a good job on the task and wants to help out. However, the cooperative member is not usually interested in a leadership role and would prefer to take instead of give directions.

<u>*Individualist Member*</u>. Some groups have an individualist member who may or may not work with the task and social directors. This team member often seems to direct the team down a path no one else wants to follow. While some team members view the individualist member as a troublemaker or someone who doesn't work within the group, the individualist member can force the team to justify what they are doing and to rethink their path. Many times a better decision or project can be achieved if the team can work successfully with the individualist member.

<u>*Floater*</u>. Unfortunately, some groups have a floater. The floater expects to do little or nothing and "float along" on the project with the goal of receiving the same reward as the members of the team who complete the task. The floater may miss meetings of the team or may attend meetings but just not complete assigned tasks. Usually, the floater has a wide range of excuses for why assignments are not completed. Groups in business and in classes do not need floaters.

Effective Team Procedures

Frequently people complain (or wish to) when they realize that a team component will be part of their assignment. The most common concern expressed is "When I work in a team, I do all the work and the others who don't do the work I do, get the same credit!" What can you and your team do to get off to the right start where everyone will have a responsible role?

A number of procedures can be used to provide an effective team experience. The procedures include determining the purpose of the group, selecting team members, getting the team started, handling conflict, and reviewing performance.

Determine Purpose of Group

What is the purpose of the team with which you are working? Usually, your main purpose is to complete a specific task. Your team will first need to determine the scope of the activity as well as the expertise which your team has to accomplish the team goals. You may also wish to include a social component such as meeting informally to discuss ideas and procedures before having a formal meeting.

Selecting Team Members

If you have an opportunity to select your team members, you may wish to visit informally with those available to try to determine who will be good team members. Keep in mind the types of diverse individuals and role holders you will wish to include. Frequently, however, someone else may select the team for you. In this case, you will wish to become acquainted with other team members as quickly as possible.

Getting the Team Started

Getting the team started effectively will be very important to the success of the group. The following ideas will be helpful.

Schedule the First Meeting. The first meeting should be scheduled so that all members can attend as all of the future activity of the team will depend on the decisions made at the first meeting. A person who does not attend the first meeting may feel no ownership in the decisions that are made and, therefore, may not contribute to the project.

Share Ideas. All ideas about how the team should proceed at any time should be shared and accepted without criticism. Even if the idea seems like an obviously poor one, avoid criticizing the person who proposed the idea. Wait for a few other ideas to appear and then evaluate each idea on its merit separately from the person who proposed it.

Explore All Options and Alternatives. Frequently, a team will meet and will need to select a topic or an activity. Within five minutes, they have decided what they wish to do. Usually in this case one individual happens to have a quick idea while the other team members can't think of something better. The first idea is not always the best. If you could not formulate an idea right away, let the team know that you will provide input when you have had an opportunity to think about it.

Allow Time to Review and Revise. Commonly, groups end up meeting fewer times than really needed so time for reviewing and revising work is limited. The goal for the team should be to provide sufficient time to review and revise work. This time management technique is especially critical if unexpected delays or problems occur through the course of the project.

Select a Team Moderator. At the first meeting, the team should select a team *moderator* rather than a team leader. Some individuals with limited experience of leading a team assume that the leader is responsible for the team and they may become dictatorial. Select a moderator to schedule meetings and keep things moving along. Later, the team may decide to select a team leader. The team should also select someone to serve as a *recorder* to keep track of the business of the team such as attendance at meetings and completion of assignments.

Determine Procedures. At the first meeting the team should attempt to resolve as many procedural issues as possible. For example, what time and day(s) will the team meet? Where will the team meet? How long will the meetings be? What are the responsibilities of the members? What schedule will be followed to complete the task? Disagreement or confusion within the team on one or more of these issues could cause problems. For example, if two members of the team show up at the library expecting to spend two hours on the task while the third member of the team is planning to stay for fifteen minutes, dissension in the team may occur.

Write an Agreement. Perhaps the most critical part of the early meetings of the team will involve preparing the team agreement. While such an agreement may not be common in the business world, it will help you learn to understand and work with the team process.

The agreement should clearly **outline the procedures** of the group, should list **what is expected** from each team member, and should **define the rewards and or penalties** in the agreement. A team may decide to penalize members who do not attend meetings by assigning them additional work or by assigning a fine of some type. The ultimate penalty might be a **dissolution** of the team which would result in two or more members completing the assignment instead of the original team.

The agreement should be clearly spelled out and signed by all team members early in the team process. Such an agreement provides confidence among the team members that the task will be successfully completed.

Handling Conflict

In every team conflict will likely occur at some point. Causes of conflict are most frequently a result of a misunderstanding, the influence of a team member, or a disagreement about the roles and procedures of team members. Usually conflict begins as a disagreement about some point or team activity. The team members may hope to maintain team harmony by avoiding a discussion of the disagreement. Unfortunately, a minor conflict can become a major issue if it is not addressed.

Confrontation occurs when the disagreement is discussed by the group. Although confrontation may cause the conflict to escalate to a higher, more intense level, resolution takes place at some point as a compromise is reached. Conflict can actually make a team stronger and the work better. However, if conflict is taken to an extreme, the team can self-destruct and have trouble successfully completing their assignment.

One of the most common issues of conflict relates to time and the stress of deadlines. This conflict can be reduced if the team allows more time to meet a deadline than one would allow for an individual. Although an individual may be able to devote hours to last minute preparation, this can be more difficult for a team as labs may close or team members may not have the same time available to commit to the project.

Tips to be a Terrific Team Member

▶ Don't prejudge other team members. When the group is first formed, people may be tempted to use stereotypes in assessing team members. If you decide at the first meeting that you don't like your team members, you will not enjoy the team experience. Give team members a chance.

▶ Attend all team meetings. You can express your ideas by following this tip. If you are unable to attend a meeting, be sure to contact the other team members so that you can find out what you should be doing—don't make them contact you!

▶ Keep in touch with team members. As a team member, you are responsible for maintaining contact with your team members by phone, e-mail, or voice mail outside of class. Do not count on team members always showing up in class for your only communication.

▶ Complete your assigned work on time or ahead of schedule. Don't make your team wait for you to complete your work.

▶ Do quality work. Make your work the best you can. Don't expect other team members to re-write your portion or be unable to use it because it is not well done.

▶ Listen to all team opinions. Weigh them carefully. To develop team synergy you must relate well to others on the team.

▶ Reduce team stress by setting reasonable time lines to complete the work. If you wait until the day before the assignment is due, you may find that the team needs more time than you have. This can cause team stress and conflict.

▶ Be there to "finish" the project. Some team members allow another member to "finish up" the assignment. Then the team member is not happy with the quality of the result. Comments such as "Ted was supposed to put in that table so it isn't my fault" do not help the final result.

Review Performance of Team Members

If the team is working on a project with a number of steps or over a longer period of time, the team may wish to evaluate the performance of the team members. If one of the team members is not keeping pace with the others, it may be helpful to let that team member know that more is expected than what the team member is providing. In all cases, the team should assess the performance of all members at the conclusion of the activity. An example of an interim evaluation is shown. The final evaluation may use a similar form or may use a more detailed one including short answer or essay comments.

Interim Evaluation

Complete the following evaluation for each member of your team and yourself. You may wish to share the evaluations with all members of the group. The ratings are (1) Poor, (2) Below Average, (3) Average, (4) Above Average, and (5) Excellent.

Name of Member	Area	1	2	3	4	5	Total
1.	Completion of assigned tasks.	1	2	3	4	5	
	Attitude in group.	1	2	3	4	5	
	Overall performance.	1	2	3	4	5	
	Suggested changes:						
2.	Completion of assigned tasks.	1	2	3	4	5	
	Attitude in group.	1	2	3	4	5	
	Overall performance.	1	2	3	4	5	
	Suggested changes:						
3.	Completion of assigned tasks.	1	2	3	4	5	
	Attitude in group.	1	2	3	4	5	
	Overall performance.	1	2	3	4	5	
	Suggested changes:						

DISCUSSION

1. List several characteristics of teams that were not discussed in the text.

2. Describe some examples of teams being used to solve problems.

3. What kinds of behavior can cause conflict in teams?

4. Is a team always a better choice than working individually?

EXERCISES

1. Assess a team of which you are a member. What are the dynamics of the group? What is the purpose of the group? Have you seen any members following the roles described? Be ready to present your information to the class.

2. As a potential entrepreneur, what can you do to encourage a cooperative work environment? What activities would discourage a cooperative environment? Develop some of your ideas and either write a brief review or be prepared to present your information in class.

3. Read a review of a successful company. Can you tell if a team or team environment was used in the company? What is your opinion of the worthiness of team communication?

4. This exercise should involve three or four other students. Discuss your team or team experiences. Try to determine what things are liked most about being in a team and what things are liked least about being in a group. Be ready to report to other groups.

PROBLEMS

1. Benoit Real Estate has a representative on the county review board. The purpose of the board is to share recent real estate information and to promote real estate development. You have been asked to join this three-year old team as Benoit's new representative. As you are getting ready to attend your first meeting, you decide to try to determine what the expected standards of behavior might be for this group. Summarize your ideas and be ready to discuss them with the class.

2. Analyze a team or task force of which you are a member. What are the behavior standards for the group? What roles appear to exist in the group? Do there appear to be any roles which were not discussed in class? Do new members cause any

changes in the behavior of the group? Be prepared to write a brief summary and/or present your information to your class members.

3. Draft an evaluation instrument which could be used to evaluate the performance of the members in any team or task force with which you are involved. Determine criteria that are important to the individual team member's success as well as criteria that will enable a project to be completed. Decide who will complete the evaluations and whether each team member should see the evaluations. Should the team member evaluation be part of the assignment grade? What suggestions could you make? You may find that this would be a good team or team project. Prepare the evaluation instrument along with your criteria to turn in to your instructor.

4. Assume you have a member of the team who is not performing up to the caliber of the other team members. Design a plan that will encourage the member to be more successful in working with the team. Be prepared to e-mail your plan to your instructor.

5. Search the Internet to find other ideas about working successfully in teams. Be prepared to give a short report on information from at least three Web sites.

DETERMINING THE RESEARCH PROBLEM

- In what circumstances would a written report be better than just explaining your ideas to someone.

- If you had to think up a suitable topic for a business report, what would it be and why?

CHAPTER OBJECTIVES

After studying this chapter, you should be able to:

1. Assess the importance of defining the problem and analyzing the audience for each report.
2. Understand the steps involved in preparing a report.
3. Organize a report using an outline format.
4. Clarify types of reports such as informational, comparative, and analytical.
5. Define the purpose of a report summary.

SELECTING A REPORT DOCUMENT

When we communicate, we convey much more than facts. As we have learned, nonverbal messages and channel selection affect the receiver's perception of our communication. Writing a report is one of the most effective ways to transmit needed data or information to others. Reports are frequently internal documents although some reports are prepared for those outside the company. Reports may take the form of a letter report, a memo report, or a formal report. Procedures concerning reports will be discussed in the next few chapters.

Understand Why The Report Is Needed

You may decide that a report is needed, or someone may assign you the task of writing one. Before you begin planning the report, be sure you understand how the information is to be used. Will it give instructions for doing a job? Will it bring the reader(s) up to date on the status of a project? Will it enable someone to make a decision? The information you present may serve one of these functions or another one; but before you can write an effective report, you have to know why it is needed and how it is to be used.

When you are assigned a report, you may need to communicate through an appropriate channel with the person who assigned it to determine the specific purpose. Are you to present information only? Are you to interpret and draw conclusions? Are you to make recommendations? Three kinds of reports are most common: informational, comparative, and analytical.

Informational

An informational report may be the one with which you are most familiar. In this category of report, your goal is to collect all the pertinent information about a subject using the most current resources. Your purpose in the report is to categorize and present the information you have found.

For example, perhaps you have been asked to explore the possibilities of doing business in a foreign country. Your informational report would include information about the culture of the country, the business environment, and any other factors that would be relevant to the business of the country. You would design your report to present this information in a logical and effective manner.

Comparative

A comparative report is more complex than an informational report. First, you must use the same procedures to collect information but you must take the report a step further and compare and contrast two or more items. You may wish to draw up lists of advantages and disadvantages as you present your collected data.

For example, you have been asked to compare the current business environments in two foreign countries. You would conduct similar research to that in the informational report, but you would add comparison information relating to the cultures and environments of the two countries.

Analytical

An analytical report is the most complicated of the reports. You will be asked to research for information, to make comparisons and contrasts, and to make recommendations. Making recommendations will require that you analyze all the data that you have collected and make a coherent decision based on that data.

After you have collected information about the two or more foreign countries, you may be asked to recommend which one your company should focus on. You make your decision based on the data that you have collected and your report should reflect that data. For instance, if all of your data seems to favor Country A as the best site for business, you would not arbitrarily select Country B as your report would not support this decision.

Determine Purpose

Before attempting to deliver your report in writing, determine your reason for sending it. The reason for sending a message may be to convey information, ideas, opinions, or feelings. You may want to inform your readers of a new process, to present additional information, to compare and contrast features or services, or to persuade the reader to act favorably on your proposal recommendations.

Each time we leave our home, we have a destination in mind— to school, to work, to the supermarket, and so on. We also have a specific route that we plan to take to reach each stop. Each report we develop should have a similar plan. Take time to analyze what you want to say, how you want to say it, and to assess the response that you want your readers to make. As you are developing your communication skills, write down your purpose and your intended outcome. Writing the purpose helps you identify the specific message and the desired outcome.

Write Statement of Purpose

First, determine if your report is to be informational, comparative, or analytical. When you determine the specific use, write a statement of the purpose or the objective to be achieved and refer to this statement often as you prepare the report.

Some good writers write this statement as a **question** to guide them in their work and then restate it as a **declarative sentence** in the finished report. Here are examples for a report to be written to enable a group to decide whether to open an additional office of the business in the same city.

> Is there sufficient need for an additional office of the McKenzie Company in Indianapolis, Indiana, to justify opening one?
>
> This study was conducted to determine the need for an additional office of the McKenzie Company in Indianapolis, Indiana.

An **informational report** might collect all the possible data about the business environment in Indianapolis and present that information so a purpose statement might be as follows: *The purpose of this report is to present current information about the business climate and suitable conditions for opening a second office in Indianapolis, Indiana.*

A **comparative report** might seek additional information. For example, if the company currently has two offices in Kansas City, you might want to design your report to compare Kansas City and Indianapolis. Your purpose statement might be: *The purpose of this report is to compare the current business environments in Kansas City and Indianapolis to assess the potential for a second site in Indianapolis.*

For an **analytical report**, you will make a recommendation about opening a second site in Indianapolis. Your purpose statement might be: *The purpose of this report is to assess the business environment in Indianapolis and to recommend the feasibility of opening a second office in the city.*

Write Factors of Problem

On any of the reports, a good technique is to follow the purpose statement with the main questions to be answered in the report:

> **Factors of the Problem**
>
> To determine the need for an additional office, these questions had to be answered:
>
> 1. Who will use the additional office? Will it increase the number of customers?
> 2. What facilities and personnel will be needed for a new office?
> 3. Is a suitable site available?

These questions, which are asked in the introductory section, are answered in the same sequence in the body of the report. Understanding the need for the report will help you to collect the right information and to design the purpose statement.

Analyze Audience

After you have determined the purpose of your message, spend a few minutes analyzing your audience. Consider these questions.

- What do you know about the people who will receive your message?
- What are their interests in your topic?
- What previous knowledge of the subject do they have?
- How will the audience respond to your report that will provide information, present a comparison, or make recommendations?
- What tone should the report convey to best convince your audience?

You may prepare a report for one reader or for a group. In most instances formal reports are read by several persons; and you may assume that more than one person will read your letters, memorandums, and other informal reports. To make a report most effective, try to answer these questions that you ask yourself about the readers:

---

1. How much do they know about the topic on which I am writing?
2. What do they know about the situation that led to the need for this report?
3. What official positions (job titles) do they hold, and what is their role in the action to be taken on the information I present?
4. Are they familiar with the terms I may need to use?

The more you know about the readers, the better you can write so that they grasp quickly and easily the information you give them. Answering these questions before developing your message will enable you to adapt your report to your audience. Some messages are more appropriate for certain groups of people than others. Put yourself in the position of the reader or your report. How would you want to learn this information? Selecting the appropriate words and tone for the report will be an easier task if you know your audience.

Gather Information

Collect and verify the information that you want to send in your message. Pay particular attention to facts and figures. Errors in price quotes, statements, dates, or proposals could be costly if misstated. In addition, such errors jeopardize the confidence readers place in you as an effective communicator.

Chapter 8 will discuss strategies for collecting report data. You can write an effective report only when you have adequate pertinent information. Begin with the knowledge you possess, and remember that other personnel of your organization can provide worthwhile facts and suggestions for the study you are undertaking. Your organization records and library holdings are valuable sources of information. Some of the most frequently used publications and methods of collecting data from people are described in the next chapter.

Your written report may use primary data that you have discovered in your investigation as well as secondary information that has been discovered by others. Add strength and authority to your reports by identifying the sources from which you collected information—publications, interviews, and so on. Collecting again the data other people have already collected and made available for use would be a waste of your time, effort, and money. Use this secondary information and give due credit to the people who provided it.

You can give the credit that is due—and often make your report more convincing—by using proper citations. Current ways of citing sources, constructing reference lists, and paraphrasing from publications and other sources are presented in Chapter 8.

Obtain exact information so that your message can include specifics instead of generalities. Specific information will enable you to include supported or supportable statements. Consider these examples:

General	Specific
We earned a significant profit last quarter.	We earned a $157,000 profit last quarter. That profit reflects a 7 percent increase over the previous quarter.
This was the best quarter we have had.	Our sales increased by 10 percent during the third quarter, the highest increase in our history.

After gathering the necessary information, plan the message organization.

Organize the Report

Organize the report by establishing the right frame of reference before writing and by composing coherent paragraphs using effective sentences and proper word choices. Organize and phrase your message with the receiver in mind.

Depending on the situation, your message may be organized in one of a variety of ways. Informational, comparative, and analytical reports may be arranged inductively, deductively, or chronologically. A report, memo, or letter arranged in an *inductive* order presents the facts first and the conclusion last. The *deductive* letter or report presents the findings first followed by the facts that led to those findings. An informational report or letter may be arranged *chronologically* with key points appearing in the order in which they occurred. The rationale for determining when to use a specific organization will be discussed in greater detail in later chapters.

Prepare the Report Draft

Prepare an initial draft of the report you want to present. As you begin working on the report, you may find it helpful to use an outline style to help you frame your key points.

Before you begin to write, think about the most important points you need to cover. Jot down notes so that you will remember these points, and then arrange them in the order in which you will present them in the finished report.

For simple memorandums and letter reports, notes on a slip of paper provide an adequate outline. For more complex reports—especially formal analytical reports—you can work better from a formal outline. A good outline not only helps to present the information in proper order, but it also helps make the writing task easy. The alphanumeric style that follows is only one of several correct styles. This style is popular and easy to follow:

```
  I.   Introduction
       A.  Point #1 for Introduction
       B.  Point #2 for Introduction
 II.   Body of report
       A.  Factor #1
           1.  Part #1 of Factor #1
               a.  Subpoint #1 of Part #1
                   (1) Element #1 of Subpoint #1
                   (2) Element #2 of Subpoint #1
               b.  Subpoint #2 of Part #1
               c.  Subpoint #3 of Part #1
           2.  Part #2 of Factor #1
           3.  Part #3 of Factor #1
       B.  Factor #2
       C.  Factor #3
III.   Conclusions and Recommendations
```

When constructing outlines, writers sometimes overlook the fact that at *least two parts must be created* when an item is divided. For example, when the information for a Roman numeral is divided, at least two letters (A and B) must follow. The information for either letter may then be divided further into two or more parts (1 and 2 and possibly 3, 4, and so on). Dividing one part does not require dividing any other part of equal rank. For example, A may not need to be divided, yet B, C, or another letter may need to be broken down to 1, 2, and so on. Further divisions—a, b, c, and (1), (2), (3), and so forth are depicted in the preceding partial outline.

You may use this alphanumeric style for either a topic outline or a sentence outline. The topic outline, which includes only a word or a short phrase for each division, is usually sufficient for a simple report. Experienced writers may also prefer a topic outline for complex reports. Here is a **topic outline**:

```
  I.   Problem orientation
       A.  Purpose
       B.  Factors
           1.  Clients
               a.  Software instruction
               b.  Software development
               c.  Hardware selection
           2.  Volume
           3.  Availability
       C.  Procedures
 II.   Facilities
       A.  Space
       B.  Equipment
III.   Personnel
 IV.   Conclusion
       A.  Summary
       B.  Conclusions
       C.  Recommendations
```

A topic outline can be extended into a sentence outline, which is a step nearer the completed report. A sentence outline such as the one that follows is especially helpful for inexperienced report writers and for experienced writers of complex reports. A portion of the preceding topic outline was made into the **sentence outline** that follows:

I. Problem orientation
   A. The purpose is to determine whether to open a computer consulting business.
   B. These factors will be studied:
      1. Clients will be interested in at least one of these areas:
         a. Software instruction on popular over-the-counter software packages will increase productivity.
         b. Software development such as specialized databases designed for a particular company will increase company effectiveness.
      2. The volume of anticipated business will require at least two employees to start.
      3. Availability to clients is a critical factor, so one employee should be on call at least 12 hours a day.
   C. The information was obtained by surveying potential clients and by studying the operation of similar companies in other cities.
II. Facilities
   A. A convenient site with two large rooms is available.
   B. Equipment and software can be obtained immediately.

A well-planned outline directs the flow of thoughts and helps the writer to arrange the information into a clear, logical order. Also, the sentence outline provides a guide to write the summary of the report.

Construct and Interpret Visuals

Much of the information in business reports is presented in sentence and paragraph form. In many reports, though, you should use graphics to present part of the data. When a well-chosen, properly constructed graphic can make a body of data easy for the readers to understand, use it. Your chief objective is to present adequate relevant information in a concise form so that readers grasp it quickly and easily.

Because graphics play an important role in business reports, an entire chapter (Chapter 10) of this book is devoted to choosing, constructing, and interpreting graphics.

Write Objectively

Give your readers facts, which may be supported by examples or clarified by analogies. Choose words that state facts precisely. When you draw conclusions from the facts in an analytical report, make clear to the readers that your conclusions are not only logical but also valid—based on the facts you present.

When you believe readers will welcome your opinions, express them in the letter with which you transmit the report.

Prepare a Report Summary

A report summary is a concise statement that describes the development of the report, the research that was conducted, the most significant findings, the conclusions that were drawn, and the recommendations that were made. The summary should stand by itself so that a reader can quickly read the key information about the report.

A well-written summary placed at the beginning of the report provides an *overview* for the busy executive. In fact, some executives read the summary in order to determine if they need to read the rest of the report. Therefore, a readable summary which highlights all of the main points and recommendations, if any, is very important.

Some major reports contain an executive summary at the beginning plus a summary at the end.

DISCUSSION

1. How are report outlines and road maps similar?

2. What are some reader characteristics not mentioned in this chapter that you may consider when preparing a report?

3. Identify three types of reports.

4. What is the value of a clear purpose statement?

5. What is the advantage of citing other sources in the report?

EXERCISES

1. The president of the student government association has asked you to work with a committee to develop a report on the most pressing issues for students on campus. The president would like you and your committee to research the issues and make recommendations for solving the problems.
   a. Write a statement of the problem in question form that you will refer to often as you prepare the report for the president.
   b. Write the statement in declarative sentence form for the completed report.
   c. Write the factors of the problem to be studied.
   d. Prepare a topic outline for the report.
   e. Develop the topic outline into a sentence outline.

2. You have been asked by the dean of your college to write a report on student absenteeism for the past six weeks. The dean is especially concerned that attendance

on Fridays seems to be low. She has asked you to study the problem and to give her a report on your findings.

a. Write a statement of the problem in question form that you will refer to often as you prepare the report for the dean.

b. Write the statement in declarative sentence form for the completed report.

c. Write the factors of the problem to be studied.

d. Prepare a topic outline for the report.

e. Develop the topic outline into a sentence outline.

3. The state has announced that a new highway bypass will be built near your city. Several local merchants are concerned that traffic will now go elsewhere for shopping. They have asked your consulting firm to try to determine how a new highway will affect customer traffic.

a. Write a statement of the problem in question form that you will refer to often as you prepare the report for the merchants.

b. Write the statement in declarative sentence form for the completed report.

c. Write the factors of the problem to be studied.

d. Prepare a topic outline for the report.

e. Develop the topic outline into a sentence outline.

4. Paul Edgeworth and his sister Polly Blade would like to open a new local business that would appeal to university students. The city is the same size of that in which your college or university is located. Paul and Polly have asked you to conduct a feasibility study of possible businesses for them to examine more closely.

a. Prepare a topic outline for the report.

b. Make the topic outline into a sentence outline.

c. Assume you have done a thorough study and are ready to write a multiple-page report in which you will recommend which businesses may be most suitable for the community.

d. List the headings you intend to use for the completed report.

5. You and several of your friends have decided to develop an investment club. Your idea is to have each member contribute a certain amount of money each month and have the various group members do research on investment opportunities. You want to conduct a feasibility study on this idea.

a. Write a statement of the problem in question form that you will refer to often as you prepare the report for the prospective club members.

b. Write the statement in declarative sentence form for the completed report.

c. Write the factors of the problem to be studied.

d. Prepare a topic outline for the report.

e. Develop the topic outline into a sentence outline.

6. You have been asked to compare and contrast three similar products. Select products of your choice.

a. Write a statement of the problem in question form that you will refer to often as you prepare the report.

b. Write the statement in declarative sentence form for the completed report.

c. Write the factors of the problem to be studied.

  d. Prepare a topic outline for the report.
  e. Develop the topic outline into a sentence outline.

7. You are interested in developing a traveling pet care business. You would travel to people's homes to give pets baths and routine care. Prepare a report that would describe your services to potential customers.
  a. Write a statement of the problem in question form that you will refer to often as you prepare the report for your potential customers.
  b. Write the statement in declarative sentence form for the completed report.
  c. Write the factors of the problem to be studied.
  d. Prepare a topic outline for the report.
  e. Develop the topic outline into a sentence outline.

8. You have been assigned to a team to investigate appropriate charities to which your corporation might contribute. Recommend at least three appropriate alternatives.
  a. Write a statement of the problem in question form that you will refer to often as you prepare the report for executive committee.
  b. Write the statement in declarative sentence form for the completed report.
  c. Write the factors of the problem to be studied.
  d. Prepare a topic outline for the report.
  e. Develop the topic outline into a sentence outline.

PROBLEMS

1. Meet with your team to discuss formative issues such as the report topic. Complete the following:
  a. Determine your team identity (such as team name, team motto, team colors, team photo, etc.)
  b. Write your team agreement (see study guide for assistance).
  c. Present the results of a. and b. in an e-mail message, in a written document, or other format as directed by your instructor.

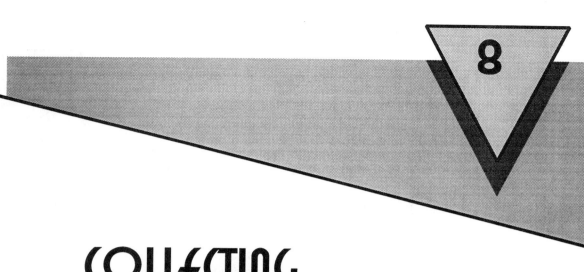

COLLECTING DATA

Critical Thinking Applications

- How does international business travel differ from domestic business travel? What sources of information should you use to learn more about this subject?

- You are concerned about the ethics and laws related to the privacy of your e-mail at work and at home. What information sources can you use to find the latest information on this topic?

CHAPTER OBJECTIVES

After studying this chapter, you should be able to:

1. Describe three methods used to acquire primary data.
2. Identify random, stratified, and systematic random sampling techniques.
3. List sources of secondary data such as journals, magazines, and government documents.
4. Locate electronic secondary sources using electronic databases and the World Wide Web.
5. Describe characteristics of three citation styles.
6. Correctly cite a document in a report.

SOURCES OF INFORMATION

Once you have determined the purpose or objective of a report you are to write, you are ready to organize your report and to collect the needed information.

You will, in most instances, possess some of the required information because the reports you choose to write or those assigned to you will be related to your work. You can write many letters, memorandums, and other short informal reports on the basis of what you already know. For some informal reports and most formal reports, you will have to collect more information.

You may collect *primary* data (information from original research) or *secondary* data (information compiled previously), or you may collect both types.

Primary Research

Techniques used to obtain primary data include *experimenting, observing, querying*, or combining two or more of these methods.

Types of Primary Research		
Experimenting	=	Doing
Observing	=	Watching
Querying	=	Asking

Experimenting

Experimenting is used extensively as an effective method of research in the physical sciences, but it is used less frequently in business. Some business situations in which experiments are sometimes conducted involve marketing research, systems and procedures studies, and communication effectiveness. Products are marketed in small areas as a trial; procedures are tried in a few cases or are simulated to test their efficiency before a complete reorganization of the current system is made; and various sales letters are tested for comparative effectiveness.

Experimenting requires a good deal of time. An experiment may be conducted by using two groups at one time: the control group performs the activities being tested in the usual way, while the experimental group uses a different way to perform the activities. Another arrangement is to have one group perform in the usual way a set of activities at one time and then have the same group perform in a new way those same activities. As a result of the experiment, one of the ways is proved to be better; or both ways are proved to be equal.

In an experiment, all factors except the variable to be tested are held constant. For example, if one group is allowed an hour to perform a task at 8 a.m. on Monday, while another group has ninety minutes to perform the task at 2 p.m. on Wednesday, the experiment has more variables than just the way the task is performed. The time of day, the day of the week, and the length of time would also be variables that could affect the experiment. A successful experiment should keep constant as many unrelated factors as possible.

Experimenting in business, when done properly, can produce results with a high degree of accuracy.

Observing

Valuable data can be obtained by observing certain activities. Office personnel or consultants may observe the work of office employees during a systems and procedures study. Marketing analysts sometimes study the traffic flows inside a specific store, among stores within a specified section of a city, or along the sidewalks.

City traffic departments observe the volume of traffic on certain streets to determine whether a traffic light is needed. Helpful data can be collected by observing numerous other activities. The examples mentioned here are only representative of the types of studies that may include data collected by observing.

One person may make all the observations, observers may work in pairs or in larger groups, or they may alternate so that some work during certain hours or days and others work at other times. The observers may use a prepared checklist for recording the data they collect, or they may just jot down notes about the activities they see.

Using the same checklist helps the researchers to observe objectively and to maintain a consistent record of observations. These techniques are especially important if more than one observer collects data for the study.

The objective of the study, the types of activities to be observed, and the work habits of the researchers are some of the factors that help you to determine the procedures to follow when collecting information by observing.

Querying

Querying is a popular method of collecting data for some types of business reports. Pertinent questions are asked orally during personal interviews or telephone interviews, or they are submitted in writing. A newer style of querying is to send queries by e-mail or to post queries to be answered on web sites.

Personal Interviews. As an interviewer, you have opportunities to ask questions of your subjects, also known as interviewees. Some advantages of asking questions during personal interviews are these:

1.   You have an opportunity to discuss any concerns the interviewees have about your reason for asking the questions. Usually, therefore, you can obtain full cooperation from the interviewees and get more information than by presenting the questions any other way. Also, many people feel complimented by being interviewed.

2.   You have an opportunity to explain the meaning of any question that seems unclear to an interviewee.

3.   You receive immediate responses to your questions.

4.   Because the interviewees may suggest items you had not thought about, you frequently obtain valuable data you are not actively seeking.

5.   You may receive answers orally that people will not put in writing.

A major disadvantage of collecting information through personal interviews is the expense involved. The time required for conducting interviews (time for both the interviewer and the interviewee) and the time required for traveling make this method too expensive for use when a large number of people are to be queried or when they are scattered over a wide geographic area.

To show courtesy and to ensure that the interviewees will be available, make appointments when you collect information through personal interviews. Appointments give the interviewees time to prepare for the interviews and to have more information ready than would be possible in impromptu visits. Prepare a list of questions to take with you. This list will enable you to ask the same questions of all interviewees.

When developing your list of questions, you may wish to ask ***closed questions*** and ***open questions***. Closed questions could include true/false, multiple-choice, or short-answer items, while open questions require essay-type responses. ***Closed questions*** usually require short answers and are useful when comparing data collected from a number of respondents. ***Open questions*** allow the interviewees to answer the questions in some depth, a characteristic that can provide insight during the interview. Arrange the questions in a logical order for recording the answers rapidly and accurately.

Closed Questions (Short Answers)	**Open Questions** (Long Answers)
How long did you work for your previous employer?	Tell me something about yourself.
What was your major in college?	How did your college education prepare you for a job in our company?
When using this procedure, how many units can be assembled each day?	In what ways could the procedure for assembling the units be improved?
How long did you work here before you were promoted?	What factors do you think led to your promotion?

By all means, be a good listener because the interviewees will want to talk about topics of interest to them. Keep the interviews friendly and informal. Formality makes people reserved and less willing to share their knowledge and feelings.

You may use a tape recorder if you have the interviewee's permission. At times it is not wise to make too many notes as your interviewee may be distracted by wondering *what* you are writing. You may not be able to write and listen intently and also observe the nonverbal cues that are quite important to understanding. Whether or not you make notes, immediately after each interview write down what you remember. When obtaining conflicting opinions, be sure to include them in your report to show the readers that the report is as bias free as possible.

Telephone Interviews. Some interviews can be conducted by telephone. You may use the same type of questions for telephone interviews as you use for personal interviews. Before you begin, let the interviewee know about how long the interview will take. If the interviewee feels that enough questions have been answered after only a few minutes and/or hangs up the phone, you may have an incomplete interview that cannot be used.

Although you can obtain some types of information more readily when talking with the interviewees in person rather than on the telephone, you can interview more people and cover a larger geographic area by telephone than through personal interviews. When these two methods of interviewing are compared, the telephone method is obviously less expensive.

Letters. When you send a letter to request data, address the letter to an individual—not to an organization—and enclose an addressed, stamped envelope for the addressee to use in returning the answers. A letter should include six or fewer questions. For more than six questions, you may use a questionnaire (see Figure 8-1).

Questionnaires. To obtain answers to several questions, prepare a questionnaire to be mailed with an introductory letter. To collect a sufficient quantity of reliable data with a questionnaire, construct it carefully by following these important points:

1. Tell who is sending the questionnaire. You may type the name and address of the sender, or you may use a letterhead. Possibly, the questionnaire and the introductory letter will be separated in the office of a recipient; and recipients should know who is to receive the information they provide by responding to questionnaires.

2. State each question clearly—so clearly that it cannot be misunderstood! To write clearly, use only the words that are familiar to the readers. Each word in the questionnaire must convey precisely the same meaning to all readers.

3. Ask only those questions the respondents are willing to answer. Omit those questions they hesitate to answer because of their religious, political, or personal views. Many people will not answer questions pertaining to age, income, or financial status.

4. Select an appropriate format for questions. Questions may require making yes/no responses, checking one response, checking more than one response, ranking responses, and rating items on a scale.

Boyett Electronics

4978 Westridge Road
Detroit, MI 48200
(313) 468-3411

August 10, 2002

Ms. Belle Polk
4230 North Howard
Detroit, MI 48200

Dear Ms. Polk

As a customer of Jackson Computer Systems of Detroit, will you please answer the following questions to help us to decide whether to enter into a computer services contract with them. We are planning to expand our computer department by outsourcing additional computer functions.

1. Was the agreed upon turnaround time always met for computer operations?

2. What difficulties did you have, if any, when you first started working with Jackson Computer Systems?

3. Knowing what you now know about their operations, would you sign a contract with them again if you had an opportunity to do so?

4. Do you believe that the confidentiality of your company information was maintained?

5. What other comments can you make about your contract with Jackson Computer Systems that may help us in deciding whether to enter into a contract with them?

We hope to make a decision on outsourcing by October 1. Your response to these questions, therefore, by September 10 would be very much appreciated.

Sincerely

Mario Ivesta

Mario Ivesta
Plant Manager

mbs

Figure 8-1. Letter Requesting Data

Question Format	Example
Check Yes or No	Are you employed full-time? ___Yes ___No
Check ONE response	Which is *most* important? ___Salary ___Challenging job ___ Work hours
Check ALL that apply	What skills do you have? ___Electronic mail ___Spreadsheet ___Word processing ___Database ___Computer graphics
Rank these items with 1 as most important	What order of importance do you place on these benefits? ___Health insurance ___Life insurance ___Dental insurance ___Retirement plan ___Child care provisions ___Savings plan
Use a scale to mark how you feel about this statement. No. 1 is Strongly Agree, and 5 is Strongly Disagree.	A job should be located close to my home. 1 2 3 4 5

5. Arrange the questions in a logical order with the easy-to-answer items first. This arrangement encourages respondents to complete the questionnaire. After they have answered most of the questions, they are more likely to answer a few hard-to-answer questions than if these items appeared earlier.

    Hard-to-answer questions near the beginning lead the respondents to believe that many of them are difficult. They are, therefore, inclined to discard the questionnaire instead of completing it and returning it to you. Many questionnaire respondents have to refer to their records for answers to some of the items on a list. They usually are unwilling to do this extra work unless they have already answered most of the questions.

6. Place the most important questions early in the questionnaire since the respondents may become tired of reading and thinking and become careless in answering.

7. When you can, supply several possible answers so that the respondent can merely make a check mark beside the answer. Provide a space for other answers, as in this example:

What was your job title on your most recent full-time job?

_____ Accountant   _____ Programmer
_____ Analyst   _____ Administrative Assistant
_____ Manager   _____ Other (specify)_____

You may design the question to include a range of responses, as in this example:

How many years have you worked for this company?

_____	Less than 1	_____	11 to 15
_____	1 to 5	_____	16 to 20
_____	6 to 10	_____	More than 20

When a question cannot be answered by using a simple check mark, ask for other short answers. People hesitate to write long answers. Some respondents ignore questions of this kind, or they give incomplete answers. Other respondents decline to complete any part of a questionnaire if some of the questions require long answers.

8. After you have listed all the questions, end with an item such as *Comments*? that permits the respondents to write comments. Although these answers are difficult to tabulate, they supply valuable information; besides, respondents like to have an opportunity to express their opinions.

You should *limit the length* of the questionnaire. Many persons will spend no more than twenty minutes completing it. Do, however, ask all essential questions for this phase of your study. Arrange the questionnaire so that it is attractive and easy to read. Material arranged neatly and with plenty of white space on the page looks short and easy to answer.

Before distributing the questionnaire, ask at least *four people to review the document* and answer the questions for you. Ask for their comments on readability and ease of answering the questions. After you receive their comments, you may wish to make changes before sending the final copy out to your audience.

Clear, concise instructions for answering should precede the list of questions. Instructions for returning the completed questionnaire may be included on the same sheet as the questions, or they may be in the introductory letter.

Send an *introductory letter* with the questionnaire to get the readers interested in the survey and to tell them the benefits they can receive by participating in it. A promise to send a summary of the findings may be the best thing to offer them to show you appreciate their help. Sometimes, however, small amounts of money or small gifts are offered for the return of the completed questionnaire. The conditions that apply to the survey and the respondents' interest will help you to determine an appropriate offer for their assistance.

Assure the respondents that all *answers will be treated confidentially*. Also tell the respondents that no personal identification is needed unless they desire a summary of the survey findings. Assure them no names or other identification will be used in the study. If possible, enclose an addressed, stamped envelope for a fast response and, of course, mention it in the letter.

Study the introductory letter and the questionnaire in Figures 8-2 and 8-3.

<u>On-line surveys.</u> You may wish to vary your technique if you are using a questionnaire through e-mail or through a web site. For best results you should ask six or fewer questions. Be sure the survey is easy to answer and that the instructions for responding are clear. For example, if you send a survey to an e-mail list of 200 people, if a person clicks reply to respond to the survey, they can easily send their response to all 200 people. This will not have the effect that you wish as those on your list will get many unneeded e-mail messages.

USA Food Retailers, Inc.
3478 Chantry Lane
Statesboro, GA 30460

February 10, 2002

(Mr., Mrs., Ms.) (First Name) (Last Name)
(Street Address)
(City), (State) (Zip Code)

Dear (Mr., Mrs., Ms.) (Last Name)

Are you interested in a wide selection of products at your local grocery store? Do you also want to pay the lowest prices for them?

If so, you may be interested to know that we are considering your community as a location for a new food store which would offer you a wide selection of products at especially low prices. Our stores are very popular in the communities in which they operate.

To help us to determine whether your community would be a good site for a new store, will you please fill out the enclosed questionnaire.

You can use the addressed, stamped envelope that is enclosed to return the questionnaire, which will take only a few minutes to complete. Your returning the completed questionnaire by March 10 would be very much appreciated.

Sincerely

Lynn Norwood

Lynn Norwood
Marketing Manager

tra

Enclosures—2

Figure 8-2. Introductory Letter

USA Food Retailers, Inc.
3478 Chantry Lane
Statesboro, GA 30460

NEW STORE FOR YOUR COMMUNITY

Please answer the following questions by placing a check mark in the appropriate space. Your comments at the conclusion of the questionnaire would be especially helpful.

1. How frequently do you go to a local grocery store to purchase groceries and related items?
    _____ Every two weeks   _____ Twice a week
    _____ Once a week   _____ More than twice a week

2. How many stores do you visit to purchase groceries and other related items?
    _____ One   _____ Three
    _____ Two   _____ More than three

3. At which time of day do you *usually* buy groceries?
    _____ 8 a.m. to 12 noon   _____ 4 p.m. to 8 p.m.
    _____ 12 noon to 4 p.m.   _____ 8 p.m. to 12 midnight

4. Would you shop in a store from 12 midnight to 8 a.m. if it were open during those hours?
    _____ Yes   _____ No   _____ Maybe

5. Please check the three things most important to you when deciding where to shop for groceries.
    _____ Quality of produce   _____ Quality of meats
    _____ Deli shop   _____ Videotape rentals
    _____ Pharmacy   _____ On-site bakery
    _____ Convenient parking   _____ Friendly service

6. How do you usually pay for your groceries?
    _____ Cash   _____ Credit Card
    _____ Check   _____ Cash Debit Card
    _____ Other (specify)_____

7. Please check any of these items that you regularly purchase at your grocery store.
    _____ Cosmetics   _____ Perfume/cologne
    _____ Flowers   _____ Toys
    _____ Hosiery/socks   _____ Light bulbs
    _____ Magazines/books   _____ Greeting cards

8. Please indicate your current yearly family income.
    _____ $10,000 or under   _____ $30,001 to $40,000
    _____ $10,001 to $20,000   _____ $40,001 to $50,000
    _____ $20,001 to $30,000   _____ Over $50,000

9. Comments: Please give us any suggestions you may have for a new grocery store in your community.

Figure 8-3. Questionnaire

If you use a web site for responses to your queries, be sure to design the questions so you can get the responses you want. If you want people to select one of three items, do not design the question so that an essay is your only response. Many software packages are now available to assist you in planning your on-line surveys.

Sampling

Several times a year news reports are given on a poll that has been conducted on a current issue. Frequently, the issue has to do with rating how well the President is performing his duties. When you look closely at the way the poll was conducted, you see that usually only a thousand people were surveyed. How can the results of such a small survey reflect the thinking of millions of people? Professional pollsters answer this question by selecting a representative sample of our country's population for their surveys.

Seldom is it possible to collect information from all the people of any large group. To try to ensure that your results speak for the entire group, you must collect information from a carefully drawn sample. You may choose a random sample, a stratified sample, or a systematic random sample.

Random. In a random sample, all individuals in the population (universe or the entire group from which a sample is taken) have equal chances for inclusion. Let's say we want to select a sample of the people whose names are in a telephone directory. One possible—though impractical—way to take this sample is to write each name on a slip of paper and drop it into a container. Shake the container thoroughly and without looking at the slips of paper draw the number of names you wish to include in the sample. While this technique is impractical, many computer programs today can generate random lists that produce the same result as drawing slips of paper.

Generally, we tend to believe that the larger the sample, the better it represents the entire population. In many instances, though, a small random sample represents the population quite well, especially when the population is small and/or homogeneous.

Stratified. To take a stratified sample, divide the names of the population into categories. For example, divide the names according to employment groups such as attorneys, physicians, and business executives. Then draw names until you have the same percentage of attorneys, physicians, and business executives as in the total population.

Choose categories that have significance for the study you are conducting. Grouping by the three professions mentioned above would have little, if any, significance when studying the brands of paint preferred for the respondents' houses.

Many professional pollsters use such groups as age, race, or gender. The pollsters could tell how women feel about an issue as compared with how men feel about the same issue. Similar responses can be drawn for age, race, and other factors.

Systematic Random. For a systematic random sample, select every nth name in the list for the entire group. First of all, shuffle ten slips of paper bearing the numbers 1 through 10 and draw one of them. If you draw the number 6, for example, select the 6th, the 12th, the 18th, and so on through the list. With this technique all names that make up the population have equal probability of being drawn for the sample.

Using a systematic random sample is appropriate if you do not have computer equipment that can generate lists of random numbers.

Processing Information

Once the information needed for a business report has been collected, it has to be tabulated and analyzed for appropriate presentation.

Tabulating. Tabulating may be required for some secondary data. The major tabulating task, however, is in processing primary data. With the widespread use of computers, the tabulating task can usually be performed in a computing center or on a desktop computer with appropriate software.

Even with computer assistance, the report writer is sometimes responsible for coding the information that was recorded on a checklist or was received in answer to the questions asked in a letter or in a questionnaire. The report writer may also be required to transfer the coded data from the original source document (letter, questionnaire, and others) into a computer. The report writer who must perform these tabulating tasks should consult an operator in the particular computing center in which the data will be processed for specific instructions for performing the coding function.

Analyzing. By cross-tabulating the answers to the questions you have asked, you can see relationships that exist between answers to any two questions. By studying an analysis of this type, you can see that some relationships are *meaningful*, while others are *meaningless*. The relationships of no value can usually be omitted from the report.

Present the significant findings in the report body and include in the appendix the detailed analyses that seem to be of little significance. (Further discussion of the appendix section of a report is discussed in Chapter 11.)

Secondary Research

Information that has already been collected, but in another form from what you intend to use it, is *secondary* data. Some of the most frequently used sources of secondary data for business reports are the files of your organization, the files of other organizations, computer databases, and publications—periodicals and books.

Organization Files

The files of your organization may include letters, memorandums, manuals, contracts, ledgers, journals, drawings, minutes of meetings, photographs, notes from conversations, and reports that contain information that pertains to your report. Do not overlook this sometimes valuable storehouse.

Other organizations may also have these various types of records that contain information you need. Possibly, someone in another organization has written a report similar to the one you are writing and would gladly share the report and other records with you.

Collecting information that someone else has already collected is usually a waste of time, money, and effort when you can work cooperatively with the people who can make the information available to you. Sharing information with other groups is one of the many benefits of maintaining good public relations with other organizations. As a note of caution, however, be sure you have permission to share any of your company information with those outside the firm. Many firms wish to maintain the confidentiality of specific items.

The more you know about business publications the more efficiently you can find information you need. Both periodicals and reference books contain valuable information. You can find your best selection of business publications in your college library. Many universities have library web sites that discuss available resources as well as strategies for searching.

Increasingly, libraries are choosing to maintain electronic records of periodicals rather than hard copies. Checking your library may also reveal databases of information with full text articles that will save you time in searching. Look for the following types of publications.

Newspapers. Most newspapers contain business information worth reading. Even the advertisements are helpful in making some business decisions. *The Wall Street Journal* is one example of a business-based newspaper.

Magazines. Some of the most popular magazines that specialize in business information are *Fortune, Business Week,* and *Forbes.* Many magazines that are written for the general public and that cover a wide variety of topics often include items that may very well be useful in business reports. You may consult various indexes to locate information in periodicals.

Journals. While magazines frequently contain articles of general interest, journals usually contain reports of specific studies. A journal usually looks different from a magazine. Magazines feature glossy covers, many articles (the author of the article is not always mentioned), and colorful ads. On the other hand, journals usually have bland covers with fewer, longer articles that always name at least one author, and have few advertisements. The journal advertisements are usually for books or conferences that relate to the purpose of the journal. If you are trying to determine if an on-line source is a journal, the article should have at least one author (many have more than one) and resources referred to in the article should be listed completely at the end of the article. Magazines do not usually list reference information.

Journals published for particular fields such as accounting, communication, economics, finance, marketing, and management contain a wealth of valuable information. Examples of journals include *The Harvard Business Review* and *The Journal of Business Communication.*

Government Publications. Local, state, and federal governments disseminate information through reports, leaflets, and larger volumes. Some of these documents are presented only once; others are published regularly. Some of the monthly publications are the *Federal Reserve Bulletin, Monthly Labor Review,* and *Survey of Current Business.* The *Statistical Abstract of the United States* is a special help to writers of business reports.

Many government reports are available on line through various government web sites such as http://www.access.gpo.gov/su_docs/locators/cgp/.

Other References. Encyclopedias, almanacs, dictionaries, directories, and handbooks are other sources of business information. Some of these references are now available online.

Internet. You may be able to do a significant amount of research through the Internet. Many libraries are now accessing databases such as the *InfoTrack's General Businessfile* or *ABI/Inform* through the Internet. Helpful business information on specific companies may be found by accessing the company's web page. The vast majority of publicly owned companies provide web pages.

Another option is to research the internet through search engines such as *Alta Vista, Excite, Google, Infoseek, Hotbot, Lycos, Link Star, Magellan, NorthernLight, WebCrawler,* and *Yahoo*. Meta search engines search more than one search engine at one time. Some of these are *All 4 One, Starting Point,* and *Savvy Search*.

Search the Search Engine

Searching strategies vary when using different search engines on the Internet. You may wish to try these techniques. Assume you are searching for your first name and your last name on the Internet. For this example, your name is Tom Link. The site might search for every occurrence of Tom and every occurrence of Link. You, however, only want the two. You might try some strategies such as putting quotations around the name "Tom Link". Or, the search engine might recognize a plus sign such as Tom + Link. If you have too many results, you might wish to narrow your search to something more manageable with additional qualifiers. You might also get different results using different search engines so you should try several of those listed in order to find information.

Card Catalog. To determine the published materials in a particular library, consult the card catalog. Traditionally, this file contained three cards for each volume of the library holdings. These cards were filed alphabetically by author, title, and subject.

More and more libraries have transferred the card entries to computers. When searching a computer card catalog, users normally have several options. They can search for ***author*** (a=jones james l), for ***title*** (t=computers today), or for ***subject*** (s=automobile). Usually, the subject is one of a predetermined list of subjects by which the card catalog is indexed.

Computer card catalogs can also be searched by a ***key word***, an advantage not available in a traditional card catalog. For example, if you needed information on tourism, a key word search (k=tourism) would generate a list of sources.

In addition, ***Boolean logic*** can be applied to key word searches. Such logic would add words such as ***and, or,*** or ***not,*** to further define the list. If the tourism key word search mentioned above generated 1500 responses, that might be too many to examine. Adding a Boolean operator to the search (k=tourism and Canada) would give a list of only the tourism entries related to Canada. This step may reduce the list to 20 responses.

The ***and*** command would combine two words so that matches must include ***BOTH*** words. An ***or*** command would search for ***EITHER*** word. A ***not*** command would exclude a word from the search. For example, if you were searching for information on workplace smoking but were not particularly interested in any legislation involving smoking your search string might be "workplace smoking NOT legislation" which could narrow your search.

Once you have found your sources, you should collect all information needed to cite them correctly in an appropriate citation style.

Citation Styles

The citation style you select for your written report will determine how you format your citations throughout the report and in any reference pages at the end. Citation style is frequently a personal choice. The most important factor is that you follow correctly the guidelines for the style you are using. Writers are frequently tempted to make up their own citation style. Such a plan can distract report readers who are familiar with accepted styles.

Certain styles have emerged for various types of documents. A widely accepted standard for reports in the social sciences (business is included) is the style proposed by the *American Psychological Association* which is known as the *APA* style. The APA style requires the author's last name and the date of the author's work in citing material within the written text. A reader of the report would see a name and year such as (Hernandez, 2002). The reader can then look at the references page if more information about the source is needed. At the end of the report, a references page lists in alphabetic order only the sources actually cited in the report. The list includes the author's last name and initials as well as information about the source. The APA style does not usually use footnotes or endnotes.

Another popular style is the one designed by the *Modern Language Association* and is called the *MLA* style. This style is popular with English writers and those who have written reports from a humanities background. In the MLA style, sources are often cited within a sentence. If Raoul Hernandez is the author, the information might read "Raoul Hernandez notes the power of advertising to move an audience (14-15)." The page numbers 14-15 are included. An alternative is to use (Hernandez 14-15) which relates the same information. The reader of the report can then look at the works cited page to see the author's name and other information about the source. The MLA style uses the author's complete name and also uses endnotes. In this style, notes throughout the text are numbered. At the end of a report is a list of the endnotes, and each number coincides with specific information about that note.

A third style discussed by Slade, Campbell, and Ballou in *Form and Style* is based on the *Chicago Manual of Style*. This style is frequently used by publishers who turn manuscripts into textbooks or by writers of formal documents such as theses and term reports. This style requires *footnotes* (notation at bottom of page) or *endnotes* (listing of notes at end of report) for citation and a bibliography.

Information about all three styles will appear in this chapter. The formal report in Chapter 11 will be cited in the APA style. You may wish to locate additional information on one of these styles. Your college library should have these manuals in the reference section.

APA Style

Publication Manual of the American Psychological Association, 4th ed. (Washington, DC: American Psychological Association, 1994).

MLA Style

Joseph Gibaldi, *The MLA Handbook for Writers of Research Papers*, 5th ed. (New York: Modern Language Association of America, 1999).

Chicago Style

Carole Slade, William Giles Campbell, and Stephen Vaughan Ballou, *Form and Style*, 9th ed. (Boston: Houghton Mifflin Company, 1994).
A Manual of Style, 14th ed. (Chicago: University of Chicago Press, 1993).

Examples of Reference Entries

When using any of the styles mentioned, you will need to compile the sources that you used for the report and place them in an appropriate format at the end of the report. In this listing, present in *alphabetic* order the printed and the unpublished works cited by footnotes or noted in the body of the report. Alphabetize by the last name of the author. When you do not know the author's name, alphabetize by the title. Also, document interviews, lectures, and other oral sources.

Each of the style manuals discussed in this chapter includes comprehensive lists of resources. Examples are provided for the most common entries in each style.

APA Style

Notice that the APA style requires only the *initials* of authors. In addition, titles of *articles* and *books* are presented with only the first letter of the title in uppercase and all of the other words in lowercase. Titles of *newspapers*, *magazines,* and *journals* are listed with key words in uppercase. If a word appears after a colon, it also begins with an uppercase letter. The volume number is underlined, while the issue appears in parenthesis. The year is near the beginning of the citation. The reference page at the end of the document is labeled *References*. See Figure 8-1 for examples of common APA entries and Figure 8-2 for examples relating to citation of electronic references.

When using the APA style, endnotes and/or footnotes are not usually included. Instead prepare a references page listing the citations used in the report. See an example in Figure 8-3. The references page should include the following: 1) Alphabetical list of all references that can be found by the reader. For example, the content of a personal interview or a personal e-mail message would not be available to the reader and should not be included in the reference list. 2) First line of entries should be indented. 3) Entries should be double-spaced when typed.

MLA Style

The MLA style uses the *first names*—not just initials—of the authors. When names of more than one author are present, the first author is listed with last name first while the other authors are listed as written. Capitalize the first words and key words in titles—do not capitalize articles (*a, an*, and *the*), prepositions (*in, to, of, between*, etc.), or coordinating conjunctions (*and, or, for, but*, and *nor*). The volume number is not underlined and the date is placed near the end of the entry. The reference page at the end of the document is usually labeled *Works Cited*. See examples in Appendix B.

An example of a *Works Cited* page is shown in Appendix B.

Chicago Style

In the Chicago style, authors *first names* are used and first and last words and key words in the title are capitalized. Do not capitalize articles, conjunctions, or prepositions. The date is usually placed last in this style. Citation is by footnote or endnote. The reference page at the end of the document should be labeled *Bibliography*. See Appendix B for citation examples.

The citation page used at the end of the Chicago style is called a *Bibliography.* See Appendix B for an example of a Bibliography.

Book with one author

Booher, D. (2001). <u>E-writing: 21st century tools for effective communication.</u> New York: Pocket Books.

Book with more than one author

Diamond, M. R., & Williams, J. L. (2000). <u>How to incorporate: A handbook for entrepreneurs and professionals.</u> New York: John Wiley and Sons.

Newspaper article, with author, discontinuous pages.

Johnson, J. (2001, May 10). A change of scenery: Campus improvement projects completed. <u>The Daily Sentinel</u>, pp. 1, 5A.

Journal article with one author

Massey, J. E. (2001). Managing organizational legitimacy: Communication strategies for organizations in crisis. <u>Journal of Business Communication, 38</u>(2), 153-182.

Journal article with more than one author

Pearce, C. G., & Tuten, T. L. (2001). Internet recruiting in the banking industry. <u>Business Communication Quarterly, 64</u>(1), 9-18.

Magazine article, with author

Dolan, K. (2001, April 16). Porcelain and portals. <u>Forbes, 167,</u> 168.

Magazine article, without author

Developments to watch. (2001, May 14). BusinessWeek, p. 121.

Edited book

Wright, J. W. (Ed.). (2000). <u>2001 The New York Times Almanac.</u> New York: Penguin Group.

Figure 8-1. APA Entries

Electronic Citations

Citing on-line sources and sources from the Internet is an area that is constantly changing. For the latest citation information, check the web sites of the various styles. For example, the web site for journals of the American Psychological Association is www.apa.org/journals. As many electronic sources are revised, moved, or removed regularly, be sure to print a hard copy of the source for documentation. Here are some examples cited using electronic citations.

Personnel communications such as e-mail, voice mail, telephone conversations, and messages from electronic bulletin boards are cited only in text–not on the reference page. Use as follows: Z. A. Northrup (personal communication, August 25, 2002). It is the writer's responsibility to verify the identity of the writer of any electronic communication.

Web sites may be cited in the text of the report and are not included in the reference page. For example, "For the latest news, I contact the CNN web site at http://www.cnn.com."

Specific documents on web sites. Citations for documents found on web sites will have similar information to that found on printed documents. In text citations, you may substitute a paragraph number instead of a page number or if neither exists, just leave out the paragraph number or page number. If you can not find a date on the web document, simple place the notation "n.d" (which stands for *no date*, where the date would be located. Be sure to always include a date that the information was retrieved from the web as information available on the web is constantly changing.

Web journal article with no date.

   Hsu, H. C. (n.d.) Earnings surprises and stock returns: Some evidence from Asia/Pacific and Europe. Business Quest 2001. Retrieved on May 15, 2001, from the World Wide Web: http://www.westga.edu/~bquest/2001/surprises.htm

Web document with no author.

   Federal Trade Commission. (2001, March 26). Identity theft: When bad things happen to your good name. Retrieved on May 22, 2001, from the World Wide Web: http://www.consumer.gov/idtheft/.

Online version of printed article. An online version of a printed document should be cited as if the document was printed rather than online assuming that the appropriate information is available. This online article was found from an online library database.

   Duran, N. (2001). In brief: General Accounting Office finds 'pretext calling' hard to track. American Banker, 166(87), p. 32.

Figure 8-2. Electronic Citations

References

Booher, D. (2001). <u>E-writing: 21st century tools for effective communication.</u> New York: Pocket Books.

Developments to watch. (2001, May 14). BusinessWeek, p. 121.

Diamond, M. R., & Williams, J. L. (2000). <u>How to incorporate: A handbook for entrepreneurs and professionals.</u> New York: John Wiley and Sons.

Dolan, K. (2001, April 16). Porcelain and portals. <u>Forbes, 167,</u> 168.

Duran, N. (2001). In brief: General Accounting Office finds 'pretext calling' hard to track. <u>American Banker, 166</u>(87), p. 32.

Federal Trade Commission. (2001, March 26). <u>Identity theft: When bad things happen to your good name.</u> Retrieved on May 22, 2001, from the World Wide Web: http://www.consumer.gov/idtheft

Hsu, H. C. (n.d.) Earnings surprises and stock returns: Some evidence from Asia/Pacific and Europe. <u>Business Quest 2001</u>. Retrieved on May 15, 2001, from the World Wide Web: http://www.westga.edu/~bquest/2001/surprises.htm

Johnson, J. (2001, May 10). A change of scenery: Campus improvement projects completed. <u>The Daily Sentinel</u>, pp. 1, 5A.

Massey, J. E. (2001). Managing organizational legitimacy: Communication strategies for organizations in crisis. <u>Journal of Business Communication, 38</u>(2), 153-182.

Pearce, C. G., & Tuten, T. L. (2001). Internet recruiting in the banking industry. <u>Business Communication Quarterly, 64</u>(1), 9-18.

Wright, J. W. (Ed.). (2000). <u>2001 The New York Times Almanac.</u> New York: Penguin Group.

Figure 8-3. APA Style End-of-Report References Page

Footnotes and Endnotes

In the **MLA** style and the ***Chicago*** style footnotes may be used. Footnote arrangements vary slightly among widely recognized authorities. Footnotes are frequently placed at the bottom of the page where the footnote number is located. A footnote provides a ready source for the citation: the report reader merely looks at the bottom of the page to find the source. Footnotes can be easily created with the leading word processing software. An example of a paraphrased passage from a government document in which a footnote was used follows:

Chicago Manual of Style Footnote

While keeping track of a company's physical assets is relatively straightforward, summarizing intellectual capital is much more complex. Intellectual capital includes such items as employees' knowledge about products and services and intellectual property.[1]

---

[1] Taylor, Christie. "Intellectual Capital." <u>Computerworld</u>, 12 Mar. 2001, 51-52.

Another technique that is frequently used in the **MLA** style is that of including endnotes. The notes are numbered throughout the text as are footnotes. The citation is not located at the bottom of the page, however. Instead, a complete list of all the numbered notes is located at the end of the report. Endnotes also can be created easily with the leading software for word processing. While footnotes and endnotes are one way of citing information, other techniques can also be used.

Using Citations When Writing

To ensure your credibility as a writer, you must cite your sources appropriately. Each time you paraphrase the material of another or use a direct quote, you must give the originator of the idea credit.

Footnotes and endnotes may be used in some citation styles but are seldom used in others. By using a combination of the author's name(s), dates, and/or page numbers, many citations can be made within the text. The **Chicago** style uses either footnotes or endnotes for citations. The following are acceptable techniques for the **APA** and **MLA** styles.

APA Style	MLA Style
Use author(s) last name(s) and the date of the source. Page numbers are only used for direct quotes. Use a comma to separate elements placed together.	Use author(s) last name(s) and the page number(s) where the information in the source is located. Put a space between the separate elements.

Correct APA Examples	Correct MLA Examples
Luggage styles have changed as the business traveler has changed (Johnson and Bayless, 2002).	Luggage styles have changed as the business traveler has changed (Johnson and Bayless 175-185).
Johnson and Bayless note that luggage styles have changed (2002).	Johnson and Bayless note that luggage styles have changed (150, 175-185).
According to Johnson and Bayless (2002), two trends related to business travel have developed in recent years.	According to Johnson and Bayless, two trends related to business travel have developed in recent years (150).
"The two factors—more women and shorter trips—have combined to make smaller cases with wheels extremely popular" (Johnson and Bayless, 2002, p. 150).	Johnson and Bayless relate "the two factors—more women and shorter trips—have combined to make smaller cases with wheels extremely popular" (150).

Just as you vary your writing style by choosing different words and phrases, you will want to vary your citation style as shown above. Remember, however, to stay within the guidelines of the specific citation style you are using.

A long paragraph which incorporates many thoughts from your research may have several citations. One of the best reasons for citing your resources is that you can quickly refer to the original source if a reader of your report needs more information on a particular point. Citing your work may also protect you from a charge of *plagiarism* which is using someone else's work or ideas as your own.

DISCUSSION

1. Give an example of an experiment that could be conducted in business.

2. List five reports for which observing would be a good primary research technique.

3. Identify three reports for which you would gather data by sending a questionnaire.

4. What steps should you use when you plan to interview several people to collect primary data?

5. What factors should you consider when determining the format to use for a questionnaire you will prepare?

6. Which is more important: primary data or secondary data? Explain your answer.

EXERCISES

1. Use the World Wide Web to find information on three companies of your choice. Be prepared to discuss your findings.

2. Do a web search on your name (use first and last, middle initial is optional) using at least three search engines. Did any of the sites have information about you or did they have information about people with your name? Be prepared to discuss this activity in class.

3. Try this web infosearch. You must find answers to these three questions using the web (other resources not permitted). Include the answers, the address of the web site where you found the information, and your name in an e-mail message to your instructor.

   A. Who is the current President of Belarus?
   B. When and where was the XV Olympiad of the Olympics?
   C. Where can you find a picture of Mars?
   D. Describe a recent Supreme Court decision.

PROBLEMS

1. You have been asked to serve as part of the pilot group to study this questionnaire (see Figure 8-4 on following page). Please make any suggestions that will be helpful before it is mailed. The topic is VCR usage.

2. You are the assistant manager of a clothing store in a college town. A limited number of college students have bought clothing at your store. You want to increase the volume of sales to the students, so you decide to observe them on campus for a week to determine the types of clothing they wear. Prepare a checklist you will use.

3. Find the names of the chief executive officers and the addresses for five Fortune 500 companies. Give the source of your information.

4. Pick a hotel chain of your choice. Find the name, address, phone number, and number of rooms for five hotels in locations of your choice.

5. Describe how a stratified sample could be taken from your class, which is the universe (population). Be ready to report your findings to the class.

6. Your company is interested in starting a life insurance plan for each of the employees. What kind of primary and secondary information would you suggest for this report? Give specific ideas. Be ready to present your information to the class.

7. Several investors are interested in starting an athletic club in your city. They have asked that you develop a questionnaire that can be administered to a sample of college students to determine what the students would like to see in an athletic club and how it would be used. You may find it helpful to work with another class member to design the questionnaire.

8. Your company is interested in profiting from the NAFTA free trade agreement between the United States, Canada, and Mexico. Do some secondary research to find five sources with information on NAFTA. Use both print sources and Internet sources.

9. You work for a company that is interested in doing business on an international scale. Access at least three government documents relating to the business climate in other countries. You may pick documents on the same country or on different countries. Report your findings to the class.

10. Use the Internet to explore a current business topic of your choice.

FRIENDLY VCR COMPANY

Name _____   Address _____
Phone _____   Social Security No._____

Please answer the following questions.

1. Do you own a VCR?
   _____ Yes   _____ No   _____ Use a friend's

2. How often do you tape television programs?
   _____ Often   _____ Every day
   _____ More than once a week   _____ Seldom

3. Do you watch rented movies on the VCR?
   _____ Yes   _____ No

4. How often do you watch rented movies?
   _____ Just on the weekends   _____ Once a week
   _____ Every couple of days   _____ Seldom

5. When you tape programs from TV, do you set the VCR to operate when you are not home? _____ Yes _____ No

6. What is the result of your taping efforts?
   _____ Always comes out right
   _____ Comes out right 90 percent of the time
   _____ Usually have a problem half of the time
   _____ Never works

7. When you rent movies, what category is most interesting to you?
   _____ Comedy   _____ Western
   _____ Thriller   _____ Drama
   _____ Funny   _____ Action
   _____ Childrens   _____ Award winners

Figure 8-4. Questionnaire for Problem 1

ANALYZING DATA

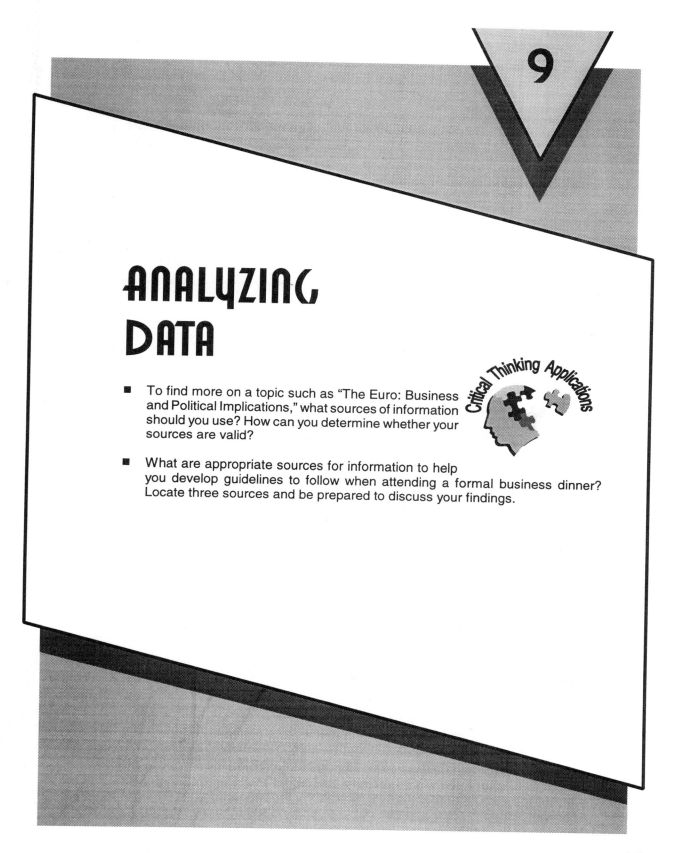

Critical Thinking Applications

- To find more on a topic such as "The Euro: Business and Political Implications," what sources of information should you use? How can you determine whether your sources are valid?

- What are appropriate sources for information to help you develop guidelines to follow when attending a formal business dinner? Locate three sources and be prepared to discuss your findings.

CHAPTER OBJECTIVES

After studying this chapter, you should be able to:

1. Paraphrase information from a primary or secondary source.
2. Document a direct quote in a report.
3. Tabulate basic primary data.
4. Abstract an article.

PRESENTING RESEARCH INFORMATION

Information collected from primary and secondary sources can be presented in a written report in a variety of ways.

When analyzing secondary information, you should rewrite and present it in your own words. Translating a primary or secondary source in to your own words is known as *paraphrasing*.

By using your own writing style, you enhance the readability of the report. Also, this practice requires a thorough study and understanding of the material you include in the report which can improve the clarity of the report.

Occasionally, you may wish to use an exact quote of primary or secondary information. Quote verbatim when the quotation adds strength to your report and when it is especially well stated for your particular writing style.

You may find it helpful to present some primary and secondary information in graphs rather than in written paragraphs. The source of such information should always be cited on the graph or chart (see Chapter 10 for further details).

Whether you paraphrase, quote verbatim, or use a graphic aid, make sure *always* to give credit to the source of the information. Give this credit by presenting the information appropriately in the text and by including citations in the proper form. A *citation*, as described in Chapter 8, will give information needed to direct the reader to the source.

Paraphrases

By paraphrasing secondary sources, you can better match the writing style to the context of the report. In addition, you may eliminate unnecessary information. Suppose you have found the following paragraphs by Johnson and Bayless (2002) in a hypothetical business resource that relate to business travelers and luggage.

Research Source

Today's business traveler is different from yesterday's traveler. Women have become a big part of the travel market in the last decade increasing from an estimated 27 to 49 percent. The length of time for journeys has also decreased from five to seven day business jaunts in 1991 to two-to-four day trips in 2002. As the business traveler has changed, so have the demands for luggage.

The two factors—more women and shorter trips—have combined to make smaller cases with wheels extremely popular. Many travelers wish to save time and reduce lost luggage by avoiding the checked baggage areas at airports and by carrying any necessary luggage on the plane.

Sales projections for new luggage show an increase in wheeled cases no larger than 21" from 22 percent of the luggage market in 1991 to 65 percent in 2002. By contrast, hard-sided large cases over 29" without wheels have gone from 40 percent of the market in 1991 to 9 percent in 2002. Clearly, the key words for today's business luggage buyer are *wheels* and *smaller.*

When paraphrasing text, one of your goals is to shorten the material, yet include the important facts you need for your report. If your report topic discusses how the business traveler has changed over the last ten years, you may wish to paraphrase the important information from above as follows:

Paraphrase #1

The stereotype image of a business traveler is that of a man who takes periodic trips of five days or longer. According to Johnson and Bayless (2002) that image has changed in two important ways: nearly half of the business travelers are women and most trips range from two to four days in length.

Perhaps, instead, you might paraphrase the information from the original source to focus on changing trends in luggage. You note that 65 percent is nearly 66 percent or two-thirds. Paraphrasing this figure may make it easier for your reader to understand the information as follows:

Paraphrase #2

Business travelers are tired of lugging around heavy, oversized suitcases. When it is time to buy a new piece of luggage, shoppers are looking for luggage that has wheels and is a smaller size. In fact, nearly two-thirds of today's shoppers will buy a case that is 21" or smaller with wheels (Johnson and Bayless, 2002).

As shown in the preceding paraphrase versions, you should put the information into your own words. Be careful, however, not to change or seriously distort the facts in the information you are citing. Each time you paraphrase, you must also cite the source of your information.

Novice report writers frequently think that a citation every few paragraphs is sufficient. On the contrary, you must *cite* each paraphrased piece of information in *each* paragraph. If you paraphrase from two sources in the same paragraph, you must cite each source. Such citations increase your credibility as a report writer and also make it easier for report readers to follow up on the valuable information you have located.

Cite the Citation Carefully in Each Paragraph of Report

In any paragraph where you have referred to another resource, you must cite the source in that paragraph. Once again, cite sources used in EACH paragraph. Do NOT write several paragraphs and then list the source(s).

Properly paraphrased information reads more smoothly, usually requires less space, and complements the writing style of the report writer. Carefully chosen direct quotations, however, may be best if you wish to use the exact words of an authority on the subject.

Direct Quotes

While paraphrasing is the preferred form for writers, a direct or verbatim quotation may add strength to the point you wish to make if the readers of your report consider the authors of the quotation to be experts in the subject. Perhaps you have decided that your report on finding the ideal luggage would be stronger with a supporting quote. A direct quote such as the following may be one way to enhance your point.

Direct Quote

"Though we travel the world over to find the beautiful, we must carry it with us or we find it not." —**Ralph Waldo Emerson**

Direct quotations can also be helpful if you feel that the writer of the quoted work related the information in a manner that was better and written more concisely than you can write.

Short direct quotations usually require quotation marks. For quotations four lines or longer, single space and indent the quote from the left and the right margins; use no quotation marks.

Introduce each quotation and use variety in the introductions. When you indicate that a statement is a direct quotation, use the exact wording and punctuation the author used. An example of an introduction and an exact quote based on the earlier resource document is described as follows:

Introduction of Long Direct Quote

Changes in the business environment in the last ten years have produced somewhat of a revolution in business travel as well as the luggage needed for travel. Johnson and Bayless (2002) report:

> The two factors—more women and shorter trips—have combined to make smaller cases with wheels extremely popular. Many travelers wish to save time and reduce lost luggage by avoiding the checked baggage areas at airports and by carrying any necessary luggage on the plane (p. 150).

Abstracting

While paraphrasing focuses on a paragraph or a few paragraphs of an article, abstracting would involve collecting all of the key points from an article. Abstracting is a good technique to use when analyzing the secondary information you collect and is a first step to deciding what information would be of value to your report.

List Citation Information

The first thing to do after you have located your full-text article from a web database or found your hardcopy resource is to determine the information that will be required for the citation. You will need as much of the following information as possible:

1. Complete name of author(s) (The APA style requires only the first and middle initials along with a complete last name, but MLA and Chicago require the complete name of the author.)
2. Date of publication
3. Title of article
4. Name of journal, magazine, or entity publishing the information
5. Publisher and place of publication for books
6. Volume
7. Issue or number
8. Pages
9. Date retrieved (if citing from a web site)
10. Web site address (if citing from a web site)

List the source information in the correct citation style at the beginning of the abstract. Remember to refer to Chapter 8 for the APA style and to Appendix B for the MLA Style and the Chicago style.

What's the issue with the volume?

One often confusing piece of citation information has to do with the volume, the issue, and the number.

The volume usually records a year's worth of issues. So, if four journals were prepared each year, you would have four issues. If an issue is sent out every month, you would have 12 issues. Not all publications use a calendar year for their volume numbers—some use an academic year. If a magazine or journal has been around a long time, they will have a high volume number. For example, *The Business Communication Quarterly* has a volume of 64 for the year 2001. Issue and number are usually the same thing. The issue for this citation is number 1 followed by the page numbers of 7-8. An APA citation would be as follows.

   Andrews, D.C. (2001). Playing a role. Business Communication Quarterly, 64(1) 7-8.

If you find a full-text article on the web with both a volume and issue number, cite the article as if it was a hard-copy article. In other words, you don't need the web site information.

Another common area for confusion in the APA style relates to when to use page numbers.

Does a Magazine Have an Issue?

Magazines frequently have volumes but not issues. It is easier to find the magazine by looking at the date. If the magazine has a volume number, be sure to use it.

Without volume number - if you have no volume or issue, use the page number notation, pp., before the numbers.

   Lavelle, L. (2001, April 16). Executive pay. Business Week, pp. 76-80.

With volume number - if you have a volume number, you don't need the page numbers notation before the page numbers. This issue of Forbes is in volume 167.

   Cook, L. (2001, May 28). Extreme exploration. Forbes, 167, 186-189.

After your citation is located at the beginning of your abstract, you are ready to proceed to the point summary.

Point Summary

In the second section of the abstract, you should list all of the key points of the article in a consistent format. This could be in complete sentences, in phrases, or in numbered items. If the article related to the job search, you might list the point summary as follows:

Point Summary

1. Employment opportunities increase as unemployment rate drops to 3.9% in Kansas City.
2. Several placement agencies are available with a number at no cost to the job seeker.
3. A new web page with job employment opportunities is located with other city information.
4. Professional opportunities are available in fields such as law and medicine.
5. Apartment complexes are being built rapidly to provide additional housing.

In completing the point summary, you should be able to find at *least five key points* to summarize your article. After you have summarized the key points, you are ready to proceed to paraphrasing key points and/or the article.

Paraphrasing Key Sections

One purpose for completing an abstract is to have a written summary of information that you can use in compiling your report. For the third section of the abstract, you will paraphrase in detail three or more of the key points listed in the point summary. Remember to use your own words in writing your paraphrase.

You may find it helpful to paraphrase by combining two or more of your key points. Your choice for paraphrasing will depend on how the article can be used in your report.

If you are working on a team report, you may wish to compare your individual abstracts after you have completed the point summary to determine which key points should be summarized effectively. In that case, you will not have two team members using the same article or using different articles but discussing the same point.

Assessment

The fourth and final section of the abstract is assessment. In this section you will assess the article and discuss its relevance to your report. You will want to discuss such issues as the quality of the article, the currency (is it new or old?), the qualifications of the authors, and any other issues which bear on the quality of the article. Be sure to note that information you found of value.

Paraphrasing and abstracting relate primarily to secondary data. How do you assess primary data you have collected?

Assessing Primary Data

Processing information you find when you look for primary data was discussed in the last chapter. One of the things you will notice about primary data is that not all of the responses will be helpful. For example, if many respondents were confused about a question you asked, you may not wish to base business decisions on the results. Another problem might be that a question you thought might generate some difference of opinion results in everyone responding with the same answer.

Depending on the size of your primary data you may be compiling the information with computer programs. However, you may also be doing smaller studies and compiling information by hand. For example, if your team conducted fifty surveys using a predesigned questionnaire, you might want to tabulate them by hand. Let's say you had the following results on a survey about working for an international firm.

Survey Question Raw Data Results of 50 Surveys

\# 1.   I would like to work at company offices in Europe.

Strongly agree-10; Agree-5; No opinion-0; Disagree-10; Strongly Disagree-25.

\#2.   I would work for a company owned by a non-USA company as long as I could stay in the United States.

Strongly agree - 20; Agree- 15; No opinion-5; Disagree-10; Strongly Disagree-0

One of the common errors made by report writers is to use raw data when presenting information. It is much more effective to use percentages. Simply divide each raw number by the total number of survey responses to that question. Be sure to mention the total number of surveys when you discuss your results. For question #1 above, the percentages would be the following:

Strongly Agree-20%;
Agree-10%;
No opinion-0;
Disagree-20%; and
Strongly Disagree-50%.

In your analysis of question #1, you could say that half of the respondents were not interested in working in Europe. Or you could combine the disagree and strongly disagree categories and say that 70% of the respondents disagreed with a statement about wanting to work in Europe. Percentages are much more effective in a case like this than is raw data. Can you compile the data for question #2? What conclusions can you draw in your analysis?

After you have collected your primary and secondary data, what is the best way to organize your information? One way to organize your data follows.

An Organizational Strategy

Sometimes the idea of working on the report can seem overwhelming. Maybe this strategy would be helpful.

Purchase colored note cards (4 x 6 or 5 x 8). You can use the color two different ways: 1) Assign a color to each team member or 2) Assign a color to each major topic to be discussed in the report. As you conduct your paraphrasing and abstracting, simply write the paraphrase on the note card (or use a cut and paste strategy from your computer printouts) on one side of the notecard. On the other side of the notecard jot down the source for this paraphrase. If you have several paraphrases from the same article, you could write the citation information once and then refer to it by an author, a number, or a letter on other cards. This could be a task that each team member completes for the research they are locating.

When the team meets with the completed cards, start shuffling them in to an order that makes sense. It is easy to make an outline from the cards (or to use the cards to fill in an outline you already have). By using this system you can quickly see where you need more research to fill in any gaps.

When you get ready to compile the report, you will find it a lot easier to type or cut and paste, your paraphrased items. If you encourage your team members to type each paraphrase (and give it an identifying letter and number–like T6 for Tammy's sixth paragraph) before the cut and paste, you might find the report much quicker to assemble than having one person type from a scrawl of illegible handwritten notes.

The next chapter will discuss graphics and techniques for presenting data in visual formats.

DISCUSSION

1. What is the difference between paraphrasing and abstracting?

2. A suggestion for organizing information for the report was given. What other ideas do you have for report organization?

3. List any advantages or disadvantages of listing only the author's initials as recommended by the APA style.

4. Give some examples of how primary data could enhance the report.

EXERCISES

1. Prepare an appropriate end-of-report reference page for these fictional sources. Use your preference of the styles listed in the text, or use the one recommended by your instructor. You may wish to refer to Chapter 8 for more details.

Type	Journal-1	Magazine-2	Book-3	Newspaper-4
Author	Jay Williams	None	Maria Ramirez	J. Cool Legend
Article	Business Writers Today	Improving the Vocabulary	Book title: 10 Steps to Success	Top Ten Business Travel Spots
Source	Journal of Writing	Person to Person	XYZ Books	Vermont Daily Times
Page	147-155	35-38	430-439	10A
Volume	24	22	Location of Publisher: New York	None
Issue	4	10	None	None
Date	2002	September 25, 2002	2002	November 8, 2002

2. Paraphrase the following information from a fictional journal article and include an appropriate citation based on one of the citation styles mentioned in the chapter. (See the table in problem 1 for Journal-1.)

> Studies of the northern region of the country indicate that 80 percent of the inhabitants are not able to write their own names much less cogent reports of value to business writers. The language barrier is also a problem as fewer than 30 percent of the populace speak any English. Of that number only about 10 percent have any degree of fluency in English. A great deal of training would be required to turn most employees into literate workers. In fact, it is estimated that reading and math skills would require a minimum of 1200 clock hours.

3. Paraphrase the following information from a draft of a fictional magazine article and include an appropriate citation based on one of the citation styles mentioned in the chapter. (See the table in problem 1 for Magazine-2.)

> There are several easy ways to improve your vocabulary. One of the most popular is to learn a new word each day. Several guides and calendars are available to help one learn this technique. The most important factor is to use the new word in all of its meanings and to speak it as well as read it throughout the day. Studies have also shown that vocabulary can be increased through reading. For those readers who are uncertain of the meaning of a word, a handy pocket dictionary is a plus when reading new information. It also never hurts to ask questions of your friends if they use an interesting word with whose meaning you are unfamiliar.

4. Paraphrase the following information from a hypothetical book and include an appropriate citation based on one of the citation styles mentioned in the chapter. (See the table in problem 1 for Book-3.)

> Success can have different meanings for different people. For some, success means an affluent life style. For others, success may mean fame and recognition. Still other individuals define success by a happy lifestyle with family and friends. As success can mean so many things to so many people, it is often difficult to define the steps to achieve success. The first and most important step, however, is to know yourself. What are your goals? What does success mean to you? Without a careful definition of this first step to success you may find yourself working diligently toward a goal you do not really want to achieve. Obviously, problems can then occur.

5. Paraphrase the following information from a draft of a hypothetical newspaper article and include an appropriate citation based on one of the citation styles mentioned in the chapter. (See the table in problem 1 for Newspaper-4.)

> Business travel has often been seen as a plus and a minus for the business person. The plus factors include the opportunity to travel to locations you have not seen before, to mingle some pleasure with business, and to meet new people. Minus factors often include the loneliness of traveling alone, hectic work schedules which do not allow you to really enjoy the place you are visiting (why go to Jamaica if you spend fourteen hours of your day working inside a plant?), and trips to places you have already seen.

The most popular business travel spots currently are Orlando, Florida; San Francisco, California; and San Antonio, Texas.

PROBLEMS

1. Prepare an end-of-report reference page that includes two books, one newspaper article, two magazine articles, and two journal articles. These references can pertain to the topic of your choice. Be sure to collect the necessary information as shown in the table in problem 1 such as author(s) names, titles of works and/or books, page numbers, dates, publishers, volume number, and issue number.

2. Prepare an end-of-report reference page that includes a book with two authors, a book with three or more authors, and a journal article with more than one author. These references can pertain to the topic of your choice.

3. Using the techniques in the chapter, create abstracts for at least two of the research articles you have located based on your report topic. Be ready to turn in your typed document to your instructor.

4.   If you have primary research data, tabulate your results. Figure the percentages for each question. Then determine which questions will be most likely to support your report. Be prepared to turn this information in to your instructor.

5.   Prepare an end-of-report reference page that includes all of your team's articles. Be sure to put them in alphabetic order. The entries should be double-spaced with the first line of each entry indented. Save and print a copy of the page for your instructor. Remember that for your final report you will include only those articles that actually served as sources for the report.

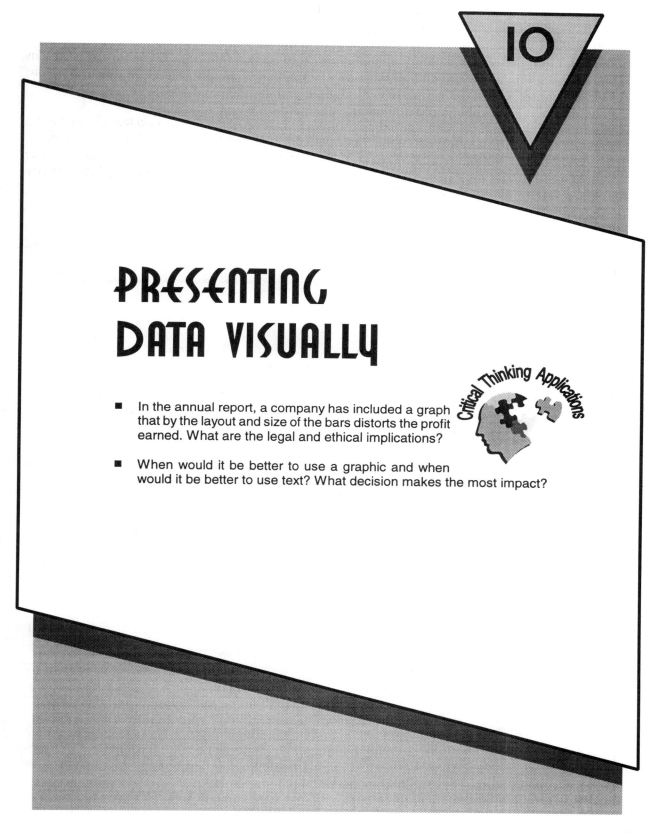

PRESENTING DATA VISUALLY

- In the annual report, a company has included a graph that by the layout and size of the bars distorts the profit earned. What are the legal and ethical implications?

- When would it be better to use a graphic and when would it be better to use text? What decision makes the most impact?

GRAPHICS

A manager had a problem that she considered a safety hazard in her computer work area. Over thirty computers were located in one large room. Computer cords and electrical cables were somewhat haphazardly arranged. In fact, some employees when moving from one part of the room to another, frequently stepped over cords that were several inches off the floor.

The manager mentioned the problem to her supervisors, but she didn't make much progress. She decided to research the problem and write a report to determine the best way to eliminate the safety hazard. She decided to take photographs of the current cable arrangement. After including the photographs in her report, she was pleased by how quickly a decision was made to remedy the hazardous conditions. When the cables and cords were confined in specially designed cable troughs, the manager took more photographs which she used in a follow-up report on the situation.

Often, graphics can be used more effectively than words in a variety of business reports. As a writer of business reports, your goal is to present accurate pertinent information so that it is easy to read and understand. Use photographs and other graphics to supplement the written text in your report. Correctly used, graphics can contribute to clarity, interest, and readability.

To use graphics effectively, construct them well and interpret them for the readers. Direct the readers to what you wish them to see in the graphic aid.

Constructing Graphics

Executives who receive numerical data through the computers on their desks can display the data in graphic form very quickly and easily and can thus interpret more efficiently than they could without the graphic form. They can study the graphics on the monitor screen, or they can print them for further use.

Various formats can be used for graphics. Whether you use one format or another, you want your graphics to be accurate, attractive, and easy to read. So that graphics are effective, make them simple and attractive. Do not try to show too much information in any one device. Choose the types that help the readers to grasp the particular points you want them to grasp.

Use a computer graphics program to develop the most professional graphic images. Such programs as *Microsoft Powerpoint, Corel WordPerfect Presentations,* and *Lotus Freelance Graphics* are designed specifically to work with computer graphics. Many other spreadsheet and word processing programs also include graphic components which can be used to enhance reports. With many graphics programs, you can create quite complicated graphs that may have little value. When working with computer graphics, take care that the information placed in the graph makes sense.

Graphics can be printed in black and white or color. Color is increasingly becoming a powerful way to focus attention on graphics. Color printing is available through some dot-matrix printers, ink jet printers, and laser printers.

Guidelines

By following the recommendations in this chapter, you can create tables and other graphics that your report readers will appreciate. These specific guidelines apply to all types of graphics.

Consider Your Audience. As with your other business messages, you must consider your audience when designing graphics. A formal table may provide the exact information that accountants wish to have. On the other hand, some audiences need less detailed information. Graphics such as maps, charts, and pictograms will provide the reader a broad picture of the subject.

Number the Graphics. When a report is to have more than one graphic besides tables, use Arabic numerals to number them consecutively. Place the word "Figure," the number, and the title above the graphic or below the graphic. (See Figures 10-3, 10-5, and 10-7.)

Give Each Graphic a Title. When possible, include in the concise, descriptive title the answers to What? When? Where? and How classified? Capitalize the main words in the title and avoid abbreviations.

Use a Source Notation. When the report readers are analyzing your graphics, they wish to refer to the source of your information. Be sure to reveal the information source by placing a notation below the graphic.

Use a Legend. Many computer software packages enable you to add a legend which can be used to define bars or lines or parts of a pie chart. Using a legend contributes to clarity for the graphic aid.

Tables

In a table, which may be either informal or formal, information is presented in columns and rows. An informal table is a useful device for presenting simple data. Like all other graphics, an informal table must have at least three items to justify its use: fewer than three items can be presented better in sentence form.

An *informal table* may consist of a simple list of items, or it may have two or three columns. While this table may have column headings and totals, it has no table number or title and is not ruled. An informal table is preceded by a lead-in sentence that is usually followed by a colon, as in these examples:

The brands studied and the number of employees who preferred each brand follow:

Wentworth	30
Brandon	14
Lerner	10

Last month's travel expenditures include the following:

Hotel	$ 1,200
Meals	950
Airfare	800
Tips	150
Total	$ 3,100

The employees gave the following responses when asked if they planned to attend the seminar:

Employees	Yes	No
Analysts	26	17
Programmers	21	11
Systems Engineers	12	23
Administrative Assistants	5	8
Totals	64	59

Seldom do you need to interpret an informal table. Sometimes, though, you may help the readers by commenting on some of the items that are included.

A *formal table*, one of the most frequently used graphics, is the only practical device for presenting a large quantity of precise information. A formal table reflects the detailed data in a form which is easy to find and to absorb. The same information presented in a paragraph form would be hard to comprehend.

You can use a formal table to compare or classify a small number of related items as well as a large number. Although you should restrict the length to only the number required to achieve the purpose for which you construct the table, the length can be more than a page. If a table is too wide for the page, present it in *landscape format* (horizontally across the long side of the page). Place the page so that the top of the table is near the binding (left side) of the report.

In a recent government document, both the enlisted military personnel and the officers were categorized by race. The following table is a subset of the larger document and concentrates on two selected groups across all branches of the military service.

Table 1
Selected Enlisted Personnel in Uniform, 2000

Service	Black Americans		Hispanic Americans	
	Number	Percent	Number	Percent
Army	115,240	29.2	34,232	8.7
Navy	62,974	20.3	29,630	9.5
Marines	25,023	16.4	20,174	13.2
Air Force	51,272	18.2	15,261	5.4
TOTAL	254,509	22.3	99,297	8.7

Source: U.S. Department of Defense, *Defense 2000*. www.defenselink.mil

While the best graphic aid for technical information is a formal table such as the preceding one, other graphic aids serve better for presenting other types of information.

In this chapter, one body of information is presented a number of ways to show how the use of graphic aids can contribute to report clarity. Envirotec has assembled information about company travel expenses for the fourth quarter of the most recent year. The travel expenses are shown in table form in Figure 10-1.

Travel Expenses for Fourth Quarter

Category	Month		
	October	November	December
Airfare	$77,000	$85,000	$45,000
Hotels	72,000	61,000	35,000
Meals	41,000	30,000	20,000
Other	10,000	10,000	8,000
Totals	$200,000	$186,000	$108,000

Source: Organizational Files, 2002

Figure 10-1. Table

Bar Charts

Use a bar chart when you want the readers to observe relative quantities more quickly than is possible by comparing large numbers. You can use bar charts also to show percentages. Each bar should be proportional to the quantity or amount it represents. The bars may be vertical or horizontal.

When comparing figures such as travel expenses for each month, a bar chart (See Figure 10-2) will provide a visual comparison. Use a stacked-bar chart (Figure 10-3 is an example) to display a number of components for each bar. Stacked-bar charts need shaded or colored components for each bar.

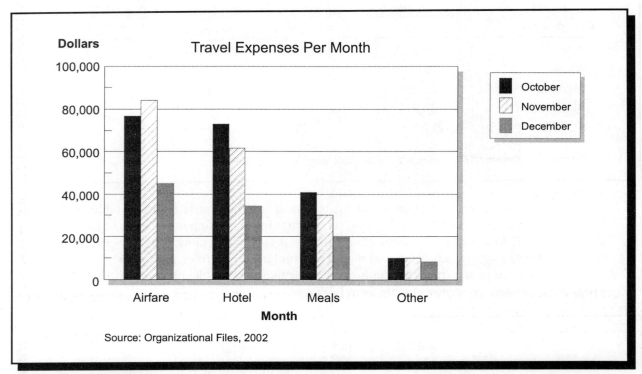

Figure 10-2. Bar Chart

Computer graphics programs can be used to make rather complex graphics. These graphics may be quite attractive, yet difficult to understand. The bar chart in Figure 10-4 is an example. One problem is that the numbers are on the right side of the chart. As English readers read from left to right, this is an awkward place for numbers. The depth of the bars makes interpreting the graph difficult. For example, how much was spent on hotel costs in November? The chart is also missing an adequate title and a source notation.

You will notice, however, that the legend on Figure 10-4 is at the bottom while other charts have placed the legend at the side. The legend may be located in any place on the chart which will enhance the legibility of the chart.

Pie Charts

A pie chart is a circle divided into segments (called slices) to show comparison of parts to one another and to the whole. Data is presented less accurately in this chart than in tables, but the generalizations are easy to see. You have, no doubt, observed in newspapers pie charts showing the sources and the distribution of the revenue for the federal, the state, or the county government.

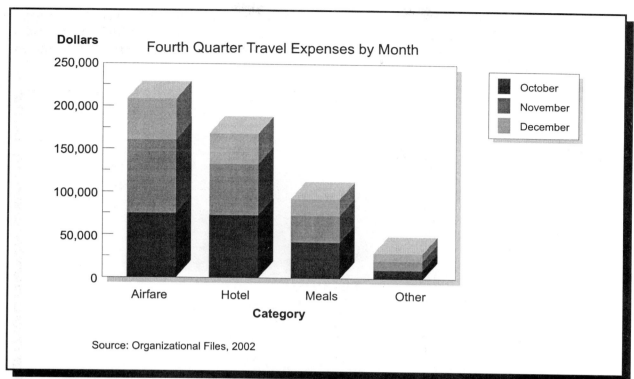

Figure 10-3. Stacked Bar Chart

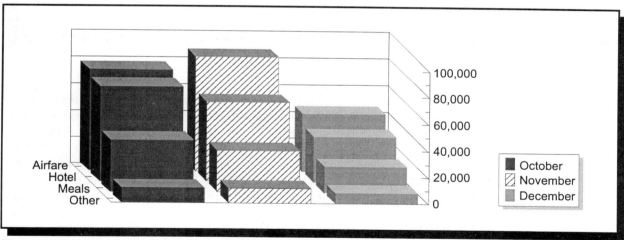

Figure 10-4. Poor Bar Chart

Whether you use a pie chart to show the breakdown of a dollar or to show percentages for other items, the percentages in the chart must total one hundred.

Suggestions for designing a pie chart follow:

1. Arrange the slices clockwise in descending order of size with the largest section beginning at the "twelve o'clock" position. With most computer graphics programs,

you have difficulty arranging the pie sections in order from the largest to the smallest. You may find it necessary to rotate the starting angle of the first piece or to key the information in a different order to achieve the effect shown in Figure 10-5.

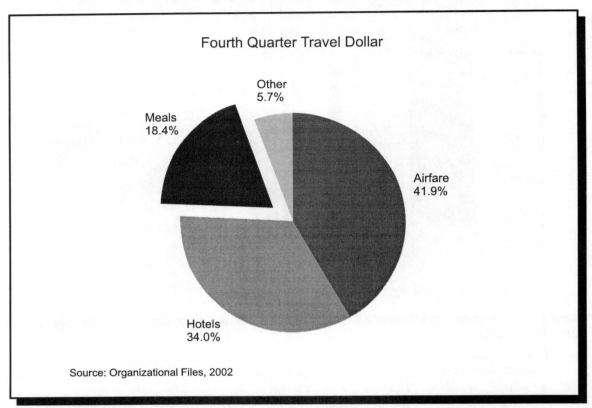

Figure 10-5. Pie Chart

2. Decide how you wish to label the sections of the pie chart. Most graphics programs will allow you to put percentages or actual figures on the chart. You may want to look at several options before making a final decision.

3. Limit the number of slices to six. Computer graphics will allow you to have more slices than six but the chart will become less clear. You may wish to combine some categories to reduce the number of pie slices.

4. Use colors, shading, stippling, or crosshatching to distinguish the portions. Use a different color or pattern for each slice of the pie.

5. If a portion is labeled "Other," place it last regardless of size.

You may wish to *explode* a piece of the pie to call attention to that element of the chart. *Exploding* occurs when one or more slices of the pie are separated from the rest of the pie. When a pie piece is exploded (as is the meals component in Figure 10-5), that item receives special attention.

Just as computer graphics programs can be used to make incomprehensible bar charts, the same effect can take place with pie charts. You may observe in Figure 10-6, which contains multiple pie charts, that the size of the pie is quite small and that the labels and percentages are more obvious than the pie. This chart could be improved by increasing the size and by using a better title and a source notation.

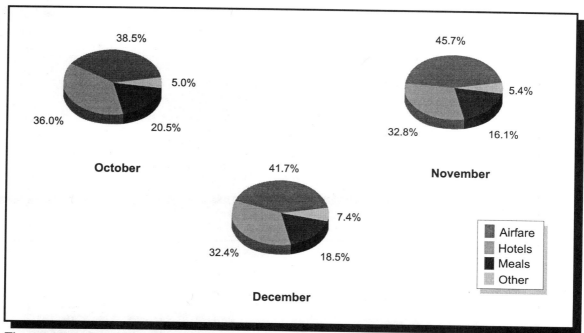

Figure 10-6. Poor Pie Chart

Line Charts

A line chart is the best graphic for showing changes in a value for a time span. This chart is made by drawing lines between points in a series. The horizontal scale is read from left to right; the vertical scale, from bottom to top. You can show two or more values on one chart (see Figure 10-7). This figure tracks the progress of each category over a three-month period. By following the line, you can determine whether the expenses for hotels increased or decreased during the time.

Computer graphics were used to create the line chart in Figure 10-8. While at first glance the chart may look fine, it has some errors. First, the categories listed on the bottom of the chart do not lend themselves to linear data. The first line shows a total for airfare and then moves to the next point (hotel), then the third point (meals), and the final point (other). A line chart should show the same category over a time span. The line should be for airfare over a three month period—October, November, December.

Other errors which make this chart ineffective are (1) the legend does not match the lines (so you don't know which line stands for which month), (2) the title is not clear, and (3) the source notation is missing.

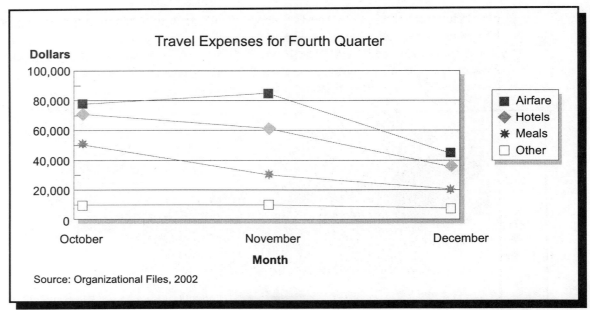

Figure 10-7. Line Chart

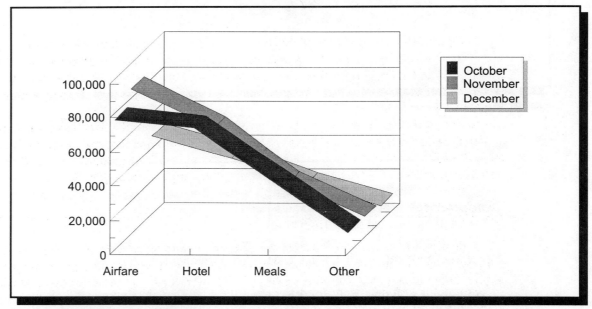

Figure 10-8. Poor Line Chart

Area Charts

Use area charts as variations of line charts. This type of chart emphasizes data that may not look as significant in a line chart. Instead of just a line or lines on the chart, the space from the base of the chart to the line (and between the lines if more than one value is represented) is filled with color or a pattern such as solid black or shades of gray, lines, crosshatching, or dots. Figure 10-9 is an example of an area chart.

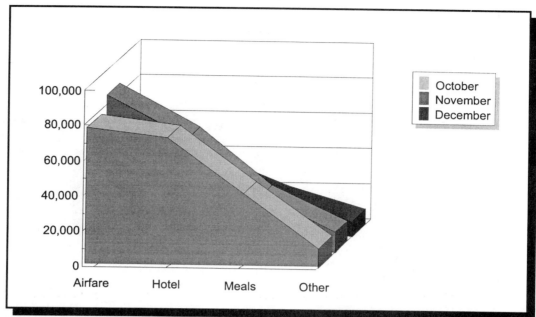

Figure 10-9. Poor Area Chart

In Figure 10-9 a difficulty with this type of chart is emphasized. While the October data is easy to read and the November data is also visible, most of the December data is hidden by the areas of the two earlier slices. In fact, this chart would be of little value in comparing the three items. Also, this chart suffers from the same misalignment of categories as did Figure 10-8.

In Figure 10-10, the arrangement which hid some sections of the chart has been adjusted so that the chart is more readable. As you may note, this realignment may require changing the order of the months, which may not be the best option for a graphic aid. As the report writer, you must choose the best approach for presenting the information.

Pictograms

A pictogram is a bar chart with pictorial symbols instead of bars. A pictogram, which quickly gains the attention of the reader, is often used in reports that go to the general public. Often a degree of preciseness can well be sacrificed and offset by the interest this graphic generates. Pictograms are frequently seen in color in such newspapers as *USA Today*.

Helpful suggestions for making pictograms follow:

1. Choose symbols that are easy to identify. They must be self-explanatory.

2. Use interesting symbols that give a clear picture. Providing a consistent symbol throughout the pictogram will make it easier for the reader to compare values.

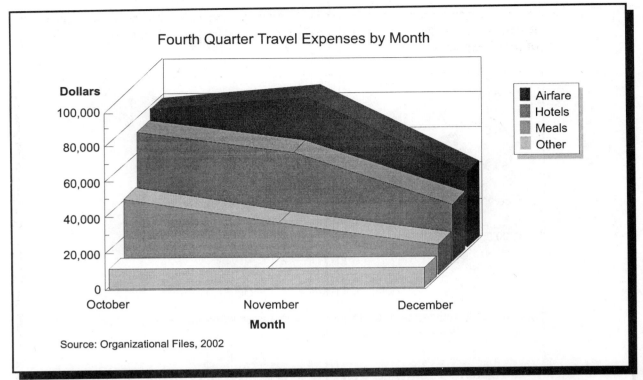

Figure 10-10. Area Chart

3. Never vary the size of the symbols; show comparison on the basis of the number of symbols. For example, you would not show a dollar symbol three times larger in one column than in another column.

4. Select the number of symbols to represent clearly the largest and the smallest quantities.

5. Rather than have more than one horizontal line of symbols, let each represent a larger number or amount so that fewer symbols are needed.

6. Avoid using a half symbol at the beginning. In fact, some chart makers portray a whole symbol for over 50 percent of a fractional value and no symbol if the fractional value is less than 50 percent. After all, pictograms are not meant to give precise information.

7. If a quantity is not large enough to have even a part of a symbol, use a dot and explain it in a note at the bottom of the chart.

8. Leave enough space between the lines to enable the readers to see the rows of symbols clearly.

The Envirotec's travel expenses for October are shown in a pictogram (Figure 10-11). A bag of money makes it easy for a reader to see what category is the most expensive part of travel expenses.

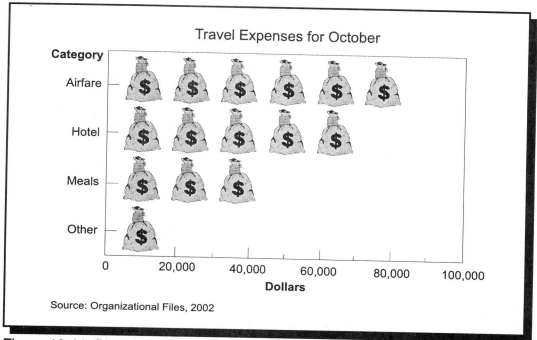

Figure 10-11. Pictogram

Some creators of pictograms advocate using different symbols for each category of information. Different symbols are used in Figure 10-12. Using different symbols, however, makes it more difficult for the report reader to draw comparisons from the visual data. The poor example of the pictogram (Figure 10-12) makes it difficult for the reader to interpret data. The goal of the report writer is to make data *easy* to read.

Maps

Any time geographic distribution needs to be visualized, no better graphic can be used than a map. A map can be drawn for an area as large as the world or as small as a part of a city.

Use these suggestions for drawing maps:

1. Select a plain outline map leaving out rivers and mountains unless they are pertinent to your message. If the map is a color map, you may wish to convert it to black and white unless you are using a color printer. Some objects in color on the computer monitor may print in solid black on a black and white printer.

   An adjustment for the printer may be needed so that the visual will be easy to read.

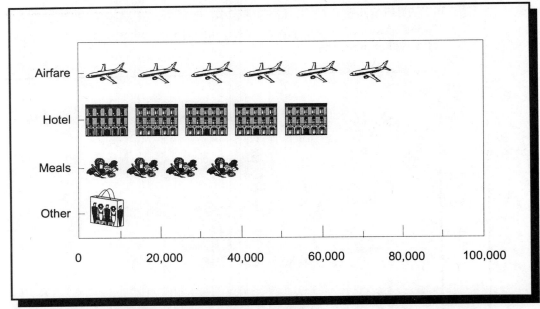

Figure 10-12. Poor Pictogram

2. Select bars, dots, circles, or other shapes to show sites at geographic points. You can even use symbols such as trees or buildings.

3. Draw lines if you want to indicate routes.

4. Use shading if you have large area sizes.

The stars on the map in Figure 10-13 represent the locations of the Envirotec offices in the United States.

Diagrams

To show a step-by-step procedure, use a diagram or flowchart. You can use symbols to represent the actual item as it flows along from one person or place to another. Use special symbols such as the American Standard flowchart symbols that are used in processing information by computer, or make your own. Most computer graphics programs provide a wide variety of symbols which can be used in designing a diagram. You may find it necessary to *rotate* or *flip* a symbol in order for it to look the way you want it to. In the diagram in Figure 10-14, the three-part arrow was rotated so that it would point in the desired direction.

Diagrams can be used to show analysis. Businesses, especially, use them to analyze their systems and procedures. The way orders are processed at Envirotec is shown in Figure 10-14. Diagrams are especially helpful in training documents and are frequently used when explaining procedures to persons who are not familiar with the company.

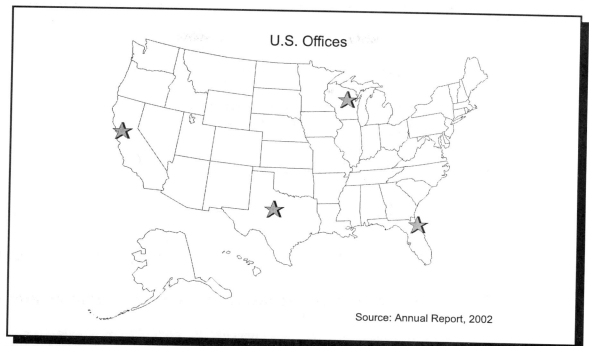

Figure 10-13. Map

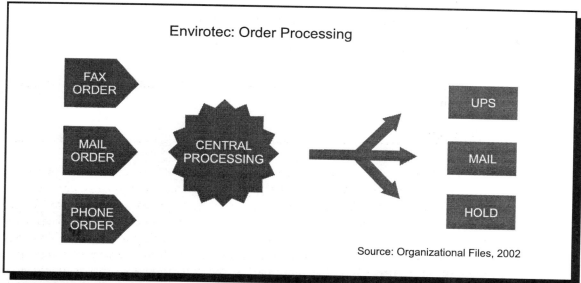

Figure 10-14. Diagram

Organization Chart

An organization chart is an effective device for showing lines of authority and span of control. Most computer graphics programs include an organization chart. To make an effective chart, follow these suggestions:

1. Place the box for the chief office at the top.

2. Place below the level of the chief office the boxes for the other positions that are on the same organizational level.

3. Continue with the remaining levels.

4. Join the boxes with solid lines to show lines of authority; use broken lines to show staff or functional authority.

5. Include the names of people as well as the names of positions unless the turnover is so great that including the names of people would be impractical.

Figure 10-15 is a partial organization chart for Envirotec. Several levels are included in the Information Systems branch while those positions are not included in Finance and Operations. A complete organizational chart may be quite large—especially if names are included.

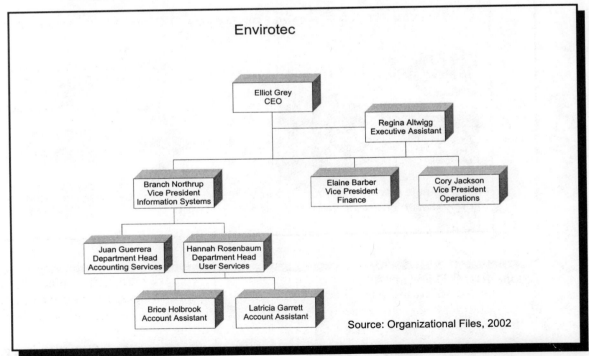

Figure 10-15. Organization Chart

Photographs and Drawings

In addition to the graphics you have seen in this chapter, photographs and drawings sometimes serve as means of presenting data in a report. Photographs and drawings can help readers to see locations and processes that cannot be described well in words. Annual reports are made clear, attractive, and interesting through the use of numerous colored photographs of products and people.

Interpreting Graphics

Even though most readers understand easily the information in a well-constructed graphic, some need help in interpreting part of it. To ensure accurate interpretation, write statements to call attention to specific points.

Without your comments, the readers may not recognize some significant meanings your information provides. Also, some readers may know so little about the particular data your report contains that you need to make interpretative comments so that they see the information in its true perspective. Write, therefore, an introduction and an interpretation of each chart, photograph, or formal table in your report.

Introduce each graphic before you present it. Use variety in the introductions, and emphasize the content rather than the graphic itself. Here are some effective ways to introduce the graphics in this chapter.

October, with $200,000 disbursed, was the most expensive month for travel during the fourth quarter (see Figure 10-1).

When examining travel expenses for the fourth quarter, Elaine Barber determined that over 18 percent was spent for meals as shown in Figure 10-5.

As indicated in Figure 10-13, the Envirotec offices, with four locations, are distributed geographically across the United States.

Orders at Envirotec are accepted by fax, mail, and phone. The order processing procedure is demonstrated in Figure 10-14.

Latricia Garrett and Brice Holbrook have the same supervisor, as shown in the organization chart displayed in Figure 10-15.

When you cannot place a graphic on the page with the introduction, place the graphic on the following page. Ideally, you would introduce the graphic, present it, and then interpret it. Because spacing often prevents this ideal sequence; part of the interpretation may precede the graphic, and part of it may follow the graphic.

No set of strict instructions can be given for interpreting the information in a graphic because no two graphics are identical and because the purpose for which reports are written differ. Always keep in mind the purpose of the report and point out significant meanings.

You may need to point out or explain trends, forecasts, or exceptions. Also, you may consider pointing out any of these factors:

similarities	high and low figures
patterns	top three figures
peaks	too low figures
troughs	mean
incongruities	median
changes	mode
number of classifications	total number of items in the graphic

You will not, of course, include all of these factors when interpreting any one graphic aid. Be sure to maintain an objective tone during your interpretation. You should point out logical information. *Do not insert your opinions in the interpretation of graphics.*

Although you show specific figures in graphics, avoid restating these specifics when interpreting nontechnical data. After all, unless a survey includes 100 percent of the population of the universe studied, the data can be only an approximation, anyway. Readers of nontechnical data are ordinarily more concerned with close approximations than with specifics, and they remember them longer. Therefore, instead of stating "This product was purchased by 31.2 percent of the residents," write such statements as "This product was purchased by slightly more than 30 percent of the residents." Or you may convert these percentages to fractions; thus "This product was purchased by almost one-third of the residents."

Do not use approximations in some reports. Accountants and others involved with budgets often expect exact figures.

Eliminate bias from your report, but help to make the meaning of the data immediately apparent by including interpretative words. You may, as an example, write "Only eighteen copiers were sold by J. Lemon last year" rather than merely state the fact, "Eighteen copiers were sold by J. Lemon last year." By including the word *only*, you tell the readers that eighteen is a small figure in comparison to expectations, to other periods, to other items, or to other sales representatives.

Instead of writing "Over 70 computers were purchased by the college in July," you may write "You may be surprised that over 70 computers were purchased by the college in July." The second statement helps to interpret, and it presents the fact interestingly.

Use interpretative words such as these judiciously. Remember that the purpose of your interpretation of a graphic is to help the readers to understand quickly the significance or proper meaning of the information you have collected and have studied carefully.

When you use graphics to simplify complex information or to add interest to a report, your readers will better understand the information you give them.

Presenting material in graphic form can enhance a report. Choosing the best graphic for any situation will make your reports easier to understand.

DISCUSSION

1. What factors would you consider in deciding whether to use a table or some other graphic to present data?

2. List some ways that graphics can be introduced to the report reader.

3. Why are pictograms often misleading?

4. What uses are made of organization charts?

5. Give some examples of subjects for diagrams.

6. Discuss the value of color in preparing graphics.

EXERCISES

1. Use a computer graphics program or a spreadsheet, database, or word processor with graphic capabilities for this problem. Make a pie chart and a bar chart of your choice. Be able to describe why you chose the specific chart type for your graphic.

2. In examining the graphs throughout the chapter, you may have noticed that October was the most expensive month for travel expenses, while December was the least expensive month. What factors do you think could cause these differences? Be ready to explain your ideas to other class members.

3. Discretionary income is that income left over after all expenses are met. Assume that you will have some discretionary income at the end of the month. Estimate how you will spend the extra funds. Present this information (or the actual amounts if you know them) in a pie chart.

PROBLEMS

1. Examine Figure 10-16, which is a bar chart for travel expenses of Envirotec. Be ready to explain how you would improve the chart.

2. The treasurer of an organization with whom you have worked has indicated that about 30 percent of the budget is for the meetings; 25 percent, for the programs; 20 percent, for the yearbook; 15 percent, for member recruitment; and 10 percent, for miscellaneous costs. Design a graphic that would better explain the status of the budget to the members of the organization.

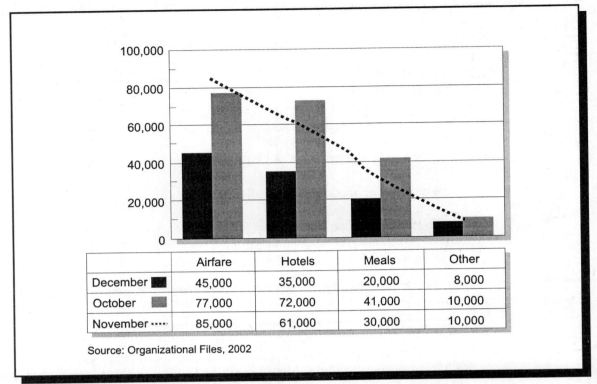

	Airfare	Hotels	Meals	Other
December ▇	45,000	35,000	20,000	8,000
October ▇	77,000	72,000	41,000	10,000
November ‧‧‧‧	85,000	61,000	30,000	10,000

Source: Organizational Files, 2002

Figure 10-16. Envirotec

3. When you interviewed the Jacobson family, you learned that their income for August was distributed this way:

Clothing	$700.00
Food	500.00
Insurance	400.00
Rent	900.00
Other	300.00

Present this information in an appropriate graphic of your choice.

4. Analyze the graphic in Figure 10-17. How could the readability and clarity of this graphic be improved. Prepare your suggestions for discussion in class.

5. Use a current almanac to collect some statistical information which could be used to prepare a line chart. Prepare a line chart and write an introduction for it.

6. Use the information in Problem 5 to prepare a stacked-bar chart. Hint: When using your computer graphics program, you may be able to select the data you have already keyed in problem 5 and copy it to the new chart.

7. Use the information in Problem 5 to design another graphic of your choice. You may wish to use only part of the data to prepare a bar chart or pie chart. Be sure to use your logic so that the chart makes sense.

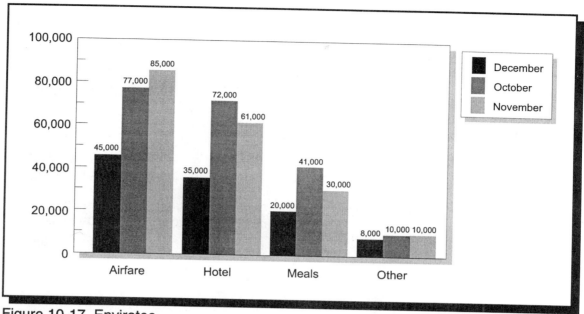

Figure 10-17. Envirotec

8.   Select a state of your choice. Choose a map. Place symbols for some of the key industries, tourist locations, or major cities on the map. Be ready to explain your decisions.

9.   Create an organization chart to show the proper relationships and lines of authority for a small business that employs people in these positions:

Chief Executive Officer
Vice-President, Finance; Vice-President, Production; Vice-President, Sales.
Two Executive Assistants report to the Vice-President of Sales.

10.   When you studied the company files, you learned the figures for the number of three-bedroom houses the Markham Construction Company built from 2000-2002. Present this information in a pictogram.

2000	12 houses
2001	28 houses
2002	20 houses

11.   Prepare a graphic of your choice (not a table) to show the number of video cameras sold by the Nguyen Appliance Store from 1999 through 2001. Those figures follow:

Model	1999	2000	2001
VHS	150	124	110
VHS-C	100	140	120
8 mm	70	100	150

12.   Write an introduction and an interpretation for the chart you prepared for Problem 11.

13. The student government association has asked for a report on traffic violations. You have obtained the following information about university traffic tickets written during the last school year. Design a graphic of your choice.

Group	Moving Violation	Wrong Zone Parking	Parking in No Parking Areas
Undergraduates	62	481	135
Graduates	20	300	101
Faculty	15	100	50
Staff	15	75	70

14. Write the introduction and the interpretation of your graphic for Problem 13 that you will include in your report to the student government association.

15. You are on a committee to improve a local tourist attraction. Use a regular, instant, or digital camera to take some photos of the attraction and use the photos to make recommendations on how the attraction could be improved.

16. Take a photo of your team that can be used on the cover page of your report.

WRITING EFFECTIVE REPORTS

- Are business reports more effective when color is used throughout the report? Describe the appropriate use of color in business documents.

- Reports frequently are written for superiors and may be forwarded to other people who are in positions of higher responsibility. What factors of courtesy should you consider when sending a report to your supervisor's supervisor?

Critical Thinking Applications

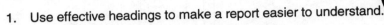

CHAPTER OBJECTIVES

After studying this chapter, you should be able to:

1. Use effective headings to make a report easier to understand.
2. Include transitions to tie your report together.
3. Write an effective informational, comparative, or analytical report.
4. Draw conclusions and recommendations based on your findings.
5. Assemble a report and all its supporting pages in correct order.

PREPARING PROPOSALS AND REPORTS

While the formal reports discussed in the last chapter are often required in business, writers are also frequently asked to prepare proposals and informal reports. Proposals and informal reports are similar to formal reports; each, however, has certain unique characteristics that will be discussed in this chapter.

Proposals

Proposals are frequently written documents in today's business. Some are written for readers inside the organization; others are written for people outside. A proposal is a sales medium; that is, it is used to sell an idea, a product, or a service. A proposal may be written to improve conditions and procedures, to increase business volume, or to secure funds for carrying out special projects.

When you write a proposal, write persuasively—not by appealing to emotions—but by presenting clear, specific, convincing information. Make your statements objective and realistic and support them with facts, figures, examples, testimonials, or whatever other evidence is needed to back up what you say.

A proposal writer may originate the idea for which the document is written, or the writer may respond to a *request for a proposal* (**RFP**) to supply a service or a product. Before you begin to write a proposal, study carefully the conditions that led to the desirability of writing it. Extensive, clear thinking is required before writing a successful proposal.

When you prepare a proposal in response to a request for proposal (RFP), by all means follow exactly the specified format. Use the specified headings in the sequence requested. These proposals are bids, and the receivers compare the various responses. You may include additional data that you believe will help to convince the readers your proposal is the one they should accept.

Write convincingly and confidently. Don't use a hard-sell approach, but provide strong support for all your statements. Assume that some readers may need to be convinced of the value of your proposal. Clear, easy-to-read, positive, courteous, well-supported statements are the best proof for the merit of your proposal.

When you originate the idea for submitting a proposal or when you have an RFP with no specified guidelines to follow, you are wise to take the following or similar steps:

1. Define the problem.
2. Discuss the problem.
3. Identify the requirements for carrying out the proposal.
4. Include a detailed budget.
5. Describe the proposed methods and procedures.
6. Define the expected difficulties.
7. Describe the proposed solution.
8. Describe the progress reports to be made.
9. Request approval.

Problem Definition

Define the problem or the need for the product or service you want to provide. You can interest the readers only when they are confident you understand the problem that exists or that you understand the product or service you want to provide. The readers may not realize that a problem exists or that they need your product or service.

Write concisely and at the same time precisely, clearly, and accurately. Use photographs, drawings, or any other graphics that help you to describe the situation that exists. Sometimes background information or a discussion of the way a problem developed is useful to the readers.

Problem Discussion

After defining the problem, discuss it to the extent that the readers will become interested and will be aware of the benefits they will derive. You may include calculations, samples, and messages from users of the service or product you propose or of other products or services you have provided. Place some of these materials (messages from users, and so on) in the appendix; but refer to them in this section of the proposal.

Requirements

Identify the tools, equipment, computers, qualified personnel, facilities, and any other support needed to carry out your proposal in a superior fashion. Identify specifically any support that you do not yet possess and supply sufficient evidence that you can acquire this support before it will be needed. You may provide facility specifications, computer capabilities, and other details that would help to support your statements that you have the resources necessary to excel in carrying out the proposal.

Place in the appendix resumes for the personnel who will hold decision-making positions in your proposed project. Prepare special resumes that highlight the capabilities needed for the particular project under consideration rather than use general resumes that may be used for other purposes also.

Include drawings of the layout of existing or of proposed facilities in those proposals for which the readers would likely want to see such drawings.

Budget

Include a detailed budget. Describe the materials needed and state the quantities; give the titles of the personnel to be involved and state the salaries they are to be paid; include a breakdown as well as a total for overhead expenses; and give detailed specifications and prices of equipment, materials, and facilities to be purchased. For all anticipated purchases, present proof that you can obtain the items at the proper times.

Estimate as accurately as you can your net financial gain to be derived from carrying out the proposal.

Methods and Procedures

Describe precisely the procedures you will follow to achieve the proposed objectives. Define each step clearly and specify the amount of time required to complete it. Specifying the number of days required for each step is better than giving a date for completing the step since one or more steps may be delayed because of action (or lack of required action) taken by the person or group for which the proposal is being carried out. Special conditions should also be addressed. For example, inclement weather could make a difference in how quickly a construction project could be completed.

Difficulties

Define the difficulties (if any) that you expect to encounter. Including this information would probably help you to convince the readers that you are realistic, that you have studied the situation carefully, and that you have had enough experience to know what to expect. Supply sufficient evidence to support your statements that even though these difficulties may arise you can fulfill your promises and achieve the stated objectives.

Proposed Solution

Your proposed solution may be stated in the section on procedures or in the problem definition or discussion. If the proposed solution has not been specified clearly with benefits pointed out to the readers, include a special section for it. Including a clearly stated positive solution is important for acceptance of the proposal.

Progress Reports

Include a schedule for making progress reports and specify the types of information each report will contain.

Approval Request

End the proposal with a confidently stated request for its acceptance. After you have written the first draft of the proposal, study it carefully to make certain nothing that would help you to convince the readers has been omitted. Also, make certain that everything you will need to fulfill your promise to carry out the proposal has been included. Hiring specialists to study the various phases of the proposed project is wise for those proposals for which large sums of money are involved.

Once you are confident that you have included all the desirable information, present it expertly. Make sure that the writing is convincing and that you use quality graphics and printing.

After you proofread the proposal with utmost care, sign the transmittal letter and other items (if any) that need to be signed. Make the desired number of copies of the completed proposal and present these copies—including the various appendixes—in an attractive manner. Using professional folders or binding the report are two presentation options.

Informal Proposals

Informal proposals can be submitted appropriately in letter form to individuals or groups outside your organization, and they can be submitted in memorandum form to readers inside your organization.

A lawn service company has designed a letter proposal for a townhome owners' association which is shown in Figure 11-1.

A well-written proposal will provide an opportunity for an idea to be implemented. Consultants who contract with companies frequently operate by writing proposals which clearly state the services they will provide and the costs involved. While proposals suggest new ideas or products, informal reports have many uses.

Informal Reports

Informal business reports are written for various purposes and can be classified by the purpose of the report. Reports—whether they are routine (periodic) or special—may be written to show progress; to evaluate products, services, procedures, or performance; to recommend action, products, personnel, and so on; or merely to present information.

Progress

Progress reports tell readers about the progress being made on a project or with an activity. Telling the owners or the future tenants about the status of the construction of a new building or the renovation of an old one is an example of progress report.

Other situations on which progress may be reported include those involving personnel recruitment; advertising campaigns; fund-raising drives; and sales of products, insurance policies, and so on. Progress reports are written for readers outside as well as for those inside an organization.

Evaluation

Evaluating is a basic management function. Evaluating products, equipment, services, procedures, and personnel must be done from time to time to continue dynamic business operations. When evaluation reports are made, decision makers analyze the results. Desirable features can be continued, while changes that are needed can be recognized. Changes may involve personnel, procedures, or any of the other factors that have been evaluated.

Grass is Always Greener Group
1347 Seabright Drive
Santa Ysabel, CA 92070

April 1, 2002

Mrs. Bonita Durwood, President
Vista Valley Homeowner's Association
149 Bright Lane
Santa Ysabel, CA 92070

Dear Mrs. Durwood

This letter will serve as our proposal for providing lawn services to the thirty townhome owners in Vista Valley. Neat, attractive, and uniform lawns add to both the prestige and value of a property development.

Basic Services

After reviewing the current lawn situation at Vista Valley, our proposal is to begin mowing all the lawns on the same day once each week beginning on May 1. The lawns will be mowed and the grass bagged and removed. The lawns will also be edged. Our high speed blowers will ensure a finished look for each home.

Maintaining the lawns on a weekly basis will not be necessary when the cooler weather of fall occurs. However, our temperate climate requires some lawn attention throughout the year. We propose to cut the lawns every two weeks from September 1 through November 1. After November 1 we will periodically examine the situation and cut the lawns as needed throughout the winter.

Extended Services

In addition to the basic services, your homeowners may be interested in some additional features. We can fertilize the lawns in the fall and early spring. We can also take care of shrubs and basic maintenance of flower beds. Trees can be examined each season for evidence of disease.

Personnel

Our firm employs 10 full-time grounds keepers as well as 25 part-time on-call workers. In order to provide maximum service, we would prefer to cut all 30 lawns on the same day. We will send out the appropriate crews to accomplish this activity. Most of our residential customers prefer to have their lawns cared for during the week so that they can enjoy them uninterrupted on the weekends.

Figure 11-1. Letter Proposal

Mrs. Bonita Durwood
Page 2
April 1, 2002

You may wish to contact some of our current customers including South Street Medical Center and the Dawn's Point Homeowner's Group. We have maintained the lawns of those two clients for the last three years.

Contract Length

We propose a two-year contract from May 1 through April 30 of the next two years. However, we would provide a contract cancellation clause at the end of the first year if either party was dissatisfied with the arrangement.

Costs

Due to the large number of lawns involved in this project, we are able to offer you a reasonable price for cutting each lawn. Our proposal is as follows:

Basic Services	$30 per home owner for each lawn cut
Extended Services	$45 per home owner for each lawn cut

Each homeowner will receive a statement after each lawn is mowed. Homeowners may choose to have the basic service or the extended service. However, once either plan is chosen it may not be altered until after the first year.

I would be happy to be present at the next meeting of your homeowner's association to answer any questions about the proposal. You may contact me at (909) 560-4109 if you need further information.

Sincerely

Justin Bartlett

Justin Bartlett
President

Figure 11-1. Continued

Recommendation

The management team requires information and ideas from one another and from individuals on other levels of the organization structure, as well as from people outside the organization. Some recommendation reports, therefore, are sent at the request of management; others are sent voluntarily.

A recommendation report usually begins with the recommendation, which is followed by facts that support it. When, however, the writers have justification to believe the readers will not readily accept the recommendation, they wisely present the facts in a convincing way first and then present the recommendation.

Because of the psychology involved in communication, guidelines only—not cut-and-dried-rules—can be followed effectively for writing any type of report, except for the simplest routine reports.

Announcements

Effective communication requires many announcements from management personnel. Announcements may involve scheduling meetings and planning sessions. Other announcements discuss mergers, new branches, promotion, transfers, proposed or adopted changes in schedules and employee benefits, new products or services, and scores of other activities.

Information

In addition to announcements, other reports are written for the sole purpose of transmitting information. The memorandum in Figure 11-2 was written to send information to a young executive who had been told a day or two earlier that she was being promoted.

Information is sent often through the various possible directions (upward, downward, and horizontal) for communication flow.

Formats

Formats for informal reports vary. They include memorandums, letters, and others.

Memorandums. Memorandums are the most frequently used reports by many groups. Because memorandums are for use inside the organization, they are quite informal in both format and writing style. Use the format shown in Figure 11-2 or in Appendix B.

Use a ***short, specific subject*** for your memorandum to help the reader immediately identify the purpose. The subject line later serves for filing identification. Capitalize the first letter in each word in the subject line except articles, conjunctions, and prepositions.

The ***message must be independent***: no part of it can depend on the subject line. For example, if you should have this subject line *SUBJECT: Meeting for First-Line Supervisors*, you could not mention merely the meeting in the message. You would have to identify the meeting as that for first-line supervisors. This practice is followed for all headings in any kind of report. The reason for this apparent duplication is that some readers focus only on headings while others skip headings and look at the text. As you will not know which type of reader will look at your report, you must include both headings and complete text.

Accuracy, completeness, conciseness, and courtesy are as important for internal messages as for those that go outside the organization.

Letter Reports. Letters—not memorandums—are often written to report information to people outside the organization. The format for these reports, which always include a subject line, is the same as that for other business letters. (See Appendix B for letter format.) As in the case with memorandums, no part of the body of the letter can depend on the subject line; the subject line serves as a guide, but the message has to be complete by itself.

When writing the letter report, use a conversational style of writing. Do not use special abbreviations and other in-house terms that may confuse people outside your organization. Include simple graphics that help make the report effective. A letter report is shown in Figure 11-3.

Often, letters are used for short recommendation reports. The usual pattern of a recommendation report is to first provide the recommendation and then to list an explanation or the reasons for the recommendation.

Multiple-Page Reports. Any of the reports described in this chapter may be more than one page, though most memorandums and letters are only one or two pages. In many instances an informal report that is longer than two pages should be written in a format similar to the one in Figure 11-4 and should be sent with a transmittal letter to the readers.

As a general rule, busy executives and others will, with very little hesitation, spend the time necessary to read a well-written short letter or memorandum. Persuasion is required, however, to get some of the intended readers to read a long report. Neatness, correctness, and interesting writing style are of utmost importance in encouraging people to read business reports. In addition to these features, which have already been discussed, organization and headings improve the readability of your report.

Good organization is especially important for business reports that are several pages in length. The ideas should be presented in a logical order so that the readers can grasp them quickly and easily. These three steps, which have been recommended for many years, still apply:

1. Tell what you are going to tell.
2. Tell.
3. Tell what you have told.

The ***tell what you are going to tell*** section should follow the report title. Make a few statements to get the readers' attention and to introduce the topics to be covered. Introduce the topics in a way that will create reader interest and help you to present the message in a logical, well organized way.

In some reports you may ask questions that will be answered in the body of the report, you may make statements that will surprise the readers, or you may simply make statements in which you feel the readers will be interested. Choose the strategy you believe is best for the particular report and for the intended readers.

The ***tell*** section is the body of the report. In this section discuss the topics in the order in which you introduced them. The degree of thoroughness with which you cover the topics should, of course, be determined by the purpose of the report, the characteristics of the readers, and the other factors involved.

MEMORANDUM

TO: Lakisha K. Jackson, Marketing Research Analyst

FROM: Bailey J. Lourds, Vice-President for Marketing   *BJL*

DATE: October 5, 2002

SUBJECT: Duties of Assistant to Vice-President for Marketing

Lakisha, congratulations on your promotion to Assistant to Vice-President for Marketing. I am looking forward to working with you when you assume your new duties on October 15.

As we discussed in the interview process, your duties will revolve around three distinct areas: budgets, market research, and motivation.

Budgets

As you know, it is important that we prepare a budget for each new product. We must pay special attention to these factors:

1. The cost of creating the product.
2. Advertising the product in newspapers and magazines, on the radio and on television.
3. The time and the expenses involved in helping our salespeople to know the product thoroughly.

Market Research

To compete with other companies and to continue to make a fair profit, we must increase our level of research. Your innovations and your ability to work well with the other analysts will enable you to excel in this area.

Motivation

A continuing activity, of course, is that of motivating the sales force. I want you to assume the primary responsibility of keeping the morale high and of detecting problems to be solved. You have already convinced me that you have excellent skills for this kind of work.

When I return on October 12, we can talk about the computer we plan to buy. In the meantime, be thinking about the furniture we should order for your new office, which will be in Suite 407.

Figure 11-2. Memorandum Report

West Town Roof Repair
148 Belle Vista Drive
Seven Corners, VA 22044

March 14, 2002

Mr. Edward D. Davis
1234 West Baybrook
Seven Corners, VA 22044

Dear Mr. Davis

SUBJECT: Replacement of Roof at 804 Ninth Avenue

As we agreed, a new roof will be installed at your property at 804 Ninth Avenue. The price we discussed was $3,000 for the complete job. Our progress to date is as follows:

1. New gray shake roof tiles have been ordered and should arrive within the next seven days.
2. A four-person crew has been lined up to begin removing the old roof on March 22.
3. The estimated completion date for the new roof is March 30.

Should you have any questions about this roof replacement, please contact me at the above address or by phoning (316) 227-3490. Thank you again for considering us for this project.

Sincerely

Wayne Ray Cookston

Wayne Ray Cookston
Manager

Figure 11-3. Letter Report

To ***tell what you have told***, summarize the key points you presented in the body. A short summary of the topics you have discussed serves as a quick review and as a desirable reinforcement for the ideas. This type of ending also helps the readers to perceive the proper relationships that exist among the major points. The report in Figure 11-4 contains the features discussed in this chapter.

For a multiple-page report, headings should be added to contribute to easy reading and comprehension. Such features encourage busy executives to read these longer reports immediately rather than to defer reading them until they have completed their other tasks. Follow the same headings guidelines for short reports that you use for formal reports.

Purpose of Formal Reports

Formal reports may be written for people inside the organization or for those outside. Usually, formal reports for internal use will go to persons above you in the organizational structure. Consistent good writing helps you win the confidence of your superiors.

Well-written reports may provide you an opportunity to show your supervisors how well you can perform. Business employees who write well have a distinct advantage over their peers who are equally well qualified except for the ability to write well.

Approach the report with your best efforts, therefore, and make your reports concise, thorough, attractive, interesting, and easy to understand.

The writing style for formal reports can be compared to the third-person writing style you may have used when writing in your English courses. In formal business reports you should:

1. Not use first person pronouns such as *I, me, my, myself, we, us,* and *our.*
2. Minimize the use of the second-person pronouns *you, your,* and so on.
3. Avoid contractions.

Because formal reports are usually long, three techniques are used to make reading easier: ***headings*** and ***transition techniques*** throughout the text, and ***additional pages*** (title page, table of contents, and so on).

Headings

Headings help readers to see at a glance how the information is organized and to know what to expect to read. In addition, headings help readers to locate the point at which they are to resume reading after an interruption. Headings also help readers to find specific sections they wish to reread and they assist readers who do not need to read the entire report in finding the sections they wish to read.

By organizing your reports well, you will probably have two or more paragraphs following each heading. In some cases, however, you may need a heading for only one paragraph.

Introduce headings to prepare the readers for the various subtopics and to make smooth transition—a feature that contributes to easy comprehension. For some reports all the headings of a section may be introduced in the first paragraph of the section, or a heading may be introduced in the last sentence of the paragraph preceding the heading.

Meeting Your Conference Requirements

Carter Hotel Convention Facilities

for

Chairs of the Convention Planning Committees

by

Linda L. Grant, Account Executive

Carter Hotel

October 16, 2002

Figure 11-4. Short Report

October 16, 2002

CARTER HOTEL CONVENTION FACILITIES

The Carter Hotel can provide a pleasant meeting environment for your conference. You will find our meeting rooms and exhibit area suitable for the diverse interests of your group. Our newly redecorated bedrooms and suites will also provide a relaxing atmosphere for your conference participants. Other conference groups have found our excellent catering service, convenient recreational activities, and effective reservations and registration procedures quite acceptable.

Since our hotel was opened nearly twenty years ago, we have hosted an average of two and one-half conventions a month. The attendance for these meetings has ranged from 73 to 546. In addition to our almost ideal location, carefully planned and efficiently operated facilities contribute to the unusual appeal our hotel has for many groups.

ROOMS AND FURNISHINGS

Some of our specially planned convention facilities are meeting rooms, exhibit areas, and bedrooms and suites.

Meeting Rooms

All the meeting rooms are on the first floor of the east wing and have easy access to the corridors, the rest rooms, the exhibit area, the parking lot, and the registration area. Each of the nine meeting rooms is fully carpeted, well lighted, and expertly decorated. The electrical outlets are spaced so that any ordinary appliance or piece of equipment can be used in any section of the room.

Each room is equipped with a temperature control switch and a lighting switch that permits the occupants to adjust the brightness of the lights to produce the desired effect for whatever activity is under way. The seating can be arranged for dining, and it can be arranged in theater style or in conference style. Some rooms are designed to be used individually; others can be combined.

Individual. Five meeting rooms are used individually. Each room will seat twenty-four persons in a conference room arrangement or forty persons when the chairs are arranged in theater style. Meals are served in only one of these small rooms; twenty persons can be served there.

1

Figure 11-4. Continued

Combinations. Four meeting rooms can be used individually, or any of them can be combined by opening the electric folding doors that separate them. Each room will seat 75 persons for dining or 150 persons by arranging the chairs in theater style.

Exhibit Area

A large exhibit area that is 116 by 130 feet is between the group of five small meeting rooms and the group of four large meeting rooms. This location is ideal for organizations meeting in any of these nine rooms. The electrical outlets are spaced 10 feet apart across the entire exhibit area.

Our sales manager will instruct Randall Brothers, a local firm, to provide any special items you need for exhibits.

Bedrooms and Suites

The 600 spacious guest rooms and suites have new plush carpets and Shaker-style wooden furnishings. Each room is equipped with a color cable television, a radio-alarm clock, a telephone, and a beverage bar. Standard-size beds are in the 300 rooms that have two beds. King-size beds are in the 290 rooms that have one bed each.

The ten suites—each of which consists of a large parlor, a bedroom, two bathrooms, and two dressing areas—also have king-size beds.

To meet the needs of guests, approximately 50 rooms are non-smoking rooms and 15 rooms are on the ground floor and are equipped to meet the standards of the Americans with Disabilities Act.

SERVICES

Outstanding catering service, recreational activities, and expert handling of room reservations and registration activities enhance the appeal of our hotel as a convention site for a group of any size.

Catering

Banquets, luncheons, breakfasts, receptions, and special meal functions at our hotel are catered by Bensen, Inc., a well-known organization. Our sales manager can arrange an appointment for any group representative to discuss menus. For any menu that you choose, the food will be excellent, while the price will be reasonable.

2

Figure 11-4. Continued

Recreation

The recreation manager will reserve tickets for you to take the regularly scheduled tours of the city, and she will arrange special tours for groups of four or more. She will also reserve tickets for you to any local theater. We are within five blocks of the three leading theaters in the city.

Classical musicians and guest artists perform nightly in our main dining room. Our pool-side sandwich buffet features music of the fifties and sixties on Friday and Saturday nights.

Reservations

All you have to do to reserve guest rooms for those attending your conference is to send us a list of their names and addresses. Or if you prefer that they make their own room reservations, we will send you a supply of forms they can use. We will confirm each reservation within one week from the time we receive it.

Registration

We provide a special registration center in the main lobby which includes tables, computers, and any other equipment you may need to register those who attend your convention. You may deposit the money you collect for registration fees in our safe for overnight protection.

SUMMARY

The five small meeting rooms, the four large meeting rooms, the 600 bedrooms and suites—along with the ideally situated exhibit area—accommodate large conventions as well as small ones. These physical features; the recreation we provide; and services such as catering, handling the reservations, and handling the registration activities account for the fact that we have hosted an average of two and one half conventions a month since we first opened our hotel.

3

Figure 11-4. Continued

Use headings to highlight **key points**, but do not rely on the heading to discuss the points. The content of a division must always be independent of the heading it follows. People who read the report text but skip the headings should obtain as thorough an understanding of the report content as they would if they read the headings, too. The headings, therefore, must be restated or paraphrased in the text that follows the headings.

While the APA style provides for five levels of headings, most business report writers should not need more than three levels. *Centered main headings* should be reserved for major sections of the report. *Underlined side headings* should be used for divisions within each major report section. *Text headings* are used only when a section with underlined side headings should be discussed in two or more subsections. Here is an example of the three types of headings.

Centered Main Headings

Centered main headings in the APA style are typed in uppercase and lowercase letters and are centered horizontally. They are not underlined.

Underlined Side Headings

The next level of heading is the underlined side heading that begins at the left margin. This type of heading is typed in uppercase and lowercase letters and is underlined.

Text heading. The rest of the paragraph immediately follows the text heading. In this level of heading, unlike the earlier headings, only the first word of the heading is capitalized. A period follows the heading.

Use short headings that indicate the **key ideas** for the sections that follow. Use consistent, parallel style; that is, if you use a word or a phrase once, use a word or a phrase for each heading of that level in the report. Or if you use a sentence for one heading, use a sentence for each heading at that level within the report. Sentence headings can be statement headings that tell the reader what the paragraph is about. Observe the headings in the following illustration.

Word or Phrase Headings	Statement Headings
Use of Proposed Equipment	Nearly One Hundred Businesses Would Use Equipment
Types of Work	Sales Presentations, Training Sessions, and Report Graphics Are Key Uses
Trainers	One Additional Trainer Will Be Needed

While headings provide the general organization plan for the report, proper transition is needed for coherence and smooth reading.

Transition Techniques

Several techniques may be used to make a transition within a report. For example, a transitional sentence placed immediately preceding or following a heading provides a transition between report sections.

Transition is also important from one idea to another within report sections. Techniques that are useful for internal transition include reference pronouns, numbered items, and transitional words or phrases.

One way to connect related ideas and achieve coherence is to use reference pronouns by making a statement and referring to it in the next sentence.

The trucks are in good condition. They were purchased last year.

Numbering items, as in the next illustration, leads the readers through a series of steps or ideas.

Most of the funds were spent on these steps: (1) testing, (2) drilling, and (3) blasting.

Transitional words or phrases such as *however, moreover, further, in addition, as a result, for that reason,* and *on the other hand* help readers to relate thoughts. Transitional words are best placed after the beginning of a sentence, however, unless they are emphatic. Examples are shown here.

She completed the new project by using the approved guidelines. They were revised, **however**, on July 1.

The managers found that the Model 8 was not fast enough for their work. They will, **therefore**, order the Model 9.

The bricks the architect recommended for the new office building were not available. **For that reason**, we chose those identified in the revised specifications.

Good transition, carefully written sentences, well-constructed paragraphs, precise wording, appropriate headings, accurate documentation, and other details of the mechanics of writing help to make the information you present meaningful to the readers.

Additional pages supplement the report body and enhance the readability of a report.

Additional Pages

Additional pages are placed both before and after the body of the report. Usually, the pages that precede the report body include these:

1. Title page
2. Transmittal letter or memo
3. Contents page
4. List of figures
5. Executive summary

The additional pages that follow the report body include the reference page(s) and possibly an appendix (or appendices). The reference materials are called references, works cited, or bibliography (depending on the documentation style you use).

The content and the preparation of the preliminary pages and the reference materials are discussed later in this chapter. The formal reports discussed in this chapter are those that are written to inform, to analyze and to recommend.

As you study the report parts, you will observe that many of them—preliminary pages and reference materials, especially—are the same as those used for formal informational reports. The body of the report includes the introduction, presentation of data, and summary, conclusions and recommendations.

Introduction

A strong introduction to the report will set the stage for understanding the findings of your research. The introduction portion normally includes an introductory paragraph or paragraphs, the purpose of the report, elements of the problem, definitions of terms (when necessary), research procedures, and scope and limitations. The report reader can better understand the report topic by reading these items.

Introductory Paragraphs. Write an introductory paragraph or two to attract the readers' attention and to encourage them to continue reading. Here is an example:

> The number of small businesses that use the computer services center has increased rapidly since 2000. Even though two additional systems were added last year, the users keep the equipment operating twenty-four hours a day six days a week. Within the past three months, several of these computer users have inquired about color printouts of graphics presentations. They need graphics services, but they cannot justify purchasing the equipment or software required to produce quality color printouts of their presentations.
>
> Should the center provide color printing capability of graphic presentations for these computer users?

If the readers are already familiar with the problem, include only a little background material. On the other hand, if some readers know little about the problem, give a more detailed explanation—but keep the explanation as concise as possible. Readers do not like to read a long introduction.

The introduction should lead naturally into the ***purpose of the report***, which is also known as the ***statement of the problem***.

Purpose of the Report or Statement of the Problem. State the problem or the objective of the report clearly so that the readers will easily understand what you are attempting to convey. Example:

> The purpose of the report was to determine the feasibility of adding color copying and printing capabilities for presentation graphics to the computer center.

Elements of the Problem. Some statements of the problem may be followed by a list of elements or factors that result from analyzing the problem statement. Examples follow:

> To determine the feasibility of adding quality color copying and printing capabilities to the computer center, answers to these questions were needed:
>
> 1. How many businesses would use the new features?
>
> 2. For what kinds of work would they use color?
>
> 3. Would the center be used more heavily at some times than at others?
>
> 4. How many trainers should be hired?
>
> 5. What type of equipment and software would best meet the needs of the clients?
>
> 6. How much would the equipment and software cost?

Questions asked in this section should be answered in the body of the report in the order in which they are asked. Therefore, the list of questions should have a logical sequence because they will determine the organization of the body of the report.

Definitions of Terms. When you have to use terms that have special meanings in a particular report, define those terms. For only one to three terms, define each one in parentheses immediately after it appears the first time in the report. See the following examples.

> Sales in the Western region (California, Oregon, Washington, Nevada, and Utah) declined by 15 percent over the first quarter.
>
> When using a PDA (personal digital assistant), complete information is critical to the success of the operation.

When you have several terms with special meanings, include a list such as this one:

The following terms are defined as they are used in this report:

Sales territory—An area of the U.S. domestic market consisting of five states.

Western Region—Includes California, Oregon, Washington, Nevada, and Utah.

Southern Region—Includes Florida, Georgia, Alabama, Mississippi, and Louisiana.

Part time employee—A person who works fewer than 27 hours per week and is not eligible for benefits.

Use parallel structure for the definitions; that is, if one definition is a fragment, the others should be fragments. If one definition is a complete sentence, the others should be complete sentences.

Research Procedures. The extent to which you cover the procedures used in collecting and analyzing information for a formal report should be based on the desires of the readers and the nature of the report. In some special purpose reports, you should describe the research method so clearly that if readers should question the validity of your findings, they could conduct the research again if they wanted to do so.

Some readers who know the researchers well and who are convinced their methods are sound prefer to have only a brief description of the research method. In such a case, they would consider a detailed description a waste of time for both the writers and for the readers. When you question the degree of coverage to present, you may be wise to present somewhat more information than is necessary rather than to present less than is needed.

The following description of the research method is for a report using primary research.

Stacy K. Fenton, director of the computing center, prepared a questionnaire (see Appendix) and mailed it to each of the 227 small businesses that have used the computing center since it was established in 1997. Within ten days, 156, or 68.7 percent, of the users returned a completed questionnaire. Seven of the computer center users that did not complete a questionnaire have merged with other organizations.

The questionnaire responses were tabulated by computer, and the results are shown in graphics and narrative in this report.

Scope and Limitations. For some formal reports, a paragraph or two may be needed to define the scope and to identify limitations. The scope sets the boundaries of the report and tells what is included. Limitations include applicable factors which may affect the report results. Limitations such as a short time frame, a small amount of money available, and/or a minimum of existing information may be mentioned to let the readers know why the report is less comprehensive than they otherwise would expect it to be. Be careful to include these factors only if they seriously affect your ability to prepare a complete report; do not use such limitations as excuses for failing to complete your assigned task.

For many reports, the statement of the purpose or objective of the report makes the discussion of the scope and the limitations unnecessary. If the purpose statement is so complete that the reader fully understands the scope and limitations of the report, additional discussion is not necessary. If, however, the reader may be unclear as to what to expect in the report, a descriptive statement is helpful.

Having prepared the readers by writing a concise, relevant, thorough introduction, you are ready to present the information you have gathered.

Presentation of Data

The best approach to writing the report is to answer any research questions. You will wish to use graphic aids when they assist the reader in interpreting the data of the report. The facts, analyses, and interpretations in the report body serve as evidence that the purpose or objective of the report has been achieved.

The report body may be only one major division of the report, or it may be divided into two or more sections. Each division should then be subdivided as appropriate. In typical business reports, the main body of material is presented in a logical, a psychological, or a chronological plan.

Logical. In the **logical** plan, which is used most frequently, major ideas are presented first with the details following. The information of lesser importance follows in descending order of importance. The logical plan works best on straightforward topics where most report readers are expected to agree with the results of the report.

Psychological. For the **psychological** plan, the information is presented according to the effect the facts are expected to have on the readers. The facts that will interest the readers most and engage them positively in the report are presented first, while the facts the readers are likely to disagree with are placed last.

The psychological plan may work best for reports in which readers are likely to disagree with your findings, conclusions, and recommendations. An explanation of the facts is given first, followed by the findings.

Chronological. The **chronological** plan is best when the readers need to know what happened in a time sequence or what events took place that resulted in certain effects (cause to effect). Because this plan is not direct and does not emphasize the most important elements, readers have to work harder to interpret and understand the significant points.

Conclusions and Recommendations

Prepare the conclusions and recommendations section of the report after you study carefully the information you gathered through primary and/or secondary sources. First, summarize the major points of your findings. Then draw conclusions and make recommendations on your interpretation of that information.

<u>*Conclusions*</u>. A conclusion is a statement of what a finding or a combination of findings means. To draw a conclusion, ask yourself, "What does this finding mean in relation to the purpose of the report?" By summarizing all the most significant findings of your study, you can base your conclusions on the information in the report. Analyze all findings thoroughly and study all possible relationships that exist among them. On the basis of this thorough study, draw conclusions that are not only logical but also valid.

The following conclusion was drawn from the executive summary of a report.

> The research findings revealed that adding a color copying and printing feature would provide at least two advantages: (1) offer a needed service for our clients and (2) upgrade our equipment and technology with the newest products.

Conclusions are usually located toward the end of the report after all of the findings of the research are presented. As conclusions are based on your interpretation of the data, you should keep them together in one location rather than scatter them throughout the report. This arrangement makes it easier for the reader to see what your findings were and what your interpretations were.

<u>*Recommendations*</u>. Base your recommendations on the conclusions—and obviously on the findings—drawn from your study. When you make alternative recommendations, present them in the order of feasibility according to your best judgment. You would normally place your most important recommendations first followed by those of lesser value.

> The recommended actions are to (1) purchase four full-color copying systems to meet the diversity of our clients, (2) schedule arrival of the systems at the beginning of the month when usage is expected to be low, and (3) hire a graphics consultant who can train our personnel in the appropriate use of color in graphic presentations.

After the body of the report is completed, you are ready to develop both the preliminary pages and the reference pages.

Preliminary Pages

After you write the report body, prepare a summary. Then prepare the preliminary pages which include a title page, letter or memo of transmittal, contents page, list of figures (when several graphics are used), and an executive summary.

<u>*Title Page*</u>. Prepare an attractive, well-arranged title page to include the report title, the name of the person or the organization for whom the report was written, the name(s) of the writer(s) of the report, and the date on which the report was completed. Make the title concise and descriptive of the report contents. The title is, in most instances, a phrase. An example of a title page is shown in Figure 11-5.

**THE FEASIBILITY OF A COMPANY RETREAT
FOR EMPLOYEE DEVELOPMENT**

Prepared for

Mr. Branch Northrup
Vice President for Information Systems
Envirotec Corporation
Dallas, Texas

Prepared by

Brice Holbrook
Latricia Garrett
Account Assistants

October 1, 2002

Figure 11-5. Report Sample Title Page

Transmittal Letter. Write a letter (or a memorandum) to transmit the report to the person for whom it was written. Identify the report and tell when and by whom you were authorized to write it. The reactions of some readers are usually affected by knowing who authorized you to write the report. For example, if a top-ranking official in the organization authorized it, the readers tend to realize quickly the need for the report.

The transmittal letter or memo serves as a document which shows when the report was finished and transmitted. You may mention a few of the most significant, the most surprising, or the most interesting findings; but do not clutter the letter by including many of them. Your specific assignment, your knowledge of the situation, and your relationship with the readers will enable you to determine the extent to which you include opinions. If the letter is used with an analytical report, you may wish to mention some of your conclusions and recommendations. Figure 11-5 has an example of a transmittal letter.

Contents Page. Prepare a contents page, which shows the page numbers where each heading of the first two levels begins. Text headings are usually omitted from the table of contents. The headings on the contents page should ***exactly match*** the headings in the report. You should use *leaders* (a series of periods and spaces) to connect the words and numbers in order to improve the readability of your contents page (see the contents page in Figure 11-5).

List of Figures. For a long report that contains three or more graphics, a list of these figures should follow the contents page. This list may be placed at the bottom of the contents page if sufficient space exists, or it may be placed on a separate page. If your report has both tables and figures, make a list of each. Check Figure 11-5 for a sample of the list of figures.

Executive Summary. Most readers want to see an executive summary of a long formal report before they read the entire report; and some of the readers read only the summary with its conclusions and recommendations.

In the summary, restate or paraphrase the statement of the purpose or the objective of the report and mention—but do not describe in detail—the research procedures used. Include the most significant findings and recommendations that resulted from your research; and integrate these concisely worded statements for smooth, easy-to-understand reading. Do not include any information in the summary that is not included elsewhere in the report.

An example of a report summary for an analytical report is shown in Figure 11-5.

After you have finished the preliminary pages, you will be ready to complete the reference materials, which follow the body of the report.

Reference Materials

Reference materials—which may include references, bibliography, or works cited and an appendix—follow the body of a formal business report. Review Chapter 8 or Appendix B of this text for the correct format for the documentation style you choose.

Place in the appendix copies of questionnaires, checklists, and other instruments used in collecting data for the report. You may also place in the appendix such details as formulas and illustrations not essential to the report text. When you include several items, you may letter them Appendix A, Appendix B, and so on.

Report Sample

The following formal analytical report is an example of a report using the APA style of documentation which was discussed in Chapter 8.

ENVIROTEC
P. O. Box 7258613
Dallas, TX 77650

October 1, 2002

Mr. Branch Northrup
Vice President for Information Systems
Envirotec Corporation
P. O. Box 7258613
Dallas, TX 77650

Dear Mr. Northrup

We are pleased to send you our report on the feasibility of company retreats for staff development purposes that you requested on August 26.

The report identifies the advantages and disadvantages of the company retreat and also includes our conclusions and recommendations. We conducted telephone interviews with training directors from twelve organizations of comparable size and mission. Additionally, we surveyed 100 Envirotec employees—25 at each branch—to determine employee interest in participating in a possible retreat. We also investigated secondary print and electronic sources for general information on company retreats.

Most companies have used some form of employee retreat for staff development purposes. The specific purposes, format, and audiences, however, varied greatly. In our opinion, a carefully planned retreat could be a useful training program for Envirotec employees.

When you have reviewed the report, Mr. Northrup, we will be glad to discuss it further with you.

Sincerely

Brice Holbrook

Brice Holbrook
Account Assistant

Latricia Garrett

Latricia Garrett
Account Assistant

Figure 11-5. Report Sample continued

Contents

iii

Figure 11-5. Continued

Figures

Figure 11-5. Continued

Executive Summary

This report analyzes the feasibility of Envirotec using employee retreats as a training program for staff development. The report was requested by Mr. Elliott Grey, CEO of Envirotec, and authorized by Mr. Branch Northrup, Vice President for Information Systems, Envirotec.

Research for the report was conducted in three ways: (1) telephone interviews were conducted with the training directors of twelve comparable organizations to determine whether they had used employee retreats for training purposes, (2) a survey of 100 company employees—25 from each branch—was administered to gauge employee interest, and (3) secondary print and electronic sources were investigated to determine current trends in company retreats.

Consistent with information obtained from secondary sources, the interviewed training directors report using employee retreats in various forms for staff development. The most frequent audience for development retreats was mid-level management, although some companies have used the retreat format successfully for motivational training of employees at all levels within the organization.

The majority of Envirotec employees surveyed indicated an interest in this form of staff development. Most expressed a preference for half-day retreats held at the work site.

The following recommendations are presented in this report.

1. Company retreats should be a component of Envirotec's comprehensive training program for employees.

2. The retreat should be scheduled as a one-day program at an off-site location.

3. Based on employee preference, the initial retreat should be content specific to improve job performance.

v

Figure 11-5. Continued

The Feasibility of a Company Retreat
for Employee Development

For many years, company retreats have been used by a variety of companies for employee training and development. These retreats have addressed the needs of top-, middle-, and lower-management personnel. In recent years many training consultants have developed specialized retreat programs and have marketed them to companies nationwide. The objectives for these programs appear to be to provide either content specific or motivational instruction.

<u>Purpose</u>

This study was requested by Mr. Elliott Grey, CEO, and authorized by Mr. Branch Northrup, Vice President of Information Systems, of the Envirotec Corporation. The research was conducted by Brice Holbrook and Latricia Garrett to determine the feasibility of using employee retreats as a staff development training program for Envirotec employees.

Conclusions and recommendations were based on the following questions:

1) How are company retreats used for staff development?
2) What are the intended outcomes of such training?
3) What retreat formats appear to be most successful?

<u>Procedures</u>

Research for the report was conducted in three ways. Telephone interviews were conducted with the training directors of twelve comparable organizations in the four cities where Envirotec offices are located: Dallas, Texas; Jacksonville, Florida;

1

Figure 11-5. Continued

2

San Francisco, California; and Green Bay, Wisconsin. A summary of the interviews is included in Appendix A at the end of this report. Additionally, 100 Envirotec employees—25 from each branch office—were surveyed to measure employee interest in company retreats as a form of staff development. Those responses are also summarized and included in Appendix B at the end of this report. Other supporting information was obtained via the Internet and from current journals and related publications.

Scope and Limitations

The findings presented in this report are limited to that data that are directly related to Envirotec Corporation and its interest in employee retreats. No attempt was made to address the relevance of employee retreats that might be suitable for other types of industries.

Company Retreats

Companies have used some form of employee retreats since 1905 when Dr. Weston Leon of the Regis Brick Works decided to have his supervisors meet in a neighboring city to review the time and motion studies of their employees. Since that time retreats have been held by companies throughout the United States in order to provide opportunities to better focus on company plans for the future (Smythe, 1997).

Traditionally, company retreats have been provided for top management personnel and have been viewed as perquisites for effective management. These retreats were typically held in exotic places and featured such leisure activities as golf, sailing, tennis, and polo (Happiness is…, 1997). Today, however, company retreats are much more serious. Bill Gates of Microsoft feels that a retreat should not be a retreat from work but rather a retreat from the office environment (Gates, 1996).

Figure 11-5. Continued

3

Reasons for Retreats

Many reasons are given for providing company retreats. Among these reasons are an opportunity to interact without distractions, an environment for socializing with colleagues, an ability to work with others for team synergy, and a venue for intensive training in a specialized area (Emery, Valmont, & Ridley, 1997).

Researchers found in a study of 100 corporate retreats that the primary reason to hold a corporate retreat was to work on new product development without distractions. No interruptions produced an environment conducive to planning and creativity (Dalton & Melton, 1998).

Twelve training directors from companies located in Dallas, Jacksonville, Green Bay, and San Francisco were interviewed by telephone to determine their use and recommendations concerning corporate retreats in their areas. Of those contacted 83 percent had held corporate retreats in the last five years. When asked for what reasons corporate retreats were held, the training directors indicated three primary reasons. As indicated in Figure 1, product development was the most frequently listed topic followed by synergy and planning.

Figure 11-5. Continued

4

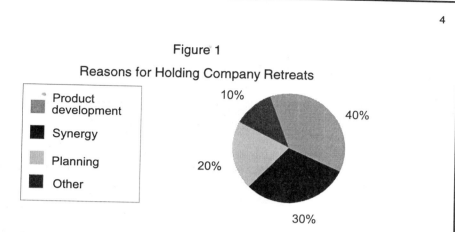

Figure 1

Reasons for Holding Company Retreats

Source: Training director interviews, 2002

Outcomes of Retreats

Company retreats quite often result in revitalized employees and greater team synergy. Teamwork, collaboration, common goals, and problem solving are often emphasized in the retreat program. Participants are given the opportunity to interact in a non-threatening environment and to brainstorm solutions to current and potential problems within their work setting (Robinson, 1998).

Over 60 percent of the Envirotec employees surveyed indicated a strong interest in gaining something from a retreat that would help them in their job performance. In addition, new product training and leadership development were the top two choices for retreat topics. Figure 2 indicates the most frequently selected retreat topics. Respondents identified their top two preferences; therefore, 200 responses are given.

Figure 11-5. Continued

5

Figure 2
Topics for Company Retreat

Topic	Number	Percent
New product training	64	32
Leadership	52	26
Motivational speakers	44	22
Company goals	22	11
Recreational activities	12	6
Team sports activities	6	3
Total responses	200	100

Source: Company survey, 2002.

Format of the Retreat

The company retreat can be arranged in a number of formats ranging from a two-hour session held on-site in a company conference room to an extensive two-day retreat held at an off-site luxury resort. Most companies choose some option in the middle. Other factors to consider include group size, cost, and facilitators (Carter, 1998).

Location. Some retreats are held on-site while others are held off-site within easy driving distance. The main advantage to the on-site location is convenience and lower costs. Minimal time is spent in traveling to the retreat location, and site costs are primarily fixed. Expenses for on-site retreats are then limited to costs for speakers, facilitators, supplies, and refreshments (Carter, 1998).

Off-site retreats are usually more favorably received by executives and less favorably received by other employees. As a result, a number of companies have chosen to fly their corporate executives to retreats as far-flung as Cancun, Mexico; or Montego Bay, Jamaica. Choices often depend on the preferences of executives involved in planning the retreat and on the perceived motivation for employees to attend the retreat. In 1997, the top corporate retreat was Hilton Head, South Carolina (Tarrant, 1998).

When surveyed, Envirotec employees favored an on-site location by a slight margin. The results were 42 percent on-site, 38 percent off-site, and 20 percent undecided.

Figure 11-5. Continued

6

Length. The most common length suggested for a retreat is one day (Carter, 19980. Employees of Envirotec were asked their preference on the length of the retreat. the greatest number (48 percent) preferred a one-half day retreat while 32 percent indicated the one-day format. Further results are shown in Figure 3.

Figure 3
Preferences for Retreat Format

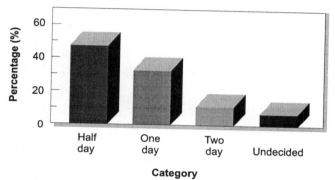

Source: Company survey, 2002.

Group size. Depending on the desired outcomes for the retreat, group sizes may vary from five to five hundred. However, if active participation is desired, groups of fewer than 12 are the ideal size (Gates, 1996). For team synergy, the complete work team should be included necessitating a larger number of people at the retreat (Emery, Valmont, & Ridley, 1997).

Figure 11-5. Continued

A large number of participants (more than 100) can easily be grouped into smaller work teams to accomplish the purposes of the retreat. When forming groups special care should be taken to provide diversity in personalities, experiences, and skill levels (Smythe, 1997).

Cost factors. Costs for retreats may be included in the overall training department budget or may receive special funding from other corporate resources. Systematic planning and budgeting is essential if corporate retreats are to be meaningful components of a company's training program (Carter, 1998).

Cost factors will vary significantly depending on location, length, and group size. A cost not often included that should be factored into the total picture is the employee replacement cost. That cost is the value of the employees' time which is being reallocated from regular work duties to retreat activities (Dalton & Melton, 1998).

Other cost factors to consider include fees and expenses for facilitators and speakers.

Facilitators. The retreat will need facilitators to organize small group sessions and to handle all of the details of the program. Some facilitators may serve a dual role as speakers or session leaders. Facilitators may be company employees, or they may be professional trainers or consultants.

Facilitators should be carefully selected for their personality, leadership, motivational ability, and technical expertise. In retreats where sensitive company issues will be explored, a decision will need to be made about whether non-company facilitators would be suitable (Happiness is…, 1997).

Figure 11-5. Continued

8

Conclusions

Based on the primary and secondary data evaluated in this report, the structure and purpose of retreats varies widely in corporate America. However, retreats are considered a viable component for corporate training programs.

The majority of companies surveyed have conducted employee retreats during the past five years. These retreats varied in purpose, length, and location.

Although the employees of Envirotec indicated that they favored a half-day format for a retreat, research indicated the most common length for corporate retreats is one day.

Other studies have found off-site locations to be preferable for providing training; Envirotec employees by a narrow margin, however, preferred an on-site meeting place.

Recommendations

Based on the above conclusions, the following recommendations are given:

1. Company retreats should be a component of Envirotec's comprehensive training program for employees.
2. Although a slim majority of employees preferred an on-site meeting place, the retreat should be scheduled as a one-day program at an off-site location, as supported by the secondary research.
3. Based on employee preference, the initial retreat should be content specific to improve job performance.

Figure 11-5. Continued

9

References

Carter, S.D. (1998). <u>The guide to the successful corporate retreat.</u> Atlanta, GA: Nolan Publishing.

Dalton, R.E., & Melton, T.R. (1998, February 15). Getting away from e-mail, fax, and phone. <u>Daily Dispatch</u>, pp. 6C, 12C.

Emery, J.R., Valmont, N.E., & Ridley, G.A. (1997). Corporate retreat: Asset in the workplace? <u>Resource Management Journal, 3</u>(2), 84-89.

Gates, B. (1996). Office 'retreat' should be work. <u>New York Times Special Features</u>. Retrieved May 14, 1998 from the World Wide Web: http://computernewsdaily.com/live/Gates/284_101096_114004_15635.html.

Happiness is golfing on company time: A look at corporate retreats. (1997, October 15). <u>Manager-at-Work</u>, pp. 70-76.

Robinson, M. J. (1998). Teambuilding experience. Retrieved May 14, 1998 from the World Wide Web: http://kanweb.com/triad/.

Smythe, B. E. (1997). Corporate retreat reenergizes the company. <u>Issues in Management, 4</u>(10), 191-198.

Tarrant, V. N. (1998). Top ten corporate retreats. <u>CEO Newsletter, 7</u>(2), 2-3.

Figure 11-5. Continued

10

Appendix A
Summary of Telephone Interviews with
Directors of Training

The appendix contains a summary of the telephone interviews conducted with twelve selected Directors of Training.

1. Have you held employee retreats for training programs during the past five years?
    _10_ Yes   _2_ No

2. To what audience did you direct your retreat?

    _3_ Top management   _2_ Middle management
    _2_ Supervisors   _2_ Training directors
    _1_ All employees   _2_ Not applicable

3. What primary topics were covered in your retreat program?

    _4_ Product development   _3_ Synergy   _2_ Not applicable
    _2_ Planning   _1_ Other

4. Where were your retreats held?
    _4_ On site   _6_ Off site   _2_ Not applicable

5. What was the average length of your retreat?
    _3_ Half day   _7_ One day
    _0_ Two days   _2_ Not applicable

Figure 11-5. Continued

Appendix B
Summary of Envirotec Employees' Surveys

This appendix contains a summary of the 100 responses provided by Envirotec employees.

Retreat Questionnaire

Please answer the following questions expressing your opinions and ideas about attending a company-sponsored retreat.

1. Have you ever attended a company retreat in your work history?
    _25_ Yes   _70_ No   _5_ Unsure

2. Would you be interested in attending a company sponsored retreat?
    _65_ Yes   _20_ No   _15_ Undecided

3. My preference for attending a company retreat would be
    _42_ on site   _38_ off site   _20_ undecided

4. My preferred length for a company retreat would be
    _48_ ½ day   _32_ 1 day   _12_ 1½ days   _8_ 2 days

5. Check your top two choices for topics at a company-sponsored retreat.
    _52_ Leadership   _6_ Team sports activities
    _22_ Company goals   _64_ New product training
    _12_ Recreational activities   _44_ Motivational speakers

6. I would prefer a small number—perhaps 10 at the retreat.
    _25_ Yes   _40_ No   _35_ Undecided

7. I would prefer a retreat limited to members of my department.
    _30_ Yes   _30_ No   _40_ Undecided

8. It is important that I learn something in the retreat that will help me in my job performance.
    _60_ Yes   _25_ No   _15_ Undecided

Figure 11-5. Continued

DISCUSSION

1. Name some types of business activities that might call for a RFP?

2. What are some examples of informal reports that were not mentioned in this chapter?

3. How can using a computer assist in recurring types of informal reports?

4. What are the advantages of using memorandums instead of letters for internal communication?

5. What are some types of proposals which would be practical for a college student to write?

6. Should a writer of an employee evaluation consider any legal or ethical situations? If so, what might they be?

7. Why is the executive summary section placed *before* rather than *after* the body of a formal report?

8. List some items that could be placed in a report appendix.

9. Describe some appropriate ways to include definitions of specialized terms in a formal business report?

EXERCISES

1. You have been asked to write a formal analytical report on employment for recent college graduates in your major. Conduct secondary research by reviewing five companies that employ graduates in your field. You may wish to examine their annual reports or other information about the companies. Conduct your primary research by interviewing five recent college graduates about their employment search. Your report should include information about the companies as well as any conclusions or recommendations about the job search process.

2. Write a formal analytical report on an issue that affects you and/or other students at school (campus computer labs, access to facilities, library hours, parking areas, or others). Use both primary and secondary data.

3. You have noticed that a number of students in your class do not bring books to class and you have wondered whether they actually own books. Conduct a study by using primary and secondary research to determine how textbooks are used in your class and/or college. In your secondary research, you may wish to focus on changing

costs of producing and marketing books. Write a formal analytical report for your instructor.

4. Identify a business problem (perhaps at your place of employment). Conduct primary and secondary research to investigate possible solutions to the problem. Write a formal analytical report.

5. Your student government association has set aside $1000 for a service or improvement project for the campus. The leadership of the organization has asked concerned students or groups to submit RFP's to determine the best use of these funds on campus. Write an RFP to describe your ideas for using the funds.

6. Redbird Crafts is an established store for those interested in hobbies and crafts in your community. The manager of Redbird Crafts is Rachel Blackwood. The store will soon be moving to a new larger building and a portion of the space will be set aside for displaying completed craft items for sale. As the space is limited, she would like to be able to have a variety in the crafts displayed as well as a consistent supply of new items as current ones are sold. Ms. Blackwood is asking that RFP's be submitted so that she can evaluate proposals. She has no specific guidelines for the RFP. You and a friend have a craft that would be eligible for this program. Write an RFP discussing the hobby or craft items you could provide.

7. Your local Chamber of Commerce is considering establishing a *Business Break-Away* program. The idea is to schedule a day trip during the week that would be a combination of business and socializing. Each trip would include a visit to a local business or one within reasonable driving distance in the morning, a luncheon at a suitable location, and an afternoon visit at another business. Transportation would be needed for those businesses outside the community. The Chamber would like to keep the first efforts small with no more than 25 participants in each event. The Chamber is looking for a director for this program who would schedule the event, recruit participants, and collect a modest fee that would cover the cost of the luncheon and any transportation. The Chamber has a budget of $500 available to start this project. As a member of the Chamber of Commerce, write the RFP detailing your ideas for the first event as well as providing other information for how you would conduct the program if you were selected as director.

8. An organization, of which you are an officer, has completed a number of activities throughout the year. You are planning a membership drive. Compose a memo describing how much the organization has accomplished. Include specific figures and statements about the year's work. The club secretary will send a copy along with recruitment information for each interested person.

9. You have noticed a pressing issue on campus which affects a number of students. After you have collected some research, organize your solution and write a proposal to the student government association. If your proposal will involve an expenditure of funds, estimate what the costs will be.

10. You are a hobbyist who enjoys woodworking. Your recent project involves making wooden cars that are about 8 to 10 inches long. You frequently paint them to match your friend's cars. One of your friends thinks that you should put an ad in the paper and take orders to make personalized cars. You have all the patterns you need to take your friend's advice. Write a letter-memo which you can use to send out to potential respondents to your ad. Mention the types of cars you can (or cannot) make, indicate costs, and also include an estimate of the time it will take to fill an order after it is placed.

11. At your workplace you have noticed that some of the beginning workers have difficulty with a task that you feel you have mastered. Write a memo report with a detailed set of instructions to accomplish the task. You may wish to include diagrams if necessary.

12. You and a classmate are interested in providing security for homes whose owners are out of town. Your idea is to work as a team and visit the homes a couple of times a day, check the appliances, check the door locks, feed any pets that are staying at home, etc. Work with your classmate to write a proposal which would detail the types of activities you could do and what the costs would be. This proposal would then be used to present a professional appearance to potential clients.

13. Your small photographic shop can now provide a new service. You can design personalized calendars. Your customer would provide 12 photos or negatives to be used for each month of the year along with a list of family holidays such as birthdays and anniversaries. Your equipment could accommodate up to 25 such events. You will then generate a personalized calendar which could be used as a Christmas gift or for personal use. In order to have the calendars for Christmas, you need to have the orders by November 1. Write a letter report which describes this service which you can send to some of your regular customers.

14. You have decided that you would like to hold a reunion with some of your friends. You plan to try to convince about 10 of them to join you for a spring break event. You are not quite sure if you want to go skiing in the mountains or if you want to go to the beach. Write a letter-report to be sent to your friends which will detail the location, costs, dates, and any other relevant data.

15. Your company office employees have expressed dissatisfaction with the poor interior and exterior lighting in the new five-story office building you moved into four weeks ago. The office workers for the five other groups that are leasing office space in the building have expressed the same concern. Your company owns the building. Study the situation carefully and write a letter to the president to describe the situation and to recommend corrective action. (The president needs to know the types of jobs that have to be performed so that he can explain them to the builder.)

16. In your sales position you are doing a lot of traveling across the metropolitan region and are frequently caught in traffic delays. You have been using your own personal

cellular phone to keep your business moving during traffic delays. You have found the service so helpful that you feel that the company should purchase cellular phones for all of its sales people who are on the road at least fifty percent of the time. Write a proposal to your supervisor discussing advantages, disadvantages, and costs of this plan.

17. You have had extensive experience in babysitting. In fact, you still do babysitting on an occasional weekend. In talking to mothers, you have discovered that many young babysitters really do not know how to handle situations that may occur. You would like to provide a workshop for potential young babysitters to give them more confidence. Your local recreation center is always offering short courses for a modest fee. Write a proposal to the recreation center, describing the workshop you would like to offer including the fee that you would charge. Include desired outcomes and objectives for the workshop as well.

PROBLEMS

1. *Envirotec*

You have been appointed to the task force on which Brice Holbrook and his associates have been studying employee compensation, including fringe benefits. The charge to the task force is to research what other companies are doing and to conduct some appropriate primary research.

First, conduct the secondary research. [You may wish to conduct this assignment by yourself or with some other members of the class.] Select three organizations; research the employee compensation and fringe benefits for the executives. Envirotec is interested in providing these benefits: life insurance, health insurance, retirement plan, and stock purchases. You may also include other benefits if you wish.

After you have completed the secondary research, you are ready to begin the primary research. Your primary research could be conducted in a number of ways. *Be sure to check with your instructor before beginning primary research as many colleges have special procedures that must be completed before research can begin.* **Any** of these options or ideas of your own might be relevant:

- Survey benefits managers of corporations in your area.
- Interview executives in a variety of companies to determine what combination of employee compensation and fringe benefits they would prefer.
- Survey managers to determine the current status of their benefits.
- Conduct an experiment by writing several similar job descriptions including variations in compensation and benefits. Ask managers which positions they would prefer based on the job description. Try to determine if benefits made a difference in the positions selected.

After you have completed your secondary and primary research, you and/or your team are ready to write a formal report. Use a documentation style of your choice or one mentioned by your instructor (see Chapter 8 for details). Be sure to include the following:

1. Title page
2. Transmittal letter or memo
3. Contents page
4. List of figures
5. Executive summary (Be sure to include conclusions and recommendations you and/or your team have made.)
6. Body of report (with findings, conclusions, and graphics)
7. References (or Works Cited or Bibliography)
8. Appendix (should include form used for primary research)

You should include within the body of the report at least one table and two graphics. Suggested graphics might be a bar chart and a pie chart. Be sure to introduce the visual aids to the readers before they see them in the report. The best approach would be to use a computer package to create the graphics.

2. *The Lindoro Company*

The Lindoro Company is a United States company whose major product is cellular phones and communication technology. While the company's products have been successful in this country, Lindoro is interested in expanding to international markets. With the passage of NAFTA, Lindoro would like to provide cellular phones and communication technology to Mexico and Canada. In addition, with the consolidation of the European Community, Lindoro would like to be able to provide similar products and services in Europe.

The Lindoro Company has asked you and other class members to conduct a study of the international market to find the best location to start selling phones. The company executives plan to begin selling to one international market and then to expand to others. You and the other class members have decided to divide the secondary research into group projects. Each group will prepare a formal report that will discuss the opportunities for selling cellular phones and communication technology in a particular market. The markets for the study include the following:

1. Canada
2. Mexico
3. France
4. Germany
5. Italy
6. United Kingdom

When conducting the secondary research, you may find government documents helpful in providing information about doing business in specific countries.

You may wish to conduct the primary research individually, as a team, or as a class as a whole. The Lindoro Company is always attempting to improve its cellular phone, which could be especially important before expanding to an international market. Interview several users of cellular phones (the brand of phone does not matter). Determine the features they find most important on a cellular phone. In addition, ask about any features they would like to have that their current phones do not have.

The Lindoro Company would like to know the following about each of the countries.

1. Is there a market for cellular phones and/or communication technology?
2. Are there any specific laws or regulations that may affect Lindoro's efforts to conduct business internationally?
3. What type of support might be expected in the country? For example, should Lindoro export phones to the country or plan to build them in the country?
4. What is the best approach to selling the product? For example, will Lindoro need to have a sales staff in the country?

You and your team should write a formal analytical report on your assigned country. Be sure to include all the preliminary pages as well as an appendix with your primary research instrument. After you have presented the results from your primary and secondary research, draw appropriate conclusions and make recommendations based on your findings. The Lindoro Company will examine each group report to determine the best market for international sales.

COMPOSING BUSINESS DOCUMENTS

■ What nonverbal communication message does a mistake in spelling send to the reader? Is correct spelling still important to communication success when spell checkers and grammar checkers are available in most computer programs? Why or why not?

■ English has been called the language of international business. What steps, if any, could a writer of documents in English take to be sure that all readers understand the message?

■ Describe courtesy and tact and the role they play in communicating in business.

COMMUNICATING CLEARLY

The primary objective for any message is to communicate so clearly that the message cannot be misunderstood. The style of expression that we choose can improve our chances of clear communication or it can reduce the success of our messages. Our writing style should be interesting and cordial enabling the receivers to concentrate on the content of the messages rather than on the way we transmit them.

Two people may convey the same message in entirely different ways. One message may have a positive, personable style, while the other may be accurate but less appealing. Language styles are the ways in which people express themselves. The way we express facts, ideas, and feelings is important—whether we express them orally or in writing.

The message we send is affected by the way we organize our thoughts into words, sentences, and paragraphs. Choosing the appropriate words for the situation, combining those words into meaningful sentences, and organizing sentences into coherent paragraphs form the basis of effective communication.

Four techniques that contribute to the clarity of communication are: (1) focusing on the reader, (2) adapting your writing style, (3) selecting words carefully, (4) constructing readable sentences, and (5) developing meaningful paragraphs.

Consider the Reader

Most people find it easier to write a message to a person with whom they are acquainted. That is because they can visualize the person who will receive the message, and they can phrase their sentences to meet the reader's level of interest, knowledge, and personal style. While it is not always possible to communicate with people with whom we are acquainted, we should still attempt to visualize the reader as we plan our message. Placing ourselves in the position of the readers will enable us to draft a letter or memo that will be acceptable to others. Factors to consider are reader references, reader viewpoint, courtesy expressions, nondiscriminatory language, and conversational tone.

References to the Reader

People enjoy personalized attention. They appreciate your using their names in your correspondence to them. Refer to people, therefore, by using proper names and well-chosen nouns and pronouns.

Written messages can be personalized by including proper names—Mr. Gardner, Linda Pipkin, Harold, Ms. Robertson, for example—within the body of the message. Observe the use of proper names in the opening sentence of a letter as illustrated below.

- *Thank you, Mr. Knop, for your assistance in selling our house.*
- *Yes, Alvis, the meeting has been rescheduled.*

If you often use the name of the person with whom you are talking, use the reader's name in a letter or a memorandum. If you seldom use people's names when talking with them, avoid using their names in the body of a letter or a memorandum. To do so would make your message sound unnatural.

Whether or not you use a person's name frequently in conversation, use the reader's name in the salutation of a letter if possible. (Letter salutations are discussed in Appendix B.) Do not, however, use the reader's name in the first sentence of a letter when you use a salutation. Read aloud the following statement. You can readily recognize the inappropriateness of using the name in both the salutation and the first sentence.

- *"Dear Mr. Harris: The bid you submitted, Mr. Harris, was accepted at our board meeting yesterday."*
- *"Dear Lisa: Your order, Lisa, arrived today."*

Do not assume all people wish to be addressed by their first name. An acceptable practice is to use the surname unless you know the reader would prefer the use of a first name. Use of a person's first name (especially a person who is not a close friend) can lead the listener or reader to believe you are insincere.

Selecting the appropriate words, tone, and channels for the message will be an easier task if you know your audience.

Reader Viewpoint

Instead of phrasing your message to show writer/sender benefit, show how the receiver will be affected. By doing so, you stress the *you* attitude. Be careful to avoid insincerity and flattery when showing reader benefit. By phrasing your message in words and tone that you would want to hear if you were the receiver, you should be able to form a sincere message that other readers would want to hear. Compare these examples.

"I" Attitude	"You" Attitude
I was happy to hear of your new store opening.	Congratulations on the opening of your new store.
We are sending you the floppy disks that you ordered today.	Your order for 10 dozen floppy disks was shipped this morning.

Courtesy Expressions

Expressions of courtesy are as important in the written word as in the spoken word. Nonverbal communication provides many opportunities to demonstrate courtesy in oral communication; whereas, only words are effective in expressing courtesy in a written message. Those words should be chosen carefully and used at the proper times.

Courtesy expressions including *thank you, please, grateful*, and *appreciate* are used frequently in business messages. Saying *thank you* shows your respect and appreciation for the reader. Excessive use of these expressions, however, leads the receivers to believe the speaker or writer is insincere, is using flattery, or is "talking down" to them.

Another way to express courtesy and to show reader benefit is to be tactful in word choice. Do not accuse, show surprise, express doubt, or pass judgment. Consider these examples.

Tactless	Tactful
If you had read the instructions that accompanied your new water dispenser, you would have known that you should replace the filter every thirty days.	As you will see from the instructions enclosed with your new water dispenser, the filter should be replaced every thirty days.
I am surprised that you had a problem installing your new water dispenser. Most of our customers do not have such problems. *or* Obviously you overlooked the instruction manual that was included with your new water dispenser. Had you read the instructions, installation would have been simple.	To install your water dispenser properly and ensure a long service life, refer to the instructions on page 36 of your manual. Most of our customers find these easy-to-read instructions complete. If, however, you have a question regarding your particular situation, please call our consumer hotline, 1-800-555-4357.
The failure of your new water dispenser to function properly is obviously due to faulty installation.	Could the problem with your new water dispenser have been created during installation? Please refer to page 36 of the instruction manual to verify that all steps were completed in the installation process. If not, simply remove the dispenser and reinstall it.

Nondiscriminatory Language

Any word that directs attention to a particular group of people may be considered discriminatory. Select words carefully to avoid gender, racial, age, or disability discrimination.

Gender Discrimination. Referring to only one gender when either sex may be the appropriate reference is called sexist language. Because sexist language offends some people, it should not be used. Traditionally, our language used noun and pronoun references to males when referring to people in general. That is not the case today. Use male noun and pronoun references only when they apply to men; similarly, use female nouns and pronouns when references apply to women. Several options are available to the writer in eliminating sexist language. Consider these alternatives: use non-gender specific nouns, use plurals, omit pronouns, restate nouns, or include both masculine and feminine pronouns.

Sexist Language	Option	Revision
The *salesman* demonstrated the stereo.	Use non-gender specific nouns	The *sales person* demonstrated the stereo.
Each student should submit *his* assignment.	Use plurals	Students should submit *their* assignments.
Each student should submit *his* assignment.	Omit pronoun	Each student should submit *the* assignment.
Coffee was served by the flight attendant. *She* also distributed peanuts to the passengers.	Restate noun	Coffee was served by the flight attendant. *The attendant* also distributed peanuts to the passengers.
Each student should submit *her* assignment.	Use pronouns for both genders	Each student should submit *his or her* assignment.

Racial Discrimination. Unnecessary references to one's race or ethnic group are another form of discrimination. Do not make such references unless the designation of race or ethnic group is the intended message. Compare these sentences.

Discriminatory Language	Nondiscriminatory Language
Charlene Lowery, the black secretary, received the Employee of the Month Award.	Charlene Lowery received the Employee of the Month Award.
The Hispanic reporter from TVTN covered the news conference.	The reporter from TVTN covered the news conference.

Age Discrimination. Unnecessary references to ages may also be discriminatory and should be avoided. Unless one's age is relevant to the message, any reference to it is inappropriate.

Discriminatory Language	Nondiscriminatory Language
John Morris, the 59-year-old coach, led his team to the championship.	John Morris led his team to the championship. *or* John Morris, the coach, led his team to the championship.
The young secretary returned my call.	The secretary returned my call.

Disability Discrimination. Another sensitive area of discrimination affects persons with disabilities. Emphasize the individuals and their abilities instead of their disabilities. Avoid using the following terms when referring to persons with disabilities.

- disabled, handicapped, afflicted
- unfortunate, victim, abnormal

Using nondiscriminatory language throughout your message will help the readers and listeners to concentrate on the content of the message rather than on the way you present it.

Conversational Tone

Letters, memos, and informal written reports should be written in a conversational tone. Use the same first- and second-person pronouns, contractions, idioms, current expressions, word choices, and concise wording that you use in oral conversation.

Personal Pronouns. Business reports are typically written using third-person pronouns while letters and memos use first- and second-person pronouns. These pronouns provide a conversational tone for the message. By following basic guidelines for using personal pronouns, you can produce conversational communication.

When making a company presentation or using letterhead stationery, you communicate as a representative of the organization that is identified through your presentation or in the letterhead. The pronouns we, us, our, and ours mean the group that makes up the organization you represent and is identified in the letterhead. Use these personal pronouns, therefore, instead of such expressions as our firm, our company, and our organization.

Eliminate the use of such wordy, impersonal, third-person expressions as "Triple J Transportation welcomes the opportunity to transport your merchandise" when you are communicating as an employee of the Triple J Transportation. Instead, say "We welcome the opportunity to transport your merchandise."

Use second-person pronouns to refer to the receiver of your message. When the receiver represents a particular organization, use such expressions as "We welcome you as a customer" instead of stilted expressions such as "We welcome your company as a customer" or "We welcome the Triangle Broadcasting Company as a customer."

Use the personal pronoun *I* when it contributes to conversational tone. The tone of your message should express an interest in the listener or reader. This interest, frequently referred to as the *you attitude,* can be established more naturally by using *I, we,* and *you* than by omitting these pronouns and thus creating a telegraphic style. "Appreciate letter of April 17" contributes less to displaying the *you attitude* than does "Thanks for your letter of April 17."

Contractions. Used in oral presentations, meetings and group activities, electronic communication, routine letters to people with whom you correspond regularly, and memos to people within the organization, contractions may add a natural, conversational tone to business messages. Limit your use of contractions in letters about employment and in those to a person whose background is not familiar to you.

When deciding whether to use contractions, keep the receiver in mind. You want the receiver to concentrate on the content of the message rather than on the delivery or writing style. If you believe the reader would like contractions, use them.

Choose contractions carefully. Such contractions as *don't, doesn't, it's,* and *won't* seem natural and in good taste for informal business messages. On the other hand, do not write such contractions as *I'd* and *you'd* since they are not commonly used in written messages.

Idioms. Well-known idiomatic expressions contribute to the conversational tone of business messages when the receiver is likely to apply the same meaning to the expression as the sender intended. When writing to someone who requested your help because of having business financial problems, the expression "When you are on your feet again" sounds not only conversational but also positive and pleasant. This idiom expresses the feeling you wish to convey. Countless other similar expressions can, when well chosen, contribute to the tone you want the message to have.

Avoid the use of idioms in international communication; most people who do not have English as their primary language attempt to interpret idioms literally. That is, a business person from Japan could interpret your statement, "When you are on your feet again," to mean "You must stand before we will help you."

Keep these points in mind when using idioms:

1. A reader who is not familiar with the idiom may be confused by your message. For example, some people may use the word *soda* to refer to a soft drink, while others may use the word *pop*.

2. If the idiom can have different meanings in different contexts, the reader may misinterpret your expression and thus make your otherwise well-written message convey an idea entirely different from the one you intended. For example, the phrase *crack the window* could be taken literally!

Be especially careful about using idiomatic expressions in messages pertaining to contracts, topics about which people are especially sensitive, and other situations in which goodwill may be adversely affected.

Current Expressions. Compare the following two columns of frequently used business expressions. As you can see, the expressions in the *outdated* column are archaic and do little to improve the overall message; the words in the *current* column are better for conversational tone. They are clear, short, and tactful.

Outdated	Current
Enclosed is	Here is
Enclosed herewith	Here is
Due to the fact that	Because *or* Since
Enclosed please find...	... is enclosed
Attached please find...	... is attached
advise *or* inform	tell
self-addressed envelope	addressed envelope
to be of service to you *or* to be of assistance to you	to help you
at the present time	now
Respectfully yours *or* Yours truly	Sincerely *or* Cordially
can be found on page 6	is on page 6

Select Words Carefully

Because your primary objective is to speak or write **so clearly that your message cannot be misunderstood** and you want the receiver to be favorably impressed by the message, select the words that will best convey your ideas. Use only those words you believe the receiver will readily understand. A listener or reader who has to ponder the meaning of a word or has to consult a dictionary to determine its meaning focuses attention on that particular word rather than on the content of the message. Avoid using any word that would divert a receiver's attention from the message content.

Words have multiple meanings; therefore, care must be taken to select words that will most nearly mean the same to the receivers as to the sender. You can bring your writing and speaking to life by using a variety of words. Select the words that are most appropriate for your audience and for the situation. Strengthen your message by using the following techniques: conciseness, tact, positive language, specificity and understandable words.

Conciseness

A desirable characteristic of business letters, memorandums, reports, and oral presentations, conciseness should not be confused with brevity. A brief message includes only the most significant points. Conciseness means all essential elements are covered adequately without excess words. Concise speaking or writing is direct and forceful, and it should be tactful. Study these examples.

Wordy	Concise
The research was conducted for the purpose of determining...	The research was conducted to determine...
I am looking forward to...	I look forward to...
They are making plans to...	They are planning to... *or* They plan to...
We learned that two programs are in existence.	We learned that two programs exist.
Six people were in attendance at the meeting.	Six people attended the meeting.

Tact

To communicate tactfully and specifically, you sometimes have to use more words than are essential for transmitting the general information. In these situations, using the extra words is worthwhile. Study the contrasting examples in these two columns:

Weak	Specific and Tactful
Thank you for your recent letter.	Thank you for writing to me on November 6.
We are glad to serve you.	We are glad to deliver your new dining room furniture.
We appreciate the opportunity to serve you.	We appreciate the opportunity to service the photocopiers in your office.
We will ship your order promptly.	We will ship the blankets the day we receive your order.
We shipped your order today.	We shipped your two desks and credenzas by Better Freight this morning.

Positive Words

Positive and specific statements enhance the effectiveness of business messages. A writer who wishes to call attention to a particular item in a catalog, a pamphlet, or any other publication may write "Turn to page 4 and read about ...." The reader is more likely to respond to the positive request for action and to read the description than if the writer used the trite wording "A description of the... can be found on page 4."

Just as the positive suggestion "Turn to page ...." encourages the reader to turn to that page, the phrase *why not* tends to make the reader think of reasons for not doing whatever is suggested. Avoid, therefore, using *why not* when suggesting that someone take positive action. Also, limit the use of negative words such as *sorry, regret,* and *unfortunately*. As is true with other negatives, though, occasionally these words can be used advantageously.

Use positive words and statements in most instances. They are usually shorter than negative expressions, they can be understood more easily, and they have greater appeal. Compare the expressions in these two columns:

Negative	Positive
Why not join us for the grand opening.	Join us for the grand opening.
Do not forget the teleconference.	Remember the teleconference.
Please do not hesitate to contact me.	Please call me to discuss these options.

Specific Words

If you have thought about a situation sufficiently to determine the real purpose of the message—letter, memorandum, report, or oral presentation—you are getting ready to convey, you should be able to use words and statements that are specific. Specificity helps to make a good impression on the receivers. They know that only those people who can think clearly can express their ideas specifically. Conversely, they know that vague or indefinite words or expressions in a business message indicate that the speaker or writer was poorly prepared for delivering it. Vagueness or rambling detracts from the effectiveness of a business message almost as much as does poor grammar. The examples in the following two columns are presented to help you convey messages specifically.

Vague	Specific
your recent letter	your letter of April 2
I appreciate your contacting me.	I appreciate your writing me. *or* I appreciate your calling me.
Thank you for your inquiry.	Thank you for your letter. *or* Thank you for writing.
as soon as possible	by August 10
under separate cover	by United Parcel Service
in the near future	before May 7

When you want a reader of your message to do something promptly, you may specify the date by which you want it done. Saying an action is to be taken within two weeks is better than saying it is to be taken "as soon as possible" or "at your earliest convenience." But because the reader may not know whether you mean two weeks from the date the letter was written or two weeks from the date it was received, specifying a date such as "by November 12" is even better.

Understandable Words

When selecting the appropriate category of language, consider the receiver. Use words that help you and your listener or reader to communicate clearly and easily. Remember that you can use simple words and still maintain the respect of the message receiver. Big ideas are much more important than big words. Use short, familiar words if they mean what you want to say. Write to express—not to impress! Consider these words:

Short, familiar (nickel) words	Complex (quarter) words
begin	initiate
told	divulge
find	ascertain
say	articulate

Why spend a quarter when a nickel will do?

Technical Words. Avoid technical and specialized words that are not familiar to the reader. Such words require the receiver to spend too much time interpreting the message.

Occasionally, specialized, technical words are appropriate and should be used. For example, an attorney communicating with another person in the legal profession should use legal terms. By using this terminology, the sender achieves clarity of expression and maintains the natural tone of a conversation the two might have. An attorney communicating with someone outside the legal profession, however, should not use legal terms the receiver does not readily understand. The people in other fields—computer technology, engineering, medicine, mathematics, and so on—should apply these same guidelines for using technical terms.

Correct Words. Familiarize yourself with similar words and distinguish the correct use of each. For example, do not confuse *their* with *there*, *principle* with *principal*, or *sight* with *site*. To do so would jeopardize your credibility as a writer. A comprehensive list of frequently misused words is presented in Appendix D. Review these words and use them correctly to improve your communication image. Use the thesaurus (a printed copy or computer software) to find alternative words to better convey your message. Do not hesitate to change a particular word to a more effective one.

Denotative and Connotative Meanings. Words, just as people, have personalities. Use both denotative and connotative meanings to show the personality of words. **Denotative** definitions are literal, factual definitions whereas connotative meanings are associated meanings. **Connotative** meanings describe emotions and thoughts the word arouses in our minds. Connotative meanings enhance denotative meanings. For example, which would you prefer to eat—a sizzling, juicy rib-eye steak or a slice of dead cow? Connotations describe people: plump versus fat, trim versus skinny, and so on. Sometimes people will make positions and situations sound more appealing through the use of connotations. Consider the realtor who promotes a house with the "lived-in look" or the homemaker who is described as a "domestic engineer."

Connotations as well as denotations are useful in precise communication. Consider the differences in meaning among these words:

Positive Connotations	Negative Connotations
inexpensive, low-cost	cheap
responsibility, task	chore
employment terminated	fired, dismissed

The words you use can have a psychological effect on the receivers of your messages. Combine psychology with grammar and communication mechanics, therefore, to get a favorable reaction to your messages. Choose words you believe will appeal (consciously or subconsciously) to your listeners or readers. Select the words that most precisely communicate your intended message. Adding life and interest to your messages will pay rich dividends.

Concrete versus Abstract Words. Choose concrete words instead of abstract words when possible. Concrete words are tangible words that can be perceived with the senses whereas abstract words are vague and subject to multiple connotations. *Chair, car,* and *office* are concrete words whereas *love, hope,* and *patriotism* are abstract words and subject to different meanings.

Word Precision. Select words with the precise meaning you wish to communicate. Avoid generalities such as *big, many, few,* and *some,* unless such words are the most precise for your situation. To communicate so clearly that you cannot be misunderstood, choose words that are not subject to multiple interpretations. The statement *"There was a big crowd at the concert."* is less precise than *"About 18,000 people attended the concert."* Perhaps in certain instances a *big crowd* could be 3,000 people!

Word Strength

Use words that enliven your message. Verbs are action words and are the strongest part of speech. Use verbs generously. Nouns are the second strongest part and should be used liberally. Use adjectives and adverbs sparingly as they add length to the sentence.

Action Verbs. Verbs expressing action are stronger words than verbs indicating a state of being. Both forms are appropriate in business writing. Exercise caution, however, to avoid using verbs indicating a state of being when action verbs are better. Compare these sentences.

State-of-Being Verbs	Action Verbs
Tyrone Jackson *is working* for the Envirotec Corporation in Dallas.	Tyrone Jackson *works* for the Envirotec Corporation in Dallas.
I *will be looking* forward to our meeting.	I *look* forward to our meeting.
All the employees *were* in attendance at the convention.	All the employees *attended* the convention.

Active Voice. Most readers prefer sentences written in the active voice (the subject of the verb does the acting) over the passive voice (the subject of the verb receives the action). Not only are the sentences that are written in active voice more interesting, but also they are shorter in most cases. Here are examples:

Passive Voice	Active Voice
The reports *were completed* by the human resources manager.	The human resources manager *completed* the reports.
The recommendations *were presented* by the task force.	The task force *presented* the recommendations.

The passive voice is appropriate and should be used to emphasize a number, a thing, or a person's name when those would normally be the object of the verb instead of the subject. The passive voice may also be used to caution or reprimand where such usage has a good psychological effect The passive voice may be helpful in conveying negative news. Consider these examples.

Passive Voice	Active Voice
Seven computers *were replaced* last month.	The company *replaced* seven computers last month.
The color copier *was purchased* by Jimmy's Book Place in September.	Jimmy's Book Place *purchased* the color copier in September.
Carlos D. Rubio *has been promoted* to the position of manager.	They *promoted* Carlos D. Rubio to the position of manager.
An office *was not locked* yesterday.	Don Iglehart did *not lock* his office yesterday.

Use passive voice when it helps you to communicate more effectively even though active voice is usually preferred.

Strengthen your writing by using verbs in the active voice. Do not camouflage a verb by adding a word ending such as *-tion* and *-ment*.

Camouflaged Verb	Direct Verb
Construction of the building required four months.	The building was constructed in four months.
Accomplishment of their goals required vision.	Accomplishing their goals required vision.
A description of the project is on page 8.	The project is described on page 8.

Using a verb instead of a derivative strengthens the sentence and also shortens it. A short sentence is superior to a long one, provided the short sentence is as courteous, as interesting, and as nearly complete and accurate as the longer one.

Redundancies. Four common redundancies in business messages are: (1) writing a number as a word and following it with a figure, (2) using both each and every, (3) including both such as, for example, and so on, with etc. in one sentence, and (4) adding a preposition at the end of a sentence. Such redundancies distract from the intended message and, therefore, should be avoided. Here are examples and revisions.

Incorrect	Correct
They shipped sixteen (16) cartons of paper today.	They shipped 16 cartons of paper today.
Each and every member is encouraged to participate in the exercise program.	Each member is encouraged to participate in the exercise program.
	or
	Every member is encouraged to participate in the exercise program.
The wellness program will include activities such as aerobics, racquetball, martial arts, etc.	The wellness program will include activities such as aerobics, racquetball, and martial arts.
	or
	The wellness program will include aerobics, racquetball, martial arts, etc.
They do not know where the computer center is at.	They do not know where the computer center is.

Selecting the proper words to precisely represent your intended message will greatly improve your chances for effective communication. Develop your vocabulary so you have a greater choice of words.

Construct Readable Sentences

Although sentence fragments occur in spoken communication, written messages should consist of complete sentences. Clear, concise, and complete sentences arranged in proper sequence form effective paragraphs. These paragraphs, arranged in proper sequence, create an effective message. In addition to the word characteristics discussed above, these sentence factors merit careful study: structure, length, transition, and accuracy.

Sentence Structure

While in short messages there is little need for variety in sentence, many business messages are sufficiently long to merit the use of a variety of sentence types. When drafting your message, consider a variety of sentence types—simple, compound, complex, and compound-complex—to make the document interesting and effective. For examples of the four types of sentences, turn to the reference section in Appendix A.

Combining simple sentences into compound or complex sentences improves the readability. The ideas in the following two simple sentences could be joined in various ways. One way to join these ideas with good transition is to use a complex sentence.

Simple Sentences	Complex Sentence
Christopher was late in arriving at his office this morning.	Because the freeway was blocked by a major accident, Christopher was late in arriving at his office this morning.
The freeway was blocked by a major accident.	

Sentence Length

Diversity in sentence length is as important as it is in sentence type. Sentences of various lengths contribute to the interest, the readability, and the overall effectiveness of a message. Some short, some medium, and some long sentences are desirable in many business letters, memos, and reports.

Although length should not be the only criterion for judging sentence quality, the average length of the sentences should be from thirteen to nineteen words. Some sentences, however, should be shorter than average; and others should be longer. Sentence length depends somewhat on the expression style of the message sender. Some people compose rather long sentences that are clear and easy to comprehend, yet other people use shorter sentences.

To assist you in determining the appropriate sentence length for a message, consider the background of the listener or reader. When sending a message to a poorly educated person or to a person who is unfamiliar with your topic, use shorter sentences than when communicating with a person who is well educated on the particular subject the message covers. Regardless of the receiver's background and the knowledge of the subject, you can use sentence length to emphasize any specific point. In messages that have several sentences, a very short sentence can be used to emphasize a point. Similarly, a longer-than-average sentence de-emphasizes an idea or thought. Vary the lengths, as well as the types of sentences.

Sentence Accuracy

For messages to be effective, they should be correct. All thoughts should be expressed in complete sentences with proper punctuation to separate dependent and independent clauses. The intended message can be transmitted in some sentences that contain errors in grammar or errors in various details of mechanics, but those sentences often carry a poor impression of the writer or speaker as well as of the organization for which the message sender works.

A few of the most common sentence errors--sentence fragments, ambiguous or unclear references, run-on sentences, and lack of parallel construction--will be discussed in this chapter. No attempt is made, however, to identify all types of errors. Refer to the reference section (Appendix A) for a more complete discussion of grammatical accuracy.

Sentence Fragments. A sentence must contain both a subject (noun) and a predicate (verb) in an independent clause. Frequently, sentence fragments appear when dependent clauses are used as independent ones. Compare these examples.

Sentence Fragment	**Sentence**
As I was driving to work this morning. (dependent clause)	I drove to work this morning. (independent clause)
	or
	As I was driving to work this morning, I saw an accident. (dependent and independent clause)

Ambiguous or Unclear References. Ambiguous or unclear references are phrases that do not refer clearly or logically to another word or phrase in the sentence. To correct these dangling modifiers, rearrange the words in the sentence to make the modifier clearly refer to the right word. Add words, if necessary, to make the meaning of the sentence clear.

Unclear Reference	Correctly-Placed Modifier
Working on the project, computer graphics were useful.	Working on the project, I found computer graphics useful.
Walking down the street, the building was quite large.	Walking down the street, she noticed that the building was quite large.

Run-On Sentence or Fused Sentence. A sentence with two independent clauses joined without punctuation between the clauses is called a run-on sentence or a fused sentence. Examine this example and the five ways it can be corrected.

Run-On Sentence	Corrected Sentence
The vice president is pleased with the progress she has scheduled a meeting for all representatives for 2 p.m. on February 7.	**1. Insert a comma and a coordinating conjunction between the clauses**: The vice president is pleased with the progress, *and* she has scheduled a meeting of all representatives for 2 p.m. on February 7.
	2. Insert a semicolon between the clauses: The vice president is pleased with the progress; she has scheduled a meeting of all representatives for 2 p.m. on February 7.
	3. Insert a semicolon and a conjunctive adverb between the clauses: The vice president is pleased with the progress; *therefore*, she has scheduled a meeting of all representatives for 2 p.m. on February 7.
	4. Write two simple sentences: The vice president is pleased with the progress. She has scheduled a meeting of all representatives for 2 p.m. on February 7.
	5. Subordinate one clause: *Because the vice president is pleased with the progress,* she has scheduled a meeting of all representatives for 2 p.m. on February 7.

Parallelism. For interest and easy comprehension, use **parallel structure:** a noun with a noun, a verb with a verb, an adjective with an adjective, a singular with a singular, a plural with a plural, and so on.

Not Parallel	**Parallel**
Kai will supply the notepads, folders, and give you a pen.	Kai will supply the notepads, folders, and a pen.
The teacher will evaluate you on the way you participate, your attendance, and by the assignments you submit.	The teacher will evaluate you on your participation, your attendance, and your assignments.
You will learn to keyboard, how to print, and saving a document.	You will learn how to keyboard, print, and save a document. *or* You will learn to keyboard, to print, and to save a document.
The manager allows time for reading correspondence, for returning telephone calls, and to check e-mail messages.	The manager allows time for reading correspondence, for returning telephone calls, and for checking e-mail messages.

Another frequent error in parallelism is the use of a singular verb with a plural pronoun to refer to a singular subject. Here are examples:

Not Parallel	**Parallel**
The Envirotec Corporation asks *their* employees for suggestions to improve company productivity.	The Envirotec Corporation asks *its* employees for suggestions to improve company productivity.

Often business writers and speakers violate the principle of parallelism when numbering items. Study these examples:

Not Parallel	**Parallel**
First, you will meet many celebrities. Secondly, you can travel to exciting destinations. And 3rd, you will gain first-hand knowledge of the business operation.	First, you will meet many celebrities. Second, you can travel to exciting destinations. Third, you will gain first-hand knowledge of the business operation.

To make parallel construction clear and effective, often we are wise to repeat an auxiliary verb, an article, or a preposition.

Poor	**Clear**
While in Germany, Marsha has visited a museum, conducted an interview, and completed research on her book.	While in Germany, Marsha has visited a museum, has conducted an interview, and has completed research on her book.

Sentence Transition

Once we have chosen words carefully and have arranged them into well-constructed sentences, we need to make certain to have good transition from one idea to the next. Good transition can be achieved in numerous ways. Some effective ways—which are illustrated in the next few paragraphs—are pronouns, conjunctions, and conjunctive adverbs.

Pronouns. Pronouns often serve as good transition, as in these examples:

Without Pronoun Usage	**With Pronoun Usage**
The members chose San Antonio as a meeting site. The members enjoy going to San Antonio often.	The members chose San Antonio as a meeting site. They enjoy going there often.
Dawn went to the movies last night. Dawn had seen the movie previously.	Dawn went to the movies last night. She saw a movie she had seen previously.

Conjunctions. Conjunctions also serve often to join thoughts naturally, as in these examples:

> Ms. Bryant would like to attend the dinner party on September 24, but she will be out of town that day.
>
> Whitney received your fax order on Wednesday afternoon, and she shipped your order this morning.
>
> William will call you on Thursday, or he will come to your office on Friday.

Conjunctive Adverbs. Conjunctive adverbs can be used effectively to show the relationship between two clauses or sentences. Observe the use of conjunctive adverbs in each of the following sentences.

	Conjunctive Adverbs
Time Connector	Katrina had to wait for her new printer to be delivered; *meanwhile*, she used the printer in accounting to print her documents.
	Alicia explained the use of the copier to Paul; *thereafter*, he copied all of the documents for the case.
Similarity	Monica completed the payroll records this morning; *likewise*, Robert printed the paychecks.
	Liz walks two miles each day for exercise; *similarly*, Brent jogs four miles each day.

Cause and Effect	The electrical storm caused a power outage in most of the city; *consequently*, traffic lights were not operating properly.
	The win record of the football team was 10-0; *therefore*, it will go to the playoffs.
Contrast	Dermid has little computer experience; *nevertheless*, he will design the database.
	Lona can begin the project today; *on the other hand*, Gray cannot start until August.

Transition is an important feature of a good style of expression. Usually, thoughts expressed in well-constructed sentences—even the short simple ones—flow smoothly from one to the other in carefully planned paragraphs.

Develop Meaningful Paragraphs

A paragraph consists of one or more statements about a major idea or topic. Generally, a paragraph is introduced with a topic sentence, which presents the major idea. The topic sentence can be at the end, however, or at any other place in the paragraph. In positive- or neutral-news business letters, memos, and reports, it is often best to have the topic sentence first. Then the following sentences support the main idea by giving evidence or by giving explanations. The added statements develop the major idea.

Organize the message based on probable reader response. If your receiver will receive your message in a positive tone, write your paragraphs in the ***direct*** or ***deductive*** order; give fact or recommendation first followed by explanation. If, however, the receiver may react negatively to your message, structure your message in the ***indirect*** or ***inductive*** order; give your explanation first followed by the recommendation.

First sentences of paragraphs receive the greatest emphasis; last sentences receive the second greatest emphasis. Therefore, place messages you wish to emphasize in these positions.

Short paragraphs are easy to read; therefore, limit the length of your paragraphs. The average paragraph length for most business correspondence is four to eight lines. Reports may have slightly longer paragraphs. Paragraphs longer than twelve lines become difficult for the reader to follow.

Write some longer paragraphs to develop an idea fully, and write some shorter ones for special emphasis. Varying the length of paragraphs helps to create interest and to improve the readability of business messages.

DISCUSSION

1. What are some idiomatic expressions you hear frequently? How could these expressions be taken literally?

2. How can you improve your vocabulary?

3. Discuss the importance of determining the purpose of the message before attempting to write it.

4. What types of information should a sender collect before attempting to draft a message?

5. Explain how word choice can affect the receiver of your message.

6. Describe ways to emphasize your message through sentence and paragraph development.

EXERCISES

Revise the following sentences to improve clarity and effectiveness.

1. The Barkley Corporation is pleased to have you as a customer.
2. I have received your recent letter.
3. We shall be happy to have your organization as a customer.
4. Thanking you in advance.
5. I'd love to hear from your company.
6. Am grateful for your help in the completion of the writing project.
7. Will you please give our representative an opportunity to give you a demonstration of our company's sanding machine?
8. A description of the modem can be found on page 4 of our catalog.
9. Due to the fact that the form must be returned before March 16, I am enclosing herewith a self-addressed envelope for your use.
10. In order to be of further assistance to you, I will contact your office in the near future.
11. Enclosed you will find complete details.
12. We look forward to an opportunity to be of service to you.
13. There are more than 500,000 people in Little Rock.
14. The sale was made by the representative.
15. Organization of the task force can be accomplished during the month of February.
16. I shall appreciate your sending the order as soon as possible.
17. The book you ordered has been shipped under separate cover.
18. Your order was processed this morning.
19. You can complete this assignment in a short period of time.
20. Why not visit our store during our special sale, which begins on October 21.

21. Please do not hesitate to get in touch with me.
22. It is a pleasure to visit you again.
23. Eighteen people were in attendance at the meeting.
24. Our organization will be glad to be of service to the Austin Company.
25. Everyone should bring their notes to the meeting.

PROBLEMS

1. Organize these sentences into well developed paragraphs.

    A. 1. In addition to monitoring what you eat, you can also assess how much you eat.
       2. If your diet is less than satisfactory, you can change it.
       3. Once you've done that, you can analyze your eating habits and decide what changes are necessary.
       4. The first step is to keep a record of what you eat for one week.
       5. Compare the quantities you eat with those recommended on the food pyramid.

    B. 1. The most common way of shopping for a gift is to go to a store and select an appropriate item.
       2. At one time or another, most business professionals are faced with buying a gift for a co-worker or supervisor.
       3. A third way to shop is to choose something from a television shopping channel.
       4. Sometimes the gift is to honor an achievement such as a promotion or sales award while at other times the event may be social such as a wedding or shower gift.
       5. Perhaps the final—and easiest—way to shop is to have a friend or relative do it for you!
       6. Another way of gift shopping would be to use a catalog: a catalog can be handy if you do not have a great deal of time to spend in stores.

    C. 1. If the stock market falls, however, you may end up with less than $10,000.
       2. The safest type of investment which will lock in your funds for a period of time is a certificate of deposit.
       3. When weighing your options, you must decide what level of risk appeals to you most.
       4. Another very safe investment which would allow you to withdraw funds as needed would be a bank savings account.
       5. Unexpectedly, you have inherited $10,000 which you wish to invest.
       6. Safe investments do not always translate into profitable investments: your money might grow faster in stocks purchased through a mutual fund.

    D. 1. A standard throughout the 70s was the rotary phone which used a dial system to input each number.

    2. Although some video phones are available today, they will probably become a standard in the years ahead.

    3. Over the years technology has improved the telephone instrument that most of us use every day.

    4. The push button phone is today's business phone of choice for the office.

    5. Perhaps the earliest phone consisted of an earpiece to listen to and a speaking portion into which to talk.

    6. However, many executives prefer the mobility of a cellular phone.

2. Patsy Rhodes, Production Manager, has given you a draft of the following letter. Please correct any errors you find in addition to editing the message for conciseness and conversational tone.

Mr. Harry M. Steiger, Manager, Hibbard Transportation Company, 1142 Bethlehem Road, Eunice, Louisiana 70535

Dear Ms. Steiger

Enclosed is a copy of our maintenence report for the month of July. You asked, when you telephoned me last week, that this report be sent to you before Monday of next week. This report, which is thirty-four pages in length, were written by Jeff Grambling and Cheryl Bradfield.

I believe that you will be especially interested in reading a description of the savings we obtained by beginning the new policies and procedures for handling fuel consumption data. You will find those results described on page 12.

It is my opinion that Mr. Bradfield and Ms. Grambling have done a fine job of the preparation of this report. If, however, you have any questions concerning the contents of this report, please do not hezitate to contact me.

Cordialy,

3. Rewrite the following letter for Mr. King correcting any errors you find in addition to editing the message for conciseness and conversational tone.

Mrs. Rebecca Hardy, 5698 Mountain Trail, Henderson, Nevada 89015

Dear Mrs. Hardy

I want to take this opportunity to thank you for calling my attention to the defect in the carrying case for the notebook computer that we sent to you last Monday. You should recieve a replacement for it in the near future. We wrote to our supplier under the date of May 8 and requested that a new case be mailed to you as soon as possible to replace the defective case that you received.

Ordinarily, we would have another case in stock; but due to the fact that this particular computer has been so popular, our supply is depleted at the present time.

We don't think you will have any problems with your notebook computer. If I may be of any further assistance, please do not hesitate to let me know.

Respectfully yours, William F. King, Order Department Manager

4.   Rewrite the following letter; edit for errors, conciseness, and conversational tone.

Mr. Anthony Young, Assistant Manager, Dillion's Office Supplies, P.O. Box 4587, Woodstock, Georgia 30188

Dear Mr Anthony Young

In referance to your recent correspondence, I am glad to tell you that the Abbott Corporation would be glad to have you visit our factory on June 11, the date you specified. Kindly tell us how many associates you plan to bring with you.

We have several girls who conduct tours of our fasility, but we have asked Ms. Gina Hillyer to serve as your hostess and to conduct your tour that day. You and your salesmen will be guests of ours for lunch.

We hope your schedule won't keep you from coming on June 11.

Cordially, Edward C. Kvapil, Director of Public Relations

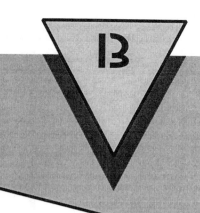

CONSTRUCTING POSITIVE MESSAGES

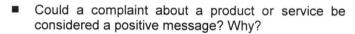

- Why should a business document begin with the most important point?

- Could a complaint about a product or service be considered a positive message? Why?

GOOD NEWS MESSAGES

Many business messages contain positive or neutral news. These messages are easy to compose because they contain news the reader is glad to receive. Common types of positive-news messages are those requesting or supplying information about products, services, or people, and those expressing goodwill.

Develop an effective positive news message that communicates clearly, concisely, and positively by planning the format, strategy, and organization before writing.

Selecting the Format

Positive messages may be written to people within your organization or to people outside the organization. Therefore, positive messages may be formatted as memos or as letters.

Memos are most often used for messages sent to people within the same organization; letters are most often sent to those outside the company. In certain situations, however, a letter is preferable for an internal correspondence. Documents of reference and personnel evaluations are frequently formatted as letters although the sender and the recipient may be within the same organization. Similarly, when the sender and the receiver, although employed by different organizations, are members of the same professional or civic organization, they may choose to use the memo format for correspondence pertaining to their joint interests.

Both memo and letter formats are less formal than most reports and use a more personal writing style including first- and second-person pronouns. Memos are frequently shorter than letters and use a specialized format that is described in Appendix B. Letters must also follow prescribed formatting standards. Turn to Appendix B to review the formats of both memos and letters.

Preparing to Write

In addition to selecting the format, a positive message should be well planned. The message should be reader-oriented, easy to read, concise yet complete, accurate in content and format, and attractively presented. for positive or neutral news messages, select an organizational strategy that presents the good news or most important point first.

Selecting the Strategy

As with reports, letters and memos may be organized in several ways. Different strategies are needed for positive, negative, and persuasive letters. Write positive news messages in the *direct (deductive)* order. The basic organization of the positive or neutral news messages are:

1. Start with the good news or most important point in the first sentence.
2. Follow with supporting details, clarification, or reasons.
3. Subordinate any negative aspects of the message within a middle paragraph.
4. Emphasize reader benefits.
5. Close with a goodwill ending that is positive, personal, and forward looking.

Message Type	Beginning	Middle	Ending
Positive (deductive approach)	most important point first; (good news)	explanation/key points	positive, forward-looking close

Determining Types of Positive Messages

Most positive and neutral messages may be classified in one of three categories: routine requests, responses to requests, and goodwill messages. Although similar, each category requires a slightly different organizational strategy.

Writing Routine Requests

One of the most common business messages written today is the request. A request may be (1) for information about a product, a service or a person; (2) for a product or a service; or (3) for a request for an adjustment to a product, service, or account.

Requesting Information. A request for information should be written in the direct (deductive) order. The organizational strategy for request letters is as follows:

Message Type	Beginning	Middle	Ending
Information request	primary request	explanation/key points	confident, positive request for a response

Begin the message with the primary request. If possible, phrase the request as a question. Follow the question with sufficient explanation so that the reader will understand why the request is being made. End with a confident request for action. Compare the following two opening paragraphs.

Slow, Indirect Start	Direct Start
We have a 2,000 square foot office that is carpeted. This carpet needs to be cleaned. I wondered if your firm would clean commercial carpets.	Does your firm clean commercial carpets? We have approximately 2,000 square feet of low plush carpet in our office to be cleaned.

If you need answers to more than one question, begin your message with the most important question and list the additional questions immediately after the explanation. Close the message with a positive forward looking ending. Show proper consideration for the reader and at the same time do yourself a favor by making it easy for the reader to understand your letter and to reply to it.

Which of the following letters is more likely to get an immediate response?

Slow, Indirect	Direct
We have a 2,000 square foot office that is carpeted. This carpet needs to be cleaned. I wondered if your firm would clean commercial carpets.	Does your firm clean commercial carpets? We have approximately 2,000 square feet of low plush carpet in our office to be cleaned.
I also need to know how much you will charge to clean these carpets and when you can do the job. We are very busy and do not want carpet cleaners to interrupt our work.	If this is a service you provide, please supply me with the following information:
We must have this work completed by the 15th, so call us by that date.	1. Do you clean after 5:00 p.m. or on weekends? We would prefer to have this work completed after our normal business hours.
	2. What are the costs associated with this project? You may want to inspect the carpet before giving us a specific bid. If so, please call me to arrange a convenient time.
	As we want to have our office cleaned by our board meeting on February 15, may we hear from you by the first of the month?

Another frequently written request is one to secure information about people. The same organizational plan applies to inquiries about people as to inquiries about products or services.

1. Begin the message with the most important question.
2. Give sufficient explanation.
3. List additional specific questions with accompanying explanation if needed. Indicate your reasons for asking.
4. Close with a request for a response.

Consider these examples.

Slow, Indirect, and Insufficient Explanation	Direct
Ms. Gina Jeffrey has applied for a position with our company and has listed you as a reference. Please tell me about your experience with her as an employee. Your prompt response will be greatly appreciated.	Would you recommend Ms. Gina Jeffrey as a customer service representative in an insurance agency? Ms. Jeffrey has applied for our customer service position and has listed you as a reference. In this position, Ms. Jeffrey will communicate extensively with customers on the telephone, by letter, and in person. She will be expected to complete her work with limited supervision. Your answers to the following questions will enable us to evaluate Ms. Jeffrey's qualifications for this position. 1. For how long and in what capacity did Ms. Jeffrey work for you? 2. How would you describe her attendance, punctuality, and work ethic? 3. Did her work require her to interact extensively with customers? If so, please evaluate her effectiveness in doing so. 4. Did Ms. Jeffrey work more effectively with others or independently? 5. Are there other factors that you could evaluate to help us assess Ms. Jeffrey for this position? As we hope to fill this position within the next two weeks, your prompt response will be appreciated.

When inquiring about people for employment purposes, remember to limit your questions to items that directly relate to the position for which you are considering them. Do not ask for opinions or information unrelated to the position.

By structuring your inquiry in question form, you give the reader an outline by which to write the response. Responses to well-written requests are easier to write. The respondent is less likely to overlook a major point when direct questions are used in the request.

Requesting Products and Services. Frequently, you will need to write requests for products and/or services. Many suppliers provide forms for merchandise orders. When an order form is available, no letter is necessary. Quite often, however, no order form is available. You may, therefore, choose to write a letter to obtain the desired merchandise. When your request is for a product, provide all the details needed to identify it.

The five essential items of information in an order letter are request for merchandise, specific identification of merchandise, cost, delivery instructions, and method of payment. First, state your request to order the merchandise; then specify the catalog number and description of the product. Supply the quantity, the size, the color, and any other variable that is applicable. Describe the cost and the method of delivery preferred. Finally, indicate your method of payment. The following letter is a good example of a request for merchandise.

Please send me the following merchandise by United Parcel Service and charge the total amount to our account—No 386670:

Quantity	Description	Price	Total
2 packages	Laser copier labels (G-15-5311)	35.99	$ 71.98
1 case	Copier toner (G15-LT77)	41.99	41.99
10 reams	Copier paper (G15-9537)	4.48	44.80
	Total		$158.77

I will appreciate your sending these items to arrive by Monday, July 18.

Write requests for services in the same way you request products. Include the specifics of the services desired and the time, date, and the exact location where the service is to be performed. The service requested in the next letter was paid for by a maintenance contract between the two companies.

Please ask one of your service representatives to come to our office this week to replace the drum on our Wellbuilt Copier. This copier, which is covered by a service agreement, is located in the Business Building, Room 229.

Our offices are open from 8:00 a.m. until 5:00 p.m. Monday through Friday. The copier will be available to service during those hours.

Requesting Routine Adjustments. Another type of request is one for an adjustment. While claim letters requesting adjustments may be considered negative news, they are written in the direct order and are considered a neutral or positive message because the business wants to know that you are dissatisfied with their product or service and wants to correct the problem. Consider the following situation:

Juanita bought a new bread machine from Acme Corporation. When the bread machine arrived, the lid was broken. Juanita had two choices: She could keep the machine and try to use it with the broken lid—she would be reminded of the defect every time she made bread and would probably complain about it to her family and friends—or she could request an adjustment from Acme Corporation to replace the machine.

When Acme Corporation received Juanita's request for adjustment, it had two choices: Acme could refuse the request. By doing so, it would probably lose a customer and get negative publicity through Juanita's complaints to family and friends; or Acme could grant the request to replace the bread machine and have a satisfied customer who would give positive advertisements about the company. If you were a customer service representative with Acme, which would you do?

Most companies prefer to have satisfied customers and are willing to grant routine adjustments.

Because of the dissatisfaction associated with the adjustment request, it is easy to let one's temper show in the letter. However, an appropriate adjustment request doesn't include angry statements or threats. A forthright statement of the problem and a request for action gives the best results.

Follow the direct order strategy for organizing an adjustment request.

Message Type	Beginning	Middle	Ending
Adjustment request (deductive approach)	most important point first; (the problem)	explanation/key points	positive, forward-looking close requesting action

Consider these two letters that Juanita could write to Acme.

Ineffective

I ordered a bread machine from your catalog. When I received it yesterday, the lid was broken. What kind of product is this? Am I supposed to pay good money for something that is broken when I receive it?

If you don't replace it immediately, I'll stop payment on my credit card.

Effective

Please replace the lid on The Allright bread machine, model #2304, that I ordered from your Spring catalog.

When my order #56432 arrived yesterday, I found the lid was damaged. One portion of the lid was attached to one hinge and the remainder was attached to the second hinge.

The instructions state the lid may be removed for cleaning; therefore, I believe I can attach a replacement lid to the machine. If you wish, I will send you the broken lid after I've attached its replacement.

As I am eager to begin using my new bread machine, I will appreciate your promptness in sending the replacement part to me.

Notice the effective letter started with a direct request indicating the action desired. Do *not* leave the reader to guess your choice of action. The direct and forthright statement of the problem is followed by sufficient explanation to enable the reader to determine the extent of the problem. The closing is positive and forward looking.

As a tactful, diplomatic writer, you should choose words carefully in order to maintain goodwill. When requesting an adjustment, therefore, avoid using negative, unpleasant words such as error, mistake, failed, and failure. Positive statements are almost always more pleasant and more effective than negative statements. Compare the expressions in the two columns that follow and ask yourself how you would react to any one of them if it were in a letter to you.

Negative	Positive
Please correct the error on the enclosed statement.	Please adjust the total on the enclosed statement.
Please fix the mistake on the enclosed statement.	Please correct the total on the enclosed statement.
Please credit my account with the $45 check you failed to record last month.	Please credit my account with the $45 check I sent to you on May 2.

Request adjustments confidently and courteously. The factors that led to your decision to write a letter should enable you to decide on the best way to organize the letter contents. You may present the request first, the explanation first, or you may present the message according to the time sequence of events.

When you feel reasonably sure the reader will readily agree that your request should be granted, **begin your letter by asking for the adjustment**. Then give your reason. Make your explanation clear and sufficient to justify the request, but do not include unnecessary details. A tone of goodwill should permeate this message. The end of the letter may very well refer confidently to the request and mention appreciation for prompt action. The following letter is an example of a successful adjustment request. Notice that the tone of the letter is positive and that goodwill is evident from the beginning to the end.

> Please adjust the balance of our account, No. 678400312. As indicated in my November 14 letter, our account had a $120 credit balance at that time. Including our November 14 order for five cases of copier paper, the current balance should be only $130 instead of $250.
>
> We will appreciate your sending a corrected statement of our account before the end of the month.

The nature of some situations is such that an explanation of the problem is needed to set the stage for an adjustment request. A reader who understands a problem usually reacts favorably to the request. The following letter illustrates the **explanation-first** approach.

Explanation First

While stored in its case, the Timekeeper watch that I purchased from you last August 18 stopped. I shipped the watch to you via UPS this morning.

I am confident that when you examine the watch, you will realize it has not been exposed to water, sunlight, nor dirt. Having worn Timekeeper watches for the past fifteen years (I have purchased at least four watches at your store), I am surprised this difficulty has developed. I realize, however, that occasionally an item may malfunction.

Please repair my watch or send me another watch to replace the one I returned to you. I appreciate your making this adjustment.

That letter brought a quick response stating that a watch had been mailed to replace the defective one. The response also included a note of appreciation for being given an opportunity to make an adjustment.

In seeking some adjustments, the writer may be wise to use a **time sequence** plan relating all the factors about the problem in the order in which they occurred. Such a plan is to be used cautiously, however, because it leads to wordiness. In this plan more details than are required to obtain the adjustment are usually included. The next letter is an example.

Time Sequence

On April 7, I purchased an E-Z Rite laser printer with built-in fax capabilities from Elsa Dillon, your representative in the metropolitan area. I am quite happy with the printer; when I used the fax, though, it did not do a satisfactory job.

I took the unit to the E-Z Rite office and discussed it with Ms. Dillon's assistant. He suggested that I leave the unit so that Ms. Dillon could check it out and call me the next day either to explain why the fax was not doing a satisfactory job or to refund my money. Since I did not hear from her for several days, I tried to call and discovered that the office had been closed.

On May 14, I called Ms. Dillon's home; her daughter explained that the family was moving out of town and that everything in the office had already been moved. She promised to ask her mother either to bring a printer/fax unit to my office or to refund the purchase price when she would be in town during the weekend of May 26.

When I tried to reach her by telephone yesterday, I discovered that her telephone had been disconnected.

Will you please send me a refund of $499 for the combination printer/fax unit.

Responding to Requests

Of all business letters, those written to comply with requests are perhaps the easiest to write. You know that the person who made the request is expecting your response and is hoping the letter contains a compliance with the request. You know, therefore, how to begin. The organizational strategy for responding to requests is similar to the strategy for initiating requests.

Message Type	Beginning	Middle	Ending
Request response (deductive approach)	good news first (most important point)	explanation/key points	positive, forward-looking close

Begin the letter by telling the reader that you are complying or that you have already complied with the request.

Here is one way to begin a reply to a request for product information.

■ *A copy of our 2002 spring catalog describing our party barges and pontoon boats is enclosed.*

If you are replying to a request for a $50 adjustment because of an overcharge, you could begin:

■ *Here is a $50 check to adjust your account.*

or

■ *Your account has been credited $50. You may use this credit on your next purchase.*

When you have enclosed materials or supplied the information for which the reader asked, the reader can readily see you have already complied with the request. Frequently, though, you must send the requested materials in a separate mailing or shipment. Be specific in telling the reader about the action you have taken. Indicate the method (parcel post, parcel service, express services, first-class mail, or others) you used to send the materials. The following opening sentence of a business letter is a good illustration:

■ *The two heavy duty electric staplers you ordered on March 26 were sent to you by priority mail this morning.*

By beginning a letter with a granting of the request, you promote goodwill, you make a good impression, and you put the reader in a good mood for reading the rest of the letter. The beginning is the most important part of a business letter; but even though the beginning is good, the tone can seem to be somewhat curt unless there is a follow-up that helps the reader realize you are complying cheerfully. Below are several sentences of the beginning of a letter supplying product information.

A copy of our 2002 spring catalog describing our party barges and pontoon boats is enclosed. The 24-foot party barges described on page 37 would be suitable for the tubing, skiing, and cruising activities you identified in your February 17 letter.

The Fun Float, Model X-242, has been very popular for use in area lakes. To examine the Fun Float personally, stop by our showroom at 31444 Northwest Parkway. Learn why our customers depend on us to provide quality recreational equipment at reasonable prices.

Having read good news in the first sentence, the readers are receptive to any sales talk you include as long as the sales talk is of possible benefit to them. High-pressure tactics, however, usually alienate readers. Follow up your compliance with the requests by letting the readers know you are genuinely interested in transacting business with them. Tell them you provide prompt, reliable, and courteous service as well as merchandise they will want to purchase.

Even though the preceding letter is short, it contains enough information to show the readers they have been given courteous consideration. The request is granted in the first sentence, and sincere concern for the reader is shown in the rest of the letter.

Responses Requiring Additional Information. When replying to some types of requests, you may have additional information, publications, or sample merchandise you think would be helpful to the reader. Send these items along with those requested.

Resist the temptation to end any letter with the trite "If I can be of any further assistance to you, please do not hesitate to contact me. " Many otherwise good letters have been spoiled by this type of ending. When you have done as much as you should do for the reader, do not suggest a request for more assistance.

Responses Requiring Greater Detail. More details are required for a letter accepting an invitation to speak to a group. The time, the date, and the place of the meeting should be specified in addition to a definite acceptance of the invitation. Anyone who invites a speaker likes to know that these details are clear to that person. Verify the date carefully; for example, make sure May 26 is Friday rather than Thursday or Saturday. An error of this nature can cause anxiety, and it usually requires additional correspondence or a telephone call.

Mentioning the length and the topic of your presentation is also helpful. Include in your reply the time you expect to arrive at the meeting place and your mode of travel, especially when tight scheduling is involved. Remember to tell the reader the special facilities (screen, overhead projector, projection system, videotape recorder, and so on) you will need for the presentation. The following letter illustrates some of these points.

I will be glad to speak to your sales managers at 2:30 p.m., on Thursday, January 23. Thank you for inviting me. Will you please have a computer projection system that supports the current version of Powerpoint software ready. I plan to show some slides to support my presentation, "Continuous Improvement in the Workplace."

Since my plane (Southwest Flight No. 1856) is scheduled to arrive in Phoenix at 12:35 p.m., there should be ample time to get to your conference center before the meeting begins.

I look forward to seeing you on January 23.

Try to reply to a letter within twenty-four hours from the time you receive it. In some instances, though, such quick responses are not feasible. For example, you may have to wait three or four days to receive the information or the materials you were requested to send. In such cases, delaying your reply until you can comply with the request may be the best course of action. If, however, you must wait somewhat longer (five days or more) to supply the requested items, reply within twenty-four hours and give the date on which you can comply with the request. Replying promptly makes a favorable impression on the reader.

When requested to do something, do it cheerfully or not at all. You are not expected to do everything you are requested to do. Some requests are unreasonable; and others, though reasonable and quite ordinary, cannot be granted because of existing circumstances. The strategy for refusing requests is discussed in Chapter 14.

Writing Goodwill Messages

Goodwill letters include those that express appreciation, greetings, or congratulations. These messages follow the direct organizational plan because in most cases, they convey positive messages.

Message Type	Beginning	Middle	Ending
Good will message (direct approach)	good news first (most important point)	benefits	warm, cordial close

Expressing Appreciation

When someone grants you a favor, express your sincere appreciation promptly. Frequently, an oral "thank you" or "I appreciate your help" is sufficient expression of gratitude. When you cannot make an oral comment promptly or when the favor you receive is somewhat out of the ordinary—or a big one, so to speak—write a letter.

This letter is easy to write. You know the purpose for writing, and you know the addressee will be pleased to receive the letter. Begin immediately with a statement of appreciation for the specific favor.

The following sentences illustrate appropriate ways of beginning a letter of this type:

- *Thank you for sharing your notes from the Quality Improvement Conference.*

- *I appreciate your help in solving the work flow problem in our office.*

Although one sentence may be all that is needed, additional comments enhance the effectiveness of the letter. The person who granted the favor obviously has a special interest in you or in the particular matters with which you were helped; therefore, a comment about the specific ways you benefitted may reveal your sincere appreciation and convince the person that the assistance was beneficial. Expressing a desire to return the favor is sometimes good for letters of this type.

These letters were written to express appreciation:

> Thank you for sharing your notes from the Quality Improvement Conference. I will use those strategies to implement our assessment program.
>
> I am returning the notes to you today by priority mail.

> I appreciate your help in solving the work flow problem in our office. The redesign of the four workstations you suggested has made a significant improvement in our information processing.
>
> Please come by to see us when you come to Athens next month. I would like to show you the new office layout.

Writing the way you talk, beginning with good news, and economizing on words are among the guidelines that apply specifically to letters showing gratitude. Some people, unfortunately, waste words and still never actually say what they mean because they begin with such wordiness as:

Wordy	**Concise**
I wish to thank you for .... I should like to thank you for .... I should like to take this opportunity to thank you for	Thank you for...

Letters that express gratitude promote goodwill. Write letters when you feel grateful and when you want to make a favorable impression on the reader.

Extending Greetings

Sending greeting cards or writing letters to show you think of people can be rewarding for them and for you. Such messages promote goodwill and enhance good public relations.

The message you send should be in keeping with the characteristics of the people involved and the occasion that prompts you to send it. You can present a message in a handwritten or a typewritten letter or by means of a printed greeting card. Printed cards may be used for general greetings to a variety of people. Letters may be reserved for special people and special events. Because of the time required to prepare a personal message, a letter would be more effective. The message may be sent from you personally or from you as a representative of your business.

Two situations for which special letters are usually preferred are welcoming new residents to the area and welcoming new clients or customers. Pay careful attention to the content, the vocabulary, and the mechanics of these messages. The following letter is typical of those mailed to new residents.

We welcome you to Raleigh and offer you the services of our all-purpose bank.

Can we help you in your relocation? A variety of financing options are available to help you acquire your new home. Harry W. Allen, our real estate loan manager, has assisted newcomers in securing home loans for the past five years; he would be glad to help you with this task. Just write to him here at the bank.

You can write without charge as many checks as you wish when the balance in your checking account with us is above $1000. We offer money market accounts as well as regular and golden savings accounts.

As I am confident you already know, Raleigh College plays an important role in the lives of our residents. We appreciate the contributions the college faculty, staff, and students make to the city; and we like to become acquainted with each new-comer. Please come by the bank for a visit when you arrive later in the summer.

A letter welcoming new customers should be short, direct, and positive. As a manager, tell the new customers that their business is appreciated and mention any existing discount policies and special sales conditions. Also outline the procedures for opening a charge account if you believe a customer qualifies for credit. Your having enough interest to send an individually prepared, personally signed letter is often sufficient to encourage the new customer to continue to purchase from your store.

A form letter designed so that minor changes can be made quickly and easily is usually effective for this type of communication. Each letter should be personalized so that it sounds as if it were composed especially for each recipient. What you, as a fair-minded store manager, would write to one new customer is what you would write to others. Use a direct, friendly style of writing.

A letter welcoming a new customer should be written within a few days after the first purchase is made. This letter, which is comparatively short, can be followed by sales announcements and other sales materials at whatever intervals seem best for the occasion. That type of item, however, should not accompany the welcoming letter.

The letter that follows was written to a customer four days after her first purchase at a large department store.

Ms. Sheri Browning enjoyed helping you make home furnishings selections when you visited our store last Friday. Any of the sales associates will gladly help you choose from our large variety of high-quality merchandise.

Your name has been added to the list of persons to receive announcements of special sales. Please remember that the 2 percent discount you received by paying cash last Friday will apply to any purchase you make from us.

We look forward to your visiting us again soon.

Sending Congratulations

Congratulate is a good word. Any of its forms connotes pleasantness. When you want to congratulate someone you do not expect to see within the next few days or when the accomplishment is an unusual one, write a letter. Write immediately and make your congratulatory remarks in the first paragraph.

Here are examples of beginnings:

- *Congratulations on your election to president of the American Purchasing Officers Association.*

- *You certainly deserve to pass the Certified Public Accountant's examination. Congratulations!*

In most situations you have enough interest in the accomplishment to write more than just a one-sentence letter. After all, you write because you are interested and want to make the reader feel good. In the sentences that follow the beginning, say something specific about the accomplishment that will let the reader know you have thought about it.

Read these examples:

> Congratulations on your election to president of the American Purchasing Officers Association. I particularly like your campaign platform to improve the electronic communication among members. Under your leadership, we can reach that goal.
>
> I look forward to seeing you at the convention in Kansas City in December.

> Passing all parts of the Certified Public Accountant's examination on the first attempt is a remarkable accomplishment. Congratulations.
>
> Because only 3 percent of the people who take that examination pass all parts on the first attempt, you have justification to be proud of your accomplishment. Your hard work in preparing for the examination obviously paid rich dividends.

Just about all congratulatory messages should be short. The following example contains a congratulatory comment, a specific reference to the accomplishment, and an expression of confidence.

> Congratulations! I was pleased to read in the News-Sentinel yesterday that you were elected president of the Jackson County Chapter of the Rotary Club.
>
> I am confident you will perform the duties of that office in your usual efficient manner.

Use letters advantageously. By writing sincere congratulatory messages, you boost the morale of the reader, make yourself feel good, and make a good impression on the reader.

DISCUSSION

1. What is the preferred organizational plan for routine requests?

2. Why should requests be phrased in the form of questions?

3. How do routine information requests differ from requests for adjustments?

4. What is meant by the phrase, "emphasize reader benefits"?

5. Give examples of goodwill messages that are appropriate for most business organizations.

EXERCISES

1. Identify violations of guidelines for effective letter-writing in the following letter.

    Enclosed you will find two copies of the report entitled "Your Future in Advertising" that you requested in your recent letter.

    Although this report usually sells for $3.75 a copy, we are glad to send two copies to you without charge. On page 17 you will find a list of the companies for whom we have prepared advertising copy within the past three years. I believe you will enjoy reading this unusual report.

    If I can be of further assistance to you, please do not hesitate to contact me.

2. In what ways can the following letter be improved?

    Miller Office Supply Co.
    1181 Broad Street
    Athens, Ohio

    Attention: Mr. James L. Miller

    Dear Mr. Miller

    I am interested in obtaining several items of merchandise for use in a class that I shall begin teaching soon. If you carry these items in stock, will you please send them as soon as possible.

    I will need 20 three-ring binders, 20 sets of three-ring index tabs, and 4 dry erase markers. If you need additional information to ship this order, please do not hesitate to get in touch with me.

    Cordially

3. What are some of the good characteristics of the letter that follows? What are the trite or wordy expressions that should be revised? What letter-writing guidelines are violated?

    Please send me two flashlights (catalog No. 30455) and two boxes of No. 2 pencils with red lead (catalog No. 3096).
    My check in the amount of $14.00 to cover the cost of this merchandise and the postage is enclosed herewith.
    Please send the above items as soon as possible.
    Thank you.

4. Improve the following sentences.

---

1. I hope that you will be able to be in attendance at the fair June 6.

2. Please return the enclosed card as soon as possible.

3. Why not visit our store during the annual sale?

4. Ms. Brown will be glad to be of service to you.

5. We are looking forward to your future orders.

6. Do not forget the meeting October 12.

7. Development of the outline was a challenge.

8. Mr. Riley W. Holtsman is the party who called you this morning.

9. You will find a description of Model No. 634 on page 8.

10. May we take this opportunity to congratulate you on your 25th wedding anniversary.

PROBLEMS

1. Compose a good news letter using the direct plan of writing. Use a different or larger font to make a letterhead at the top of the page. The company name is Ballentine Investments, 1722 Plymouth Lane, Riverside, California 92515. Send the letter to Hamilton Toys, 2122 London Way, Harrisonburg, Virginia 22807. You are in the business of recommending promising investments to your clients. You recently heard about a toy company which is making wooden reproductions of famous old toys. You feel that the company would be a good investment and would like to recommend it to your clients. Ask the company for 50 copies of their annual report so you can distribute it to interested investors. Also ask for any special information about purchasing stock in the company. Use your name as the person writing the letter. Your title is Investment Manager.

2.   Use the direct letter plan to compose a good news letter. Design an appropriate letterhead. The company name is Alpha Beta Books, 4578 Tremendous Drive, Hays, Kansas 67601. Send the letter to The Roots Place, 3099 Forrest Lane Way, Columbus, Mississippi 39701. You are a bookseller who just received a shipment of 24 copies of *Researching the Past* from the Roots Place, a company that does genealogical research. You noticed that four of the books are missing pages 1-50 while the other books seem fine. Write a letter asking The Roots Place to send you four books to replace the incorrect ones. You would like the books in time for your May 5 in-store signing event by the author. Use your name as the person writing the letter. Your title is Manager.

3.   In a recent edition of *Achieve*, a sporting news publication, you read an article about the 10 best camping sites. The article contained pictures and descriptions of several locations you would like to visit. One site was particularly appealing to you—the north rim of the Grand Canyon. You might want to try that spot for your summer vacation if you had additional information. Write a letter to the author of the article, asking the specific questions you would need answered before making the decision to camp there. Address your letter to David Harlan, Associate Editor, *Achieve*, P. O. Box 348, Boulder, CO 88402.

4.   Rewrite the letter from Exercise question 1. Supply any specific information you wish to add without changing any of the facts that are presented in the letter.

5.   Rewrite the letter from Exercise question 2. Supply any specific information you wish to add without changing the facts that are presented in the letter.

6.   Write an appropriate letter ordering the supplies described in Exercise question 3. Supply any specific information you wish to add without changing the facts that are presented in the letter.

7.   As a college student with limited work experience, you are very much interested in an advertisement you saw for the university's internship program. According to the ad, you can earn college credit for work experience in selected workplaces through this program. You believe the practical work experience would be a perfect complement to your general business degree but you need additional information. Write a letter to the program director requesting additional information. Information that would help you make your decision includes, among other things, the minimum qualifications for program eligibility, the credit a student could receive, the course requirements, the time frame, the location, rate of pay, and job responsibilities. Write to Dr. Margaret McComas, Director of Internships, Central State University, P. O. Box 785, State University, TX 77754 to find out more about this program.

8.   Today you received a letter from Thomas A. Gresham requesting information about Jane Manglicmot, one of your former employees. Mr. Gresham is considering Jane for a sales position with his cellular phone company. You believe Jane would be an excellent sales representative in that she has an outgoing personality, is self motivated, and is quite bright. Write a letter to Mr. Gresham at A-1 Cellular Phone

Company, 7259 East Columbia, Sullivan, MO 63063. Supply any additional details you wish to add without changing the facts of the case.

9.   Assume one of your classmates is interested in joining an organization (professional organization, sorority, fraternity, civic or special interest group) of which you are a member. Write a memo describing the organization and the benefits of membership.

10. While you were washing your car yesterday, a patch of paint on the back of the side mirror came off exposing a one-inch circle of bare fiberglass below. You were extremely surprised and disappointed. You knew of no reason for the paint to peel as the mirror had not been damaged or scraped. Your car is two years old and, therefore, no longer covered by a warranty. Nevertheless, you expected the paint to last longer than two years. Write a letter to Bobby Thomas, the body shop manager of the dealership where you purchased the car, requesting that the mirror be repainted without charge. Supply any reasonable details, but do not alter the facts of the situation. The manager's address is Expressway Motors, 6790 Northeast Expressway, Springfield, MO 64501.

11. You are Professor Mosley, who conducted a short correspondence workshop last Saturday morning for the office staff of the General Insurance Company. This morning you received a letter from Annette Long asking you to recommend a good book on letter writing. Since you have taught business communications courses for several years, you have a large up-to-date library. Recommending a book on letter writing will, therefore, be an easy task for you. Reply to the letter and send Miss Long the information she will need to obtain a copy. Do not send her a book. Include any comments that would be appropriate for this letter. Her address is General Insurance Company, First National Bank Building, 624 Market Street, Tuscaloosa, AL 37402.

12. You are the president of a club, a fraternity, or a sorority. You asked an assistant to the president of your college or university to speak to your group at a special meeting last night to tell those attending about the plans for landscaping the residence halls section of the campus. Write a thank you letter to the assistant for speaking to your group. Refer to a specific item in the presentation so that the reader of your letter will know you are not sending a form letter that you send to all the speakers you invite. Supply the necessary information to complete the letter.

13. You are the assistant manager of McKechney Office Products, 789 North, Flagstaff, AZ 80017. Today you received from Elroy S. Braun an order for a fax machine and portable phone. You can ship these items immediately. This order is the first one you have received from Mr. Braun, whose address is Route 8, Tempe, AZ 80106. Write to him. In your letter let him know that you are glad to have him as a customer.

14. You are the manager of the production department of Phillips Manufacturing Company. You learned when reading the local newspaper this morning that Jerry E. Hutton, who was your capable assistant manager more than three years, was

elected this year's chairman of the United Way Fund in your city. You know he was elected to this office because he is well organized and is well liked and admired by many civic leaders and business personnel.

Write to him; congratulate him; wish him luck; and assure him you are confident he will have a successful fund-raising campaign this year. His address is 2627 White Road, Deerfield, MI 48112.

15. You heard an unusually good presentation last night when you attended a regularly scheduled monthly meeting of the Administrative Management Society. The speaker, Ms. Inez M. Missling, talked about psychological effects that technology is having on today's office workers. Ms. Missling, a consultant with Anderson, Radford, and Smith Consultants, Inc., has done extensive research on this topic. Not only is she well informed, but also she presented her many worthwhile ideas clearly, convincingly, and entertainingly.

Write to Ms. Missling at Anderson, Radford, and Smith Consultants, Inc., 1148 Water Valley Road, Tulsa, OK 79211. Tell her you enjoyed the presentation and congratulate her on doing an outstanding job of presenting her ideas. Mention a specific point or two that you learned from her remarks.

16. You are a first-line supervisor in a large manufacturing company. A young man, Jason O. Kline, who entered the company training program at the same time you entered it two years ago has been promoted to the position of assistant manager of the Transportation Department. He is a likable person and is quite competent. You are, therefore, happy to learn of his recent promotion.

Because the organization for which you work is large, you usually see Jason only about once a month. Write a letter and congratulate him on being promoted.

17. As public relations director of the First State Bank of Morrow, Georgia, write a letter congratulating one of your customers, Lana Wilson Bryant, on passing the Georgia Bar Examination, which was held last month. You read about her achievement in the Morrow Public Dispatch. Her address is 32210 Belvedere Road, Morrow, Georgia 30260.

18. Yesterday you learned from the director of the management training program for your company that Sarah N. Henry, who entered the training program about thirteen months ago, has been promoted to the position of assistant manager of the Shipping Department. You supervised some of the work to which Sarah was assigned during her training period, and you are favorably impressed by her performance. Send her a memorandum and congratulate her on her promotion.

CONVEYING NEGATIVE MESSAGES

- How can one maintain goodwill while denying a request?

- Being told "no" doesn't have to be a negative experience. Why?

Critical Thinking Applications

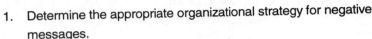

CHAPTER OBJECTIVES

After studying this chapter, you should be able to:

1. Determine the appropriate organizational strategy for negative messages.
2. Identify the five-point strategy for presenting negative messages indirectly.
3. Write a buffer for an indirect message.
4. Propose suitable alternatives to requests.

POLITELY SAYING NO

Regardless of how efficiently your organization is run or how much you are interested in helping other people, you will occasionally receive requests with which you cannot comply; or it may be possible to comply though you believe you should not. Your responses to these requests are somewhat difficult to write, but you can reply in a way that will still maintain goodwill. Letters of that type are discussed in this chapter.

Good public relations is important in any business endeavor or in any activity involving other people. A good reputation for you and for the organization you represent can be established and maintained by handling all transactions efficiently and tactfully. The tone of your message is important, especially in negative messages. Your attitude is reflected in the tone of your letters. Be careful, therefore, to develop the appropriate attitude before drafting your negative news messages. With practice, it is possible for you to decline a request and at the same time maintain the goodwill and friendship of the person who made the request.

Consider your negative news message as a sales document. In negative messages, you are trying to "sell" your decision. It is your responsibility to convince the reader that your decision although contrary to the request is fair, reasonable, and perhaps even the best course of action. Respond in a way that will make the requesters feel just as good toward you and your organization as they would feel if you complied.

Before attempting to respond negatively to a request, try honestly to see the situation from the other person's point of view. Why did the person make the request? A high percentage of the requests that business people receive are made by fair-minded people who ask for only those products or services they believe the recipient can provide. Some people, however, make unreasonable requests that the receiver cannot afford to grant. Such requests made by fair-minded individuals are the ones you should treat with care.

As you plan your organizational strategy for the negative message, analyze your audience. How will your reader respond to your message? Perhaps your reader wants a direct answer; if so, use the direct order strategy discussed in Chapter 13. Typically, the direct order is appropriate when the negative news is minor, when you are writing to a superior who wants a direct report, or when you want to emphasize the negative news.

Negative News Presented in Direct Order

Consider these examples: (1) a memo to the assessment committee members notifying them that the meeting has been postponed for one week; (2) a memo to your superior explaining that employee benefits costs will increase 12 percent during the coming year; or (3) an adamant "no" to an individual who won't accept your decision not to chair a civic fund raising activity. In each of these cases, the direct order is preferred.

Use the direct order for minor news that carries little, if any, emotional message. If the reader won't likely be disappointed with the message, a direct order is preferred. If, however, the reader may be disappointed or angry with the response, an indirect strategy (inductive approach) is better.

Compare the organizational strategies of the direct and indirect order.

Message Type	Beginning	Middle	Ending
Positive	most important point (positive news)	explanation additional key points	positive forward-looking close
Negative—no/little emotional response	bad news with brief rationale	explanation alternative	neutral or positive close
Negative—uncertain or disappointed response	neutral opening (buffer)	explanation decision alternative	neutral or positive close

When using the direct approach, include a brief rationale in the first sentence with the negative news.

Avoid: The software training class has been canceled. The next class will be held on Thursday, October 17.

Use: Because of the delay in installing new software on the system, the software training class scheduled for Thursday, October 10, has been rescheduled for Thursday, October 17.

Avoid: Employee benefit costs will increase 12 percent next quarter.

Use: The increase in insurance premiums as well as the addition of dependent child care will result in a 12 percent increase in employee benefits costs next quarter.

Follow the initial statement of negative news with sufficient explanation for the reader to fully understand the problem and the decision. Offer alternatives or substitutions as appropriate. Close with a positive statement related to the topic but not directly related to the negative decision.

Consider this example.

As a result of the popularity of the Comfort E-Z workstation chairs, your shipment of thirty blue ergonomic chairs will be delayed until October 17. The rose, gray, and black chairs are available for immediate shipment. If one of these colors fits your decor, you could be using them by June 25.

Negative News Presented in Indirect Order

Use the indirect order when presenting negative news to readers who will be disappointed or angry with your decision, or to readers you do not know. Most often, the indirect strategy is used in negative messages to subordinates and to customers.

Follow this basic *five-point strategy* when writing indirect messages.

1. Begin with a neutral buffer.
2. Show reasons for decision.
3. Give decision (expressed or implied).
4. Provide alternatives (if available).
5. End with positive or neutral statement that doesn't refer to decision.

Begin with a Buffer

A **buffer** is a neutral statement that helps the writer get in step with the reader. Be careful when drafting the buffer of your message not to sound too negative—nor too positive. A buffer that implies a positive response sets the reader up for a greater disappointment when reading the decision.

Consider one of these types of buffers:

Type of Buffer	Example	Letter Purpose
Good News	Beginning May 24, you may exercise 24 hours a day at the Fitness Center.	Increase in monthly rates
Agreement	Maintaining an attractive lawn during these hot summer months is challenging.	Increase in monthly water rates
Appreciation	Thank you for ...	Refusing request for speaking engagement
Specific fact	Midville has had a 38 percent increase in the number of automobile accidents during the past year.	Increase in auto insurance rates
Compliment	Congratulations on your being named business manager of the Tiger Rag!	Refusing request to advertise in high school newspaper

Show Reasons for Decision

Follow the initial buffer statement with supporting information that leads directly into an explanation of the *reasons* for the refusal—not the refusal itself. Present your reasons honestly and convincingly. Avoid the "I" emphasis by stressing reader benefit. If possible, explain how the reasons (and ultimately the decision) will benefit the reader instead of the writer.

Avoid hiding behind company policy. Company policies are developed by the company and can be changed by the company. If you have several reasons for saying no, limit your explanation to those that are strongest and most believable to the reader.

Give Decision

After you have supplied the reasons, give your decision. That decision may be implied or expressed. If your reasons are logical and complete enough to remove all doubt about the decision, the refusal may be implied. If, for example, you have been asked to speak at a meeting in Philadelphia on September 11 and you have said that you will be in Seattle on that date, an expressed decision is not needed.

If the explanation does not remove all doubts about the decision, however, and there could be a question regarding your response, state the refusal. Use positive language and subordinate the decision by placing it within a paragraph. Do not put the decision in the first or last sentence of the paragraph as these are positions of emphasis.

Provide Alternatives

When you cannot grant a request or fill an order with the product requested, tell the reader what you can do. You may be able to offer an alternative or a substitute, comply with the request at a later date, or recommend another source of supply.

Alternatives. If possible, suggest an alternative or recommend a substitute. Your willingness to assist the reader will build goodwill and soften the disappointment of your negative news.

Suppose you are asked to speak on a selected topic to a group on a specified date. If you have another commitment for that date, you may logically agree to speak at another time, provided the meeting could be rescheduled. In this case, your offering to speak at a later time may be a good alternative.

The Chamber of Commerce selected me to attend a meeting in Toronto, Ontario, on May 9, 10, and 11.

Could your chapter of the Business and Professional Women meet at some time other than Thursday evening, May 9? I would be glad to speak to your group on the topic you suggested, "The Customer-Oriented Organization" at any time I am free.

I realize that you may have to retain the May 9 date for your meeting so you will, no doubt, have ample time to find another speaker for that occasion.

If you know the group is especially interested in having a particular topic discussed on the date you have been invited to speak, you may suggest an alternate speaker if you know someone whom you believe could present a good speech on the topic. Under some circumstances you may want to consult the person you plan to recommend before making the recommendation. Be sure, though, to exercise special care in handling the situation so that the suggested alternate will not be embarrassed or offended if not invited. Also, make your suggestion in a way that the reader of your letter would not feel obligated to invite the person you recommend. Often, program planners have more than one speaker in mind so that they can choose an alternate if the first person they invite declines.

When you suggest an alternate speaker, make it easy to invite the person by sending the full name, mailing address, and telephone number. You also may offer to get in touch with the person you suggest. Do give reasons for recommending the alternate. Tell some of the characteristics—knowledge of the subject, ability to speak, and so forth—of the person you recommend.

When offering to speak on another date, be as considerate of the reader as you are when recommending another speaker. The reader may have already made plans for the future meetings and would not want you to speak at any other time. To avoid an embarrassing situation, make it easy for the reader to proceed with any plan without feeling obligated to accept your offer to speak later.

Product Substitutions. Substitutions are possible alternatives when you have inadequate inventory, when the reader has requested a discontinued item, or you have a better item available.

If the customer writes that an item must be received by a specific early date, you can suggest a substitute item if you believe the substitute is satisfactory. Give specific reasons why you believe the substitute will be satisfactory. Merely telling the reader that the substitute should be satisfactory is not sufficient unless that person is already familiar with the item or already has a great deal of confidence in your judgment.

The writer of the following letter offered a substitute.

The Model 5100 answering machine is more popular this year than the Model 4100 because it has a digital display with caller identification. The new model has all the other features the Model 4100 has and sells for only $15 more, which is a small sum when applied to a purchase of this amount.

We can send the Model 5100 to you immediately. August 17 is the earliest date on which we can send a Model 4100. A strike in the manufacturer's plant last month has prevented our obtaining a supply of that model.

A Model 5100 answering machine will be on its way to you the day we receive your approval to send it.

Almost always your reason for suggesting an alternative can be presented without using a single negative word or negative connotation. Omit such negative terms as *unfortunately, regret, sorry, cannot, not, will not be able*, and *unable*. Contrast the negative expressions with the positive expressions in the two columns that follow:

Negative	**Positive**
The scanner cannot be shipped until May 13.	The scanner can be shipped on May 13.
Why not consider this substitute.	By considering this item, you....
...will not be available until...	...will be ready to mail on...

When you cannot provide the requested product or service and have no suitable substitute to recommend, you may be wise to encourage the customer to wait until you can comply with the request. Begin the explanation by telling when you can comply and then explain in a positive, tactful manner the reason for the delay. A positive explanation omits delay, inconvenience, failure, and other negative words.

A sales presentation on an additional item may be included in letters explaining delays. Resale information on the product that was ordered may also be desirable. Consider this example.

A supply of the best seller *Adventures in Outer Space* by Malcom Hegwood is scheduled to arrive at our store on December 15. We can, therefore, send a copy to you that day so that it will reach you before Christmas.

I am confident your grandson will be pleased with your gift. This book has received some of the best reviews of any children's publication within the past five years. Because it has been enjoyed by so many adults as well as by teenagers, I suspect that you, too, would enjoy reading it.

The demand for this book has been so great that our first supply, which we received on November 8, was exhausted before the end of the week.

We will gift wrap your copy of *Adventures in Outer Space* with a paper that appeals to many young men so that it will be ready for you to put under the Christmas tree.

Outright Refusals. Most requests are legitimate, yet there are those that you cannot grant or that you choose to decline without offering a substitute or another alternative. For example, you may be asked to contribute to a fund you do not care to support because you do not agree with the objectives of the group conducting the fund-raising campaign. You may be requested to grant credit to a person with a poor credit record. You may receive an employment application when you have no appropriate job openings.

Study the situation thoroughly to determine whether to suggest one or more appropriate alternatives before declining a request of any kind.

Closing

Close your letter with a pleasant, positive, and specific statement that does not refer to your decision. Avoid using words that create doubt. Many otherwise well-written letters suggesting an alternative are spoiled by using such words as *hope, trust,* or *if* in the last paragraph in a way that makes the reader doubt the alternative will be satisfactory. Contrast the negative and the positive ending paragraphs in the two columns that follow:

Negative	Positive
I hope you will be pleased with the Model 22, which we believe is superior to the model you ordered.	Ray Adams, who serves your area, will bring a supply of revised order forms when he comes to your office next week.
We trust you will be pleased with this substitute.	A fall edition of our catalog will be mailed to you on June 4.
If you like this new model as much as the one you requested, we will be happy to fill orders for it.	We look forward to receiving your next order.

Don't apologize for your decision. If you must apologize, you made the wrong decision. Don't refer to the negative situation that the reader experienced. Avoid trite expressions such as "If I can be of any further assistance..." You weren't of assistance this time!

Negative statements at the end of an otherwise good letter cause the reader to concentrate more on your declining a request than on your willingness (and possibly even eagerness) to help in whatever way you mentioned earlier in the letter.

Note that in each of these positive endings no reference is made to the refusal.

- *We wish you the best of luck in your fund-raising campaign.*
- *Please give us an opportunity to exhibit our machines at your next annual convention.*
- *We heartily endorse the work your organization does.*

Remember always that as a person of strong character you should uphold your convictions. People respect you for this strength of character. When you receive a request with which you do not choose to comply, you can decline in a firm, clear, tactful, straightforward manner. Tact is an important trait of successful business people.

Whether you comply with a request, offer a substitute or other alternative, or make an outright refusal, apply the letter-writing guidelines in this book.

DISCUSSION

1. Give examples of negative messages that should be written in the direct order.

2. Give examples of negative messages that should be written in the indirect order.

3. What are some of the requests business people may likely receive that they would have to refuse to grant?

4. Sometimes customers request adjustments to which you feel they are not entitled, yet you grant the adjustments anyway. What are some advantages to granting these requests?

EXERCISES

Improve the following sentences.

1. I hope you will be pleased with the substitute, which is superior to the product you ordered yesterday.

2. Any of our salesmen will be glad to be of assistance to you in the selection of the furniture for your new office.

3. Due to the fact that the schedule was changed, we will be unable to attend the meeting.

4. I have received your offer, and I regret to inform you that I shall be unable to accept.

5. The tapes you ordered cannot be sent until May 30.

6. We hope this arrangement will not be inconvenient for you.

7. You will find a self-addressed envelope enclosed.

8. The lawn furniture you mentioned in your inquiry of February 8 will not be manufactured until March 15.

9. In the event that we receive a shipment earlier than January, we will send the compact discs you ordered immediately.

10. The cost of doing business continues to go up; therefore, prices must go up.

PROBLEMS

1. Use the indirect plan to write a negative news letter. Design an appropriate letterhead for your supply firm–Talbott Supplies, 14987 Baltimore Road, Stevens Point, Wisconsin 54481. Ms. Lenora Dawson, 2917 Lacey Terrace, Stevens Point, Wisconsin 54481, recently purchased from your company a digital camera that she intended to use to take pictures to be used on her computer system. Your company sent her a bill of $699 for the camera. Today she sent you a check for $549 and a newspaper rebate coupon for a $150 discount on the camera she bought. The newspaper coupon was generated by the camera manufacturer–not your company. In reading the coupon, you see that it should be returned with proof of purchase to the manufacturer. However, the coupon expired nearly a month ago on March 25. You would be unable to honor the coupon anyway as it was a rebate from the manufacturer.

Write her a letter informing her that you can not accept the rebate coupon. In fact, she still owes you $150. Offer an appropriate alternative, but do not give away anything for free. In addition, do not offer a discount on purchases. Use your name in the closing. Your title is Assistant Manager.

2. Write the following letter with an indirect plan. Create an appropriate letterhead for your company Furn and Fix, 3098 Norton Lane, Macomb, Illinois 61455. Your company sells furniture and fixtures to retail businesses. You extend credit to companies with good credit reputations who have been in business for at least one year. You evaluate each case on an individual basis. Mr. Douglas Walter, The Collectible Place, 2214 Venture Drive, Macomb, Illinois 61455, has written to establish credit with your company for his new business. You are concerned that his business has only been in operation for three months. You would like to keep him as a cash customer and then look at his application after he has been in business for a year. Write an appropriate letter. Your title is Assistant Manager.

3. As the Service Department Manager, you frequently deal with customers who have problems with equipment. Write a letter to Mr. Michael Dillon, Box 195, Kinsley, Kansas 67547. Design an appropriate letterhead for your firm–Ellington Electronics, 349 Wyatt Earp Boulevard, Dodge City, Kansas 67801. Mr. Dillon purchased your top of the line stereo with CD-disc changer and remote control as well as a dual cassette tape deck with AM/FM radio and surround sound speakers 18 months ago. As far as you know, he has been pleased with the unit until now. The system comes with a one-year warranty. Now, the tape deck is not working correctly as one of the units seems to tear up the tapes. Mr. Dillon expects you to fix the unit at no charge because he indicates in his letter that your company is known as a top of the line company with the best service. While you agree on the quality of your service, you can not repair the unit at no charge. Use an indirect plan for the letter.

4. You are the owner and manager of a small motel and campground in a popular resort area. Brent Wooten and his family have come to your motel for a two-week vacation each summer for the past five years. Year after year they have written to you in February to reserve the same efficiency apartment. Because your motel is perhaps the best in the area, all space for the summer months is reserved by May 1 each year.

    The Wootens wrote to you in February, but discovered on April 16 that the letter had not been mailed. They called your office that day while you were on a business trip. When you returned to the office this morning, your assistant told you that the Wootens had called and that all motel space for the entire summer had been reserved by April 10. A few good campsites, however, are still available for some weeks during the summer.

    You would like to help the Wootens, and you would like for them to return to your motel next summer. Write to them.

5. Bob Johnson purchased a car from you two years ago. Today you receive a letter from him stating that a "patch of paint" had peeled off the back of his side mirror while he was washing the car. His claim was not the first one of that kind that you had received. In fact, you have received similar letters from three other customers. You have contacted the manufacturer to see what adjustment should be made; however, you have not yet received a response. You really don't know whether the company will pay for the painting, so you can't grant Mr. Johnson's request. What are your alternatives? Write to him at 1005 Prairie View, Lincoln, NE 54439.

6. You are the manager of the BuildRite Lumber Company. Three years ago, your company adopted the policy of not advertising in area high school yearbooks. With thirteen area schools to support, the cost of such advertising was significant. Besides, you aren't aware of any business that you've received resulting from such an ad. Basically, the money was just a donation. Today, you received a letter from Julie Willis informing you that she is the new business manager of her high school yearbook and asking you to buy an advertisement in this year's edition. You must respond to her request, but this one isn't easy. Julie's dad is a major building contractor in town, and he buys a substantial part of his materials from you. Julie's address is 2471 Westwind, Batesville, AR 72501.

7. Assume you are the Vice President of Community Affairs for First State Bank in your community. Today you receive a letter from Robert Samuels, a local businessman and scoutmaster of Troop 19. The letter, signed by Scoutmaster Samuels and 12 of his troop members, requested the use of the bank's board room for the troop's weekly meetings.

    You must refuse their request because the room is too lavishly furnished for active young boys. Furnished with plush cream carpet and upholstered swivel executive chairs, it was designed for adult use. Before you respond to Scoutmaster Samuels, consider possible alternatives. As you write your courteous refusal, remember that the parents will no doubt read your letter. Write to Mr. Samuels at his business address, Brown Insurance Company, 9210 South University Avenue, Waco, TX 76203.

8. One of your responsibilities as the local television meteorologist was to speak to area elementary children about weather phenomena. When you assumed the position eight years ago, you created a pseudo character, Wendal the Weather Wizard, to make your presentations more entertaining. Wendal is now widely recognized and enjoyed by children of all ages for his humorous and informational presentations. In fact, Wendal is in great demand at area schools and civic organizations with more requests than he can manage. Recently, you were promoted to the general manager's position and no longer have time to be Wendal. Today you received a letter from Ms. Dorothy Evans, the third grade teacher at Westside Elementary. Ms. Evans asked Wendal the Weather Wizard to visit her class on September 16. With your new responsibilities, you cannot continue to be Wendal. Write to Ms. Evans and her third-grade class.

9.   As owner and general manager of MKC Manufacturing, you received a letter this morning from Jimmy Newsom requesting replacement seats for his 1986 runabout boat. He said that he was extremely pleased with the original seats you had manufactured; therefore, he was ordering the replacement seats "exactly like the original ones" from you. While you are pleased to have such a satisfied customer, you have a problem. The seats that were put in the 1986 models were upholstered seats covering wooden frames. That process has been discontinued. The seats which are used today are molded fiberglass. The fiberglass seats are more durable than the wooden ones were, but they also cost more—about twice as much. Write to Mr. Newsom proposing to substitute the fiberglass seats for the wooden seats. His address is 18 Horseshoe Lake Estates, Dothan, AL 43139.

10.   The principal of the high school from which you graduated has asked you to chair the alumni association for the coming year. As the chair, you would be actively involved in the homecoming activities, athletic events, and honors programs. Although you are honored by the request, you don't believe you have the time to devote to such a commitment this year because of your busy college schedule. You may be interested in that role in a few years after you finish college. Write to the principal. Supply additional details as appropriate for the problem.

11.   You are the chair of the benefits committee for your company. As such, it is your responsibility to inform the employees of an 8 percent increase in their insurance premiums beginning September 1. Supply the necessary details to write the memo.

12.   As the department head, each year for the last five years you have arranged a Christmas dinner for employees and their spouses/guests at a local restaurant. Employees pay for their individual meal expenses but the group is given a private dining room and buffet. As prices have gone up each year, attendance at the dinner function has dropped. This year you have 12 people interested in participating. The restaurant requires a minimum guarantee of 15 people to prepare the buffet. Use the direct strategy to write the members of the department indicating that you are canceling the event due to lack of participation.

13.   For the past several years, fourteen employee parking spaces have been available in a lot adjacent to your building. Additional parking was available in a larger lot approximately one block south of your building. This summer, the lot with the fourteen spaces has been closed due to the construction on a nearby building. The building expansion has claimed six of those spaces. Now that the lot can be reopened, you have decided to reserve the remaining eight spaces for visitors. Write an appropriate memo.

CREATING PERSUASIVE MESSAGES

- If an employee writes a letter to a customer filled with misleading information about a new product, is the company liable for any damages? Discuss issues affecting the employee and the company.

- How do persuasion and manipulation differ?

PERSUASIVE STRATEGIES

The ability to persuade can contribute to success in business. Executives, as well as personnel on the lower levels of the organization chart, know that much more can be accomplished through persuading (convincing—but not begging) people than through attempting to drive them.

While all successful communication can be considered persuasive to a degree, certain types of communication require a greater degree of persuasion than others. Persuasive messages may be written in the **direct** or **indirect** order. To determine the better strategy, you must first assess your purpose in writing the message.

Choose a strategy based on your responses to these questions:

1. Who is your reader?

2. What do you want the reader to do?

3. What is the knowledge and attitude of the reader on this subject?

4. What effect will your message have on the reader?

5. Will the reader object to your proposal? If so, what objections will you have to overcome?

6. What level of credibility do you as a writer have with this reader?

The Reader

Identify your audience. What characteristics do you know about the reader? What is the approximate age of the reader? What is the educational level? What interests does the reader have? Some degree of stereotyping may be necessary if the reader is not a personal acquaintance. For example, young executives will usually be more interested in proposals/products that will enable them to move ahead in their careers even though risks may be higher, whereas older readers may be more interested in security and stability.

Similarly, a person with a higher education level may better understand complex proposals than a person with a limited education. The content of your message should be adjusted according to the reader characteristics.

What current knowledge of or interest in the subject does your reader have? Fewer details will be needed to persuade a person who is knowledgeable about the subject than would be necessary for the one who is not familiar with your topic.

How will your proposal affect the reader? Are you asking for a commitment of resources (time or money)? If so, can you show that the benefits will outweigh the cost commitment? Will the action you request be easy for the reader to take?

The Writer

Assess your strengths for writing the message. Do you fully understand your proposal or product? What are the strengths—weaknesses—of the plan? What are the reader's alternatives? By analyzing potential objections BEFORE you write, you will be prepared to overcome the readers' opposition while they read your proposal.

Examine your credibility as a writer. People are more easily persuaded by a person they see as trustworthy, knowledgeable, or powerful. If your reader doesn't know of your credibility, you will want to structure your message to supply convincing facts and figures as evidence of your knowledge. If, however, the reader recognizes you as an expert on this subject, less documentation of convincing evidence will be needed. For example, which person would be perceived as more credible on the subject of corporate income taxes—a local bookkeeper or a corporate consultant with the IRS?

The Appeal

Consider the variety of appeals that can be used in persuasive writing. Common appeals are logical, emotional, positive, negative, and personal benefit.

Logical appeals focus on one's practical and reasoning ability. Logical appeals are rational concepts such as safety, efficiency, durability, and economy whereas *emotional* appeals focus on intrinsic feelings of well being such as success, achievement, happiness, joy, prestige, or excitement. Even the most knowledgeable businessperson who uses logical problem solving may also respond to an emotional appeal. Consider these examples:

Logical:	Earn a credit up to 1 percent of your purchase amounts and pay only 9.9 percent APR fixed rate with your new Access card.
Emotional:	Imagine having extra money to spend at the end of the year—up to 1 percent of your purchase amounts on your new Access card. And you could spend that money on anything you choose—from a vacation in the Caribbean to gifts for your loved ones.

Other appeals include positive or negative approaches. The positive approach shows the reader the positive benefits of responding to your request; whereas the negative approach emphasizes the consequences of not responding to your proposal. Use the negative approach sparingly and only with unique audiences where its use would be the most effective.

| **Positive:** | The skies are sunny and the retirement picture is bright. By opening your individual retirement account today, you can enjoy the blue skies and a bright financial picture in your retirement. |
| **Negative:** | Without Social Security, where will you be? With a federal retirement system that is nearly depleted, how will you manage in your retirement years? |

The personal benefit appeal is useful in persuasive writing. This appeal focuses on the direct benefits the reader will enjoy. It shows how your proposal will solve one of the reader's existing problems or create a better environment. Those benefits may be personal safety, security, social status, or a sense of well being. Answer the question that most readers have when they first view a proposal: What's in it for me? Show the readers how they can benefit directly.

| **Personal:** | Join the Fitness Center today and enjoy a higher energy level, a firmer body, and a little less weight! In just 45 minutes a day, you can be a new person. |

The Action

Determine the action you want the readers to take. Don't leave the readers to guess what they are to do. Are they to attend a meeting, place an order, write a check, or visit a demonstration? Make the action clear and easy to take.

Perhaps several different actions are required to accomplish your goal. Identify the intermediate action that will eventually lead to the ultimate action desired. Assume, for example, your ultimate desired action is for the readers to buy a car. Your request for them to visit your showroom for a test drive will be more successful than a request to purchase the car. At the showroom, the next action request will be addressed.

The Strategy

Persuasive messages may be written in the direct order if (1) the readers are inclined to listen objectively to your proposal, (2) they know your credibility as a writer, and (3) the proposal is long and complex (resulting in the request being buried within the report). Internal requests are frequently written in the **direct** order—particularly those addressed to superiors who are inclined to listen to the request.

Other persuasive messages—particularly those addressed to individuals who may not be interested in your proposal or who may not know your credibility—should be written in the **indirect** order. Compare the persuasive letter strategies with the earlier strategies you've studied.

Message Type	Beginning	Middle	Ending
Positive	most important point (positive news)	explanation additional key points	positive forward-looking close
Negative—no/little emotional response	bad news with brief rationale	explanation alternative	neutral or positive close
Negative—uncertain response	neutral opening (buffer)	explanation decision alternative	neutral or positive close
Persuasive—direct	request	interest/desire	request for action
Persuasive—indirect	attention	interest/desire	request for action

A Persuasive Approach

The indirect strategy used in effective persuasive messages differs slightly from the indirect strategy of the negative news message. Consider a four-point approach to persuading the reader. Make certain the message does these four things:

1. Gain the reader's attention.
2. Generate interest in your proposal/product.
3. Create a desire for the proposal/product.
4. Motivate the reader to act.

Getting Reader's Attention

Most readers receive more unsolicited mail than they want. Persuasive messages are generally unsolicited; that is, the reader is not expecting to receive the message. As a result, an attention-getting opening is needed to attract the reader to your message. Attention-getting devices are limited only by the imagination of the writer and may emphasize the design, format, or content of the message. Choose a device you believe will appeal to the particular group to whom you are writing. Among the almost unlimited number of devices are headlines, letter formats, alterations, attachments, and enclosures.

For some persuasive messages you can use a catchy slogan, a question that creates interest, or another type of headline to get the recipient's attention.

Right on Time, Every Time!

Be the first to be last!

Where would you go if you no longer had a home?

These headlines may be near the top of the page, in the margin, in a diagonal position, or in any other position that will stand out. You can use a special color to make a headline more prominent.

One letter writer obtained the desired attention by burning the upper right-hand corner of the letter that began with the headline "This letter contains HOT NEWS!"

A story, a quote from a famous person, or a striking announcement catch the reader's attention as well.

It's Christmas morning and the children are opening their presents. See the delight in Erica's eyes as she opens her dream castle. Wasn't Kelby surprised to see the bicycle? But wait, what about those children who have no presents?

"Ask not what your country can do for you, but what you can do for your country." *John F. Kennedy*

A cure for cancer can be yours!

Perhaps you can gain the reader's attention by asking a rhetorical question or by making a statement of common interest. By using a rhetorical question, you cause the reader to think about your topic. Do not use a yes-no question as that does not require much thinking. Consider these examples.

Yes-No Response:	Do you want to save a tree?
Rhetorical Question:	Where will we find the trees to make the paper that we need for our copying machines in 2015?
Common Interest:	Ten tons of paper are used each day in office copying machines in Centerville.

Regardless of the specific attention getting technique you choose, the opening should directly relate to the remainder of the message and should flow naturally into generating interest for the proposal or product.

Generate Interest

Follow the attention opening with sufficient explanation to create interest in your request. Using the focus initiated in the first sentence, develop your request. Explain why the request is important and create a desire for the reader to comply with your request. To create interest in and a desire for a product or a service, describe the appearance of the product and tell about unique features or opportunities. For some items you can effectively compare the size with an item that is familiar to the readers. For example, saying a calculator is about the size of a credit card helps most readers to visualize the size of the calculator, whereas specifying the exact dimensions—2⅛ by 3½ inches—would not.

Create a Desire

Create a desire for the reader to accept your proposal or purchase your product. Put the readers in the message by explaining how they can use the product or service in their daily lives.

> Available in sky blue or candy apple red, the X34 convertible puts you in touch with nature. Feel the wind blowing through your hair while the sun radiates on your back.

Give examples of situations in which they can use the product and when appropriate, tell how other people use the item. You can usually enclose leaflets, pictures, and other material to help describe the appearance of a product and to show how it is used.

Motivate Action

Motivate the reader to take some form of action: accept your proposal, donate time, place an order, visit your showroom, request more information, and so on. Confidently ask for the desired action. If you aren't convinced that the reader should act, you won't be able to convince the reader!

Close your letter with a clear concise statement of the action desired. Make the action easy. If the reader is to respond to you, enclose an addressed stamped envelope for convenience. If the reader is to call or to fax a response, include those numbers in the closing paragraph.

Common Persuasive Messages

Messages usually requiring sufficient persuasion to justify an indirect strategy include those that are written to invite, to request, to solicit, and to sell a product or a service. Each type uses a slightly different approach as described in the following section.

Persuasive Invitations

When you invite people to speak to a group, to serve on a committee, or to submit suggestions or recommendations, you compliment them. Inviting them lets them know you believe they have the ability to do what you are asking them to do. You can, therefore, extend invitations in a straightforward manner without feeling in any way apologetic.

Frequently, though, persons you invite need to be convinced that they should accept the invitations. You have to assure them they have the ability to carry out the assignments you are asking them to accept, or you have to assure them their completing the assignment(s) will benefit them or someone else.

Write invitations so clearly that the readers know exactly what you are asking them to do and when, where, and how they are to do it. Facts are almost always more useful than opinions in persuading people to accept invitations. Therefore, give one or more reasons for selecting them as participants. State the benefits they can expect to receive and possibly explain how their participation will contribute to the success or welfare of others. Write persuasively, cordially, and confidently. When you use the positive approach, the recipients are more likely to accept. Study the letter that follows.

Your presentation at the Association for Business Communication's annual conference in Cincinnati in October of 2002, was so informative to the two members of our organization who heard you speak that they highly recommended you to be the keynote speaker for our state meeting in Corpus Christi on Thursday, July 14, 2003. We will meet at 6 p.m. in the Seaside Room of the Bayfront Hotel. About four hundred members will attend.

Could you give the same presentation, "Minding Your Manners on Electronic Mail," you gave at the Cincinnati meeting? Our representatives liked the content of that presentation and the way in which you delivered it.

We will pay your expenses and give you an honorarium of $300. I will be glad to reserve you a room at the Bayfront Hotel for the night of July 14.

As our preliminary program must go to press by the end of the month, please call me by the 25th to let me know whether you can speak to our group. My telephone number is 936 555-3407.

Persuasive Requests

Requests are among the most common types of persuasive messages in business. Requests are a part of the normal business operations and are made by business personnel, homemakers, educators, and others. Many requests—routine and special—are made by writing letters. Routine requests were discussed in Chapter 13. Some requests, however, require greater persuasion.

When requesting something that is generally available, you have to use very little persuasion. Just use a courteous tone. Show proper consideration for the reader and at the same time do yourself a favor by making it easy for the reader to understand your letter and to reply to it.

More persuasion is required in special requests than in those that are routine. Use the indirect strategy to gain the reader's attention first. Follow the attention opening with sufficient explanation to create interest in your request. Using the focus initiated in the first sentence, develop your request. Explain why the request is important and create a desire for the reader to comply with your request.

Often, the effectiveness of special request letters can be enhanced by telling how the addressee will profit by complying. For example, some letters that are mailed to ask that a questionnaire be completed and returned contain promises to send summaries of the findings of the questionnaire survey. Since the writer sends the questionnaire to only those people who are genuinely interested in the survey, the writer can logically assume the recipient would like to have a summary of the findings.

You've had a hectic day. Every time you resolved one hassle today, two more problems surfaced. Finally, it's 5:00 and time to relax. But wait. You still have to drive home. Traffic will be at a standstill. More hassles, more stress. What can you do to reduce this stress? Join a car pool.

By sharing the driving responsibilities with your colleagues, you would face traffic hassles twice weekly instead of twice daily. On the other days, you could relax, enjoy a conversation with friends, or even read the paper on the drive home. By joining a car pool, you can also reduce your car maintenance and fuel costs.

At the request of several employees, we are organizing company car pools. You will be given the names of three people who live in your community and are interested in forming a car pool.

Simply answer the following questions and e-mail them to me by May 15. You can be enjoying hassle-free commuting within two weeks.

Persuasive Solicitations

Letters are used frequently for soliciting funds or services. When soliciting funds or services for an organization that is well known to the reader, the letter-writing task is much easier than when you have to describe the organization and its activities. A reader who has already been convinced that the organization is worthwhile needs little more than enough information to learn the kind of help you are seeking. The following letter, written in the direct order, was mailed to a civic-minded business person who had contributed on several occasions to the group that mailed the letter.

The Civic Action Club is soliciting the help of the business people in our city again this year to send children of low-income families to summer camp.

As you already know, this two-week program includes educational and recreational activities especially planned for the group. We have received applications from 36 deserving boys and girls from nine to eleven years of age. To permit all of them to participate, we must increase our existing fund by $700 before May 1.

Can you help again this year? Any contribution you make will be appreciated as much as ever.

Obviously, more information is needed for a letter to a person who is not already familiar with the organization or its activities. Use the indirect strategy. Keep the letter short yet complete, courteous, and interesting. Business people, as well as other citizens, receive so many letters of this nature they may not read the entire letter if it is long. On the other hand, they do not contribute the help that is solicited unless the letter contains adequate information in a well-written style.

An attention-getting device of some kind is needed for a letter that solicits. Attention getting is obviously not enough. To be effective, messages must hold the readers' interest and convince them that the purpose for which the solicitation is made is worthy of their help. Once you have convinced a reader you are soliciting for a worthwhile cause, make it easy to contribute. Give the exact name to whom the check should be written. Or if a service is to be contributed, give complete instructions on where, when, and how the service is to be provided. To encourage a quick response, enclose an addressed envelope.

Sales Messages

Good sales messages require careful planning and writing. Usually such messages are planned, drafted, and then edited by several people to ensure they have the right information, the right tone, and the right appeal. Plan your message by identifying the audience, assessing the product, selecting the primary selling point, and determining the desired action to be taken.

Determine as many traits as you can that are common to the people whose names are on your mailing list. The greater the number of these traits, the easier it is to write a letter that appeals to the readers. Select the appeal that best fits the audience. If you are writing to a well informed audience, a logical appeal may be used. If the audience is affluent, the emotional appeal is also appropriate in that cost is less of a consideration.

Study your product. What is it? How is it used? What are its strengths and weaknesses? How is it different from comparable products? Once, these questions have been answered, you are ready to select a primary selling point.

The *primary selling point* is the general theme of the message. It is impossible and impractical to describe every aspect of your product. To attempt to do so fragments your message. Instead concentrate on a few major qualities and combine those into one general theme. Assume you are selling notebook computers. If your audience consists primarily of experienced business users, convenience and time-saving features make a good primary selling point. If, however, your audience consists primarily of computer novices, ease of operation and maintenance may be a better primary selling point.

Next, select the action that you want the audience to take. This action may be to place an order, to visit your showroom to see a product or a demonstration, to ask that a representative visit a home or a work place to demonstrate a product or a service, or to request additional information about the item you are selling.

You are now ready to draft your sales letter. A well-chosen attention getter is of utmost importance in a sales letter; but that device alone cannot accomplish the purpose of the letter, which is to sell a product or a service. Follow the attention getting device with a carefully written message that creates interest in the item you are attempting to sell. Provide convincing evidence that prompts the reader to take the desired action. Refer to Figure 15-1 for an example of a sales letter.

Keep sales letters short and minimize the number and the length of enclosures. Do, though, use whatever enclosures are needed to describe adequately the product or service. You can advantageously use pictures, drawings, and descriptive writing on carefully chosen colored paper to supplement the sales information in the carefully written letter.

Make the action easy by enclosing a card or return envelope. Providing the means for response greatly improves your response rate.

Bristol First Consolidated Bank
2789 Main Street
Bristol, IN 46507

July 15, 2002

Mr. Dale Needham
4509 Guildford
Bristol, IN 46507

Dear Mr. Needham

Next August when the blistering summer weather descends on Bristol, you will be ready to make your escape for 10 days of refreshingly cool weather viewing spectacular ice formations on the route of the *Alaska Queen.*

We are offering a vacation account plan starting August 1 which will provide you an opportunity to deposit $100 on the first of each month for twelve months. With this investment, you may join the bank's cruise next year on August 1-10. Should you wish to take others with you on the cruise, you may deposit additional funds each month or encourage them to open their own accounts.

On February 15, we will ask that you commit $300 as a deposit for each person who will participate in the cruise to Alaska. If you decide not to go on the cruise at that time, you can use your funds for a different vacation or continue to save them for future vacations to be sponsored by the bank.

The vacation accounts currently draw interest at the same rate as our Golden Savings accounts. We can also arrange automatic withdrawal from your regular checking account to the vacation account. You will be surprised how quickly your vacation account grows.

Please examine the enclosed brochure with further details about the vacation account plan and send in your authorization form today. Next year, you, too, can be looking for a warm jacket in August as you and your friends from Bristol tour scenic Alaska!

Sincerely

J. B. Madison

J. B. Madison
Vice President of New Accounts

Figure 15-1. Sales Letter

DISCUSSION

1. What steps can you take to make it easy for the recipient of your letter to respond to your special request?

2. Why is audience analysis important in persuasive writing?

3. What are some attention-getting items that can be included or attached to sales letters to attract attention?

4. Give examples of persuasive messages using the logical, emotional, positive, negative, and reader benefit appeals.

EXERCISES

Improve the following sentences.

1. Settlement of the claim cost our company in excess of $500,000.
2. There are four desks that are to be removed from the fourth floor.
3. Our comptroller, whose name is Tina Owens, will represent us at the meeting in Switzerland.
4. Our company has only one office in the state of Idaho.
5. For the sum of $450, he can refinish the desk.
6. Please arrange the names in this list in alphabetical order.
7. By attaining a realization of the reason the problem existed, they could effect a solution to it.
8. Madge will be able to tabulate the data in a short period of time.
9. Due to the fact that the rental charges are being increased, we made the decision to move to a new location.
10. The book which you ordered yesterday has been shipped by parcel post.
11. We only have four copies of the book to send you.
12. There will be an opportunity for each employee to study the manual before it is printed in final form.
13. It is our hope that you will tell the manager if you want to be considered for the job so that she will know the exact number of applicants.
14. The dietitian recommended vegetables such as peas, beans, asparagus, etc., for the employee cafeteria.
15. They need more time to outline the report, to collect the data, and for writing a rough draft.

PROBLEMS

1. As director of the local humane society, you are trying to find homes for animals that are at the shelter. These animals are examined thoroughly, treated if necessary, and bathed when they are brought to the shelter. Many of them would make wonderful pets; some are even housebroken. If homes are not found for them, they are disposed of through euthanasia after two weeks. Write a persuasive letter to an audience of your choice encouraging them to adopt a pet.

2. You are responsible for obtaining a speaker for the annual spring banquet for athletes at your college. Invite an inspirational coach or athlete. Use your imagination and supply any information that you need to write a persuasive letter.

3. Your campus organization is sponsoring a Christmas toy drive for children from low-income families. You have worked with the Human Services Department and have identified more than 100 children who will probably not receive Christmas presents this year. Write a letter that can be personalized and sent to the faculty and staff of your university requesting donations of money, toys, and/or time (to wrap and distribute gifts). Supply additional details as needed, but do not alter the facts of the problem.

4. Each year, local fishing enthusiasts sponsor a "Get Hooked on Fishing" tournament for children seven to twelve years of age at the Sandy Flats Marina. Approximately 40 boats will be needed this year to accommodate the children and their sponsors. Write a letter that can be sent to each boat owner whose boat is kept in the Sandy Flats Marina, asking for the use of the boat for this tournament. If they desire, the owners may participate in the tournament as sponsors.

5. As director of the local chamber of commerce, you are excited about a new program. This year, the chamber is holding a dinner and awards program for area high school seniors recognizing them for their accomplishments. Write a letter to chamber members asking them to sponsor one or more students for the dinner. Additionally, you want the members to attend the dinner and sit beside "their" graduate. The cost is $15.00 per person.

6. You and two of your friends are building five chalets on a 12-acre tract in the beautiful Cascade Mountains. These chalets are in a secluded wooded area near a stream that several fishermen have referred to as "the fisherman's paradise," and they are about 40 miles from the nearest city, which has about 60,000 residents. Excellent ski slopes that are used by avid skiers provide entertainment during the winter. Other recreational facilities are also available.

   The chalets will be ready for use by June 1. Each chalet will accommodate six people. Each one is attractively furnished and has the modern conveniences of city living. You will rent them on a weekly or a monthly plan. Because of their attractiveness, their location, and the beauty of the surrounding area, you expect them to be used most of the year. Reservations for them will have to be made several months in advance.

Write a letter to be personalized and mailed to 200 skiers and fishermen who have enjoyed the ski slopes and streams of the Cascade Mountains the past eight years. You may enclose a descriptive brochure, but place most of the essential information in the letter.

7. Design an appropriate letterhead for your company Swingline Traders, 124 Blanca Road, Murfreesboro, Tennessee 32132. Write a persuasive letter using an indirect strategy. The letter will go to Petrina Chan-Nui, 2309 Grand Avenue, Butte, Montana 59701-4916. Petrina is the owner of a small gift shop called *Chance of a Lifetime*. You have just received some new unique items that you think her customers might like to buy. Select one item described by your instructor or one item of your choice. Use an attention getting opening. Your goal is to convince her to buy the selected item to sell to customers in her store. For the first order only, you will give her one item free for each twelve items she buys. You may determine the price of the item and describe appropriate selling points. Close the letter with your name. Your title is Sales Manager.

8. As program chairperson of the Franklin, Maryland, chapter of the Administrative Management Society, invite Sam T. Collier to speak at your monthly chapter meeting three months from now. Because he has done a great deal of work in the team building area, you want him to talk on that subject. Many of the executives in your region have expressed an interest in learning more about this popular concept. Mr. Collier is vice-president of Office Consultants, Inc. His address is 1125 Park Avenue, Bennington, NY 12783. Add any information that is necessary for you to write a good letter inviting Mr. Collier to speak to your group.

9. As a member of the student advisory council for your department, write a letter to alumni soliciting funds for the department's scholarship fund. Supply other information as appropriate to the problem.

10. You are the assistant manager of the Way-Off Campus Bookstore. Select an item in your inventory that you feel would be especially attractive to college students and would also encourage them to visit your store. Write an appropriate persuasive message to be distributed to college students to encourage them to come in to your store to see the item.

11. Your campus organization is small and fund raising is always a challenge. You have thought about having a two-day event on campus for the sole purpose of fund-raising. Write a letter to the presidents of the other campus organizations asking them if they would be interested in participating in this fund raising event where activities such as bake sales, raffles, and games could be held. Be sure to use an attention getting opening.

12. Your store is starting a new program to offer a credit card to recent college graduates who have been employed full time for at least one year. Your plan is somewhat different from other credit cards. For each month that the balance is paid in full, card holders earn points which can be redeemed for prizes at the end of each plan year. If a card holder does not wish to pay the full balance each month, however, a nominal payment of four percent of the balance is required. Create a letter which could be sent to potential card holders. You may also create a persuasive presentation graphics slideshow which can be used at key locations in the store to interest potential card holders.

PREPARING RESUMES AND APPLICATION LETTERS

- A job applicant is hired based on information in a resume which indicated the applicant was a college graduate. After five very successful years on the job, it was revealed that the employee never graduated from college. What are the ramifications for the employer and the employee?

- How do you determine the best structure for your resume?

CHAPTER OBJECTIVES

After studying this chapter, you should be able to:

1. Investigate the job search process including developing a network of contacts.
2. Create a job application letter to accompany the resume.
3. Describe three types of resumes: chronological, functional, and combination.
4. Discuss components of the resume including personal information, education, and work experience.
5. Examine ethical issues related to resume design.
6. Prepare a resume appropriate for your qualifications.

INITIATING THE EMPLOYMENT PROCESS

What kind of career do you want to develop? What skills and abilities do you have that will help you to get a job that will be the first step along your career path?

Employers screen applicants carefully to determine those who can contribute significantly to the employers' goals. To compete successfully with others who will apply for the jobs you want, you owe it to yourself to do as much as you can through study and work experience to make yourself an appealing applicant for an employer.

What knowledge, skills, and special attributes can you offer? Study your background including your accomplishments, education, skills, work experience, and personal traits so that you can present your qualifications in a way that will convince an employer you will be a valuable asset for the company.

As you prepare to seek employment, remember that employers are seeking employees who will best help them accomplish their objectives. Learn the requirements for the job you want and then present your qualifications to fit those requirements. After you decide what kind of job you want, the next step is trying to find an available job.

The employment process consists of a number of key components including networking, on-line job research, company research, job factors, types of resumes, resume components, ethics and the resume, the resume format, electronic resumes, posting resumes electronically, and writing an application letter.

Networking

Developing and maintaining a network is one of the most important things that you can do in the job search process. The majority of jobs are found by networking. Networking involves establishing a series of business contacts who may know of job openings in which you are interested. When developing your network, you may wish to consider contacting the following:

1. Current or former employers
2. Current or former teachers
3. School placement officers
4. Friends and relatives
5. Individuals who may have assisted you with college activities and/or assignments

If you have lost contact with some of these individuals, you should communicate with them about your progress since you last talked to them. As the job search begins, notify your network of individuals that you are looking for a job. Tell them the type of job you are interested in as well as when you would be ready to begin working.

In addition to your network contacts, you may learn about employment possibilities from newspaper and journal advertisements as well as posted jobs. Many universities schedule interviews with businesses through the campus placement center which may be an additional avenue for employment contacts. When you find a company in which you are interested, you should conduct some research to learn about the company.

An increasingly important place to look for jobs is through employment postings on the World Wide Web. By selecting a search engine and using key words such as "jobs" and "employment," a wide variety of job related sites can be located. Many sites post jobs or provide information about the job search process. Many companies provide resume builder features which allow a person to send their employment information directly to a company so that it will become part of the company's employment database.

On-Line Job Research

The World Wide Web is gaining increasing importance as both a job information source and a way to connect potential employees with potential employers. The number and quality of job sites varies. Two categories of web sites are career resources and job search sites. **Career resource sites** help job seekers better understand a career and help determine what jobs might be suitable or of interest to the job seeker. These sites are excellent to use when first thinking about careers and future employment. The second category of web sites are **job search sites**. These sites list and describe actual jobs and provide avenues for application. In addition, corporations often offer **resume builders** that allow applicants the opportunity to key in information to build a resume with a specific company. This information is connected to the company's database of potential job seekers.

A number of sites will give you lists of job-related sites. When searching for your own list of sites, the key words "job search", "career resources", and "jobs" may be helpful. The following tables provide ten web sites for career resources and ten web sites for job search sites. These sites are just a beginning point. You will be able to find many more sites as well.

Career Resource Sites	
http://www.analyzemycareer.com	Analyze My Career - offers career guidance and testing
http://www.brainbench.com	Brainbench - opportunity to assess skills, certification tests
http://www.careerfairs.com	CareerFairs - provides current information on career fairs in sales and technology
http://www.careerjournal.com	CareerJournal - from *Wall Street Journal*. Includes career articles.
http://www.careerperfect.com	Career Perfect - locating careers, includes e-resume ideas
http://stats.bls.gov/ocohome.htm	Occupational Outlook - U.S. Dept. of Labor source for the outlook on jobs
http://www.quintcareers.com	Quintessential Careers - provides tools for career and job seekers
http://www.referencenow.com	Reference Now - helps you build a file of references to use for employers
http://www.salary.com	Salary - gives salary information for various jobs by region and type
http://www.vault.com	Vault - career resources, provides message board to discuss employment trends and ideas

Job Search Sites	
http://www.brainbuzz.com	Brainbuzz - information technology jobs site
http://www.careerbuilder.com	Career Builder - post resume, job tips, job articles
http://www.headhunter.net	Headhunter - nationwide job posting, can post resume
http://www.hotjobs.com	Hotjobs - details jobs in many categories
http://www.thingamajob.com	Thingamajob - career management information as well as job seeking for information technology
http://www.jobs.com	Jobs - post resumes, career transition information, lists jobs, job seeking hints
http://www.jobsinthemoney.com	Jobs in the money - lists professional finance jobs
http://www.kforce.com	Kforce - searches other job sites for professional business jobs
http://www.monster.com	Monster - global site, job advice for different career stages, job listings, post resumes
http://wjo.wantedjobs.com/wjo/search.jsp?cb=wjo	Wanted Jobs - searches other job sites, offers job seeker services such as apartments

Company Research

Before you send an application letter to an organization, discover some of the important facts about it. Find out how long the organization has been in business, its location, the types of products or services it provides, its recent growth, and its prospects for the future. Your university library and/or placement center can supply you with a variety of sources about various types of organizations. The following references may be particularly helpful.

1. Company information through company sites on the World Wide Web
2. Company annual reports
3. Publications such as *BusinessWeek, Fortune, Forbes,* and *The Wall Street Journal*
4. Various business directories available in your college library

Job Factors

What should you consider when looking for a job? Some of the factors to consider are opportunities for growth through the job, the type of work in which you are especially interested and for which you are well qualified, working atmosphere, location, salary, fringe benefits, and the opportunity to continue formal education. You may also be interested in other factors such as the company's stand on the environment, the opportunity for on-site day care or elder-care, and the company's involvement in the community.

What is the best job for you? The best job will be one which meshes your attitudes, beliefs, and preparation with the goals of the company. Most placement experts would agree that it is better to wait for the job that "feels right" than to take the first job offered.

An important point to keep in mind is that if the job is one you want, it will also be desirable to other highly qualified people. Competition for good jobs is strong; therefore, put forth your best efforts when applying. Submit your application as soon as you can after you learn the job opportunity exists.

Most jobs are obtained through a combination of written communication and interviews. When you write an application letter, your objective is to present effectively enough information to impress the reader favorably so that you will be invited for an interview. Send a resume along with the letter. By enclosing a resume, you can keep the letter short and still present adequate information in a neat, orderly arrangement. Prepare the resume before you write the letter.

Types of Resume

The *resume* which is sometimes called a vita or a data sheet serves several purposes. A good resume (1) enables an applicant to give in an easy-to-read form a great deal of job-related information, (2) helps prospective employers to determine whether the applicant merits a job interview, and (3) permits prospective employers to get a good idea of the applicant's ability to organize and present information. When keying a resume, any format that looks professional, is consistent throughout, and is suitable to the job will work well.

Most resumes are one of three types: *chronological, functional,* or *combination.* While the chronological resume is the most traditional, one of the other choices may be more valuable for a particular applicant or a particular position. The three styles are described as follows.

Chronological Resume

A chronological resume lists information about the applicant in a chronological order with the most recent information first. When describing the applicant's education, the resume would include the most recent college first (see the example in Figure 16-1).

Education
> Stephen F. Austin State University, Nacogdoches, Texas. Graduated with B.B.A. degree in General Business, December 2002.
>
> Angelina Junior College, Lufkin, Texas. Completed general education requirements, August 1998-May 2000.
>
> Henderson High School, Henderson, Texas. Diploma, May 1998.

Figure 16-1. Applicant's Education

In the chronological resume, work experience is listed with the most recent job first. Employers find the chronological resume to be valuable when they wish to see a logical progression of work experience and education. For those applicants whose work experience falls into a chronological pattern, this type of resume is preferred (See the example in Figure 16-2).

Some applicants, however, may have gaps in work history or may wish a job that is not an obvious choice based on their previous experience and education. These applicants may prefer to use a *functional resume*.

Functional Resume

The functional resume groups the applicant's skills in a series of categories that relate to the job the applicant is seeking. The applicant does not necessarily include the dates or places of all educational endeavors or work experiences (See Figure 16-3).

Applicants who have been out of the work force due to family responsibilities or military experience may find the functional resume a more effective way of outlining their qualifications. The functional resume can also be used to show how the applicant's qualifications match that of a specific job (See example in Figure 16-4).

Combination Resume

The combination resume combines facets of both the chronological resume and the functional resume. An applicant who has a strong chronological record of education may wish to list education in that manner. If the same applicant has held numerous part-time jobs or has not worked much during college, a functional approach to the work experience component may be more effective. A combination resume can also be tailored to fit the requirements of a specific position.

Jeffrey James Winstead
442 Stallings Drive
Nacogdoches, TX 75961
(936) 560-2109

OBJECTIVE

To obtain a position in a financial institution which will enable me to contribute both to the company and to my own personal growth.

EDUCATION

Stephen F. Austin State University, Nacogdoches, TX, December 2002. B.B.A. degree in Finance. Minor: International Business
G.P.A. in major: 3.4 (4.0 scale)

EXPERIENCE

First State Bank, Shreveport, LA. Internship. Summer 2002. Responsibilities: Maintain safety deposit records, open and close accounts, and work with loan customers.

Brentwood Motors, Lufkin, TX. Bookkeeper. August 1998-May 2002. Twenty hours per week. Responsibilities: Prepare payroll, issue purchase orders, pay bills, and maintain accounts.

County Pool, Nacogdoches, TX. Lifeguard. Summers 1996-1998. Responsibilities: Develop work schedule for lifeguards, train and supervise new lifeguards, and maintain safety conditions of pool area.

ACTIVITIES AND AWARDS

Alpha Kappa Psi. Pledge trainer.
Beta Gamma Sigma. Inducted into business honor society.
Dean's List, four semesters
Scholarship for academic performance

REFERENCES

Dr. J. L. Lincoln, Finance Professor
Stephen F. Austin State University
P.O. Box 13079
Nacogdoches, TX 75962
(936) 468-3194

Ms. Teri Greenwood, Supervisor
Brentwood Motors
1411 Timberland
Lufkin, TX 75901
(936) 634-8491

Mr. Curtis Cole, Owner
Brentwood Motors
1236 N. First Street
Lufkin, TX 75901
(936) 637-0347

Figure 16-2. Chronological Resume

Computer skills
Worked with a variety of software programs including Lotus, Word, WordPerfect, and Powerpoint both in school and on the job. Used Powerpoint to design a promotional presentation about a new service offered by a real estate firm.

Academic preparation
Graduated from an accredited university with a bachelor's degree in business. Completed minors in International Business and French. Served as salutatorian of high school class.

Figure 16-3. Applicant Skills

By studying yourself carefully and deciding which attributes, achievements, and work experience will best suit the job for which you are applying, you may select the most promising resume design for the particular job. Although there are no prescribed rules in resume design, most applicants select several key components to include in the resume (See Figure 16-5).

Resume Components

All of the resume styles address basic content areas including education, work experience, personal information, and references. Many resumes, however, use different titles for these areas or break them into small sections. Use your originality in designing a resume to meet your needs.

Personal Information

The types of personal information to place on the resume vary among applicants. Be sure to include your full name, address, and telephone number. If you are living away from home temporarily, you may show two addresses and telephone numbers—temporary and permanent. As communication in the job process is important, you may also decide to include an electronic mail address or fax address. If you have a personal web page suitable for viewing by prospective employers, you may wish to include that address.

A married woman will need to decide how to list her professional name. Some women replace their middle names with their maiden name. Others use a hyphenated name.

The best step to take in choosing items of personal information is to study the requirements for the job and then ask yourself, "If I were an employer, what information would help me to decide whether I would like to interview this applicant?"

Omit any information that would not help the prospective employer in determining your qualifications for the job. Information such as height and weight may have little value in most jobs.

Employers are not to discriminate during the hiring process on factors of race, age, gender, religion, national origin, marital status, or physical disability. You may wish to eliminate personal references in these areas.

Lynica Gerold
407 Shoal Creek Place
Austin, TX 78757
(512) 458-0461

OBJECTIVE

To employ managerial skills and experience in a position as a manager of a medium sized retail establishment.

QUALIFICATIONS

- Four years as assistant manager with a multiculturally diverse retailing firm with sales of $25 million per year.
- Extensive experience using computer software including Lotus for management analysis.
- Designed training programs for new employees.
- Adept at developing rapport with all levels of employees.

EXPERIENCE HIGHLIGHTS

- Developed marketing strategy which increased store sales 15 percent during one quarter.
- Combined two departments resulting in a savings of over $50,000.
- Revised procedures to speed credit approvals for customers.

WORK HISTORY

- Assistant Manager, The Box Store - 4 years
- Sales Clerk, The Box Store - 2 years

EDUCATION

B.S. degree - Business Administration - University of Texas - Austin

REFERENCES

Available upon request.

Figure 16-4. Functional Resume

T. L. Hernandez

<u>Temporary Address</u>
4879 Kingwood
Phoenix, AZ 85072
(932) 560-3409

<u>Permanent Address</u>
3271 Haviland Lane
Atlanta, GA 30367
(404) 387-6083

Objective

A position in industrial sales which will utilize both technical and sales background.

Professional Education

University of Kansas, Lawrence, KS. M.B.A. August 2002.

Kansas State University, Manhattan, KS. B.S. in Mechanical Engineering. May 1994.

Related Experience

Simon Engineering. Kansas City, KS. May 1997-July 2002.
Installed new processing equipment and repaired equipment in a five state area.
Trained new employees. Participated in yearly trade show in Atlanta.

U.S. Army Corps of Engineers, May 1994- April 1997.
Completed training course and participated in activities throughout the United States.
On special assignment as part of UN Peacekeeping Troops.

Sales Experience

Sold industrial equipment as part of a team concept utilizing a sales person and an industrial technician. Answered customer questions about operating capacities of available products. Team received quarterly sales award.

Organized fund raising auction for major local charity which earned $62,000.

Completed analysis during M.B.A. program of sales departments of several large industrial firms.

Personal Traits and Communication Skills

Active member of local Toastmaster's organization to develop speaking ability.

Fluent in Spanish and French.

Organized study groups during M.B.A. program to facilitate the learning experience.

Outgoing and friendly personality has been an asset in engineering career.

References

Available upon request.

Figure 16-5. Combination Resume

Goal or Objective

A component included in some resumes is the objective or goal statement. That statement can be either short term or long term. A goal statement is especially helpful when it is unclear from your qualifications what type of job you may be seeking. The following example includes both short- and long-term elements.

Goal

To obtain an entry-level accountant position that will provide experience in auditing so that within the next three years, I will be able to pass the CPA examination.

Education

The background in formal education is often the most impressive part of the resume for a college student or a recent graduate. This section—when it appears to be the applicant's strongest attribute—should be placed before the sections for work experience and references.

Include in this well-organized record of education the name and location of your college or university, years of attendance, anticipated graduation date, academic major and/or minor, and any activities, awards, or honors. If you feel it is to your advantage, you may wish to include your overall scholastic average and the average in your major field.

You can strengthen this section of the resume by listing courses you have taken that apply specifically to the job that you are applying for. As you will observe when studying the sample resumes in this chapter, you can list courses in addition to those in your major field of study. Studying the job requirements will help you to decide whether to include names of courses and, if you do, which courses to list and how to list them.

Activities, awards, and honors are an important part of your education and can make a favorable impression on employers. Rather than attempting to list all accomplishments, select only those activities you believe indicate you have a well-rounded background or that demonstrate how your out-of-class experiences contribute to your competence in the particular job being sought.

As a general rule, the record of your educational background should include secondary education as well as any education after high school graduation. When using a *chronological resume,* show the school name, location, and dates of attendance. If you apply for a job within a few years after graduation from high school, including data on high school academic achievements and outstanding extracurricular activities may be worthwhile. Ordinarily, however, the name, location, and dates of attendance cover sufficiently the high school background for a college graduate. If, however, you do not wish to reveal your age, you should either not include dates or omit the high school information.

Work Experience

An applicant who has work experience that would probably be more beneficial than formal education for a particular job should present the work experience section first on the resume. Applicants who have worked several years since attending college, graduate school, or a professional school usually present their record of work experience before that for formal education. In addition, college graduates who attended college part-time while working full-time may wish to stress the work experience component.

Under work experience show the dates of employment, the nature of your work, the names and addresses of employers, and possibly the names of your immediate superiors. Make specific statements about your work. For example, give the title of your job and list specific duties such as greeting customers, demonstrating products, and meeting sales targets.

Which should you list first—the title of your job or the name of the employer? If you believe the prospective employer will be more favorably impressed by a job title accompanied by a list of specific duties than by the name of the employer, list the job title first. On the other hand, if the prospective employer knows that your present or former employer hired only outstanding workers, you may list the name of the employer before the job title. Use *parallel structure*. For example, when you show the job title first for a present or a former job, list the job title first for all other work records on your resume. In addition, be consistent in providing the same information for each job listed.

When you provide the name of your immediate superior, the prospective employer may wish to contact that person by telephone or by letter to obtain information about you. Your immediate superior can supply more specific, helpful information than can the personnel director or others who have only a general knowledge of your performance. A former supervisor's statements about a specific task you performed or about a special trait you possess means much to a prospective employer.

You will also want to include any *internships* you completed as part of your course of study. Be specific in describing the experiences you obtained as part of the internship. If you have had limited work experience, include a record of part-time and summer jobs. If you have had no work experience for which you were paid a wage or a salary, include an account of work for which you received no pay. You may very well mention activities such as helping carry out a project for a civic club or serving as an officer for a club, a fraternity, or a sorority.

The work experience does not have to be related directly to the job you are seeking. If you have worked as a laborer or in a job unrelated to your major after school, on weekends, or during summers, include this experience on your resume. Referring to these jobs may help convince the prospective employer you are willing to work. Willingness to work and to perform some of the less desirable tasks as well as those you enjoy is a characteristic employers like. One employer indicated that he would rather interview a student who had spent his or her college years working as a cashier in the local grocery store rather than a student with a better academic record who had no work experience.

Experience in lower-level jobs is helpful for a person who desires a management position. Because employees look at a situation from a vantage point different from that of management personnel, your previous experiences working at that level help you to understand the thinking of the employees at different levels of the organization's structure. You can, therefore, manage more effectively than you could without this understanding.

You may be wise to omit some of the many short-term jobs you may have held if including them would clutter your resume. Do not, though, omit a job solely because it seems to have little or no relationship to the job you are seeking.

Make your resume interesting. Emphasize any item that would help you to convince the prospective employer you are well qualified for the job for which you are applying, and de-emphasize any item that does not help you make a favorable impression. Active verbs contribute to the interest quality of a resume. Use active verbs, therefore, and use parallel structure. Instead of saying "Was responsible for closing the warehouse on Friday evenings," say, "Assumed responsibility for closing the warehouse on Friday evenings." Among the numerous active, interest-creating verbs are these:

assumed	conducted	coordinated
designed	established	maintained
increased	created	installed
instituted	equipped	provided
originated	devised	formulated
prepared	supervised	verified
revised	developed	generated

Give specific information, and use parallel structure throughout your resume. For the chronological resume, present the experience record in chronological order with the most recent date first.

Another trend in resume design is to replace action verbs with specifically focused accomplishments. For example, instead of saying "trained ten employees", you would focus on an accomplishment of your training activities. Perhaps you could say "developed new training program for employees which resulted in a 25 percent reduction in employee turnover during the first six months of the new program." This style of listing your accomplishments requires that you keep detailed records of your work experience.

References

Many prospective employers write, telephone, or converse in face-to-face situations with an applicant's references—people who know a good deal about the applicant's work experience, education, or personal traits. Prepare, therefore, a list of three to five people who can give and are willing to give prospective employers an accurate evaluation of your qualifications for a job. Give the names (as they sign them), job titles, business addresses, and telephone numbers.

You may include this information on your resume, or you may send this information when the prospective employer requests it. More and more applicants today—especially those for jobs other than those at the entry level—prefer to supply references upon request. A reason for including the names on the resume, though, is that it saves time for employers who want to contact those people. If you omit the names from your resume, have them ready to mail the day you receive a request for them. One appropriate way to arrange a reference sheet as shown in Figure 16-6. Transmit this sheet with a letter, which may be similar to the one in Figure 16-7.

Lynica Gerold
407 Shoal Creek Place
Austin, TX 78757
(512) 458-0461

REFERENCES

Mr. Milton Clifford   Employer
Manager
The Box Store
497 Main Street
Austin, TX 78757
(512) 458-3498

Ms. Elise Black   Supervisor
Department Head
The Box Store
497 Main Street
Austin, TX 78757
(512) 458-3497

Dr. Allen Moore   Major professor
College of Business
University of Texas
Austin, TX 78757
(512) 458-3378

Figure 16-6. References Page

Lynica Gerold
407 Shoal Creek Place
Austin, TX 78757

November 15, 2002

Mr. Bob Westphal
Human Resources Director
The Benson Company
7941 Utica Road
Dallas, TX 75222

Dear Mr. Westphal

Thank you for contacting me about your managerial position. As you requested, I am including the names, addresses, and telephone numbers of three references who can provide you with further information about me.

I look forward to hearing from you after you have had an opportunity to visit with my references.

Sincerely

Lynica Gerold

Lynica Gerold

Enclosure

Figure 16-7. Letter to Accompany References

Your list of references depends somewhat on your background. If you have had a considerable amount of work experience, include the names of two or more employers—present or former. If you have had limited work experience, consider including the names of two or more professors. Ordinarily as a recent college graduate, you should list the name of a professor in your major or your faculty advisor. Employers usually expect this listing because your major professor or faculty advisor probably knows a good deal about you.

By all means, list the names of people who will give you a good recommendation. When choosing between two people who are about equally well prepared to give you a good recommendation, choose the one who you believe can write the better letter and will write promptly. Receiving recommendations early gives an applicant an "edge" over another applicant whose letters of recommendation arrive later.

While past or present employers are usually the best references, you may wish to consider others who may be able to speak about your character. You should avoid listing relatives as references. When a reference's job title does not indicate the reason you gave that name, add a note explaining your relationship with the person. If the relationship is unclear, the reader may not understand the value of the person as a reference.

If you are unsure if your potential reference remembers you clearly, try to remind them of experiences they might remember. For example, if you have asked a college professor to serve as a reference, you might wish to recall a specific project you completed in a certain course taught by that professor.

Be sure to ask **permission** from your references before you list their names on your resume. At the time you ask them to serve as a reference, you may wish to give them a copy of your updated resume and let them know what type of position you are seeking. Also, update them on changes in your life since you last talked to them. Be sure to share any name changes with your references. By keeping your references informed as you proceed through the job search, they will be able to provide a more responsive reference for you when employers call.

When you are applying for a job you are very interested in, it is a good idea to contact your references and let them know they may be receiving a call from a specific company. You may wish to share with them any particular information that would help them do a better job of providing a reference.

Other Areas

Because employers look for applicants who can produce, you may wish to include the percentage of your college expenses you earned if you earned a significant percentage of them. You can present this information in personal information, in experience, or in education.

You may also want to include your experience with computers and other technology. You could list the information in a section called *Computer Skills* or a similar topic. You may wish to include software packages and hardware that you have worked with either through your work experience or education. Be specific by including the names of hardware and/or software packages including the versions you used. If you do not wish to use a separate section for your technology-based information, you might want to include the information as part of your education or experience sections.

If you have earned scholarships or awards or have been involved in professional, campus, or civic organizations, you may wish to use an *Awards and Activities* section. The name of this section should reflect the information you have decided to include.

If you have had other life experiences which have been valuable, you may wish to include them. For example, if you are fluent in another language or have traveled extensively, you may wish to include this information at some point in the resume. Some people place this information in an *Interests* section which might also include hobbies or leisure activities. If you feel the information relates directly to job performance, you may wish to list it as part of the experience or education section of the resume.

Ethics and the Resume

You may choose any style of resume which best meets your qualifications. Certainly you wish to portray yourself in the best light possible in the employment process. However, everything you list on the resume should be *true information*. Many employers express concern about the ethical practices of those developing resumes.

The most common problem in recent years has been a trend toward *inflating* the applicant's qualifications. For example, a person who graduated from a two-year college with an associate degree might list that he or she graduated from a four-year university instead. This is clearly an unethical and illegal representation. Recently, one state politician inflated the resume to indicate that the baccalaureate degree was conferred with honors when, in fact, the person was more than a semester short of the hours needed to graduate. In this case the individual felt compelled to resign the political position after the true academic background became public knowledge.

Other inflation problems also occur. A common one is for applicants to inflate work experience. A bus person at a restaurant might list the job as assistant manager. As former employers are the references who will most likely be checked, inflating the work experience can be a fatal mistake. Once a potential employer catches an applicant in a lie, the entire application becomes suspect.

A third area for inflation is in academic ability such as grade point average or in scholarships and awards. A student with a GPA of 2.5 should not list the GPA as 3.7 as the GPA is easily verified by transcripts. A better practice would be to not list the GPA if the applicant feels it is not advantageous.

Many employers base their hiring decisions on the total packet of information available to them which may include an application form, and any communication from the applicant such as the application letters and resume. For that reason, an ethics violation on the resume could later turn into grounds for dismissal from a job. Most application forms have a place for the applicant to verify that this information is true to the best of the applicant's knowledge. When designing the resume, assume that the same statement applies to the resume as well. Prepare an accurate resume which reflects the best of your abilities and qualifications.

The Resume Format

While no one resume format is required, successful resumes have several things in common. The resume should be well organized with the appropriate information easy to find and to read. In addition, a laser printer should be used to print the resume. Most business resumes are printed on white or off-white high-quality paper. Although some resumes are printed on different colors of paper, conservative choices are usually the best guide. While no more than two different typefaces or fonts should be used, bolding, italics, and underlining can assist in the readability of the resume.

Although some experts might argue that the resume should be no longer than one page, a resume that is easy to read and is well organized may be up to two pages long. When preparing a resume that will be longer than one page, be sure to place the most important information early in the resume to insure that it will be quickly noticed. A two-page resume should also have an appropriate heading at the top of the second page in case the pages become separated.

Electronic Resumes

Some companies have started working with *electronic resumes*. The most common procedure is to scan applicants' resumes and then to organize them for quick reference. Large companies with thousands of resumes from applicants are finding this procedure very helpful.

If you know that your resume will be scanned, you will want to use a single font and avoid bolding and italicizing information as most scanners have difficulty translating special features on resumes. You may find it helpful to have two forms of your resume—one for traditional companies and one for those companies who scan resumes.

Electronic resume management software matches key words. Therefore, be sure to use appropriate key words in your resume that will lead to the type of job you wish. Most electronic software is designed to work with chronological resumes so functional resumes often cause difficulties in computer systems. You will also find it a good idea to place most of your key words early in the resume as some software packages will search only the first 100 words or so for the key words. If you belong to any professional organizations, also include them. If a search is conducted based on professional membership, you would like your resume to be on the list. An example of an electronic resume is shown in Figure 16-8.

Posting Resumes Electronically

You may decide to post your resume on a World Wide Web site. One option would be to publish your resume as a link to your personal web page. Several companies offer potential employees the opportunity to post resumes at job or employment sites. Some postings are free. Many, however, require a fee to post a resume for a specifed length of time–perhaps 90 days. Check carefully into the cost and the audience for the site. If a very focused group reads the site, it may be worth your time to pay to post your resume.

As mentioned earlier, many companies also provide a resume builder tool which provides you with blanks to key in information. When you are finished, you can send your resume directly to a specific company.

Before you post your resume electronically, you should follow some common sense guidelines. Be sure to date the resume. Sometimes it is difficult to remove a resume once it is posted as others may forward it to different sites. You do not want your new employer to find you have a resume posted online apparently looking for a new job when you have just started. A date helps to resolve this problem.

Jeffrey James Winstead
Nacogdoches, TX 75961
email: jjwinstead@hotmail.com

OBJECTIVE

To obtain a position in a financial institution which will enable me to contribute both to the company and to my own personal growth.

KEYWORDS

B.B.A., Finance Major, Minor in International Business, banking, open and close accounts, prepare payroll and purchase orders, Stephen F. Austin State University, Beta Gamma Sigma, Dean's List, academic scholarship, work with loans and customers, bookkeeper.

EDUCATION

Stephen F. Austin State University, Nacogdoches, TX, December 2002.
B.B.A. degree in Finance. Minor: International Business
G.P.A. in major: 3.4 (4.0 scale)

EXPERIENCE

First State Bank, Shreveport, LA. Internship. Summer 2002.
Responsibilities: Maintain safety deposit records, open and close accounts, and work with loan customers.

Brentwood Motors, Lufkin, TX. Bookkeeper. August 1998-May 2002. Twenty hours per week. Responsibilities: Prepare payroll, issue purchase orders, pay bills, and maintain accounts.

County Pool, Nacogdoches, TX. Lifeguard. Summers 1996-1998.
Responsibilities: Develop work schedule for lifeguards, train and supervise new lifeguards, and maintain safety conditions of pool area.

ACTIVITIES AND AWARDS

Beta Alpha Psi. Pledge trainer.
Beta Gamma Sigma. Inducted into business honor society.
Dean's List, four semesters
Scholarship for academic performance

REFERENCES

Available and furnished upon request.

DATE: December 1, 2002

Figure 16-8. Electronic Resume

Do not include confidential information such as your social security number or your exact address. As you do not know who may access your resume, you may be wise to include your name, city, and either an e-mail or phone number at which you can be contacted. Also, do not include detailed information such as names, street addresses, and phone numbers about your jobs and references in a posted resume. You do not want someone to see your completely detailed and excellent resume and have them decide that they will assume your identity.

Once you post your resume, it is important that you keep it updated, that you follow up on contacts, and that you remove it from job databases when you have completed your job search.

Application Letter

Having studied the organization to which you plan to apply for employment and having prepared a resume, you are ready to write the application letter. The purpose of the application letter is to focus on two or three of your major accomplishments and to encourage the reader to examine your resume. Your resume should ALWAYS be accompanied by an application letter. The letter is usually no more than three to five paragraphs in length. A well-written application letter should include the following sections.

Opening Paragraph

When you know of a specific job, the first paragraph should clearly state the job in which you are interested. You may wish to say who told you about the job or how you learned about it. An employer who advertises through journals, newspapers, or radio likes to know the advertisement has received responses. Many employers like to receive applications from friends, relatives, or acquaintances of present or former employees. Try to determine, however, if the friend whose name you wish to use is in good standing with the company. If not, you may prefer not to mention a name.

If you do not know if a vacancy exists, use another type of beginning to gain favorable attention. These opening sentences have been used in successful application letters:

Is your firm looking for a qualified sales representative with a record of success in the industry? If so, please consider my qualifications.

Stacey L. Westville, your sales representative for this area, told me you usually hire several extra sales people for the summer months. I am interested in applying for a sales position.

Middle of the Letter

In the middle section (between the first and the last paragraphs) convince the prospective employer that you understand the job requirements and that your qualifications fit those requirements. Try to match your qualifications as closely as possible with the requirements that the employer has listed for the position.

As you state your understanding of the job requirements, be careful that you do not appear to be telling the reader what the company needs. Contrast these general examples to ones that are more focused on the job requirements.

General	Focused
The position requires someone who can communicate effectively.	My communication skills were developed during the two sales positions I held during my college career.
I can understand why you want a college graduate for this position.	After completing my college degree in business, I am ready to apply the knowledge I have learned.
Your ad asked for a dependable person—that is me!	After successfully completing my college courses while working approximately 20 hours per week, I consider myself a dependable person.

Even though your background has been outlined on the resume, use the middle paragraphs of the letter to emphasize your best qualifications. In addition to convincing the reader that you have skills and knowledge that will enable you to contribute to the employer's objectives, let the reader know you are energetic and eager to work.

Do not give the impression you are conceited, but do not sell yourself short. Remember, no one thinks more highly of you than you think of yourself. Do all you can to show you have the proper blend of self-confidence and modesty to succeed. What is the blend that suits your personality and the job you are seeking?

Call the reader's attention to the resume you have enclosed by mentioning a specific item on the resume. These ways have been used:

> My business education at the University of Florida is detailed in the enclosed resume.
>
> I have gained confidence in the retail field through my position at Benson Brothers as described on my resume.

Closing Paragraph

In the last paragraph ask confidently—not presumptuously or pleadingly—for an interview. If you can go for an interview at any time, say so when you ask for an opportunity to discuss your qualifications for the job.

Perhaps you will be in the vicinity of the interviewer's office during certain dates and would like to have an interview then. Mention this arrangement. If that office is far away, you may suggest the possibility of an interview when a representative is in your region.

Sometimes an arrangement such as this is advantageous to the prospective employer, especially if the company is paying your travel expenses.

Letter Examples

Study the first draft of your letter and make any needed revisions. The prospective employer knows your application letter represents your **best efforts** in writing. In other words, the reader knows no other letter you would write would be better than the one you write to apply for a job.

Choose words that fit the occasion, and write in a style that reveals your personality. Do not copy someone else's letter. The reader wants to know about you. You have to use the pronoun I to tell about yourself, but do not use it unnecessarily. You can use I and still maintain the you attitude by emphasizing the excellent work you can do for the employer.

Your grammar should be impeccable. Strive for a good command of the English language when speaking; but even those minor errors that creep in occasionally in everyone's speech because of chance, changing thoughts before finishing a sentence, or for any other reason should be eliminated from the application letter. Including a misspelled word is inexcusable as it shows a carelessness about both excellence and the job search.

You should use computer spell checkers and grammar checkers to review your letter. In addition, ask someone whose opinion you value to review your application letter to find any undetected errors as well as to determine the clarity of your writing style.

By all means, include your return address above the date on the letter. The reader will know that a letter sent to that address will reach you. Therefore, do not use the trite expression "write to the address given above." If you believe you will be at another address when the reader replies, specify the address to be used.

Try to learn the name and the job title of the officer in charge of employing someone for the job you are seeking. If you cannot learn from a friend or from printed materials the employing officer's name, call the organization. Ask the person who answers the telephone to give you the name and the title of the person to whom you should send an application. Verify the spelling of the name. Address your letter to that person. If you cannot learn the name, however, address the letter to the "Director of Human Resources."

Center the letter on the page. An attractive, well-written letter no longer than one page in length helps to command favorable attention. Use the same laser printer and quality paper you used for the resume.

You can apply the suggestions in this chapter and still use originality in your letters. Sample application letters are shown in Figures 16-9 and 16-10.

Once you have printed the letter, signed it in ink, and mailed the application letter and resume, you can give additional thought to the interview you requested in the final paragraph. If you are invited to go for an interview, you have been successful in your first step—writing the letter and the resume—of the application process.

Jeffrey James Winstead
422 Stallings Drive
Nacogdoches, TX 75961

December 1, 2002

Ms. Carole Owens
Bank of North America
4780 Park Circle West
San Mateo, CA 94404

Dear Ms. Owens

Are you looking for a dependable assistant loan officer who can relate well with the public? Dr. J. L. Lincoln, my finance professor, told me this morning that you plan to employ an assistant loan officer to begin working on January 2. Please consider my application for that job.

For the past three years, I have worked part-time for Brentwood Motors in Lufkin, TX, as a bookkeeper. This work fascinates me; and I am challenged by the demands that are made, especially during the financial activities at the end of each quarter and the end of the year.

During the summer of 2002, I completed a finance internship with First State Bank in Shreveport, LA. I found my first experience working in the banking environment to be very rewarding. I especially enjoyed learning to know the bank customers and assisting them in their banking needs.

In addition to my work experiences during college, I have maintained a 3.4 scholastic average in my major on a 4.0 scale. As you can well imagine, I have learned to budget my time. I look forward to applying the finance courses I took in college to a full-time job.

Dr. Lincoln and the other references listed on the enclosed resume have said they will be glad to give you an evaluation of my qualifications for a financial position.

Will you discuss with me the possibilities of working for you? I could come to your office at almost any time that would be convenient for you.

Sincerely

Jeffrey James Winstead

Jeffrey James Winstead

Enclosure

Figure 16-9. Application Letter

T. L. Hernandez
4879 Kingwood
Phoenix, AZ 85072

August 1, 2002

Mr. George Trent
Human Resources Director
The Greenville Corporation
1 Vista Place
Atlanta, GA 30369

Dear Mr. Trent

Please consider me an applicant for the industrial sales position you have open. Mr. Duane Stewart, your regional representative, informed me of the opening.

My work experience includes three years with Simon Engineering in Kansas City as the technical engineer for industrial equipment. In that position I had an opportunity to work with the sales representatives which so sparked my interest in sales that I decided to go to graduate school.

As part of my MBA from the University of Kansas, I completed an analysis of sales departments of several large industrial firms which gave me a broader view of the industrial sales field. I am looking for a position which will allow me to combine my technical knowledge as an engineer with the business aspects of sales in an industrial sales environment.

I would like to have an opportunity to discuss my qualifications further in an interview at your convenience. You may contact me at (404) 387-6083.

Sincerely

T. L. Hernandez

T. L. Hernandez

Enclosure

Figure 16-10. Application Letter

DISCUSSION

1. Describe the value of using an electronic resume.

2. What elements should you include in the resume?

3. Describe the chronological resume, the functional resume, and the combination resume. How would you decide which would be the best choice?

4. Should you include personal information in your letter or resume? If so, what?

5. Describe selecting your references and deciding whether to include them on the resume.

EXERCISES

1. A friend has asked for your help in creating a resume. Work with this information and the guidelines in this chapter to create an acceptable resume.

   Linda L. Lorenzo is going to graduate from your university this spring. She graduated from Toledo Bend High School four years ago and was the valedictorian of her class. In college she has majored in Marketing with a minor in Psychology. Her grade point average is 3.5 on a 4.0 scale. For the last two years she has worked at H.E.B. (a grocery store chain) in the deli department. Last summer she completed a two-month internship in the marketing department of Horizon, Unlimited, a local marketing firm. Before she worked at H.E.B. she worked for three years on a part-time basis at the county library primarily in the cataloguing department. In high school she was President of the French club. She has continued her interest in French by completing 12 additional hours in French in college. In college she was in the Marketing Club and was the membership director last year. This year she was named to Beta Gamma Sigma, the business honor society. During her first two years of college she was a member of the university volleyball team. Her interests include sports such as volleyball and swimming and her hobby of making scrapbooks for family and friends.

PROBLEMS

1. Create a chart which will show your network of support individuals to help you in your job search. Group together those from the same companies or same fields. You will use the chart to determine in which areas you have strong contacts and which areas you need to develop others. Be ready to explain your chart to the class.

2. *Fortune* magazine publishes yearly lists of the 500 largest firms in the country. Select a firm listed by *Fortune* from a current list. Do extensive research on one of these organizations: consider applying for the job of your choice even though you do not know whether a vacancy exists. Prepare an effective resume to send with your application letter. Address the letter to a person you have not met and include that person's job title.

3. Prepare a resume and application letter which describe your current qualifications. Assume that you will use the resume and application letter to apply for an internship and/or a scholarship.

4. Select another format (chronological, functional, or combination) for the resume you created in Problem 3. Revise the resume to fit the new format. Ask three of your friends to look at both resumes and tell you which one they prefer and why. Report your results in a memo to the instructor.

5. Revise the resume you created in Problem 3 so that you could post it to an online service through the World Wide Web. Be sure to consider security and confidentiality issues. Post your revised resume at a job site if you feel it is appropriate.

6. Prepare a list of three to five references which you will use as either a second page for your resume or as a list which will be mailed later to a prospective employer. Be sure to use day time addresses and phone numbers and complete names.

7. Evaluate a fellow class member's resume and letter of application and make suggestions for improvement.

8. Do some research on the status of *electronic resumes* in the community in which you plan to work. Revise the resume you created earlier so it could be used as an effective electronic resume which could be mailed to an employer.

9. Do some research on companies by using the World Wide Web. Explore at least three companies and share your findings in a memo to the instructor or an oral presentation to the class.

10. Use the attachment feature on electronic mail to send your resume to a person of your choice.

11. This chapter lists ten career web sites. Explore these web sites and find an additional five sites. Prepare to make a brief report to the instructor or class.

12. Ten job search web sites are included in this chapter. Research these sites and additional job search sites of your choice to make your own top ten list. List the site name, address, and a brief summary of what you can find on the site.

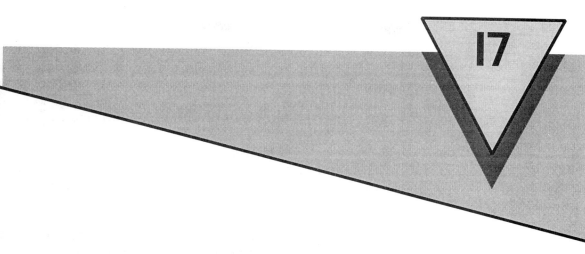

INTERACTING WITH EMPLOYERS

Critical Thinking Applications

- A personnel director is hiring a new employee. Two candidates have equal qualifications and have both indicated their religious affiliations on their resumes. The personnel director has openly criticized one of the religions as little better than a cult. The person hired has the same religious faith as the personnel director. Is the personnel director's action unethical, illegal, or neither?

- What strategy should you use if an interviewer asks you a question you know to be illegal?

PREPARING FOR EMPLOYMENT

The interview and employment process provides an excellent opportunity for you to use your oral and written communication skills. Preparing an effective resume and application letter were the first step in the written process. The job interview is the oral communication component. The interview is followed by a written thank you to the interviewers.

An invitation to participate in an interview—a major part of the employment process—is, of course, the response you want from your resume and application letter. When you are invited to an interview, you can assume the employer has been favorably impressed by your resume and your cover letter and possibly by recommendations from the people whose names you listed as references.

In many companies, you will go for a **series** of interviews. Early interviews may be screening techniques to call back only the most serious candidates. During your interview you may meet several people and you may be interviewed by more than one person. Try to remember as many names as possible and jot them down as soon as you can as you may see these individuals in subsequent interviews. You will make a good impression if you can greet them by name.

An overview of the interview process is shown in Figure 17-1. The interview process has three phases which are (1) preparing for the interview, (2) participating in the interview, and (3) following up the interview. In addition, you will look at accepting a job offer, declining a job offer, writing a letter of resignation, and the role of e-mail in the job search process.

Preparing for the Interview

Thorough preparation for an interview includes studying the organization, anticipating interview questions, and deciding questions to be asked.

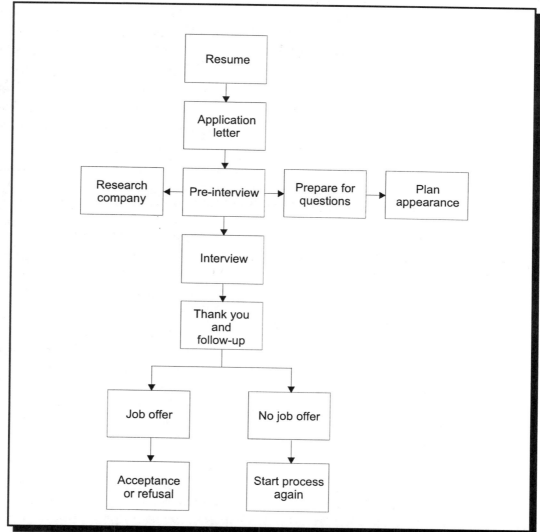

Figure 17-1. Overview of Interview Process

Study the Organization

To prepare an impressive resume and a cover letter, you had to know something about each organization to which you applied for employment. Continue to study the organizations. You can study annual reports, which are usually easily accessible and are quite informative. Additional information may be located on the company's home page on the World Wide Web.

University placement offices and libraries have valuable information about companies. You may wish to look at recent magazine, and newspaper articles which discuss the company. Such articles should help you understand issues of concern to the company.

Another valuable resource is to contact present and former employees of the organization—if you know some. They can frequently provide valuable information.

A thorough grasp of company information may also show that you were interested enough in the company to do research—a fact which may set you apart from other candidates. The more you know about the organization, the more intelligently you can talk and the more effectively you can listen during an interview. In addition, being thoroughly acquainted with the organization will help you feel confident and thus present yourself well.

Anticipate Interview Questions

Remember that no two interviews are identical. You may not be asked any of the questions you have anticipated, but you may be asked some of them. Studying carefully those you anticipated should help you to answer others that arise. Don't simply memorize answers to expected questions, but think about them carefully and formulate good answers. Making thorough preparation early will enable you to respond without wasting time and without appearing to be slow or poorly informed. Do, though, take the time necessary to think before replying to a question. Remain poised and exhibit self-confidence without appearing to be cocky. The interviewer will observe your listening skills and your nonverbal skills.

Several types of questions may be asked during the interview. Perhaps you might find that an analogy with college testing is appropriate in that you could find true/false, short answer, essay, or case problem questions.

Type of Question/Example	*Explanation*
True/False Example: I see you are graduating from college this semester with a major in General Business.	These questions are usually used for verification of material you have already submitted and are frequently asked in the early portion of the interview because they should be easy to answer.
Short Answer Example: What was your major in college? *OR* I see you were on the Dean's List. How many semesters did that involve?	This type of question usually asks for a short response which is fairly obvious and easy to answer. Such questions are often used to try to put the applicant more at ease.
Essay Example: Why do you think we should hire you? *OR* How do you see your career developing in the next five years?	An essay question turns the control of the interview over to the person who is asked the question. The applicant has a chance to structure a question to discuss the valuable points just as one would on a good essay exam.
Case Problem Example: Your full-time position involves reporting to two different supervisors. Each one has seemed pleased with your work and has started assigning you additional work. You find your performance is suffering because you can not seem to determine which jobs have priority and it seems like you are working two jobs instead of one. How would you handle this situation?	In this type of question, the applicant is asked how he/she would respond to a specific scenario encountered on the job. This question may be difficult to prepare for. Be sure to give yourself a few moments to think it through before you start answering. Case problems may involve practical problems such as the one described in the example or may include ethical or legal issues.

Numerous interviewers, after greeting the applicants, have begun the process with an **essay** question by saying, "Tell me something about yourself." Persons who make this statement want to learn about your traits that would help you excel on the job and that would help you fit in with the work environment. For example, if you are goal oriented, you may say so and then identify a few specific goals you have set for yourself and have attained. You could mention the steps that you planned in order to reach the goals. Or, you might decide to briefly outline your educational and work experience that have prepared you for this particular position. Most employers do not want you to spend this time saying very much about your hometown, your family, or other personal interests not specifically related to the job. Be sure to focus on your strengths and assets to the company.

Some additional questions that have been reported by a number of applicants include:

Typical Essay Questions

1. What do you know about our organization?
2. How did you hear about us?
3. Why do you want to work for us?
4. Why do you think you would like this particular job?
5. What are your strengths as they relate to this job?
6. What are your weaknesses as they relate to this job?
7. Why should we hire you?
8. What are your goals for your career five years from now? ten years?
9. What kind of computer experience have you had?
10. What was your favorite course(s) in college? *OR* What was your favorite task(s) in your last job?

Applicants who are ready to answer such questions will have a distinct advantage over those who have not considered their answers.

As many professional books on employment easily available in bookstores include extensive lists of questions, employers are trying to find alternatives to typical questions to determine if an applicant can apply their knowledge. An increase in the use of case problem questions has been reported by some applicants.

Select Questions You Wish to Ask

Interviewers guide the interviews and ask most of the questions, but you should prepare some to ask at appropriate times. Some interviewers ask for questions at various points within the interview; others invite them near the end. Sometimes you may inquire spontaneously without distracting the interviewer.

Write your questions so that you will remember them, but don't read from your notes during the interview. One question you would probably like to have answered is "What would be some of my early assignments?" Another question may be "What are likely paths to follow for career advancement?" If you expect to travel, you may ask about the portion of the time you should expect to be out of town; to what destinations you may go; and whether attending special seminars, training sessions, and so on will be part of your job.

If during the interview the next step to be taken in the employment process has not been identified, you may ask what that step is. The type of job you are seeking, the location, and other factors will help you to think of suitable questions to ask.

All of your questions should indicate that you are genuinely interested in getting the job. You want the interviewer to know you are eager to work and to contribute to the success of the organization. Don't give the impression you are interested only in what can be done for you. The best practice is not to ask about salary, vacations, retirement plans, and other fringe benefits until the interviewer mentions them.

Although salary may not come up in the first couple of interviews, you should determine an acceptable range for the job through your research efforts. Be sure to account for your geographical location and for the type of job. In most situations the interviewer should mention salary first unless a job has been offered with no mention of salary—at that time, the applicant could bring up the salary issue.

Participating in the Interview

The first minute or so of an employment interview is a crucial time. Make the most of it by dressing well, pronouncing the interviewer's name correctly and clearly, shaking hands firmly, using good posture, making eye contact, and using pleasant facial expressions. Be sure to be on time. Try to be yourself.

As first impressions are extremely important in an interview, your appearance can play a major role as you are introduced to key individuals. Here are some interview suggestions.

	Some Do's and Don'ts on Interviews
DO	Be prepared by researching the company.
	Extend your hand for handshakes at the beginning and end of interview.
	Wear business attire appropriate for the job and the situation.
	Ask pertinent questions.
	Write a thank you letter after the interview.
DON'T	Be late. Allow sufficient time for parking, security, etc.
	Wear excessive jewelry.
	Apply overpowering perfume or cologne.
	Wear an outfit you have never worn before–wear it at least once before the interview.
	Use interviewer's first name unless invited to do so.

Appearance

Most interviewers expect an applicant to dress up for the interview—perhaps at or slightly higher above the level he or she would wear in a day-to-day work situation. If you know how the present successful employees dress, dress in an equivalent fashion.

Clothes should be clean, well pressed, and in excellent condition. Also, they should fit well. Conservative clothes for both men and women are usually the preferred style. Exceptions may occur in more creative jobs such as advertising or fashion design.

Shoes (including soles and heels) should be freshly polished. You may wish to carry an attaché case or a portfolio. Not only would this item make it easy for you to carry extra copies of your resume and other pertinent documents, but also it may help you to project the image of a professional. A woman should not try to carry both a business case and a purse.

In addition to appropriate business clothing, applicants should have clean, well-groomed hair and hands. Your hair style should help you to project the image of an employee rather than that of a college student. You should feel comfortable shaking hands and sitting correctly. Leaning forward in your chair can convey a sense of interest and eagerness in what the interviewer has to say. Jewelry, cologne, and perfume should be understated.

Many job applicants purchase or carefully select an interview ensemble which gives not only the impression they wish to convey but provides confidence in their appearance.

Initial Steps of the Interview

Most on-campus interviews for college students and recent graduates are held in offices designated by the placement director. Company on-site interviews are held in the office of the human resources director or the office of the prospective supervisor.

Wherever the interview is held, arrive from five to ten minutes before the designated time. Allow sufficient time for parking and for passing through building security. Arriving too early tends to give the impression that you are overly nervous. Arriving late without good reason would certainly create a poor impression. Go alone to the interview unless you are asked to bring your spouse with you.

When you arrive for an on-site interview, introduce yourself to the receptionist and give the name of the person you are to meet. Also, identify the job you are seeking. If you do not know the correct pronunciation of the interviewer's name, ask the receptionist to pronounce it for you. Treat everyone with courtesy. You will not know who will be asked to express an opinion about you. You should exhibit your best manners at all times.

As you wait for an interview, maintain good posture and try to look relaxed. Usually, reading materials are available. Read those that pertain to the organization so that you can learn more about it and so that you can exhibit keen interest in it. Don't try to engage anyone in conversation.

The Actual Interview

When the interviewer arrives (or when you are escorted into the office), stand, of course, and smile and shake hands. A grip firm enough to signify enthusiasm, but not so firm that it signifies nervousness, contributes to a good first impression. Stand until you are asked to be seated. The interviewer usually indicates the place for the applicant to sit if more than two chairs are in the room.

First impressions can be important—you should not smoke or chew gum. Avoid placing anything on the interviewer's desk unless you are invited to do so.

Interviewers want to learn as much as they can about your qualifications for the job and your likelihood of fitting in with the business environment. They want to see how well you communicate both nonverbally and verbally. Erect, yet relaxed posture means much in a successful interview. Although you are not expected to look directly into the interviewer's eyes throughout the conversation, your doing so part of the time is impressive. Don't try to be overconfident. Some anxiousness is expected of applicants.

Answer questions honestly and tactfully. Give short answers, but talk enough to show that you can communicate clearly, confidently, and comfortably. Even though you will be asked some questions you have not anticipated, having thought carefully about those you did anticipate will help you to answer others and to remain poised.

Keep note writing during the interview to a minimum. You won't appear alert and interested if you spend your interview time writing down everything. You would be wise, however, to write extensive notes immediately after leaving the office. Keeping notes is especially helpful if you are involved in several interviews over a short time span.

Ethics and the Interview

The same ethical standards that applied to the design of the resume and application letter should also apply to your behavior during the interview. You will wish to paint the most attractive picture of yourself that you can, but be sure that the information you give is honest and can be verified.

Overstating your contribution to a project or activity can come back to haunt you. Some questions the interviewer may ask are to verify information you included in your resume. Obviously, if you provide a different answer during the interview than you did on your resume, a red flag appears.

If you wish to clarify some information or discuss a difficult situation that caused you to be dismissed from a previous job, do so toward the end of the interview when you will have an opportunity to raise any issues which should be discussed. You will be in a better position if you bring up a difficult issue than if an interviewer who is impressed with your interview calls a former employer and receives a negative report.

Another ethical issue concerns statements you might make about former employers or colleagues. You will not gain any advantage by saying negative things about others. A statement such as "my last boss discriminated against me" will not find favor in an interview situation. Interviewers may feel that, if hired, you will say negative things about this company at your next interview. Follow the maxim "If you can't say something nice, say nothing at all."

Conclusion of the Interview

When the interviewer indicates by words or gestures that the interview is over, leave promptly, but not in a rush. Shake the interviewer's hand with a firm grip and express appreciation for the opportunity to discuss your qualifications for the job. Use this closing opportunity to find out what will happen next in the interview process.

If the receptionist or others you have met are near your exit route and you can conveniently make a cordial parting comment to them without interrupting their work, do so for good human relations.

Following Up the Interview

Once an interview for employment has been completed, further communication should follow. This additional communication may include letters in which you thank the interviewer, accept a job offer, decline a job offer, or resign a job.

Usually, the first step to take after an interview is to write a letter in which you thank the interviewer for discussing with you your qualifications for the job. Write this letter promptly—usually within twenty-four hours after you return to your home. The content of the letter is governed by the results of the interview as shown below.

Dear Ms. Michaels

I would like to thank you and Mr. North for your consideration during my interview today for the position of assistant manager of your Towne East store. I was especially impressed by the high morale of the store employees and the location of the store.

In fact, after the positive experience of the interview, I think employment with your company would be very attractive. I look forward to hearing from you after you have finished your other interviews.

Sincerely

If you were offered the job during the interview and you accepted the offer, write immediately. After thanking the interviewer for the enjoyable visit, state the exact title of the job you have accepted, the starting salary, and the date you will report for duty. In addition, include any extra terms that were agreed upon. Say you look forward to working in that position. Of course, you would not accept an offer if you did not look forward to the job; but saying so provides a courteous, goodwill ending for the letter. See the example letter on the following page:

Dear Ms. Michaels

Thank you for the courtesy you and Mr. North extended during my recent job interview for assistant manager of your Towne East Store. When I accepted your job offer, I knew that I would enjoy working for your organization.

My understanding of the assistant manager position is that I will report to the headquarters office on June 1 for a three-week training course. My yearly salary of $34,000 which will include health insurance is to begin at that time. After my six-months probationary period, I am eligible for additional benefits such as profit sharing and life insurance.

Again, I look forward to joining your organization.

Sincerely

If you signed a contract that specifies the job title, the terms of payment, and the beginning date of employment, do not restate all these points in a letter. Usually, you need to restate the job title as an immediate reminder if the employer has hired persons for several job classifications within the past few days. Too, you could hardly express genuine enthusiasm for working without stating the title of the job you have accepted.

Frequently an applicant is in the process of interviewing with several companies when a job offer is made. If you were offered the job and you promised to let the interviewer know by a specified date whether you will accept the offer, confirm your promise to give your decision by that date (and specify the date). State the job title. The following letter is an example.

Dear Mr. Kilian

Thank you for interviewing me yesterday for the job of assistant manager of your Oak Park store. I am convinced I would be challenged by the work you and Mr. Atkins, the store manager, described; and I am favorably impressed by all the employees I met.

As I mentioned to you, though, I am committed to go out of town next Monday for another interview. I appreciate your offering me the job, and I will certainly let you know my decision by Thursday, May 24.

Sincerely

If you were given forms (job application, expense statement, and so on) to complete, return them with the letter. Remember, however, when something is worth enclosing, it is also worth mentioning in the letter. If you have to wait three or four days to obtain all the information necessary for completing the forms, delay writing the letter to thank the interviewer until you can enclose the forms. If you must wait longer to obtain the information, write the thank-you letter immediately and mention the date on which you expect to return the completed forms.

If the interviewer is to let you know by a specific date whether you will be offered the job, say that you look forward to hearing the decision by the date that was mentioned (and specify the date). Try to add something about your qualifications that will help to convince the prospective employer you are the person for the job. Of course, use discretion to keep the reader from thinking that you are overzealous or that you are trying to exert pressure for an offer of employment.

Accepting a Job Offer

Promptness is important in accepting an offer of employment. Although applicants most frequently agree to accept an offer of employment in person or over the phone, you will wish to confirm the terms of employment in writing. In some cases, however, your employer may indicate that he or she will send a confirmation letter or a contract.

If you decide to write a confirming letter, address it to the person who made the offer unless you are instructed to send it to someone else. Be sure that in the letter you state definitely and cheerfully that you accept the offer. State the job title, the salary, and the date on which you are to begin working. Existing circumstances may, of course, require your including additional information.

The essential points of a job acceptance letter are in the example that follow.

Dear Mr. Lee

I am happy to accept your offer as an area salesperson for COMPTCO in the Irving, Texas, area. I understand that my base salary of $26,000 per year will begin on my first day of employment—July 1. In addition, I will be eligible for a 2 percent sales commission on all sales over $100,000 during my first year.

After my sixty day training and probationary period, I will be eligible for company health benefits, life insurance, and retirement.

I appreciate the information you sent about housing and plan to look for housing the first weekend in June.

Again, I look forward to joining your company.

Sincerely

What should you do if you believe you have a good chance of being offered another job that would be better? This question, of course, has no specific answer. Some applicants have requested permission to delay acceptance, and their requests were approved. If you choose this alternative, be fair. Request permission to delay only a short time, and do this only when you are sincerely interested in the two jobs—the one offered to you and the one you believe will be offered to you.

Employers want their employees to be well satisfied with their jobs, and many are willing to wait a reasonable length of time for a decision if they do not have to fill a vacancy immediately. Some college seniors who wrote letters similar to the one that follows were granted the request. You will observe that the letter has a positive, cordial tone.

Dear Ms. Blanchard

Working as a junior accountant for you definitely appeals to me, and I appreciate your job offer. Could I wait two weeks, however, until August 1 to give you my decision? I have an interview scheduled with another company on July 26 and would like to keep that appointment.

Will you please let me know if the date for this decision is acceptable to you?

Sincerely

Declining a Job Offer

In many instances a job is offered to an applicant a few days after an interview. If you receive a letter containing a job offer you wish to decline, reply immediately (within twenty-four hours) and say you decline the offer. You may give the reason for your decision, but you do not have to. If the reason is a pleasant one, you may very well state it. Do not mention unpleasantness when rejecting an offer. See the following example.

Dear Ms. Wilson

Thank you for offering me a position as assistant manager in your San Antonio store.

As I mentioned in our interview, the location of the store was not a primary factor in my selection of a job. However, yesterday I received an offer for a comparable position in my hometown area of Houston. Remaining in the Houston area at this point in my career has more advantages than moving to San Antonio; so, for that reason, I have accepted the Houston offer.

I was very favorably impressed with your company and hope we have an opportunity to meet again in the future.

Sincerely

By declining promptly, you make a favorable impression on the "would-be" employer. That person will appreciate your thoughtfulness and fair-mindedness in declining quickly so that someone else can be employed soon. Probably, the interviewer has considered another person who also has good qualifications for the job; and your promptness in declining the offer may enable the interviewer to hire the other well-qualified applicant.

Writing a Letter of Resignation

When you are accepted for a new job, you may find it necessary to resign from your previous job. Most people change jobs several times during their lives.

You hope, of course, that you will change jobs only because you have an opportunity to move into a better situation. The situation may be better because you are going to a job that pays a higher immediate salary, offers a better chance for advancement in salary or prestige, provides an opportunity to use your skills and knowledge to greater advantage, or provides an opportunity to do the kind of work that is most satisfying to you. Or you may be going to a geographic area that is especially appealing to you. You have very little difficulty in writing a letter of resignation when leaving a pleasant situation.

Ordinarily, address the letter of resignation to your immediate superior. In some organizations, however, all such letters are addressed to the director of human resources. Reviewing the company policy will help you to determine the officer who should receive the letter.

The conditions existing at the time you resign help you to determine just what to include in the letter. State specifically the last day you are to work on the job you are leaving and state the job title. Write a letter that leaves a good impression on those who will read the letter. The letter will be filed in your personnel folder and may be read by several persons at various times. See an example of a resignation letter in Figure 17-2.

Sometimes a person may resign under unpleasant circumstances. The resignation letter is about as important as the application letter because it is often the last document that goes into the writer's personnel file in that organization. If you should resign because of unpleasantness, make the tone of your letter of resignation as pleasant as it would be if you were leaving under pleasant conditions. Do not dwell on the unpleasant aspects.

The Role of E-Mail in the Job Search Process

With advancing technology gains the protocol of the job search process often adapts. You may find yourself meeting someone who gives you a business card and says "E-mail me your resume." In an order of priority, a thank you letter would be the best but a thank you e-mail message would be better than no message at all. You may find yourself using e-mail with questions about the posted job or to arrange the details of the interview(s)

You may receive a job offer, accept a job, or refuse a job by e-mail. You learned that a fast response in letting potential employers know of your acceptance or refusal decisions is important. You may wish to accept a job by e-mail and follow it with a more formal letter. Or, you may choose to send the more formal letter as an attachment to e-mail.

What should be your guideline for using e-mail? If the employer encourages the use of e-mail, you should follow his or her guide. If you plan to use e-mail during the job search be sure you are using your e-mail address (not a friend's) and be sure your address is professional (not cooldude@collegeguys.com).

Pleasant Hill Industries
4612 Commercial
Emporia, KS 66801

October 1, 2002

Dr. Justin Wilmington
Human Resources Director
Pleasant Hill Industries
4612 Commercial
Emporia, KS 66801

Dear Dr. Wilmington

As you may have heard, the Alnovive Corporation is opening a new office in the city. I have decided to accept a position with them that offers both a higher salary than my current position and new challenges. I would like my resignation to take effect two weeks from now on October 15.

I have found the five years that I have worked with Pleasant Hill Industries to be a period of personal growth and fulfillment. As you know, I began in an entry-level position and have now moved up to a higher position with more responsibilities. I would especially like to commend my supervisor, Ms. Daria Ford, for serving as a mentor to me during my years at Pleasant Hill Industries.

If you wish, I will be happy to provide any necessary training to the person who is hired in my place.

Sincerely

N. J. Belton

N. J. Belton
Assistant Department Manager

Figure 17-2. Letter of Resignation

DISCUSSION

1. List some questions you can anticipate in an interview that were not mentioned in the chapter.

2. What factors relating to appearance are important for a successful interview?

3. List any rationale for writing a letter confirming a verbal job offer.

4. Describe some advantages or disadvantages of writing a thank-you letter after an interview.

5. What is the value of a letter of resignation?

6. What elements should you include in a thank-you letter?

EXERCISES

1. Interview a professional who holds a job similar to one you would like to have. Ask about the interview process and ask for any tips. Be ready to give an oral report to the class.

2. Work with a team member to practice interviewing skills. Take turns asking each other interview questions. Be sure to include practice shaking hands.

3. Do some research. What would be appropriate for you to wear to an interview? What would not? Be ready to report to the class.

4. Arrange an appointment to discuss your career options with someone who is a member of your network of contacts.

5. Conduct a focused search on the World Wide Web for information about careers, jobs, and/or employment which are of value to you. Be prepared to share your information with the class.

6. Select a city of your choice where you may be interested in working. How much information can you gather from the World Wide Web about the city before your interview. Hint: Check Chamber of Commerce web sites or Convention and Tourism sites for information.

7. Visit your campus placement office and see if you can schedule any on-campus interviews.

PROBLEMS

1. You had an interview this morning for a job for which you are qualified. As another applicant is to be interviewed next week, you are to be notified within two weeks as to whether you will be offered the job. Write a letter thanking the person for the interview and let the interviewer know you are still very much interested in obtaining the job. Having had an interview, you know the name of the person to whom you are writing.

2. At the conclusion of the interview you had last Friday, the personnel director (and of course you remember her name) told you she would let you know within two weeks whether she would offer you the job. You received her letter today offering you the job. Write a letter accepting the offer.

3. During an interview last week, you were offered the job for which you applied. You promised to let the interviewer know your decision within two weeks. Yesterday (one week later) another company offered you a job that you prefer. Write a letter to decline the employment offer given to you during the interview last week.

4. Assume that for the past two years you have been working for the Western Travel Company. You will need to make some reference to the kind of work you have been doing. You have an opportunity to take a better job with another company. Use your imagination! Why is the job better? When will you resign? What is the name of the other company? Have you profited by working two years for the Western Travel Company? Add anything that is appropriate. Write a letter of resignation. Remember that this letter will be placed in your personnel file. Perhaps this letter will be the final good impression that you will make on the people who work for the Western Travel Company.

5. Write a practice resignation letter from your current job or from an earlier job.

6. Design a form that will help you keep track of information from interviews from several companies. Provide categories for key information so you can use this form to tabulate your interview experiences.

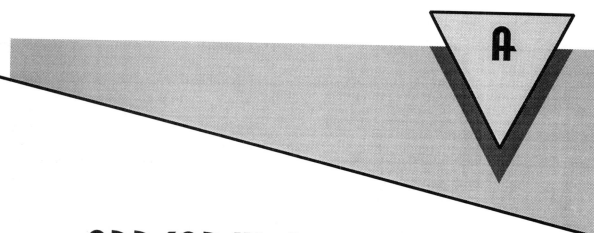

APP€NDIX A
APPLYING GRAMMAR PRINCIPLES

Although not inclusive, the following section gives basic guidelines for correct writing:

1. Sentence Structure
2. Punctuation
3. Line divisions
4. Capitalization
5. Numbers
6. Abbreviations
7. Forms of Address

GRAMMAR

SENTENCE TYPES

Simple, compound, complex, and compound-complex sentences are discussed and illustrated in the next few paragraphs.

Simple

A simple sentence is the same as an independent clause: it contains a subject and a verb. Simple sentences express one complete thought. Use more simple sentences than any other kind, but do not bore the reader by using simple sentences exclusively.

- *Marty completed the project last week.*
- *The team will meet Friday.*

Compound

A compound sentence is made up of two or more independent clauses (simple sentences). Use a compound sentence to express closely related ideas. Join the independent clauses by the appropriate coordinating conjunction or by a semicolon.

Coordinating conjunctions. When the independent clauses of a compound sentence are parallel in meaning, use one of the coordinating conjunctions *and, or, but,* or *nor.*

- *Sarah input the data, and Alicia proofread the report.*
- *Lois will go to the mall at noon, or she will shop after work.*
- *Mike delivered the plans this morning, but Adam will not review them until Monday.*
- *Shandra did not come to work Monday, nor did she call her supervisor.*

Semicolon. A semicolon may be used instead of a coordinating conjunction to join the independent clauses of some compound sentences. In these cases the main ideas in the two clauses should be closely related, the clauses should be short, and the clauses should be in the same voice—active or passive.

- *Samantha wrote the letter; Stephen signed it.*

Conjunctive Adverbs. Another way to join independent clauses in a compound sentence is to use the semicolon followed by a conjunctive adverb. Choose a conjunctive adverb that expresses the proper relationship between the ideas in the independent clauses.

Consequently and *therefore* are two of the many conjunctive adverbs that show result. *Moreover* means additional, and *however* and *on the other hand* indicate contrasts.

- *Their store will remain open until 7 p.m. each weekday until Christmas; consequently, they must employ additional salesclerks for that period.*
- *The assembly lines will close temporarily on July 16; therefore, the specifications for your automobile must reach us before July 5.*

Complex

A complex sentence is made up on one independent clause and at least one dependent clause. The sentence may begin with the dependent clause, or it may end with the dependent clause.

- *When you learn to keyboard quickly and accurately, you can use a variety of software packages effectively.*
- *You can use a variety of software packages effectively when you learn to keyboard quickly and accurately.*

Compound-complex

A compound-complex sentence is made up of two or more independent clauses and at least one dependent clause. Here are examples:

- *If you return the card before April 30, your order will be shipped by May 5; consequently, you will be enjoying your new lawn furniture by Memorial Day.*
- *We have shipped the four electric drills you ordered on May 6; and because you are a preferred customer, the Mailing Department has placed your name on the list to receive copies of all brochures we produce.*

Use variety in the types, as well as in the lengths, of the sentences in business messages.

Agreement

Subjects, verbs, and pronouns must agree in person--singular or plural.

Subject/Verb Agreement.

The verb of the sentence and the subject must agree in person.

- *Bill is moving to Oklahoma City this month.*
- *The Jeffersons were on vacation last week.*

Compound Subjects

Compound subjects joined by *and* normally use the plural form of the verb. When compound subjects are joined by *or* or *nor*, the verb form is determined by the part of the subject that is closer to the verb.

- *Marcus and Bill work well together.*
- *Neither of them prefers to work late.*
- *The teacher or the students give software demonstrations daily.*

Collective Nouns

Collective nouns such as team, class, board, committee, and jury may require either singular or plural verbs. If the members are acting collectively, a singular verb is preferable. If, however, the members are acting individually, the plural verb form is correct. To avoid awkward sentences using the plural verb form, restructure sentences to indicate individual action.

- *The committee is meeting this afternoon.*
- *The team have not resolved the problem.*
- *The team members have not resolved the problem.*

Pronoun/Subject Agreement

A pronoun that represents the subject must agree in number and gender with that subject.

- *Marty will send his proposal to vice president today.*
- *Motorists should be aware of their surroundings while driving.*

Indefinite Pronouns

Indefinite pronouns such as each, every, either, and neither require singular verbs.

- *Each of the respondents was given a notepad.*
- *Neither of them was satisfied with the outcome.*

PUNCTUATION

Period

Use a period to indicate the end of a sentence, for abbreviations, and for enumerations.

End of Sentence

Use a period at the end of a declarative sentence (a statement), an imperative sentence (a command), a polite request, and an indirect question. Space once after the period at the end of a sentence if you are using word processing software. For typewritten text, space twice after the period.

- *The storm raged throughout the morning.*
- *Write your name in the upper right corner of your paper.*
- *Will you please make your reservation by September 7.*
- *He asked me when you would return.*

Abbreviations

Use a period to indicate that a letter or a group of letters represents a word or a group of words not spelled out. Space once after a period following an abbreviation.

Mr., Mrs., Ms., Dr., No., a.m., p.m., Ph.D., Co., C.O.D., f.o.b.

When several initial letters are used together as an abbreviation for a group of words, the abbreviation can be written in all capitals without periods.

- *ABC (The Association for Business Communication)*
- *IRS (Internal Revenue Service)*

Decimal Point

Use a period to separate dollars from cents in sums of money that are expressed in figures. No space is placed between a decimal point and the numbers of the amount.

- *$8.32*   *$7.94*   *$375.68*

Do not use a decimal point with an even sum of money except in a series when at least one of the items includes cents.

- *$5*   *$30*   *$23*
- *The books cost $41.75, $56.00, and $67.95.*

After a Figure

Use a period after a figure that is used to enumerate tabulated items. Space twice after the period.

- *You may send your message by any of the following:*
    1. *E-mail*
    2. *Fax*
    3. *Delivery Service*

Question Mark

Review these uses of the question mark.

Direct Question

Use a question mark at the end of a question to which a verbal response is expected. Space once after the question mark at the end of a sentence if you are using word processing software. For typewritten text, space twice after the question mark.

- *What time will Jeremy's plane arrive?*
- *Have you used the scanner today?*

Do not use a question mark after a courteous request that is stated as a question.

- *Will you please attend the meeting on August 9.*
- *Would you send me a copy of the catalog that you described in your November 7 presentation.*

Within Parentheses

A question enclosed with parentheses within sentence is followed by a question mark, but it does not begin with capital letter.

- *I will bring the brochure (have you seen it?) to the meeting.*

Multiple Questions

When several questions are abbreviated because they could be stated in the same way, use a question mark after each one.

- *How many of your employees work on Monday? on Saturday? on Sunday?*

Exclamation Mark

Use an exclamation mark after a strong exclamatory word, phrase, clause, or sentence. You can also use the exclamation mark to indicate that you are excited. Be careful not to overuse this form of emphasis. Space once after the exclamation mark at the end of a sentence if you are using word processing software. For typewritten text, space twice after the exclamation mark.

- *Stop! Run! Hurry!*
- *The presentation was a tremendous success!*

Comma

Space once after a comma that follows a word or a figure, but do not space after a comma that is used within a group of figures.

Introductory Subordinate Clause

When a sentence begins with a subordinate clause, use a comma between the subordinate clause and the independent clause. Space once after a comma that follows a word or a figure.

- *If the price is low, I will purchase the land.*

Ordinarily, do not use a comma between the clauses when the independent clause precedes the subordinate clause.

- *I will purchase the land if the price is low.*

Direct Address

Use a comma or commas to set off a word that is used as a direct address.

- *Diane, will you visit with Ms. Brogan about the discrepancy?*
- *I believe, Mr. Shaw, that the repairs can be made by August 26.*
- *You will like this report, Benjamin.*

Appositive

Use a comma or commas to set off a nonrestrictive (nonessential) appositive. A nonrestrictive appositive is not needed to identify the noun or the noun substitute to which the appositive refers.

- *Please call Jerry Mize, our consultant.*
- *Jennifer Jernigan, the company auditor, will present the report.*

Do not use commas to set off an appositive that is restrictive (essential) for identifying the noun or the noun substitute to which it refers.

- *I believe your son Stefan is taller than his brother.*

Nonrestrictive (Nonessential) Clause

Use a comma or commas to set off a nonrestrictive (nonessential) clause. A nonrestrictive clause is not needed to identify the noun or the noun substitute it modifies.

- *The president, who lives three blocks from the office, walks to work each day.*
- *The inventory report, which was updated by Debbie, has been misplaced.*

Do not use commas to set off a clause that is needed to identify the noun or the noun substitute it modifies.

- *The man who mowed my lawn last year has moved to Santa Fe.*

The clause is needed to tell which man has moved .

Compound Sentence

Ordinarily, use a comma before the coordinate conjunction that joins the independent clauses of a compound sentence when a subject is expressed in each clause.

- *Tyrone and Shonda worked late yesterday, and they completed the report on schedule.*
- *Tyrone and Shonda worked late yesterday and completed the report on schedule.*

Note: When the independent clauses are short, the comma may be omitted.

- *Rene' wrote the check and Joy mailed it.*

Series

Use a comma between items (figures, words, or groups of words) in a series. A series consists of three or more items.

- *We have shipped the paper, the books, and the notebooks you ordered last week.*
- *The business executive may spend the day writing letters, talking with customers, and supervising others.*

Parenthetical Expression

Use commas to set off a parenthetical expression that tends to cause the reader to pause for that expression.

- *The project will be supported, however, by several civic groups.*
- *A two-thirds majority of the residents, on the other hand, thought the tax rate was too high.*

No comma is needed if the parenthetical expression would not tend to cause the reader to pause.

- *The consultant is also of that opinion.*

Direct Answer

Use a comma to set off the direct answers yes and no.

- *Yes, I will serve on the committee.*
- *No, you will not be required to pay the special fee.*

Introductory Phrase Containing a Verb Form

Use a comma after an introductory phrase that contains a verb form.

- *Having studied the assignment, he was ready to solve the problem.*
- *To get the most out of your courses, you must study every day.*

Long Introductory Phrase. Use a comma after a long introductory phrase even though the phrase contains no verb.

- *Within the next few weeks, they will make some major changes in their service delivery.*
- *Throughout Charles C. Hamilton's childhood, he was influenced by the writings of his parents.*

Introductory Adverb. Use a comma after an introductory adverb that is to be emphasized.

- *Ordinarily, the office is open until 6:00 p.m.*

Coordinate Adjectives. Use a comma between coordinate adjectives.

- *She is a courteous, charming person.*
- *The brightly colored, loosely woven materials are very popular.*

Omission of Common Element

Use commas to indicate the omission of a common element in the second and succeeding clauses of parallel structure.

- *History had an enrollment of 76; English, 87.*
- *Mr. Harley coached baseball; Mr. Sams, football; and Mr. Holt, basketball.*

Short Informal Quotation

Use commas to set off a short informal quotation.

- *The speaker said, "You are good listeners."*
- *When the supervisor says, "I have news for you," we know what to expect.*

Abbreviation, Etc.

Use a comma before the abbreviation etc. at the end of a sentence, and use a comma before and after that abbreviation within a sentence.

- *The discussion of fringe benefits will include insurance, vacations, etc.*
- *They discussed insurance, vacations, etc., at the meeting on Tuesday afternoon.*

Addresses

Use a comma between parts of addresses that appear on the same line. When the city and the state are given in a sentence, use a comma after the state.

- *1234 Midway Road, Suite 404*
  Midville, GA 36523
- *The sales supervisor will meet you in Lincoln, Nebraska, on June 6.*

Dates

Use a comma between the day and the year when the month, the day, and the year are expressed. Also, use a comma after the year.

- *On January 6, 2002, the company adopted the new policy.*

Do not use a comma after the day or the year unless both are expressed except, of course, when the comma is needed because of some other punctuation principle.

- *On January 6 the company adopted the new policy.*
- *In 2002 the company adopted the new policy.*
- *When you called my home on January 26, I was attending a meeting in Philadelphia.*

The comma is needed because of the introductory subordinate clause.

Large Figures

Use commas to group digits in three's for large figures such as sums of money and items that can be counted.

- *The estate is at least $2,800,000.*
- *Do you know that 17,891 people visited this site last summer?*

Two Series of Figures

Use a comma between two series of figures when each figure is so large it should be written as a figure rather than as a word.

- *In 2002, 16,719 people visited this park.*
- *For a circulation of 5,255, 267 carriers will be needed.*

Adverbial Clause Interruption

Use commas to set off an adverbial clause (or a long phrase) that interrupts a main clause.

- *The contract, after it was reviewed by the attorney, was signed by the vice president.*
- *We hope that, with a continuing decrease in interest rates, real estate sales will increase.*

Contrasting and Opposing Expressions

Use commas to set off contrasting and opposing expressions with a sentence.

- *She is not the owner, but the manager.*
- *Kelly is the interviewee, not the interviewer.*

Tag Question

Use a comma to separate a tag question from the rest of the sentence.

- *This book is the one Kim recommended, isn't it?*

Name and Position Title

Use a comma to separate a position title from a name.

- *Address the letter to H. Glenn Morris, information specialist.*

Compound Sentence Containing a Conjunctive Adverb

When a conjunctive adverb appears at the point where two independent clauses are joined, use a semicolon before and a comma after it.

- *The windows were shipped on Thursday; therefore, we can install them on Monday.*

When, however, the conjunctive adverb appears within the second clause, use a semicolon at the point where the clauses are joined and commas before and after the conjunctive adverb.

- *The windows were shipped on Thursday; we can, therefore, install them on Monday.*

Semicolon

Space once after a semicolon.

Compound Sentence Containing a Comma

Many good writers use a semicolon before the conjunction that joins the independent clauses of a compound sentence when a comma is used at some other point in the sentence.

- *When you learn punctuation principles, you will be prepared to punctuate accurately the sentences in your communication; and you will be prepared to help other writers who seek help on this feature of effective writing.*
- *A thorough understanding of the rules of proper punctuation contributes to your self-confidence; and it enhances your ability to write interesting, easy-to-read messages.*

Compound Sentence with No Coordinating Conjunction

Use a semicolon to join the independent clauses of a compound sentence when no coordinating conjunction is used to join them.

- *The writer applied the principles expertly; he had studied them thoroughly.*
- *They prepared these examples for you; use them advantageously.*

Compound Sentence with Independent Clauses Joined by a Conjunctive Adverb

Use a semicolon when the independent clauses of a compound sentence are joined by a conjunctive adverb.

- *He learned the interest rate had been increased; consequently, he did not borrow the money.*
- *We received the contract for providing the concessions at the state tournament; therefore, we must employ additional food service personnel.*

Series

Use a semicolon to separate the items of a series when a comma is used within one of the items.

- *Within the next seven or eight weeks, the personnel manager will employ a receptionist; four data input clerks; and six well-trained, experienced administrative assistants.*

Enumeration

Use a semicolon before such expressions as *namely, for example, i. e., e. g,* and *that is* when the expression introduces an enumeration.

- *The interior decorator emphasized the use of the warm colors; namely, red, orange, and yellow.*

Illustration

Use a semicolon to introduce an illustration that is a complete sentence and is preceded by such expressions as *that is, namely, e. g., i. e.,* and *for example.*

- *Jerri's assistant works efficiently; for example, he takes the initiative to make decisions when his superior is out of the office.*

Colon

Space twice after a colon except when it is used within a group of figures.
The names of the most popular letter styles follow: extreme block, modified block, and AMS simplified.

Salutation

Use a colon after the salutation of a business letter that is formatted with mixed punctuation. The colon is not used after the salutation, however, when a letter is formatted with open punctuation and no comma follows the complimentary close.

- *Dear Ms. Gray:*
- *Dear Mr. Hartley:*

Time

Use a colon to separate the hour from the minutes when you express time in figures.

- *8:30 a.m.*   *4:45 p.m.*

Quotation

Use a colon to introduce a long formal quotation.

- *The contract stated: "For all materials that are provided by the contractor, the owner will pay the purchase price plus 10 percent."*

Series of Items

Use a colon to introduce formally a series of items.

- *Please answer the three questions that follow:*

  1. *How many people do you employ?*
  2. *What is the average weekly income of your employees?*
  3. *How many people received promotions in your organization last year?*

Explanation or Illustration

Use a colon to introduce an explanation or an illustration that is an independent clause.

- *The reason for his great success is obvious: he works night and day.*

Hyphen

Do not space before or after a hyphen.

Word Division

Use a hyphen when dividing a word at the end of a line of writing.

- *work- ing*
- *plan- ning*
- *under- stand*

Compound Adjective

Use a hyphen to form a compound adjective before a noun that is **modified** by the compound adjective.

- *the past-due account*
- *the easy-to-read sentences*
- *a two-week vacation*

Do not use a hyphen to join words that form a compound modifier that precedes the noun it modifies when one of the words is an adverb that ends with ly.

- *the widely recognized authority* (*Widely* is an adverb ending with *ly*.)
- *a well-known speaker* (*Well* is an adverb, but it does not end with *ly*.)

Do not use a hyphen to join compound adjectives that appear after the noun they modify.

- *The account is past due.*
- *The speaker is well known.*

Use a hyphen with each term for which a common element normally follows.

- *two- and three-week vacations*

Compound Word

Use a hyphen to join words that are used as a unit. (Consult an up-to-date dictionary when you question the use of a hyphen for words of this type.)

- *sister-in-law*
- *father-in-law*

Prefix

Use a hyphen with some prefixes such as self-, ex-, and re-. (Consult an up-to-date dictionary when you question the use of a hyphen for words of this type.)

- *self-confident*
- *ex-spouse*

Compound Numbers

Use a hyphen in compound numbers that are written as words.

- *forty-seven*
- *ninety-four*

Apostrophe

Space once after an apostrophe that follows the last letter of a word. Do not space after an apostrophe that comes between two letters.

Contraction

Use an apostrophe to form a contraction.

- *can't for cannot*
- *won't for will not*
- *couldn't for could not*

Possession

Use an apostrophe and an s with nouns that do not end with *s* to show possession.

- *student's paper*
- *Mrs. Gottshall's assistant*
- *children's clothing*

Also use an apostrophe and an s with pronouns-except possessive pronouns-to show possession.

- *someone's car*
- *anybody's guess*

Do not use an apostrophe with possessive pronouns:

- *my, mine, our, ours, your, yours,*
- *their, theirs, his, her, hers, its*

Show possession by adding an apostrophe to plural nouns that end with an s or a z sound.

- *years' experience*
- *Joneses' property*

Use only an apostrophe to show possession for words that end with an *s* or a *z* sound unless you expect the pronunciation of a second *s* or *z* sound.

- *Joan Childress' secretary*
- *Lois's desk*

Joint Possession

Use an apostrophe with the final name only to signify joint possession.

- *Kim and Rick's home*
- *Barnett and Bradshaw's store*

Individual Possession

Use an apostrophe with each name to signify individual or private possession.

- *Kim's and Rick's homes*
- *Barnett's and Bradshaw's stores*

Compound Nouns

For compound nouns show the possessive for the final word.

- *father-in-law's office*

Parentheses

Supplementary or Parenthetical Elements

Use parentheses to set off elements that are included as parenthetical or as supplementary information not to be emphasized.

- *In many instances polysyllabic words (including those of a specialized, technical nature) should be used.*

When a complete sentence is enclosed with parentheses within a sentence, the parenthetical sentence does not begin with a capital letter; and it does not end with a period.

- *He learned that one of the three vice-presidents (he does not know which one) will attend the convention in Atlanta next week.*

Numbers or Letters Within a Sentence

Use parentheses to enclose numbers or letters that introduce items given in paragraph form.

- *These three guidelines are emphasized: (1) Write promptly. (2) Determine the purpose of the letter. (3) Keep the reader in mind.*

Dash

Space once before and once after a dash that is made by striking the hyphen once. Do not space before or after a dash that is made by striking the hyphen twice.

Appositives, Clauses, and Parenthetical Elements That Contain a Comma

Use dashes to set off an appositive, a clause, or a parenthetical element that contains a comma.

- *Betsy Rayburn--frequently referred to as the most competent, most courteous, and most intelligent member of the staff--will represent us at the convention.*

Sudden Break or Abrupt Element

Use dashes to set off a sudden break in thought or an abrupt element.

- *The owner, the officers, or all the employees of an organization--provided the total number is small--may attend the conference.*

Quotation Mark

Three rules apply to spacing quotation marks.

    a.   **Comma and period.** When a comma or a period is used with an ending quotation mark, place the punctuation mark inside the quotation mark.

- *When the prospect said, "I would have to see it to believe it," the salesman gave him an impressive demonstration of the machine.*
- *The secretary wrote, "My employer will be in his office on Thursday morning."*

    b.   **Colon and semicolon.** When a colon or a semicolon is used with an ending quotation mark, place the punctuation mark outside the quotation mark.

- *When my administrative assistant was asked to comment, he said, "The problem was solved by Jim, the chief engineer"; and he handed the representative the report that described a solution.*

- *The names of the following senators were mentioned in the article "Today's Top Brass": Manning, Oliver, and White.*

c. **Exclamation mark and question mark.** Place the exclamation mark or the question mark outside the quotation mark when the quotation is not a question or an exclamation.

Place the punctuation mark inside the quotation mark when the quotation is a question or an exclamation.

Quotation Marks

Direct Quotation

Use a quotation mark at the beginning and at the end of a direct (verbatim) quotation whether it was originally spoken or written.

- *The personnel manager said, "We need a person who is well trained for this particular task."*
- *"You seem to be well qualified for the job," replied the recruiter.*

When you interrupt a quotation by inserting words, use quotation marks to enclose each part of the quotation.

- *"We need a person," said the personnel manager, "who is well qualified for this particular task."*

Quotation Within a Quotation

Use apostrophes to set off a quotation within a quotation.

- *Jason Smallwood wrote, "When Bob Haley replied to my request on April 6, he said, 'Yes, you may use my name as a reference when you apply for employment with Big State Company.'"*

Multiple-Paragraph Quotation

When you quote more than one paragraph in a letter or a memorandum, use a quotation mark at the beginning of each paragraph and a quotation mark at the end of the final paragraph of the quotation.

- *Jason Smallwood had this to say in his letter of April 6:*

  "We have spent a great deal of time preparing for this program, and we believe the speakers we have chosen are the best that can be obtained.

  "Please encourage the employees in your department to send their reservations before May 15. Cards they may use to reserve rooms are enclosed."

Special Meanings

Use quotation marks to enclose words that have special meanings in the context in which they are used.

- *The "Other" sector of the chart includes responses not reflected above.*

Ellipses

Direct Quotation

Use ellipses to indicate the omission of one or more words from the direct quotation. Ellipses can be used in these three ways:

a. Three periods at the beginning of a quotation signify that the beginning of the quotation has been omitted.

   - *The writer said, "...   he will gladly make the adjustment for you."*

b. Three periods within a quotation signify that the beginning and the end of the quotation are given but that some part of the statement is omitted.

   - *His letter stated, "October 28 was the tentative deadline, but ... we will accept the offer you made on October 30."*

c. Four periods at the end of the sentence signify that the final word or words of the quotation are omitted.

   - He wrote, "Your check for $14 has been credited to your account. . . ."

Brackets

Within Parentheses

Use brackets to enclose parenthetical expressions within material that is already enclosed with parentheses.

- *According to the representative, the message (we do not know what type of message [letter, telegram, or telephone call] he sent) contained an explanation of his plans.*

Within Quotations

Use brackets to enclose statements within quoted material when the statements that are enclosed were not made by the person whose quotation is presented.

- *Julian Ramsey replied, "I refuse to give an explanation for my actions [we do not know the reason for his refusal] in regard to that particular matter."*

To Mark an Error

Use brackets with *sic* or the correct information to show that an error appears in quoted material.

- *"The house was built in 1967 [sic] by the Hayes Construction Company."*
- *"The house was built in 1967 [1976] by the Hayes Construction Company."*

END-OF-LINE DIVISIONS

Between Syllables

Divide words between syllables only.

- *prob- lems*
- *sen-tence*

Between One-Letter Syllables

When two 1-letter syllables come near the end of a line, divide between them.

- *situ- ation*

After Single One-Letter Syllables

Generally, divide a word immediately after a single one-letter syllable.

- *cate- gories*
- *situ- ate*

Exceptions.—Divide immediately before the single one-letter syllable a, i, or u when it is followed by the syllable ble, bly, cal, or cle-

- *reli- able prob- ably   cler- ical   mir- acle*

Hyphenated Words

When a word is already hyphenated, divide only at the existing hyphen.

- *sister-in- law or sister- in-law   not sis- ter-in-law*
- *self- confidence   not self-con- fidence*

Between Double Consonants

Divide between double consonants except when a suffix such as *ing* or *er* follows a double consonant in the root word.

- *com-merce   call-ing   plan-ning   tell- ing*

Sums of Money

Do not divide sums of money.

- *$100,000   not $100,- 000*

Minimum of Two Letters at End of Line

Avoid dividing a word so that only two letters are at the end of the line.

- *in- crease*
- *re- ceived*

Minimum of Three Letters on Following Line

Divide a word so that at least three letters are at the beginning of the next line.

- *print- ing*
- *print- ers not   print- er*

Dates

Avoid dividing dates; but when a date must be divided, divide only between the day and the year.

- *November 10,   1996 not November   10, 1996   or   Nov-ember 10,1996*

Proper Names

Avoid dividing a proper name; but when a name must be divided, divide immediately before the last name.

- *Leon J. Henderson   not   Leon / J. Henderson*

Contractions

Do not divide contractions.

- *don't   not   don-'t*

Excessive Divisions

- Avoid excessive word divisions at the line endings.

Consecutive Lines

- Avoid dividing words at the ends of more than two consecutive lines.

Last Word on Page

- Do not divide the last word on a page.

CAPITALIZATION

Sentence Beginnings

Capitalize the first word of a sentence.

- *Our representative will visit your store next week.*

Proper Nouns

Capitalize proper nouns. Capitalize only the name of a name with a prefix.

- *Jones, Steinway, Brown, Paz, Dietz,*
- *de Haas, von Braun*

Capitalize words that form a part of a proper name even though these words would not be capitalized when used in other contexts.

- *the Mississippi River*   *but river*
- *the Comer Building*   *but building*
- *Maple Avenue*   *but avenue*

Do not capitalize the plurals of such words.

- *the Tennessee and the Ohio rivers*
- *the Blanton and the Hamilton buildings*

Capitalize a word when it is understood that the word refers to a proper name.

- *We toured the University campus while we were in Lexington.* (In this context the word university refers to a specific university, the University of Kentucky.)
- *He will enroll in a university next September.* (In this context no specific university is designated.)

Geographic Area

Capitalize words that are used to designate a geographic area, but do not capitalize words that are used to designate directions.

- *We will reside in the South.*
- *They will drive south on Interstate 65.*
- *His accent indicates that he is from the Middle East.*
- *The house faces east and is well shaded by several large trees.*

Specific Course Titles

Capitalize specific course titles, but do not capitalize course titles of a general nature.

- *Thirty students are enrolled in Marketing 432 this term.*
- *Thirty students are enrolled in marketing this term.*

Personal Titles

Capitalize any title that immediately precedes the name of the person to whom the title refers.

- *The letter was addressed to Mrs. Robert A. White.*
- *The article was written by Professor May.*

Days and Months

Capitalize the days of the week and the months of the year. Do not capitalize seasons of the year unless they are personified.

- *They will meet on the first Thursday in October.*
- *The group will meet sometime during the spring.*

Titles of Chapters, Articles, Books, and Periodicals

Capitalize the principal words in titles of chapters, articles, books, magazines, newspapers, and other publications. Conjunctions, articles, and prepositions are not usually capitalized.

- *Did you read the chapter that is entitled "Safety In Investments"?*
- *I enjoyed reading your second newspaper article, "Organizational Controls."*

You may write the title of a book in italicized uppercase and lowercase letters, or you may write the book title in all capitals not underlined. Be consistent in your choice and use the same style for all books in the document.

- J. Fred Rich wrote two books, *Investing in the Stock Market* and *The First Million*.
- I read the book A CRISIS AT THE OFFICE last week.

Salutations

Capitalize the first word as well as titles and proper nouns in the salutation of a letter.

- *Dear Mr. Hayes*
- *Mr. Roberts*
- *Dear Ms. Roberts*

Complimentary Closings

Capitalize only the first word in the complimentary close of a letter.

- *Sincerely*
- *Cordially*
- *Very sincerely yours*

Numbers in Business Papers and Legal Documents

Capitalize numbers expressed in words in business papers and legal documents.

- *Three Hundred Sixty-three Dollars*
- *One Thousand Four Hundred Ninety-two Dollars*

Quotations

Capitalize the first word of a quotation unless the beginning of the sentence is omitted from the quotation.

- *Teresa Allen wrote, "The stationery will be shipped on the 26th of June."*
- *Kevin Hunter said "...the merchandise is ready to be shipped."*

Pronoun I

Capitalize the pronoun I in any context.

- *I will let you know whether I can attend the meeting.*

Parts of Published Works

Capitalize the major parts volumes, documents, and plays.

- *Volume 11*
- *Unit 6*
- *Act 111, Scene 11*
- *Article V*

Special Abbreviations

Capitalize the abbreviations for college degrees.

- *He earned B.S. and M.A. degrees at an accredited college.*

NUMBERS

Sentence Beginning

Always express a number as a word when it is used to begin a sentence.

- *Eight players reported for practice on Tuesday afternoon.*
- *Forty-three members voted for the change.*

Large Round Numbers

Express large round numbers in words.

- *At least two thousand people attended the meeting.*

Small General Numbers

Use words for numbers ten and below.

- *We ordered eight printers last week.*
- *My assistant mailed 23 brochures yesterday afternoon.*

Streets and Avenues

Use words for street and avenue numbers that are ten or below.

- *259 East Ninth Street*
- *286 West 22 Street*
- *2911 Tenth Avenue*

House Numbers, Page Numbers, Model Numbers, Graphic Numbers, and Standard Measures

Use figures for house numbers except one-page numbers, model numbers, graphic numbers, and standard measures except time.

- *12 Market Street*
- *6 feet*
- *One Park Avenue*
- *8 gallons*
- *page 332*
- *pages 22 and 23*
- *32 degrees*
- *Model 8*
- *two weeks*
- *Figure 4*
- *four hours*
- *8 by 11 inches*

Percentages and Sums of Money

Use figures as the preferred way to express numbers for percentages and for sums of money.

- *At least 8 percent of the employees preferred the new model.*
- *The pencils cost 10 cents each.*
- *You may spend as much as $65 a night for a single room.*

Time

Use figures to express time except when the word o'clock follows the hour that is specified. Use a colon and zeros only when minutes are expressed in the sentence.

- *He will open the office at 8 a.m.*
- *He will close the office at 12 o'clock on Saturday.*

Dates

Use figures to express the day when the month precedes the day.

- *They moved into that building on December 8, 1990.*

When the day precedes the month, use a figure with *st, d, nd, rd,* or *th*; or use words to express the day.

- *1st of May*
- *4th of May*
- *third of May*

Separate Series

When two small numbers appear together and represent different items, use a figure for one of the numbers and a word for the other.

- *four 2-page letters*
- *4 two-page letters*

ABBREVIATIONS

Only a few abbreviations are acceptable for business messages. Those that are acceptable are preferred over spelling in full. Use these abbreviations:

- *Mr.   Mrs.   Dr.*
- *No. or no. (when it precedes a figure). For example, I prefer style No. 16 instead of I prefer style number 16.*
- *Co. and Inc. (in an inside address when writing to an organization that abbreviates these words on its stationery)*
- *YMCA, SPCA, and other abbreviations for long names (when the abbreviations and the names they represent are well known by the recipient of the message)*
- *The state/territory/province name in an address when the ZIP Code follows (Only the two-letter abbreviations recommended by the post office are acceptable.) A list of those abbreviations follows in Figure 1.*

Spell in full the days of the week; the months of the year; and words in the inside address of a letter such as avenue, street, road, and one-syllable words that indicate direction:

- *126 North 18 Street* **but** *717 Fifth Avenue, S.E. (two-syllables)*

State/Territory	Abbreviation	State/Territory	Abbreviation
Alabama	AL	North Dakota	ND
Alaska	AK	Ohio	OH
Arizona	AZ	Oklahoma	OK
Arkansas	AR	Oregon	OR
California	CA	Pennsylvania	PA
Connecticut	CT	Puerto Rico	PR
Delaware	DE	Rhode Island	RI
District of Columbia	DC	South Carolina	SC
Florida	FL	South Dakota	SD
Georgia	GA	Tennessee	TN
Guam	GU	Texas	TX
Hawaii	HI	Utah	UT
Idaho	ID	Vermont	VT
Illinois	IL	Virginia	VA
Indiana	IN	Virgin Islands	VI
Iowa	IA	Washington	WA
Kansas	KS	West Virginia	WV
Kentucky	KY	Wisconsin	WI
Louisiana	LA	Wyoming	WY
Maine	ME		
Maryland	MD	**Canadian Provinces**	
Massachusetts	MA	Alberta	AB
Michigan	MI	British Colombia	BC
Minnesota	MN	Labrador	LB
Mississippi	MS	Manitoba	MB
Missouri	MO	New Brunswick	NB
Montana	MT	Newfoundland	NF
Nebraska	NE	Northwest Territories	NT
Nevada	NV	Nova Scotia	NS
New Hampshire	NH	Ontario	ON
New Jersey	NJ	Prince Edward Island	PE
New Mexico	NM	Quebec	PQ
New York	NY	Saskatchewan	SK
North Carolina	NC	Yukon Territory	YT

Figure 1. Two-Letter State Abbreviations

FORMS OF ADDRESSES

Business Forms of Address

When addressing correspondence to people in business situations, follow these guidelines.

Use an appropriate courtesy title for the person to whom you are writing. The proper forms of address and salutations are given on the following page.

Addressee	Letter Address	Salutation
Man	Mr. (Full name)	Dear Mr. (Surname)
Woman	Ms. (Full name)	Dear Ms. (Surname)

Do not include a courtesy title with your name. Exception: A women who prefers to be addressed as Miss or Mrs. instead of Ms. should include the preferred courtesy title in parentheses preceding her name in the signature block.

- *(Miss) Sharon Long*
- *(Mrs.) Joyce McMillan*

Although there is a trend toward informality in addressing government officials, the forms of addresses and salutations used for those people are still somewhat different from those used for business personnel. Appropriate address forms and salutations for nonbusiness personnel follow.

Address	Salutation

President of the United States.

The President	Dear Mr. President:
The White House	
Washington, D.C. 20500	

Vice-President of the United States.

The Vice-President	Dear Mr. Vice-President:
United States Senate	
Washington, D.C. 20510	
Or	
The Honorable... (name in full)	
Vice-President of the United States	
United States Senate	
Washington, D.C. 20510	

Chief Justice of the United States.

The Chief Justice of the United States	Dear Mr. Chief Justice:
The Supreme Court	
Washington, D.C. 20543	

United States Senator.

Honorable (name in full)	Dear Senator (surname):
United States Senate	
Washington, D.C. 20510	

United States Representative.
    Honorable (name in full)   Dear Mr. (surname):
    House of Representatives   Dear Ms. (surname):
    Washington, D.C. 20515

Governor.
    The Honorable (name in full)   Dear Governor (surname):
    Governor of.. (name of state)
    (Capital city), (State name) (zip code)

Mayor.
    The Honorable . . . (name in full)   Dear Mayor (surname):
    Mayor of the City of (name of city)
    (City), (State) (zip code)

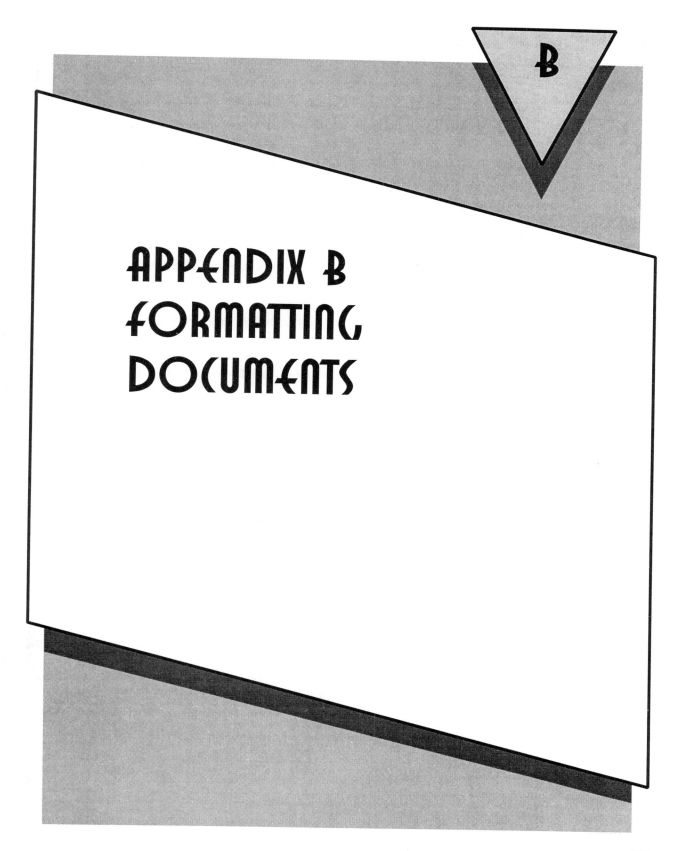

APPENDIX B
FORMATTING
DOCUMENTS

REPORTS

For a report of any kind, a good format not only provides for an attractive appearance, but it also contributes to readability and reader acceptance. Pay careful attention to margins, spacing, headings, pagination, proofreading, color, printing, and copying and binding. Refer to Chapter 11 for examples of various types of reports including the formal report.

Margins

Leave ample margins—one to one and a fourth inches for the top, bottom, left, and right. This spacing produces a good appearance that does not seem crowded, and it leaves space for the readers to make notes in the margins if they care to. Alternating text and graphic illustrations helps to keep the pages open and easy to read.

If you intend to bind the report on the left side, you may wish to allow a wider margin on that side of the page. Margins of one and one-half inches on the left and one inch on the right provide a balanced look for bound reports: the lines appear to be centered horizontally on the page. Notice, however, that this technique works only if you intend to print the report on one side of the paper.

Spacing

Formal reports may be double spaced or single spaced. When using the APA style, indent the first line of each double-spaced paragraph one-half inch. While the sample report in Chapter 11, is double spaced, it could have been single spaced. When reports are single spaced, paragraphs are not indented—insert a double space between paragraphs.

The title page often has a two-inch top margin. Space the information down the page so that it looks attractive. Long titles are frequently divided into two or more shorter lines to enhance the appearance of the title page.

An executive summary is always single spaced and ordinarily should be limited to one page. After all, the purpose of the summary is to *summarize*.

A heading should have a double space before and after it (except for third-level headings). No heading should follow another heading without at least one paragraph intervening. A paragraph of only one sentence may be sufficient to lead from one heading to the next.

For spacing references, footnotes, and quotations, refer to Chapter 8 and examples later in this appendix. If a paragraph will not fit on one page and has to be divided, leave at least two lines on the first page and carry at least two lines to the next page. Some word processors automatically follow this guideline if you turn on the Widow/Orphan protection feature.

Citation Styles

A formal report should use an appropriate citation style. Three of the most frequently used styles are the APA (American Psychological Association), the MLA (Modern Language Association), and the Chicago style. Examples of the APA style are illustrated in

Chapter 8. General guidelines for the MLA style and the Chicago style are included here. Further information can be found in the style manuals notes in Chapter 8 that are available in your college library. The MLA examples follow in Figures 1 and 2 while the Chicago Style is shown in Figures 3 and 4.

Book with one author

Booher, Dianna. <u>E-Writing: 21st Century Tools for Effective Communication.</u> New York: Pocket Books, 2001.

Book with more than one author

Diamond, Michael R., and Julie L. Williams. <u>How to Incorporate: A Handbook for Entrepreneurs and Professionals.</u> New York: John Wiley and Sons, 2000.

Newspaper article, with author, discontinuous pages.

Johnson, Johnny. "A Change of Scenery: Campus Improvement Projects Completed." <u>Daily Sentinel</u> [Nacogdoches, TX] 10 May 2001, 1+.

Journal article with one author

Massey, Joseph E. "Managing Organizational Legitimacy: Communication Strategies for Organizations in Crisis." <u>Journal of Business Communication</u> 38.2 (2001) : 153-182.

Journal article with more than one author

Pearce, C. Glenn, and Tracy L. Tuten. "Internet Recruiting in the Banking Industry." <u>Business Communication Quarterly,</u> 64.1 (2001): 9-18.

Magazine article, with author

Sellers, Patricia. "Get Over Yourself." <u>Fortune</u> 30 Apr. 2001: 76-88.

Magazine article, without author

"Developments to Watch." <u>Business Week</u> 14 May 2001: 121.

Web journal article with no date.

Hsu, H. Christine. "Earnings Surprises and Stock Returns: Some Evidence from Asia/Pacific and Europe." <u>Business Quest 2001</u> 15 May 2001 <http://www.westga.edu/~bquest/2001/surprises.htm>.

Online government publication.

United States. Federal Trade Commission. <u>ID Theft: When Bad Things Happen To Your Good Name.</u> Mar. 2001. 15 May 2001 <http://www.consumer.gov/idtheft/>.

Figure 1. MLA Entries

Works Cited

Booher, Dianna. <u>E-Writing: 21st Century Tools for Effective Communication.</u> New York: Pocket Books, 2001.

"Developments to Watch." <u>Business Week</u> 14 May 2001: 121.

Diamond, Michael R., and Julie L. Williams. <u>How to Incorporate: A Handbook for Entrepreneurs and Professionals.</u> New York: John Wiley and Sons, 2000.

Hsu, H. Christine. "Earnings Surprises and Stock Returns: Some Evidence from Asia/Pacific and Europe." <u>Business Quest 2001</u> 15 May 2001 <http://www.westga.edu/ ~bquest/2001/surprises.htm>.

Johnson, Johnny. "A Change of Scenery: Campus Improvement Projects Completed." <u>Daily Sentinel</u> [Nacogdoches, TX] 10 May 2001, 1+.

Massey, Joseph E. "Managing Organizational Legitimacy: Communication Strategies for Organizations in Crisis." <u>Journal of Business Communication</u> 38.2 (2001) : 153-182.

Pearce, C. Glenn, and Tracy L. Tuten. "Internet Recruiting in the Banking Industry." <u>Business Communication Quarterly</u>, 64.1 (2001): 9-18.

Sellers, Patricia. "Get Over Yourself." <u>Fortune</u> 30 Apr. 2001: 76-88.

United States. Federal Trade Commission. <u>ID Theft: When Bad Things Happen To Your Good Name.</u> Mar. 2001. 15 May 2001 <http://www.consumer.gov/idtheft/>.

Figure 2. MLA Style End-of-Report Citation Page

Book with one author

Booher, Dianna. <u>E-Writing: 21st Century Tools for Effective Communication.</u> New York: Pocket Books, 2001.

Book with more than one author

Diamond, Michael R., and Julie L Williams. <u>How to Incorporate: A Handbook for Entrepreneurs and Professionals.</u> New York: John Wiley and Sons, 2000.

Newspaper article, with author, discontinuous pages.

Johnson, Johnny. "A Change of Scenery: Campus Improvement Projects Completed." [Nacogdoches, TX] Daily Sentinel, 10 May 2001, 1+.

Journal article with one author

Massey, Joseph E. "Managing Organizational Legitimacy: Communication Strategies for Organizations in Crisis." <u>Journal of Business Communication</u> 38, no.2 (2001): 153-182.

Journal article with more than one author

Pearce, C. Glenn, and Tracy L. Tuten. "Internet Recruiting in the Banking Industry." <u>Business Communication Quarterly</u>, 64, no. 1 (2001): 9-18.

Magazine article, with author

Sellers, Patricia. "Get Over Yourself." <u>Fortune</u>, 30 Apr. 2001, 76-88.

Magazine article, without author

"Developments to Watch." <u>Business Week</u>, 14 May 2001, 121.

Web journal article with no date.

Hsu, H. Christine. "Earnings Surprises and Stock Returns: Some Evidence from Asia/Pacific and Europe." <u>Business Quest 2001</u> 15 May 2001 <u><http://www.westga.edu/~bquest/2001/surprises.htm>.</u>

Online government publication.

United States. Federal Trade Commission. <u>ID Theft: When Bad Things Happen To Your Good Name</u>. Mar. 2001. 15 May 2001 <http://www.consumer.gov/idtheft/>.

Figure 3. Chicago Style Entries

Bibliography

Booher, Dianna. <u>E-Writing: 21st Century Tools for Effective Communication.</u> New York: Pocket Books, 2001.

"Developments to Watch." <u>Business Week</u>, 14 May 2001, 121.

Diamond, Michael R., and Julie L Williams. <u>How to Incorporate: A Handbook for Entrepreneurs and Professionals.</u> New York: John Wiley and Sons, 2000.

Hsu, H. Christine. "Earnings Surprises and Stock Returns: Some Evidence from Asia/Pacific and Europe." <u>Business Quest 2001</u> 15 May 2001 <u><http://www.westga.edu/~bquest/2001/surprises.htm></u>.

Johnson, Johnny. "A Change of Scenery: Campus Improvement Projects Completed."<u>[Nacogdoches, TX] Daily Sentinel,</u> 10 May 2001, 1+.

Massey, Joseph E. "Managing Organizational Legitimacy: Communication Strategies for Organizations in Crisis." <u>Journal of Business Communication</u> 38, no.2 (2001): 153-182.

Pearce, C. Glenn, and Tracy L. Tuten. "Internet Recruiting in the Banking Industry." <u>Business Communication Quarterly,</u> 64, no. 1 (2001): 9-18.

Sellers, Patricia. "Get Over Yourself." <u>Fortune,</u> 30 Apr. 2001, 76-88.

United States. Federal Trade Commission. <u>ID Theft: When Bad Things Happen To Your Good Name</u>. Mar. 2001. 15 May 2001 <http://www.consumer.gov/idtheft/>.

Figure 4. Chicago Style End of Report Page

Headings

You may use three levels of APA style headings in your report. (Check the manuals mentioned in Chapter 8 for other styles.) Type the first-level heading centered across the page with uppercase and lowercase letters. Capitalize each major word except articles, conjunctions, and short prepositions. The second-level heading follows the same guidelines except it begins at the left margin and is also underlined. The third-level heading is a paragraph heading. Underline these headings and capitalize only the first word. Indent the heading from the left margin to be consistent with paragraph indentions. The text of the paragraph immediately follows the third-level heading. See the following example of three levels of headings.

First-Level Report Heading

Include text information here about what will be discussed in first level of report.

Second-Level Report Heading at Left Margin

Include text information here about what will be discussed in second-level headings of the report.

Third-level heading at beginning of paragraph. The rest of the paragraph follows the third-level heading. In third level headings, unlike those on the first level and second level, only the first word of the heading is capitalized. A period follows.

Pagination

Use lowercase Roman numerals for preliminary pages. Center the number horizontally at the bottom page margin. While no page number should appear on the title page, assign a number to it. Use Arabic numerals for the other pages beginning with the body of the report. While the most-used numbering system for the body of the report has the page number at the upper right side of the page, you may use any appropriate page numbering plan including page numbers at the bottom of the page.

Proofreading

Proofreading is critical in the success of your report. Most word processing packages have spell checker features that find many errors. The spell checker will not, however, find the kinds of spelling errors that result from incorrect word choices such as those in the following illustration.

When practicing her oral report, she will *sea* whether *here* audience can *here* her. If she does not speak loudly, her *instruction* will probably deduct *pints*.

As you proofread your work, placing a colored sheet of paper below the line you are reading may be helpful. If you proofread on the computer screen, move your cursor to the line you are reading.

Several word processing packages also are accompanied by grammar checkers which provide an additional opportunity to check your work for accuracy. Grammar checkers may point out errors in subject and verb agreement or in word choice.

Writers often have difficulty proofreading their own work. You may wish to ask someone else to read your report carefully before you submit it to the person(s) for whom you wrote it.

Color

You can use color to enhance the appearance of your report and to highlight some points. Several word processing programs allow you to determine the color of the text. Presentation graphics programs also provide color capabilities. You must, however, have a printer that is capable of printing your color choices. If your report is to be copied, make certain that the copier will reproduce satisfactorily the colors you use.

If the report is printed, you can use color to enhance the appearance and to encourage people to read it. You can use colored headings, stationery, and illustrations of various types. Annual reports use color to highlight company performance. When appropriately used, color can make reading long business reports easier.

Printing

A laser printer produces a sharper, darker image than do most other printers. Color laser printers will print color graphics and photographs in the most attractive manner. The quality of ink jet printers is also acceptable for many reports. The paper you choose for the report may depend on the type of printer you use. A smooth finish on paper is more suitable for laser printing while some papers with a rougher finish work better with ink jet printers.

Copying and Binding

Use a copying method that produces neat, clear copies on a high-quality paper and place the completed report in paper or plastic covers. Spiral binding is preferred. A spiral-bound report can be handled easily, and it can be opened so that minimum space is required for displaying any page. If facilities for spiral binding are not available, use a loose-leaf cover.

LETTERS

The overall appearance of your document will affect the readability and reader acceptance. A document that is accurately formatted on quality letterhead will be more favorably received than one that is confusing or difficult to read. Use appropriate equipment and supplies to prepare an attractive document.

The majority of business letters are written on company letterhead. The letterhead may be commercially typeset and printed or it may be computer formatted and printed on a laser printer when the document is printed. Regardless of the method of preparation, the letterhead should include the company name, address, telephone number, web address, and any other pertinent information about the company. The paper used for letterhead stationery and envelopes should be a quality bond paper. The document should be printed on a laser or inkjet printer. Dot matrix printers do not produce the quality print necessary for attractive correspondence.

Letter Format

The format of the letter is the first thing the reader notices. The letter should be centered on the page; that is, the left and the right margins should be approximately equal, and there should be about as much space below the letter as above it. All margins—sides, top, and bottom—should be at least one inch and may be wider for short letters.

Letter Styles

Common letter styles used in business today include the full block, the modified block, and the simplified formats. The full block style is the most commonly used format today. The modified block format is considered the most traditional.

Full Block Style. In the full block style letter, all lines begin at the left margin. The date and the closing lines begin at the left margin and the paragraphs are not indented. Use the block style letter for most of your correspondence. This letter format is illustrated in Figure 5.

The Simplified Style. The simplified style is similar to the full block style in that all lines begin at the left margin. The salutation and the complimentary close, however, are omitted. A subject line, typed in all capital letters, is required. The sender's name and title are also capitalized. This letter style is particularly effective when the name or the gender of the addressee is unknown. Refer to Figure 6 for an example of the simplified style.

The Modified Block Style. Paragraphs within the body of the modified block style letter may begin at the left margin or may be indented five spaces. The date, the complimentary close, and the sender's name begin at the center point as illustrated in Figure 7. Considered a traditional format, the modified block letter may be used effectively when corresponding with conservative receivers.

Standard Letter Parts

All letters should include the following parts and spacing unless otherwise indicated.

- Letterhead with sender's address information - press enter key twice after last line
- Date - press enter key 3 or 4 times after date is typed
- Letter address - press enter key twice after zip code is typed
- Salutation - press enter key twice after salutation is typed
- Body - press enter key twice after each paragraph
- Complimentary close - press enter key 3 or 4 times after closing is typed
- Name of writer - press enter key one time after name is typed
- Title of writer

Fine Collectibles
4646 Axenty Way
Redondo Beach, CA 90278
(213) 555-1440
Fax (213) 555-4848

July 31, 2002

Mr. Clint King
The Collection
8359 South Sanibel Street
Gladstone, OR 97027

Dear Mr. King

Please send me a copy of your recent catalog, Collecting Spoons, that was advertised in this month's edition of *The Collector*. A check for $8.95 is enclosed for shipping and handling.

A number of our customers collect spoons. As the miniature spoons seem especially popular, we are interested in expanding our line.

Sincerely

Alexandria VanCleave

Alexandria VanCleave
Manager

Figure 5. Full Block with Open Punctuation

Fine Collectibles
4646 Axenty Way
Redondo Beach, CA 90278
(213) 555-1440
Fax (213) 555-4848

July 31, 2002

The Collection
8359 South Sanibel Street
Gladstone, OR 97027

REQUEST FOR CATALOG

Please send me a copy of your recent catalog, Collecting Spoons, that was advertised in this month's edition of *The Collector*. A check for $8.95 is enclosed for shipping and handling.

A number of our customers collect spoons. As the miniature spoons seem especially popular, we are interested in expanding our line.

Alexandria VanCleave

ALEXANDRIA VANCLEAVE-MANAGER

Figure 6. Simplified Format

Fine Collectibles

4646 Axenty Way
Redondo Beach, CA 90278
(213) 555-1440
Fax (213) 555-4848

July 31, 2002

Mr. Clint King
The Collection
8359 South Sanibel Street
Gladstone, OR 97027

Dear Mr. King:

Please send me a copy of your recent catalog, Collecting Spoons, that was advertised in this month's edition of *The Collector*. A check for $8.95 is enclosed for shipping and handling.

A number of our customers collect spoons. As the miniature spoons seem especially popular, we are interested in expanding our line.

Sincerely,

Alexandria VanCleave

Alexandria VanCleave
Manager

Figure 7. Modified Block with Mixed Punctuation

Letterhead. A letterhead contains the name and the address of the organization for which it was printed. If you do not have letterhead stationery, you should use your computer to create an appropriate business or personal letterhead. Include the name, street address, city, state, and ZIP code. You may wish to include phone and fax numbers as well as an e-mail address or World Wide Web page address. Here is an example of an appropriate letterhead.

Clifton Services
1005 Oakdale
Rockford, IL 61125
(304) 478-1455
www.cservices.net

___

Date. Print the date—month, day, and year—approximately ½ inch below the letterhead. Do not abbreviate the month.

Letter Address. Begin the letter address three to four lines below the date. Include in the letter address the same information you write on the envelope. You should usually include the addressee's: (1) name; (2) house or apartment number; (3) street, avenue, route, or post office box number; (4) city; (5) state (two-letter abbreviation); and (6) zip code. The job title and the company name are needed in some addresses.

If known, include a courtesy title (Miss, Mr., Mrs., Ms., Dr., Professor, and so forth) before the person's name in the letter address, as in these examples:

___

Mr. James C. Young
3497 N.W. Freeway
Tulsa, OK 74103

Dr. Barbara Horton
893 Ridgebrook
Athens, GA 30603

___

If you do not know the correct courtesy title, omit it. People are less offended when their titles are omitted than when their titles are incorrect.

Salutation. When addressing a letter to a person rather than to an organization, you should in most instances use a three-word salutation—Dear + courtesy title + surname. If, however, you and the addressee are on a first-name basis, you may use a two word salutation—Dear + first name. Do not use Dear Sir; it is outdated.

Salutations such as Dear Sir, Dear Madam, or To Whom It May Concern are either outdated or inappropriate when writing letters to persons whose gender is not known.

___

The recommended salutation for writing to a company when you do not know who will read the letter is to eliminate Dear and use the following:

Ladies and Gentlemen

___

Body. Single space paragraphs and double space between them. Don't indent the first line in full block or simplified formats. You may indent paragraphs that are formatted in modified block style.

Complimentary Close. Sincerely is the most popular complimentary close. Closes such as Yours truly, Very truly yours, and Respectfully yours are outdated and should be avoided.

Name of Writer. When typing a business letter, type your name three to four lines below the complimentary close or four lines below the last line of the letter if a complimentary close is not included. Remember, do not include a courtesy title (Mr., Dr., and so forth) in your signature; a woman, however, may use a courtesy title enclosed in parentheses if she prefers not to be addressed as Ms.

Remember to sign each letter with a pen using black or blue ink above your printed name.

Title of Writer. Include the title of the writer on the line below the typed name in full block or modified block style. The title of the writer is placed on the same line as the name of the writer in the simplified format.

Special Letter Parts

In addition to the letter parts described in the preceding paragraphs, these special parts are sometimes needed:

- Attention line
- Subject line
- Position title
- Enclosure notation
- Special mailing notation
- Postscript
- Other

Attention Line. Usually, a letter is addressed to a specific person. When, however, you address a letter to an organization but wish to direct the letter to a particular person within the group, use an attention line. In the full block and modified block formats, type the attention line between the last line of the letter address and the salutation. When using the simplified format, type the attention line as the second line of the letter address. Even though you use an attention line, always use a salutation that is appropriate for the first line of the letter address, as in this the example on the following page:

Full Block or Modified Block Format:	**Simplified Format:**
Pioneer Printing Company 7800 Industrial Boulevard Carrolton, TX 75000	Pioneer Printing Company Attention: Mike Laidlaw 7800 Industrial Boulevard Carrolton, TX 75000
Attention: Mike Laidlaw	NEW PRODUCT RELEASE
Ladies and Gentlemen:	

Subject Line. So that the reader can see at a glance the subject of the letter, you may place key words in a subject line. By including account numbers, policy numbers, and similar references, you can assist the addressee. Place this line between the salutation and the body of the letter. The word subject is optional. Here is one example:

```
Croskroft Copying Service
1441 Grandview Road
Deming, NM 88030

Ladies and Gentlemen

SUBJECT: Manuscript Submissions
```

Position Title. When using a letterhead and writing as a representative of the organization for which the letterhead was designed, show the title of your position on the line immediately below your name or on the same line, as in these examples:

```
Sincerely                           Cordially



(Mrs.) Elisa J. Maddox             Jason T. Lovins, General Manager
Program Director
```

Enclosure Notation. If you include an item inside the envelope with the letter, print the word Enclosure positioned at the left margin and a line or more below the signature line. When sending more than one enclosure, use the word Enclosures followed by the number of items you are sending. Itemizing or describing the enclosures is desirable when they are especially important or when you believe the person opening the envelope may overlook an item. Here is an example with multiple enclosures:

```
Sincerely



Ms. Shirley G. Claborn
Manager

Enclosures  3—Approval form
                Revised manuscript
                Addressed envelope
```

Postscript. If you use a postscript, place it two lines below the last part of the letter. The original purpose of the postscript was to present ideas that were inadvertently omitted in the body of the letter or ideas that occurred to the writer after dictating the letter. The postscript is still used occasionally for these reasons, but the chief reason today for using it is to emphasize an idea. Because it is short and in a position that makes it stand out from the rest of the letter, it gets special attention. Use postscripts sparingly. You may use or omit the abbreviation P.S. Here are examples:

Enclosure

Mail your order by Friday to take advantage of the sale price.

Copy Notation. You may send a copy of a letter to a third person. Usually, you would like the addressee of the letter to know you are sending a copy to another person. If so, print two spaces below the final notation on the page the words "Copy to" followed by the name of the person who is to receive the copy. Here is an illustration:

---

rbs

Enclosure

Copy to Ms. Tiffany Svebeck

Multiple Page Letters

For a multiple-page letter, use letterhead only for the first page. The second page of the letter should include a header rather than the letterhead. Include these three items in the header of the second and succeeding pages:

- Addressee's name
- Page number
- Date

You may wish to use your software's header feature to create the second page heading. Leave at least two blank lines between the header and the body text. The header may be arranged horizontally or vertically, as in the following examples.

Vertical second page heading

Mrs. Robert Samuels
Page 2
April 15, 2002

Horizontal second page heading

Mrs. Robert Samuels   2   April 15, 2002

Use the vertical arrangement for the full block or the simplified format. Either arrangement is acceptable for the modified block format that has indented opening and closing lines.

Letter Punctuation

Use conventional punctuation for the body of a business message. Punctuate the salutation and the complimentary close of a letter according to either of two styles—mixed and open. For **mixed punctuation** use a colon after the salutation and a comma after the complimentary close.

For **open punctuation** use no punctuation mark after the salutation or the complimentary close. Open punctuation is generally preferred with the full block format. Do not use a comma after the salutation in a business letter. The use of the comma to end a salutation is reserved for personal letters.

MEMORANDUMS

Letters may go to persons inside the organization as well as to those outside. Memorandums go to primarily those inside the organization. Some organizations have prepared forms on which memorandums are written, which may resemble the letterhead or may be an entirely different heading. Most word processing software programs have memorandum templates that have been preformatted to include the key headings used in memos.

Because memorandums go to persons within the group, the format is quite informal. Courtesy titles for the receivers are not necessary (though they are sometimes used when addressing superiors), and the message is not centered vertically on the page.

Align the names of the sender, the receiver, the date, and the subject line approximately one-half inch to the right of their headings. The vertical alignment makes these items easy to read.

Notice that no salutation or complimentary close is used. Other notations such as reference initials, enclosure notations, and copy notations are the same as those for letters. Although no signatures on memorandums are required, most writers sign them by placing their initials by their name. The initials may follow the body of the message; usually, however, initials are placed beside the sender's name as in Figure 8.

The headings for the second and succeeding pages are the same as those for a letter and are typed on plain paper. If headings are needed within the body of a long memorandum to help the reader locate certain information quickly, they may be added. The popular format described here provides for easy preparation and easy reading.

MEMORANDUM

To: Mitchell Jeffrey
             Sales Representative

From: Rebecca Bradshaw *RB*
             Fiscal Affairs

Subject: Monthly Expense Report

Date: March 10, 2002

To receive reimbursement for your February travel expenses, please submit your expense form by Friday, March 13. Be sure to include your receipts along with your daily expense statement.

Checks will be issued on March 25 for expenses reported March 13. Expense statements received after March 13 will be paid on April 25.

You may send your report to me or to my assistant, Victor Flores.

Figure 8. Memorandum

ENVELOPES

Regardless of how well a letter is written, it is of no value until it is delivered. The envelope address should be identical to the letter address within the letter and should be in the approximate horizontal center of the lower half of the envelope. The return address should be in the upper left-hand corner.

Follow these basic guidelines:

1. If the address contains an attention line, type it as the first line of the address.
2. Use only capital letters, eliminate all punctuation, and use block format (see Figure 9).
3. Include the city, two-letter abbreviation for the state, and the ZIP code in the last line.
4. When you use a plain envelope, print your address in the upper left-hand corner.

Fine Collectibles
4646 Axenty Way
Redondo Beach, CA 90278

MR CLINT KING
THE COLLECTION
8359 SOUTH SANIBEL STREET
GLADSTONE OR 97027

Figure 9. Envelope

For an attractive letter to retain its good appearance, it must be folded properly if it is to be mailed in a business envelope.

The standard letter fold consists of only two creases.

1. Place the letter face up on a desk and bring the bottom edge of the letter up toward the top edge so that roughly one third of the page is left uncovered. Crease the letter at this point.

2. Bring the top edge of the letter down over the bottom one third of the letter that has already been creased. The top edge should come to within about one quarter of an inch from the crease you have already made. Hold the top edge in this position as you make the second and final crease in the letter. The folded letter is now slightly smaller than a long (No. 10) envelope and, therefore, can be placed easily into the envelope.

APPENDIX C
RECOGNIZING COMMONLY
MISSPELLED WORDS

The following words are commonly misspelled in business documents. Study them carefully to avoid errors.

accommodate
acknowledgment
advisable
appropriate
attorneys

bankruptcy
beneficial
bibliography
business
calendar

candidate
category
chronological
collateral
column

commitment
committee
competent
congratulations
conscientious

conspicuous
convenience
corporation
courteous
deficit

deficiency
dilemma
discrepancy
efficient
eligible

embarrassing
emphasize
enthusiastic
equipped
exceed

existence
extracurricular
extraordinary
familiar
fascinate

feasible
February
genuine
grammar
grievance

guaranteed
honorarium
illegible
inevitable
interfered

interpret
itinerary
jeopardize
legible
marital

mediocre
misspell
morale
necessitate
ninety

noticeable
occasion
occurred
pamphlet
parallel

parliamentary
participate
perseverance
personnel
precede

preferred
prerequisite
presumptuous
prevalent
privilege

proceed
promissory
questionnaire
receive
reciprocate

recommend
recurrence
referred
reimbursement
remunerate

repetitive
representative
restaurant
retrieval
seize

separate
similar
sincerely
sophomore
specific

statistics
studying
temporary
tentative
transferring

truly
twelfth
unanimous
undoubtedly
verbatim

APPENDIX D
MASTERING FREQUENTLY
USED WORDS

To communicate accurately, use words correctly. The following list gives a brief definition and illustrates correct usage of similar words.

1. **accede** — to agree or to consent — Micah will accede to work on Saturday if she does not work on Friday.
   exceed — to go beyond — Leslie will not exceed the speed limit because of her fear of getting a speeding ticket.

2. **accept** — to receive — Mark will accept the award on Byron's behalf.
   except — to exclude — Everyone in the class passed the test except Shawn.

3. **access** — to admit, to approach — Tanya has access to classified information.
   excess — surpassing limits — Clean the excess glue from the model car before it dries.

4. **addition** — the result of adding — His addition error resulted in an overcharge.
   edition — an issue of a publication — All students are required to read the latest edition of *Newsweek*.

5. **advise** — to counsel, recommend — The doctor advised Wilma to exercise more.
   advice — recommendation — The banker gave me advice on my financial situation.

6. **affect** — to influence — Will smoking affect a person's health?
   effect — a result, to create — The effect of the smoking ban was cleaner air.

7. **a lot** — much, many — Amanda has a lot of money in her checking account.
   allot — allocate, assign — Each team should allot three weeks to this project.

8. **among** — use with three or more — The work was divided among the four assistants.
   between — use with only two — The choice was between Saturday or Sunday.

9. **amount** — masses that cannot be counted — A large amount of water poured over the dam.
   number — items that can be counted — A large number of people attended the meeting.

10. **anxious** — worried — I was anxious to get home before the thunderstorm started.
    eager — enthusiastic — I was eager to get home and have a relaxing dinner.

11. **any** — use with three or more — Any of the three desks will be available Tuesday.
    either — use with only two — Either of the two desks will be available Tuesday.

12. **can** — able to do — The President can veto congressional bills.
    may — permission — Anyone who wants an extra day off may have one.

13.	**capital** **capitol**	city of government a building used by government	The capital of Texas is Austin. Congress assembles in the Capitol.
14.	**choose** **chose**	to select past tense of choose	I am not sure which answer to choose. I chose the correct answer on the test.
15.	**cite** **sight** **site**	to quote to see; a view a place	Cite reference sources in your paper. Jim and Jane visited the sights of London. The engineers selected the site by the river for the power plant.
16.	**complementary** **complimentary**	serving mutually flattering	The carpet and the furnishings were complementary to the room design. The concert received complimentary reviews.
17.	**compose** **comprise**	create, make up consists of, composed of	Dimetria composed a poem describing Barbara. The book comprises fifty poems in her honor.
18.	**continual** **continuous**	regular occurrence without interruption	The doctor prescribed a continual low fat diet. Mark gazed at the continuous slope of the property.
19.	**counsel** **council**	to give advice governing body	Faculty counsel students on study habits. The student council will discuss the year's events.
20.	**discrete** **discreet**	individually distinct showing good judgment in conduct or speech	A discrete variable should be used to solve this equation. Politicians are discreet when talking about certain issues.
21.	**disinterested** **uninterested**	not affected by not interested	It seems that many politicians are disinterested in all efforts to find a peaceful solution. Ruth was totally uninterested in the proceedings.
22.	**each other** **one another**	use with only two use with three or more	The two employees helped each other. The three employees helped one another.
23.	**envelop** **envelope**	to wrap a packet for a letter	She will envelop the guests with her Southern hospitality. I need an envelope in order to mail this letter.
24.	**farther** **further**	a greater distance additional	New York is farther away than Florida. I need further information to complete my analysis.
25.	**fewer** **less**	use with items that can be counted use with things that cannot be counted	Fewer people choose to drive than to walk. There is less water in this lake than normal.

26.	**fiscal**	financial matters	U. S. businesses are regulated by fiscal policy.
	physical	of the body	My doctor says that I need to engage in more physical activities.
27.	**formally**	in a formal manner	Buck formally advised his entire team to reevaluate their status.
	formerly	at a time that has passed	Susan formerly worked as a secretary.
28.	**good**	an adjective	The assistant does good work.
	well	an adverb	The assistant works well with others.
29.	**interoffice**	from one office to another	Ambrin Inc. has interoffice computer networks.
	intra office	within one office	The Finance department has an intra office intercom.
30.	**it's**	contraction of it is	It's a very nice day.
	its	of or belonging to it	The company is forming its own research team.
31.	**lay**	to put or to place	Lay the newspaper on the table.
	lie	to recline	Jana needs to lie on the couch for a while.
32.	**loose**	free, unattached	Velma found a loose paper on the desk.
	lose	to fail to keep	How did Harry lose the paper in the copy room?
33.	**marital**	pertaining to marriage	Rita changed her marital status on her W-4 form.
	martial	military; relating to war	The territory was under martial control.
	marshal	an officer	Greg is the parade marshal.
34.	**may be**	might be	Rachel's shoes may be in my closet.
	maybe	perhaps	Maybe John will go to the mall with us.
35.	**moral**	ethical	Luther has high moral standards.
	morale	a mental attitude	The morale of Patti's team is low because she hasn't motivated them.
36.	**neither**	use with only two	Neither Wanda nor Bonnie was in the office today.
	none	use with three or more	None of the team members understood the play.
37.	**percent**	use after a figure	Only 5 percent of the employees attended the meeting.
	percentage	use without figures	A large percentage of the employees have life insurance.
38.	**personal**	private	Dr. Gershwin keeps his personal files in his credenza.
	personnel	employees	All personnel must complete the drug testing by noon.

39.	**perspective**	mental outlook	What is your perspective on the presidential nominees?
	prospective	likely	Tina is a prospective client of hers.
40.	**precede**	to go before	It is good to precede a speech with an anecdote.
	proceed	to continue	The work can proceed on the building site.
41.	**principal**	school official	Mr. Howdy was my high school principal.
	principle	basic truth or belief	A business student masters each principle of economics.
42.	**quiet**	free from noise	All areas of the library should be very quiet.
	quite	completely	I don't think that everyone is quite finished.
	quit	to discontinue	Pam quit her job today.
43.	**respectfully**	marked by respect	I respectfully ask your permission.
	respectively	each in the order given	The memo was sent to Bob and Judy, respectively.
44.	**role**	a part	She assumed the role of receptionist and answered the telephone.
	roll	to rotate, a list, bread	Please add Mike's name to your class roll.
45.	**some**	unspecified amount	Bring me some paper, please.
	sum	an amount of money, result of adding	The sum of the equation is 76.
46.	**some time**	period of time	You need to give her some time.
	sometime	at some indefinite time	Come and visit us sometime.
47.	**stationary**	fixed, not moving	The exercise bicycle is stationary.
	stationery	letterheads, envelopes	Please type the letter on company stationery.
48.	**suit**	clothes; court action	She is wearing a new suit.
	suite	a group of items; a set	We are located in suite 211.
	sweet	pleasing to the taste	Strawberry cheesecake is sweet.
49.	**their**	possessive for they	Bob and Cindy received their mail.
	there	in or at that place	Was Emily there when you arrived at the office?
50.	**to**	a preposition	It is time to take out the trash.
	too	more than enough, also	There are too many people in the elevator.
	two	a number	Louise has two cars.

INDEX